I0084144

MAYFLOWER

Day by Day

Compiled by

W. Becket Soule

HERITAGE BOOKS
2025

HERITAGE BOOKS

AN IMPRINT OF HERITAGE BOOKS, INC.

Books, CDs, and more—Worldwide

For our listing of thousands of titles see our website
at
www.HeritageBooks.com

Published 2025 by
HERITAGE BOOKS, INC.
Publishing Division
5810 Ruatan Street
Berwyn Heights, MD 20740

Copyright © 2025 W. Becket Soule

Heritage Books by the author:

*Centennial History of the Society of Mayflower Descendants
in the State of North Carolina, 1924–2024*

Mayflower: Day by Day

Passengers of the Fortune *(1621)*

All rights reserved. No part of this book may be reproduced or
transmitted in any form or by any means, electronic or mechanical,
including photocopying, recording or by any information storage and
retrieval system without written permission from the author, except
for the inclusion of brief quotations in a review.

International Standard Book Number
Paperbound: 978-0-7884-4732-7

for
L.T.W.

Table of Contents

INTRODUCTION

2020 was certainly the year of disappointments, not the least of which was the four-hundredth anniversary of the landing of the *Mayflower*. Planning had begun decades before, and numerous not-to-be-missed events were scheduled. COVID lockdowns and quarantines brought most of these to a screeching halt, although some managed to survive in a modified form thanks to virtual transmission, podcasts, and other remote technologies.

The new presentations and forms, however, meant that the *Mayflower* "narrative" (to use a tired, hackneyed, and over-used phrase) was tightly controlled by a small group, who used it – or perhaps "hijacked it" would be more appropriate – for partisan purposes. It became obvious to me, and regretfully so, by the middle of 2020 that *none* of the commemorations or remembrances even mentioned the *Mayflower*. This led my curiosity to ask what my ancestors were doing, right now, four hundred years ago. That led to the first postings of what became Mayflower Day by Day: a longer or shorter post daily from the beginning of August 2020, when the Leiden Pilgrims left Holland, to December 2021, when the *Fortune* left Plymouth to return to England (eventually).

These snippets were posted on the Facebook pages of the Canadian Society of Mayflower Descendants, the Society of Mayflower Descendants in the State of North Carolina, and on the website of Soule Kindred in America, beginning on 6 September 2020. Some days there were only a dozen or so views; on other days the number topped one thousand (counting re-postings). The comments were interesting, and usually quite well researched. The original posts were taken down not long afterwards, but many people have asked for them to be preserved together in one place, so that they could go through the journey again.

This is not at all a work of scholarship, but more a reflective perusal of a wide variety of sources to go deeper into the details of the Pilgrim story and experience of 1620-21. It is certainly a personal reflection, based on forty years of reading and research and discussion.

One particularly over-wrought discussion, or argument, in the comments had to do with the calendar used. As several postings noted, two calendars were used simultaneously in Europe in this period, and they were out of sync by ten days, as well as manifesting other differences. The Julian calendar was used in some countries into the twentieth century (and thus in Russia the Bolshevik October Revolution actually took place in November), and is still used by several Eastern Christian Churches. But since almost everyone who was reading the posts used the Gregorian Calendar, I did so as well, and modified the dates so that it would be possible to determine what was happening *exactly* four hundred years ago on that date. This brought about a certain amount of anxious and angry online screaming, because "the Pilgrims did not use the Gregorian calendar." This is only partially true, since Leiden used the Gregorian calendar, and the Pilgrims there must, perforce, have followed suit. Many presenters made much on 11 November 2020 that "exactly four hundred years ago" the Mayflower Compact was signed – which is actually not true. But saying that the Mayflower Compact was signed "exactly three hundred ninety-nine years, three hundred fifty-five days ago" lacks a certain punch.

This brings up one of the most intriguing questions that I considered in this project, and one which I have not successfully or even sufficiently answered to this day. About a quarter of the men on the Mayflower above the age of about 20 did *not* sign the Mayflower Compact. It also appears that some men signed, but under duress and coercion. The story of the Mayflower Compact is frequently presented as a marvellous, fraternal gathering in which everyone agreed to be bound by common consent. But a dozen or so men did not sign, and I came back over and over again to the question of what happened to them. Did they go back to England? Did they simply blend in to the structures of the Plymouth Colony, willing to be governed without their consent? The story presented, at least since Daniel Webster in the nineteenth century, is that the Mayflower Compact was a proto-Declaration of Independence or Constitution, all rolled in to one, and it has been celebrated as such for two hundred years. But is this accurate, or even partially true? I still have not reached a conclusion.

The texts for each day remain as they were originally posted, with minor corrections and alterations. The citations have for the most part been dropped from the text to the footnotes. A list of all passengers on the voyage, and not simply those who have descendants, is included as an appendix. Extensive quotations are made from William Bradford's journal, *Of Plimmoth Plantation*, and from *Mourt's Relation*: in some cases the spelling is modernised, in others it is not, particularly when the original spelling is significant to make a point. Both of these works (in several editions) are listed in the bibliography at the end, but individual citations are not put in the text – the date should be sufficient to locate the original citation.

Two gentlemen in particular should be acknowledged, although both of them have gone to their eternal reward and, alas, will not be able to read my heartfelt gratitude. The Reverend Peter J. Gomes, the Plummer Professor of Christian Morals at Harvard Divinity School, the Pusey Minister at Harvard's Memorial Church, and loyal son of Plymouth, first suggested this project to me over thirty years ago, and I can almost hear him chuckling at some of the entries. He died in 2011 and is still sorely missed. Jeremy Dupertius Bangs, a scholar of rare erudition and humane instincts, read each and every one of these posts when they came out, and his comments were frequently longer than the original post; his comment that it was "well researched" was high praise indeed. His death in 2023 leaves a significant void in Pilgrim scholarship.

Numerous others have assisted in ways large and small, and while the good points are the result of so many others' aid, any errors or deficiencies are entirely my own.

I hope that this story provides a way for us, four hundred years later, to join our ancestors on that famous journey.

W. Becket Soule

Maggie Valley, North Carolina

29 December 2024

JULY 1620

FRIDAY, 24 JULY 1620

Preparations

Preparations had gone very, very badly. In a letter of 10 June, the Leiden Pilgrims complained that a ship had not even been hired or purchased yet, and the group was not being informed about what was being done. "The colony, even before it began, was fully mortgaged for seven years. [Robert] Cushman's justification for having made that arrangement consisted of high flown rhetorical flourishes."[1] To make matters worse, in addition to the leaders of the Leiden group seeking to travel as a bridgehead for the congregation, there were three agents in England (Weston, Cushman and Carver), often working at cross purposes and frequently acting without consulting each other: the project was haemorrhaging money. The *Mayflower* was finally engaged, and, against Weston and Cushman's advice, Carver went to Southampton to engage what crew he could at the last minute and assemble provisions. Plans were made to transport 150 settlers. The Leiden congregation had decided that only a minority would go: John Robinson, as the minister, would remain, and William Brewster, as the elder, would go.

SATURDAY, 25 JULY 1620

Mayflower *departs London*

Robert Cushman and Christopher Martin, agents of the chartering-party, came aboard the *Mayflower* this morning at London. The crew finished lading; the passengers who embarked at London went aboard and got under way for Southampton. Dropped down the Thames to Gravesend with the tide: vessels leaving the port of London always, in that day, "dropped down with the tide," tug-boats being unknown, and headway against the tide being difficult in the narrow river by sail power alone.

SUNDAY, 26 JULY 1620

Mayflower *at Gravesend*

The *Mayflower*, now at Gravesend, took aboard a pilot for its route down the English Channel. Favouring wind.

---

[1] Bangs, *Strangers and Pilgrims*, 594

MONDAY, 27 JULY 1620

Mayflower *in English Channel*

Set course S.W. by W. Favouring wind. The *Speedwell* heads for the Netherlands.

TUESDAY, 28 JULY 1620

Mayflower *headed to Southampton*

The *Mayflower* reaches Southampton Water, a tidal estuary north of the Solent and the Isle of Wight in England. It was formed by the rivers Test major, Itchen and Hamble minor which flow into it, and became an inlet of the sea at the end of the last ice age when sea levels rose, flooding many valleys in the south of England.

WEDNESDAY, 29 JULY 1620

Mayflower *in Southampton*

The *Mayflower* arrived at Southampton and came to anchor just outside of the harbour. Both the *Mayflower* and the *Speedwell* would lay at anchor a day or two offshore, before hauling in to the quay. The *Mayflower* undoubtedly lay at anchor until after the *Speedwell* arrived, to save expense.

THURSDAY, 30 JULY 1620

Mayflower *at Southampton*

Lying at Southampton off north end of "West Quay."

Pilgrims gather for departure at Leiden

Edward Winslow wrote in *Hypocrisie Unmasked* that "They that stayed at Leiden feasted us that were to go at our pastor's house, it being large; where we refreshed ourselves, after tears, with singing of Psalms, making joyful melody in our hearts as well as with the voice, there being many of our congregation very expert in music; and indeed it was the sweetest melody that ever mine ears heard." Pastor John Robinson preached his last sermon to the whole congregation, a third of which prepared to leave tomorrow; about twenty-five years later, Winslow remembered Robinson saying, "We are now ere long to part asunder, and the Lord knoweth whether ever he should live to see our faces again ... he charged us before God and his blessed angels, to follow him no further than he followed Christ; and if God should reveal anything to us by any other instrument of his, to be

2

as ready to receive it, as ever we were to receive any truth by his ministry; for he was very confident that the Lord had more truth and light yet to break forth out of his holy word. He took occasion also miserably to bewail the state and condition of the Reformed churches who were come to a period in religion and would go no further than the instruments of their reformation."[2]

FRIDAY, 31 JULY 1620

Mayflower *at Southampton*

Lying at Southampton. John Carver, Robert Cushman, and Christopher Martin, three of the agents, are now here. Outfitting ship, taking in lading, and getting ready for sea.

Embarkation of the Leiden Pilgrims

The initial embarkation was at Leiden, doubtless upon the Dutch canal-boats which brought them from a point closely adjacent to Pastor Robinson's house in the Klock-Steeg, in the garden of which were many of their houses, to Delfshaven.

---

[2] Winslow, *Hypocrisie Unmasked*, 127.

AUGUST 1620

Mayflower *at Southampton*

> *Mayflower* lying off the West Quay, Southampton.

Leiden Pilgrims en route to Delfshaven

Passing out of the gates of Delft and leaving the town behind, the Leiden Pilgrims still had a good ten miles of canal journey ahead of them before they reached their ship and came to the final parting, at Delfshaven, their point of embarkation in the *Speedwell*. Below Delft the canal, which from Leiden is the Vliet, then becomes the Schie, and at the village of Overschie the travellers entered the Delfshaven Canal, which between perfectly straight dykes flows at a considerable height above the surrounding pastures. Then after passing through one set of sluice gates after another, the Pilgrims were finally lifted from the canal into a broad receptacle for vessels, then into the outer haven, and so to the side of the *Speedwell* as it lay at the quay awaiting their arrival. "When they came to the place" [Delfshaven], says Bradford, "they found the ship and all things ready; and such of their friends as could not come with them [*from Leiden*] followed after them; and sundry also came from Amsterdam (about fifty miles) to see them shipped, and to take their leave of them."

The Pilgrim company took their farewells, and Winslow records: "We only going aboard, the ship lying to the key [quay] and ready to sail; the wind being fair, we gave them [their friends] a volley of small shot [musketry] and three pieces of ordnance and so lifting up our hands to each other and our hearts for each other to the Lord our God, we departed."[3]

Goodwin says of the parting: "The hull was wrapped in smoke, through which was seen at the stern the white flag of England doubly bisected by the great red cross of St. George, a token that the emigrants had at last resumed their dearly-loved nationality. Far above them at the main was seen the Union Jack of new device."[4]

---

[3] Winslow, *Hypocrisie Unmasked*, 91.
[4] Goodwin, *Pilgrim Republic*, 51.

SUNDAY, 2 AUGUST 1620

Mayflower *at Southampton*

Lying off Quay, Southampton.

Speedwell *en route to Southampton*

On the "German Ocean." Wind fair. General course due West, toward Southampton. Sails set, running free.

MONDAY, 3 AUGUST 1620

Mayflower *in Southampton*

Lying off West Quay, Southampton.

Speedwell *en route to Southampton*

Fair. Wind moderate. The *Speedwell* is in Dover Straits and the English Channel, in sight of Dover Cliffs.

TUESDAY, 4 AUGUST 1620

Mayflower *in Southampton*

Lying off Quay, Southampton. Waiting for *Speedwell* to arrive from Holland.

Speedwell *en route to Southampton*

Hugging the English shore, the *Speedwell* enters Southampton Water.

WEDNESDAY, 5 AUGUST 1620

Southampton Harbour

The *Speedwell*, having on board some 70 passengers and lading for Virginiacame to anchor in the Port of Southampton near the ship *Mayflower*, which had arrived from London a week ago, off the north of the West Quay.

THURSDAY, 6 AUGUST 1620

Mayflower *and* Speedwell *in Southampton Harbour*

The *Mayflower* and the *Speedwell* are at anchor in port of Southampton. The *Speedwell* was "warped to berth at the quay" near the *Mayflower*, to transfer lading, i.e., they passed the ends of ropes to the shore and, once those ends had been tied to bollards or rings on the dock, they pulled on the ropes to bring the ship into its berth. Some of the cargo of the *Speedwell* is here transferred to the larger ship *Mayflower*; doubtless the cheese, "Hollands," and other provisions, ordered by Cushman.

Thomas Weston presented the Leiden group with revised

terms: he now claimed that circumstances had changed and it was necessary to alter the original agreement. He had hoped to obtain a fishing monopoly for the settlement, but that was no longer possible. Many of the merchant adventurers, Weston maintained, now wanted to back out. For the merchants in London to supply the necessary funds, the Pilgrims must agree to dedicate all their time to working for the company. Instead of having two days a week to themselves, they must spend seven days a week working for the company. The Leiden group objected, maintaining that the new terms "were fitter for thieves and bondslaves than honest men." Making matters worse, Robert Cushman had agreed to Weston's terms without consulting the rest of them back in Leiden.

FRIDAY, 7 AUGUST 1621

Bickering in Southampton Harbour

Mayflower and *Speedwell* lying at anchor at Southampton.

Bradford gives an account of the bickering and recrimination at Southampton, when all parties had arrived: "After a joyful welcome, and mutual congratulations, with other friendly entertainments, they fell to parley about their business, how to dispatch with the best expedition; as also with their agents, about the alteration of the conditions. Mr. Carver pleaded he was employed hear at Hampton, and knew not well what the other had done at London. Mr. Cushman answered, he had done nothing but what he was urged too, partly by the grounds of equity, and more especially by necessity, otherwise all had been dashed and many undone. And in the beginning he acquainted his fellow agents herewith, who consented unto him and left it to him to execute, and to receive the money at London and send it down to them at Hampton, where they made the provisions. The which he accordingly did, though it was against his mind and some of ye merchants, that they were there made. And for giving them notice at Leyden of this change, he could not well in regard of the shortness of the time; again, he knew it would trouble them and hinder the business, which was already delayed overlong in regard of the season of the year, which he feared they would find to their cost. But these things gave not content at present."

The Leiden group refused to honour the agreement signed by John Carver on their behalf. Pastor Robinson had rather too strenuously given instructions, which it now began to be seen were not altogether wise. Cushman was censured, and there was evidently some acrimony. "Mr. Weston, likewise, came up from London to see them dispatched and to have the conditions confirmed. But they refused, and answered him that he knew right well that these were not according to the first agreement, neither could they yield to them without the consent of the rest that were behind. And indeed they had special charge when they came away, from the chief of those that were behind, not to do it. At which he was much offended, and told them, they must then look to stand on their own legs. So he returned in displeasure, and this was the first ground of discontent between them. And whereas there wanted well near £100 to clear things at their going away, he would not take order to disburse a penny, but let them shift as they could." Without Weston to provide them with the necessary funds, they were forced to sell off "some of their provisions to stop this gap, which was some three or four-score firkins of butter," between 3360 and 4720 lbs., or more than two tonnes, "which commodity they might best spare, having provided too large a quantity of that kind," before they could leave Southampton.

SATURDAY, 8 AUGUST 1620

Preparations at Southampton

Lying at Southampton. The *Mayflower* is ready for sea this day, but was obliged to lie here on account of the leakiness of the *Speedwell*, which required re-trimming. Some of the passengers transferred from *Speedwell* and vice versa. Christopher Martin was chosen by passengers their "Governour" for the voyage "to order them by the way, see to the disposing of their provisions, etc." Robert Cushman was chosen his "Assistant." The Mayflower now has 90 passengers and the Speedwell 30.

NOTE: there was *no* list of passengers, for either vessel, generated at the time. William Bradford's 1651 list as an appendix to his journal is our only extensive and fairly complete list of passengers from the *Mayflower*, which needs to be read alongside the 1623 division of land. There is no list of passengers from the *Speedwell*; there were (probably several) rearrangements of passengers between the two vessels before the *Speedwell* was abandoned. Lists purporting to be of the passengers on the *Speedwell* are modern (nineteenth and twentieth century) and are a "best guess" of who was, at one point or another, on that ship.

7

This is particularly unfortunate when we try to determine who came from the Netherlands to England on the *Speedwell* in August, but in September decided not to crowd on to the *Mayflower* for the final voyage. We know about Robert Cushman and Elizabeth Warren and her daughters (who would not have been on the *Speedwell* coming from Holland since these all were in England already), but what of eighteen year old Philip Delano (Philippe De la Noye)? Was he in England already, or did he come with the Pilgrims from Holland and, after the *Speedwell* was abandoned, decided to stay in England and get the next ship over a year later (the *Fortune* in the autumn of 1621)? Our research has not turned up any contemporary documents that can answer that question.

SUNDAY, 9 AUGUST 1620

Lying at Southampton

Kept the Sabbath on board the two ships.

The Pilgrims did not assent to the new conditions, imposed by Weston, until Cushman came over to Plymouth in the *Fortune* in 1621, and by dint of his famous sermon on "Sin and Danger of Self-Love" (more about that later) and his persuasion, induced them to sign: them they were also advised to by Robinson. All business up to this time had been done between the Adventurers and the Pilgrims, apparently, without any agreement in writing. It was probably felt, both by Robinson and the Plymouth leaders, that it was the least reparation they could make Cushman for their cruel and unjust treatment of him, realizing at length that, through all vicissitudes, he had proven a just, sagacious, faithful, and efficient friend. There does not appear to be any conclusive evidence that any articles of agreement between the Adventurers and colonists were signed before the *Mayflower* sailed

MONDAY, 10 AUGUST 1620

Lying at Southampton

Letters received for passengers from Holland. One from the Leiden Pastor [John Robinson] was read out to the company that came from that place; there was also a cover letter to John Carver: "I have a true feeling of your perplexity of mind and toil of body, but I hope that you who have always been able so plentifully to administer comfort unto others in their trials, are so well furnished for your self as that far greater difficulties than you have yet undergone (though I conceive them to have been great enough)

8

cannot oppress you, though they press you, as the Apostle speaks. The spirit of a man (sustained by the spirit of God) will sustain his infirmity, I doubt not so will yours. And the better much when you shall enjoy the presence & help of so many godly & wise brethren, for the bearing of part of your burden, who also will not admit into their hearts the least thought of suspicion of any the least negligence, at least presumption, to have been in you, what so ever they think in others. Now what shall I say or write unto you & your goodwife my loving sister[5]? even only this, I desire (& always shall) unto you from the Lord, as unto my own soul; and assure your self that my heart is with you, and that I will not forslowe my bodily coming at the first opportunity. I have written a large letter to the whole, and am sorry I shall not rather speak then write to them; & the more, considering the want of a preacher, which I shall also make some spur to my hastening after you. I do ever commend my best affection unto you, which if I thought you made any doubt of, I would express in more, & the same more ample & full words. And the Lord in whom you trust & whom you serve ever in this business & journey, guide you with his hand, protect you with his wing, and shew you & us his salvation in the end, & bring us in the meanwhile together in the place desired, if such be his good will, for his Christs sake."

TUESDAY, 11 AUGUST 1620

Lying at anchor at Southampton

The *Speedwell* was retrimmed a second time to overcome leakiness.

The conclusion of Robinson's letter to the whole company, read yesterday: "Sundry other things of importance I could put you in mind of, and of those before mentioned, in more words, but I will not so far wrong your godly minds as to think you heedless of these things, there being also diverse among you so well able to admonish both themselves and others of what concerns them. These few things therefore, and the same in few words, I do earnestly commend unto your care and conscience, joining therewith my daily incessant prayers unto the Lord, that he who hath made the heavens and the earth, the sea and all rivers of waters, and whose providence is over all his works, especially over all his dear children for good, would so guide and guard you in

---

[5] Robinson was married to Bridget White, the sister of Carver's wife.

your ways, as inwardly by his Spirit, so outwardly by the hand of his power, as that both you and we also, for and with you, may have after matter of praising his name all the days of your and our lives. Fare you well in him in whom you trust, and in whom I rest. An unfeigned well-willer of your happy success in this hopeful voyage, John Robinson." Bradford included this in his journal, adding, "This letter, though large, yet being so fruitful in itself, and suitable to their occasion, I thought meet to insert in this place."

WEDNESDAY, 12 AUGUST 1620

Lying at anchor at Southampton

Speedwell still leaking. Re-trimmed again. Passengers are assigned to each ship. Landed several tonnes of butter, which were sold as determined.

THURSDAY, 13 AUGUST 2020

Lying at anchor at Southampton

Receiving passengers, finishing loading and unloading, etc. Some of the principal Leyden men were assigned to Speedwell. After Weston's departure, in a huff, the settlers had a meeting and resolved to sell some of such stores as they could best spare, to clear port charges, etc., and to write a general letter to the Adventurers explaining the case, which they did.

FRIDAY, 14 AUGUST 1620

Preparing to leave Southampton

Both ships lying at anchor at Southampton, making ready to leave. Speedwell nearly ready for sea.

Heard that the King's warrant had issued to Sir James Coventry, under date of 23 July, to prepare a Patent for the Council for the Affairs of New England to supersede the Plymouth Virginia Company, Sir Ferdinando Gorges and Sir Robert Rich the Earl of Warwick among the Patentees.

SATURDAY, 15 AUGUST 1620

Departure from Southampton

The Mayflower weighed anchor, as did the Speedwell, and in company dropped down Southampton Water. Took departure from Cowes, Isle of Wight, and laid course down the Solent to the English Channel. Wind dead ahead, then baffling (a wind that frequently shifts from one point to another). General course S.W.

by S.

SUNDAY, 16 AUGUST 1620

Ships in English Channel

Head winds, and wind baffling; slow progress, beating down the English Channel ("beating" is a nautical term meaning to sail upwind by tacking repeatedly, which, given the contrary winds, was the only way to make progress). Both ships passed the Bill of Portland, an important way-point for coastal traffic: Portland Bill is a narrow promontory (or "bill") at the southern end of the Isle of Portland, and the southernmost point of Dorset, England. From Roman times, beacon fires were lit to warn ships of the danger of the Bill. George I granted permission for a lighthouse to be built there in 1716, and eventually three lighthouses were built on the promontory, but there was nothing when the *Mayflower* and *Speedwell* passed.

MONDAY, 17 AUGUST 1620

Ships in English Channel

Wind contrary. Beating out the English Channel. *Speedwell* in company with the *Mayflower*.

TUESDAY, 18 AUGUST 1620

Speedwell still leaking

The *Speedwell*, sailing in company with the *Mayflower*, starts to leak badly. Wind still contrary. Beating out the English Channel: very slow progress.

WEDNESDAY, 19 AUGUST 1620

Water rising inside the **Speedwell**

Speedwell leaking badly; *Mayflower* within sight, travelling in company. Wind still contrary. Beating out the English Channel: very slow progress.

THURSDAY, 20 AUGUST 1620

Detour to Dartmouth

Speedwell still leaking badly; water rising in the hold, gaining on pumps. Signalled the *Mayflower*, in company, which hove to. On consultation of Masters Reynolds of the *Speedwell* and Jones of the *Mayflower* and the chief of passengers of both ships, it was concluded that both should put into Dartmouth, being the nearest port. Laid course for Dartmouth with wind ahead.

11

Wind fair.

FRIDAY, 21 AUGUST 1620

Ships bearing up to Dartmouth

Wind fair and ahead. *Speedwell* leaking badly. *Mayflower* and *Speedwell* bearing up to Dartmouth.

SATURDAY, 22 AUGUST 1620

Speedwell *and* Mayflower *arrive in Dartmouth*

Mayflower made port at Dartmouth. The *Speedwell* was in company, and came to anchor in the harbour. Russell says: "The ships put back into Dartmouth, August13/23."[6] Goodwin says:[7] "The port was reached about August 23." Captain John Smith strangely omits the return of the ships to Dartmouth, and confuses dates, as he says "But the next day after leaving Southampton the lesser ship sprung a leak that forced their return to Plymouth." Cushman's letter, written the 17th, says they had then lain there "four days," which would mean, if four full days, the 13th, 14th, 15th, and 16th (all old style).

SUNDAY, 23 AUGUST 1620

Lying at anchor in Dartmouth Harbour

Mayflower lying at anchor with *Speedwell* (leaking badly) in Dartmouth harbor. No passengers, except leaders, were allowed ashore. Cushman, in his letter to Edward Southworth, written at Dartmouth on 17 August, says that Christopher Martin, the "governour" of the passengers in the *Mayflower*, "will not suffer them the passengers to go ashore, lest they should run away." This probably applied especially to such as had become disaffected by the delays and disasters, the apprenticed ("bound") servants.

MONDAY, 24 AUGUST 1620

Fixing the Speedwell

The *Mayflower* lying at anchor in Dartmouth harbour; the *Speedwell* at the quay, taking out lading for a thorough overhauling.

TUESDAY, 25 AUGUST 1620

Lying at anchor, Dartmouth Harbour

Speedwell being thoroughly overhauled for leaks.

---

[6] Russell, *Pilgrim Memorials*, 15
[7] Goodwin, *Pilgrim Republic*, 55.

WEDNESDAY, 26 AUGUST 1620
Lying at anchor, Dartmouth Harbour

The *Speedwell*, being thoroughly overhauled for leaks, was pronounced "as open and leaky as a sieve." The carpenters found a loose plank three feet long and admitting water freely, "as at a mole hole"; the seams had also opened some. There was much dissatisfaction and discontent between the passengers and the ship's "governour" Christopher Martin, between whom and Robert Cushman, the "assistant," there is constant disagreement. Cushman portrays the contemptible character and manner of Martin very sharply, and could not have wished to punish him worse for his meannesses than he did, by thus holding him up to the scorn of the world for all time. He says, *inter alia*: "If I speak to him, he flies in my face and saith no complaints shall be heard or received but by himself, and saith: 'They are froward, and waspish, discontented people, and I do ill to hear them.'"

THURSDAY, 27 AUGUST 1620
Lying at anchor, Dartmouth harbour

The *Speedwell* being searched and mended. Sailors offended at Christopher Martin because of meddling; there is also some dissension among the chief of the passengers. Cushman's letter, written in Dartmouth and dated August 17 (o.s.) says: "The sailors also are so offended at his ignorant boldness in meddling and controlling in things he knows not what belongs to, as that some threaten to mischief him. ... But at best this cometh of it, that he makes himself a scorn and laughing stock unto them."

FRIDAY, 28 AUGUST 1620
Lying at anchor in Dartmouth Harbour

The *Speedwell* still being repaired, although it is now judged by the workmen that mended her to be sufficient for the voyage.

A plaque in Bayards Cove to the two ships reads, in part: HERE, OFF BAYARD'S COVE, THE MAYFLOWER (180 TONS) WITH LONDON COLONISTS, AND THE SPEEDWELL (80 TONS) WITH LEYDEN PILGRIMS - SOME 122 IN ALL - LAY AT ANCHOR FROM AUGUST 23 (NEW STYLE) TO ABOUT AUGUST 31, 1620. THESE SHIPS HAD SAILED FROM SOUTHAMPTON ON AUGUST

15. THEY PUT IN AT DARTMOUTH TO REPAIR THE LEAKING SPEEDWELL. THEY SAILED FROM DARTMOUTH FOR AMERICA'

SATURDAY, 29 AUGUST 1620

Ships lying at anchor

Mayflower and *Speedwell* lying at anchor in Dartmouth harbour (Bayard's Cove). *Speedwell* relading.

SUNDAY, 30 AUGUST 1620

Lying at Anchor, Dartmouth harbour

Both ships lying at anchor in Dartmouth harbour.

Although the *Speedwell* was abandoned after trying to cross the Atlantic, it has appeared in art a remarkable number of times. The dramatic scene before the *Speedwell*'s departure from Delfshaven is depicted in "The Embarkation of the Pilgrims" by Robert J. Weir in the Capitol Rotunda in Washington, D.C., and the same scene is reprinted on the back of the rare US $10,000 bill. You can tell that this is the *Speedwell* and not the *Mayflower* because the name of the ship is visible under Pastor Robinson's knees. The evocative 1971 painting by Leslie Arthur Wilcox, now at Pilgrim Hall, was included in our chronicle a couple of days ago. That painting, as well as another painting of the *Speedwell* leaving Delfshaven, appeared on two commemorative stamps from the Isle of Man in 1992: Wilcox's painting is on the 28p postage stamp. There are several websites giving a more complete survey of the Pilgrims in postage, but to my knowledge these are the only two stamps with the *Speedwell*. Oddly enough, these stamps were issued in 1992 to commemorate the five hundredth anniversary of Columbus' discovery of America: since the Isle of Man had no connection with Christopher Columbus, they used their next best and commemorated Myles Standish (who, it is claimed, was a Manxman).

MONDAY, 31 AUGUST 1620

Ships lying at anchor in Dartmouth Harbour

Ships still lying at anchor at Dartmouth Harbour. The overhauling of the *Speedwell* has been completed, and the cargo has been replaced. Making ready to go to sea.

SEPTEMBER 1620

TUESDAY, 1 SEPTEMBER 1620

Lying at anchor, Dartmouth Harbour

Both ships lying at anchor in Dartmouth Harbour, both ready for sea. Bradford says: "Some leaks were found and mended and now it was conceived by the workmen and all, that [the *Speedwell*] was sufficient, and they might proceed without either fear or danger." Bradford indicated that they must have left Dartmouth "about the 21st" [o.s.] of August (or 31 August n.s.). Captain John Smith gives that date, though somewhat confusedly. Arber says:[8] "They actually left on 23 August." Goodwin says:[9] "Ten days were spent in discharging and re-stowing the Speedwell and repairing her from stem to stern," which would indicate that they left on 23 August/2 September.

WEDNESDAY, 2 SEPTEMBER 1620

Mayflower *and* **Speedwell** *weigh anchor*

Both ships weighed anchor and set sail. Laid general course W.S.W.

THURSDAY, 3 SEPTEMBER 1620

Fair wind

Mayflower, with the *Speedwell* in company, pass Land's End with wind fair. General course W.S.W.

FRIDAY, 4 SEPTEMBER 1620

Speedwell *leaking*

Speedwell starting to leak dangerously; *Mayflower* in company. Course W.S.W.

SATURDAY, 5 SEPTEMBER 1620

Speedwell *and* **Mayflower** *divert to Plymouth*

Observations showed ships above 100 leagues [345 miles] W.S.W. of Land's End. *Speedwell* leaking badly; hove to, and signalled the *Mayflower*, in company. On consultation between masters, carpenters, and the principal passengers, it was decided to put back into Plymouth and determine whether the pinnace is

---

[8] Arber, *Pilgrim Fathers*, 343.
[9] Goodwin, *Pilgrim Republic*, 55.

seaworthy. Put about and laid course for Plymouth.

SUNDAY, 6 SEPTEMBER 1620

Ships reach Plymouth (England)

Wind on starboard quarter. *Speedwell* and *Mayflower* arrive in Plymouth together, and come to anchor.

SUNDAY, 6 SEPTEMBER 1620

Speedwell *and* Mayflower *arrive in Plymouth together*

The *Speedwell*, the smaller of the two ships (according to William Bradford, a "smale ship of 60 tune"), had sprung a leak the day before when the ships were about 100 leagues (345 miles) out, and both ships decided to turn back. They arrived back in Plymouth harbour together today.

MONDAY, 7 SEPTEMBER 1620

In Plymouth Harbour

Both the *Mayflower* and the *Speedwell* have arrived and are at anchor in Plymouth harbour. From "the *Speedwell's* Log" for August 28 [o.s.]/September 7 [n.s.]: "At anchor in Plymouth harbor. Conference of chief of Colonists and officers of *May-flower* and *Speedwell*. No special leak could be found, but it was judged to be the general weakness of the ship, and that she would not prove sufficient for the voyage. It was resolved to dismiss her the *Speedwell*, and part of the company, and proceed with the other ship."

TUESDAY, 8 SEPTEMBER 1620

Who was on which ship?

While we know who the passengers on the *Mayflower's* voyage to the New World were from William Bradford's list which he compiled about 1651 (over thirty years later), and we know that some of the passengers on the *Speedwell* stayed in England after the ships turned back, there is no full, separate, list of original passengers on the August sailings of the *Speedwell* or the *Mayflower*. There was no passenger manifest for the two ships that has survived, or even for the *Mayflower* itself for its voyage to New England: after all, who would check the manifest or passenger list once they reached Massachusetts? The only list of passengers is the one compiled by Bradford in 1651 for *Of Plimoth Plantation*, for those who had made the 66 day voyage to Massachusetts. William Bradford and his wife were almost

16

certainly on the *Speedwell*, as shown by his account of the embarkation; likewise, Edward Winslow's full account of the embarkation ("Hypocrisie Unmasked") also suggests that he and his family were *Speedwell* passengers. William Brewster and his family were likewise probably on the *Speedwell*.

WEDNESDAY, 9 SEPTEMBER 1620

Mayflower Conspiracy Theories

It is certain that the *Speedwell* sprung a leak in the Atlantic, causing it to return to Plymouth along with the *Mayflower*. What caused the leak? The most frequently mentioned possibility is that it was "over-rigged" and had on too much sail which caused a strain on the masts, and which then caused holes and leaks to develop. Prior to the voyage, the *Speedwell* had been refitted in Delfshaven in Holland and had two masts. Nathaniel Philbrick suggests that the crew used a mast that was too big for the ship, and that the added stress caused holes to form in the hull. William Bradford wrote that "the leakiness of this ship was partly by her being overmasted and too much pressed with sails," but attributes the main cause of her leaking to actions on the part of the crew. Robert Cushman wrote from Dartmouth in August 1620 (as soon as the *Speedwell* returned) that the leaking was caused by a loose board or plank approximately two feet long. There is a persistent rumour of sabotage, either by the captain or the crew, but there is no proof. We shall revisit the question about sabotage in a few months when we look at the decision to drop everyone off in Massachusetts.

THURSDAY, 10 SEPTEMBER 1620

Why did they turn back?

If the *Speedwell* had not been overmasted, both she and the *Mayflower* would have arrived early in the fall (probably by the middle of October) at the mouth of the Hudson River, and the whole course of New England history would have been entirely different. It does appear, however, that most of the leaders of the community (Bradford, Brewster, Cushman, Winslow, and their families) were on the *Speedwell* when it started to leak; letting the *Mayflower* continue on its way by itself, to arrive in New Amsterdam before the weather turned bad, was not a good or viable option, since that would have deprived the emigrant community of its religious and commercial leaders ("the cheefe of them that came from Leyden," in Bradford's words).

FRIDAY, 11 SEPTEMBER 1620

Cargo transfers

Cargo was transferred from the *Speedwell* to the *Mayflower* in Plymouth harbour, continuing for the next few days. John A. Goodwin notes [10] that "it was fortunate for the overloaded Mayflower that she had fine weather while lying at anchor there ... for the port of Plymouth was then only a shallow, open bay, with no protection. In southwesterly gales its waters rose into enormous waves, with such depressions between that ships while anchored sometimes struck the bottom of the harbor and were dashed in pieces."

SATURDAY, 12 SEPTEMBER 1620

Final determinations

As the transfer of cargo from the *Speedwell* to the *Mayflower* continued, passengers were reassigned. Robert Cushman and Thomas Blossom, and their families, decided to stay in England. While Elizabeth (Walker) Warren and her five daughters stayed in England, her husband Richard, a London merchant who had probably provided part of the financing for the voyage to New England, was included among the *Mayflower* passengers, with the hope that his wife and children would join him later. (They came to him on the *Anne* in 1623, and Richard and Elizabeth subsequently had sons Nathaniel and Joseph at Plymouth.) Philip Delano (Philippe de la Noye), part of the Leiden community and a passenger on the *Speedwell*, also stayed in England and took passage the following year on the *Fortune*. In all, eleven people from the *Speedwell* boarded the *Mayflower*, leaving 20 people to return to London. From what we can tell, most of those 20 eventually did reach the New World.

SUNDAY, 13 SEPTEMBER 1620

Speedwell/Swiftsure

This was the final day of cargo transfer from the *Speedwell* to the *Mayflower*. The *Speedwell* was built in 1577, under the name *Swiftsure*, as part of English preparations for war against Spain. She participated in the fight against the Spanish Armada.

---

[10]Goodwin, *Pilgrim Republic*, 57

18

During the Earl of Essex's 1596 Azores expedition she served as the ship of his second in command, Sir Gelli Meyrick. After hostilities with Spain ended, she was decommissioned in 1605 and renamed the *Speedwell*. According to William Bradford, the *Speedwell* was sold at auction in London after 1620, and after being repaired made a number of successful voyages for her new owners. The *Swiftsure/Speedwell* had thus previously crossed the Atlantic several times when it started leaking in August 1620, making its peril all the more mysterious.

MONDAY, 14 SEPTEMBER 1620

Speedwell *leaves for London*

All of the *Speedwell*'s passengers who were to cross the Atlantic now being on board the *Mayflower*, the *Speedwell* departed for London. Christopher Martin had been made "governour" of the passengers on the *Mayflower* for the voyage, and Robert Cushman his "assistant." It is evident from Cushman's letter of 17 August 1620 that Martin had become obnoxious to both passengers and crew, particularly regarding provisioning and payments and rendering financial accounts to the Leiden contingent: "If I speak to him, he flies in my face and saith no complaints shall be heard or received but by himself, and saith: 'They are froward, and waspish, discontented people, and I do ill to hear them.' ... The sailors also are so offended at his ignorant boldness in meddling and controlling in things he knows not what belongs to, as that some threaten to mischief him ... But at best this cometh of it, that he makes himself a scorn and laughing stock unto them." It seems that when the passengers were all gathered in the *Mayflower* after the *Speedwell*'s departure there was a new choice of officers (though no explicit record has been found of this), as Cushman had vacated his position and gone back to London, and we will see that on November 11 [o.s.]/21 [n.s.] the colonists "confirmed" John Carver as their "governour," showing that he had been previously chosen for this position; the likeliest day for this selection is today.

A number of historians have commented that the *Speedwell*'s return to London is a sign that some passengers, tired of staying on the ships for a month and a half and not getting very far, just "gave up and went home." There are indications that the captains (Jones for the *Mayflower* and Reynolds for the *Speedwell*) refused to allow passengers to go ashore while the ships were

19

anchored at Plymouth to prevent anyone from "running away." It is nonetheless evident (a) that no one did sneak away -- Bradford would almost certainly have called attention to any defections in his narrative if they had, and (b) most of the 20 who left Plymouth for London on the *Speedwell* did eventually get to New England: some (the Warren women, Cushman, and Delano) within a year or two, and others (Blossom and Kenelm Winslow) after more than a decade.

As I have mentioned before, given the mortality rate of the first year, it is highly likely that even if these 20 passengers had somehow managed to squeeze on to the *Mayflower*, most (particularly the women) would have died during "the great sickness." The fact that they stayed in England and came over later meant that they survived -- for if they had not, I would not be here. Such is the role of contingency in history.

TUESDAY, 15 SEPTEMBER 1620

Quarters Assigned

Some of the principal passengers aboard the *Mayflower* went ashore in Plymouth and were entertained by other Separatist brethren on this, their last full day in England ("having been kindly entertained and courteously used by divers friends there dwelling," *Mourt's Relation*). The passengers were all assigned quarters today on the *Mayflower*, which must have been a daunting task. There were 102 passengers, and a crew of perhaps 35 men, for a total of about 135 men, women and children (along with two dogs). However, at about 180 tons, the *Mayflower* was considered a smaller cargo ship, having travelled mainly between England and Bordeaux with clothing and wine, not an ocean ship, and not designed to carry passengers. A good, strong ship was at least 300 tons, which made the Mayflower relatively small. Some had better quarters than others, some much more and heavier furniture, while some had bulky and heavy goods for their personal benefit (such as William Mullins' cases of "boots and shoes"). The assignments were in a large measure determined by the requirements of the women and children: analysis of the list shows that there were nineteen women, ten young girls, and one infant requiring special consideration. Of the other children, none were so young that they couldn't readily bunk with or near their fathers in any part of the ship in which the men might be located.

WEDNESDAY, 16 SEPTEMBER 1620
Mayflower *sets sail for the New World*

The *Mayflower* weighed anchor, "the winds coming east north east, a fine small gale" (*Mourt's Relation*); laid course WSW "for northern coasts of Virginia." Bradford wrote: "Now all being compact together in one ship, they put to sea again with a prosperous wind, which continued diverse days together, which was some Encouragement unto them, yet according to the usual manner many were afflicted with seasickness." Most of the Pilgrims had now already been living onboard the ships for nearly a month and a half.

THURSDAY, 17 SEPTEMBER 1620
Mayflower *under full sail*

The *Mayflower* comes in with wind ENE. Light gale continues. Made all sail on ship. Unhappily the early chroniclers familiar with the *Mayflower* have left us neither a representation nor even a general description of the ship, and little data from which to reconstruct her outlines and details. Tradition chiefly places her in one of the few classes into which the merchant craft of her day were divided, her tonnage and service being almost the only other authentic indices to this class. Bradford states little more than that a vessel, which could have been no other, "was hired at London, being of burden about 9 score [tons]." It is extraordinary that all writers keep silence even as to the ship's name; no specific description exists from Smith, Bradford, Winslow, *Mourt's Relation,* and the other contemporaneous or early writers of Pilgrim history.

FRIDAY, 18 SEPTEMBER 1620
Mayflower *under full sail*

No one can state with authority the *Mayflower's* exact rig, model, or dimensions; but there can be no question, from even the meagre data and the prints we possess, that all these were very standardised. Her hundred and eighty tons register indicates in general her size, and to some extent her probable model and rig. In that era, the ships of each class closely corresponded to each other. Like all vessels having high stems and sterns, she was unquestionably "a wet ship" — upon this voyage especially so, as Bradford shows, from being overloaded, and hence lower than usual in the water. Bradford says, quoting the master of the

21

Mayflower and others: "As for the decks and upper works they would caulk them as well as they could, ... though with the working of the ship, they would not long keep staunch." She was probably not an old craft, as her captain and others declared they "knew her to be strong and firm under water;" and the weakness of her upper works was doubtless due to the strain of her overload, in the heavy weather of the autumn gales. Bradford says: "They met with many contrary winds and fierce storms with which their ship was shrewdly shaken and her upper works made very leaky."

SATURDAY, 19 SEPTEMBER 1620

Mayflower *under full sail*

The *Mayflower*'s galley, with its primitive conditions for cooking, existed rather as a place for the preparation of food and the keeping of utensils, than for the use of fire. The arrangements for cooking were exceedingly crude, and were limited to the open "hearth-box" filled with sand, the chief cooking appliance being a tripod-kettle of the early navigators. This might be set up in any part of the ship where the "sand-hearth" could also go, and the smoke be cared for. It not infrequently found space in the forecastle, between decks, and, when fine weather prevailed, on the open deck. The bake-kettle and the frying-pan were only slightly less important than the kettle for boiling.

Her ordnance doubtless comprised several heavy guns, mounted on the spar-deck amidships, with lighter guns astern and on the rail, and a piece of longer range and larger calibre on the forecastle; this was the general disposition of ordnance on merchant vessels of her size in that day, when an armament was a *sine qua non*. Edward Winslow in his "Hypocrisie Unmasked" ([1646] 91) says, in writing of the departure of the Pilgrims from Delfshaven, on the *Speedwell*: "The wind being fair we gave them a volley of small shot and three pieces of ordnance," by which it seems that the *Speedwell*, of only sixty tons, mounted at least "three pieces." The *Mayflower*, being three times the size, may have carried more.

SUNDAY, 20 SEPTEMBER 1620

Mayflower *under full sail*

The *Mayflower* comes in with wind ENE. Gale continues. The *Mayflower* now surpassed the point at which it had turned back on 5 September when the *Speedwell* had begun to leak, two weeks before. The *Mayflower* was square-rigged with a beakhead bow and high, castle-like structures fore and aft which protected the crew and the main deck from the elements — designs that were typical of English merchant ships of the early 17th century. Her stern carried a 30-foot high, square aft-castle which made the ship difficult to sail close to the wind and not well suited against the North Atlantic's prevailing westerlies, especially in the fall and winter of 1620; the voyage from England to America took more than two months as a result. *Mayflower*'s return trip to London in April–May 1621 took less than half that time, with the same strong winds now blowing in the direction of the voyage.

MONDAY, 21 SEPTEMBER 1620

Passengers' Ages [Part One]

The actual and comparative youth of the majority of the leaders — "the Pilgrim Fathers" — is a matter of comment, even of surprise, to most students of Pilgrim history, especially in view of what the Leiden congregation had experienced before embarking for America. Four men were over 50, five men were between 41 and 50, 21 men were between 31 and 40, seven men were between 21 and 30 years old. The largest age group was the teen-aged boys aged between 10 and 18, with about 24 in all, or about one-quarter of the total passengers -- more about them as time goes on. Only nine could have been over forty, and of these Carver, Chilton, Martin, Mullins, and Priest died within a few months of landing, leaving Brewster, Warren (who died early), Cooke, and Hopkins as the "seniors." Winslow celebrated his twenty-fifth birthday during the crossing, Dr. Fuller was about 31; Bradford was only 31 when chosen Governor, Allerton was 32, and Standish 36. They were certainly "old heads on young shoulders."

TUESDAY, 22 SEPTEMBER 1620

Mayflower *under full sail*

First day of Autumn. Fine, warm weather and the "harvest-moon." The shorter than usual lag time between moonrises around the full Harvest Moon means no long period of darkness between sunset and moonrise for days in succession. The usual equinoctial storms seem to have been delayed, but the danger increased significantly now that the calendar has passed into autumn.

WEDNESDAY, 23 SEPTEMBER 1620

The name "Mayflower"

There were 26 different vessels bearing the name *Mayflower* in the Port Books of England during the reign of James I (1603–1625); it is not known why the name was so popular. Even more strange is the fact that Bradford does not mention the name of the ship on which he came to America, even once, in his *Of Plimoth Plantation*. In his record of 1629 he speaks of a ship called the *Mayflower* (along with the *Talbot*) commissioned by the Massachusetts Bay Company, but this is different than the ship which brought the Pilgrims to Plymouth. The earliest authentic evidence that the ship which bore the Pilgrims across the North Atlantic in the late autumn of 1620 was the *Mayflower*, is the heading of the "Allotment of Lands" — happily an official document — in March, 1623. It is more than a little remarkable that, with the constantly recurring references to "the ship," the all-important factor in Pilgrim history, her name should nowhere have found mention in the earliest Pilgrim literature. Bradford uses the terms the "bigger ship," "larger ship," and "first ship"; Winslow, Cushman, Captain John Smith, Morton, and others mention simply the "vessel," or the "ship," when speaking of the *Mayflower*, but in no case give her a name.

* * *

In the Land Distribution of 1623, property is given to various settlers according to when they arrived: each of the ships are named. In the first lot, it is stated: "The Falles of their grounds which came first over in the May-Floure, according as their lotes were cast ." Caleb Johnson notes, "In 1623, the Pilgrims divided up their land. The people mentioned in the Division of Land came on the *Mayflower* (1620), the *Fortune* (1621), and the *Anne* (1623). A couple may have arrived on the *Swan* (1622) or the *Little James* (1623), but these were small ships carrying mostly cargo. The Division of Land is recorded in Volume XII of the *Records of the Colony of New Plymouth*.[11] Each family was given one acre per family member." This would appear to be the first definite indication of the name of the ship.

---

[11] Reprinted in *MD* 1:227-230

THURSDAY, 24 SEPTEMBER 1620
The Mayflower *before the Pilgrims*

The identity of Captain Jones' *Mayflower* is based on records from her home port, her tonnage (est. 180–200 tons), and the master's name in 1620 in order to avoid confusion with the many other *Mayflower* ships. It is not known when and where the *Mayflower* was built, although late records designate her as "of London." She was designated in the Port Books of 1609–11 as "of Harwich" in the county of Essex, coincidentally the birthplace of *Mayflower* master Christopher Jones about 1570. Records dating from August 1609 note Christopher Jones as master and part owner of the *Mayflower* when his ship was chartered for a voyage from London to Trondheim in Norway and back to London. The ship lost an anchor on her return due to bad weather, and she made short delivery of her cargo of herring. Litigation resulted, and this was still proceeding in 1612. According to records, the ship was twice on the Thames at London in 1613, once in July and again in October and November, and in 1616 she was on the Thames carrying a cargo of wine, which suggests that the ship had recently been on a voyage to France, Spain, Portugal, the Canaries, or some other wine-producing land. Jones sailed the *Mayflower* cross-Channel, taking English woolens to France and bringing French wine back to London. He also transported hats, hemp, Spanish salt, hops, and vinegar to Norway, and he may have taken the *Mayflower* whaling in the North Atlantic in the Greenland area or sailed to Mediterranean ports.

FRIDAY, 25 SEPTEMBER 1620
The Mayflower *before the Pilgrims (continued)*

After 1616, there is no further record which specifically relates to Jones' *Mayflower* until 1624. This is unusual for a ship trading to London, as it would not usually disappear from the records for such a long time. No Admiralty court document can be found relating to the Pilgrims' voyage of 1620, although this might be due to the unusual way in which the transfer of the pilgrims was arranged from Leiden to New England; some of the records of the period might also have been lost. Jones was one of the owners of the ship by 1620, along with Christopher Nichols, Robert Child, and Thomas Short. It was from Child and Jones that Thomas Weston chartered her in the summer of 1620 to undertake the

Pilgrim voyage. Weston had a significant role in the *Mayflower* voyage due to his membership in the Company of Merchant Adventurers of London, and he eventually travelled to the Plymouth Colony himself.

SATURDAY, 26 SEPTEMBER 1620

Chartering the Mayflower

In 1619, the Leiden Separatists first met with Thomas Weston, a representative of the London investors, who conveyed his fellow investors' willingness to finance the Separatists' colony in the New World. The Separatists sought to build an autonomous community based on New Testament principles; Weston and his fellow investors were interested in the Colony of New Plymouth, but more so in New England and her natural resources. Arlene Spencer writes, "That Weston invested his own money in a business as an individual along with other investors who together owned a company through joint stock was not new. What was relatively new was this: as individuals, those investors were not necessarily wealthy, courtiers, nor aristocracy anymore. This was a recent emerging economic engine in England: the first of what eventually becomes the middle class. The practice came about because then, in recent prior decades, English merchants had learned from their more affluent and successful Dutch competitors, as an individual trader, no longer to trade solely in one good (i.e. wool cloth, coal, or fish), but instead to diversify trade goods, buying different kinds of goods and then selling those goods by, crucially, creating and maintaining trade routes through relationships with trade partners within Britain and internationally."[12] The actual contract for the *Mayflower* has not survived; most of what we know about Weston, the financial arrangements, and the chartering of the *Mayflower* is told to us in William Bradford's first hand account, *Of Plimoth Plantation.* Others of Weston's contemporaries, such as Winslow (*Good Newes From New England*), Pratt (*A Declaration of the English People That First Inhabited New England*), and Morton (*Mourt's*

---

[12] Arlene Spencer, "New Evidence: Was Thomas Weston, Seventeenth Century London Merchant among the First to Sail Fish to Virginia's Starving Colonists?"
https://globalmaritimehistory.com/thomas_weston_merchant/ (Accessed 12 December 2024).

Relation) wrote about this but none had the personal dealings with Weston and the Merchant Adventurers that Bradford had. From these works we only learn about Weston and the Merchant Adventurers during the years 1619-1623: these are the years Weston was involved in the founding of Plymouth and an attempted second colony, Wessagusset. More about all this next month; tomorrow we will try to figure out how much this all cost.

SUNDAY, 27 SEPTEMBER 1620

How much did this cost?

It is probable that the exact stipulations of the contract will never come to light, and we can only roughly guess at them by a somewhat difficult comparison with the terms on which the *Lady Arabella*, the "Admiral" or flagship of Winthrop's fleet, was chartered in 1630, for what is substantially the same voyage (of course, without expectation or probability of so long a stay on the New England coast), though the latter was a much larger ship. The contract probably named an "upset" or total sum for the "round voyage," as was the case with the *Lady Arabella*. Winthrop enters among his memoranda, "The agreement for the *Arabella* £750, whereof [blank] is to be paid in hand [*i e. cash down*] the rest upon certificate of our safe arrival." The sum was doubtless considerably in excess of that paid for the *Mayflower*, both because she was a much larger, heavier-armed, and better-manned ship, of finer accommodations, and because ships were, in 1630, in far greater demand for the New England trade than in 1620, Winthrop's own fleet including no less than ten. The adjustments of freight and passage money between the Adventurers and colonists are a matter of much doubt and perplexity, and are not likely to be discovered by further research. The only light thrown upon them is by the tariffs for such service on Winthrop's fleet, and for passage on different ships at a little later day. It is altogether probable that transportation of all those accepted as colonists, by the agents of the Adventurers and "Planters," was without direct charge to any individual, but was debited against the whole. But as some had better quarters than others, some much more and heavier furniture, while some had bulky and heavy goods for their personal benefit, it is fair to assume that some schedule of rates for "tonnage," if not for individuals, became necessary, to prevent complaints and to facilitate accounts. Winthrop credits Mr. Goffe—owner of two of the ships in 1630—as follows:—"For ninety-six passengers at £4, £384. For thirty-two tons of goods at £3 (per ton). For passage for a man, his wife and servant, (3 persons) £16/10, £5/10 each."

MONDAY, 28 SEPTEMBER 1620

How much did this cost? (continued)

Goodwin shows the cost of transportation at different times and under varying conditions: "The expense of securing and shipping Thomas Morton of 'Merry Mount' to England, was £12 7 0," but just what proportion the passage money bore to the rest of the account, cannot now be told. The expense of Mr. Rogers, the young clergyman brought over by Isaac Allerton, without authority, was, for the voyage out: "For passage £1. For diet for eleven weeks at 4s. 8d. per week, total £3 11 4" [A rather longer passage than usual.] Constant Southworth came in the same ship and paid the same, £3 11 4, which may hence be assumed as the average charge, at that date, for a first-class passage. The expenses of the 35 of the Leiden congregation who came over in the *Mayflower* in 1620, and of the others brought in the *Lion* in 1630, were slightly higher than these figures, but the cost of the trip from Leiden to England was included, with that of some clothing. In 1650, Judge Sewall, who as a wealthy man would be likely to indulge in some luxury, gives his outlay, one way, as, "Fare, £2 3 0; cabin expenses, £4 11 4; total, £6 14 4."

On calculating historical equivalents of prices: Note that prior to 15 February 1971 ("Decimal day," or "D-day"), monetary amounts in the UK were expressed as pounds (£), shillings (s.) and pence (d.), where £1 = 20s. = 240d. After 1970, there were 100 pennies in a pound, so one (new) penny = 2.4 old pence. Often one knows the price, cost, or value of something in a particular, historic year, and one wants to know the value of this money amount in another year (such as the present). The measure often used is the price of a "bundle" of goods and services that a representative group of consumers buys or earns. In the UK that measure is usually taken to be the "retail price index" (RPI), which corresponds to what is called the "consumer price index" in other countries. While it is tricky (and well-nigh impossible) to calculate exactly modern equivalents, a guess is that £1 sterling in 1620 is equivalent to £210 sterling today (and thus about $275 US or $360 CAN at current exchange rates -- which is somewhat misleading). Thus the £5 10s. mentioned yesterday as the per person amount for passage on one of the ships of the Winthrop fleet in 1630 would convert in 2020 to £1,155 = $1,970.63 CAD = $1,472.03 USD.

TUESDAY, 29 SEPTEMBER 1620

The Mayflower Crew

Charles Banks estimated that the *Mayflower* had a crew of about 50: 36 men 'before the mast' (crew) and 14 officers on the captain's staff.[13] This included the following officers: four mates, four quartermasters, surgeon, carpenter, cooper, cook, boatswain and gunner. Many other writers, however, conclude that there were perhaps a little more than half that number, with the crew being reduced to permit more passengers. The entire crew stayed with the *Mayflower* when it wintered-over in Plymouth in 1620-1621, with about half of them dying during that time, including the gunner, boatswain, three of the four quartermasters and the cook. That she had no chaplain goes without saying. The Pilgrims had their spiritual adviser with them in the person of Elder Brewster, and were not likely to tolerate a priest of either the English or the Romish church on a vessel carrying them. The identity of several key officers under the captain has been well established: two Masters Mates with previous New World sailing experience were John Clarke, age 45, and Robert Coppin. They were assisted by Masters Mates Andrew Williamson and John Parker. John Alden, possibly a distant relative of Christopher Jones, was the ship's cooper. He was sent early to Southampton, to buy provisions for the journey and "cooper" them in casks. Alden remained in Plymouth when the crew returned to England. An important person on the captain's staff that Bradford oddly neglected to mention was the ship's surgeon, a young man just out of apprenticeship as a London Barber-Surgeon by the name of Giles Heale. His name appears as a witness to the death-bed will of William Mullins in February 1621. Another person that Bradford also did not mention who is recorded as possibly being a principal officer of the *Mayflower* (due to his title) is a man identified only as "Master" Leaver. He is recorded in *Mourt's Relation*(1622) as rescuing Pilgrims lost in a forest in January 1621.

---

[13] Banks, *English Ancestry*, 18-19

WEDNESDAY, 30 SEPTEMBER 1620

Relations with the Crew

There were daily prayer services each morning, led by Elder William Brewster, the spiritual leader of the group. These consisted principally in singing psalms and reading Scripture. Given the cramped accommodations on the ship, these services took place on deck when the weather was good, but wherever they could when the weather was bad. These services were crucial to the maintenance of morale among the passengers during very difficult times. During this time, the crew had to continue with their duties as usual, and this caused a significant amount of friction during the journey. While most of the passengers were extreme Protestants of various descriptions, the stories of the hostility during the voyage between passengers and crew suggests that very few of the crew were likeminded -- and the crew, apparently, were not at all shy about displaying this difference in religious attitude to the passengers.

OCTOBER 1620

Relations with the Crew (continued)

William Bradford wrote, "And I may not omit here a special work of God's providence. There was a proud and very profane young man, one of the seamen, of a lusty, able body, which made him the more haughty; he would alway be contemning the poor people in their sickness and cursing them daily with grievous execrations; and did not let [*i.e., refrain*] to tell them that he hoped to help to cast half of them overboard before they came to their journey's end, and to make merry with what they had; and if he were by any gently reproved, he would curse and swear most bitterly."

FRIDAY, 2 OCTOBER 1620

First Death

Bradford continues his story of the "proud and very profane young" seaman: "But it pleased God before they came half seas over, to smite this young man with a grievous disease, of which he died in a desperate manner, and so was himself the first that was thrown overboard. Thus his curses light on his own head, and it was an astonishment to all his fellows for they noted it to be the just hand of God upon him." We can readily imagine this first burial at sea on the *Mayflower*. There does not appear to have been any funeral ceremony, since the crew lacked a chaplain and the Pilgrims viewed funeral ceremonies and prayers for the dead as worthless remnants of Papism: the comments of Separatist ministers upon the death of Elizabeth I are somewhat shocking to modern ears in their rejection of prayers for the dead. William Elliott Griffis says "the Puritans cared next to nothing about ceremonies over a corpse, whether at wave or grave."[14] The *Westminster Confession of Faith* (1647) stated, "Prayer is to be made for things lawful; and for all sorts of men living, or that shall live hereafter: but not for the dead, nor for those of whom it may be known that they have sinned the sin unto death" (XXI.IV, citing II Sam 12:21, 22, 23 with Luke 16:25, 26; Rev. 14:13). Bradford's phraseology in this case would seem to support the

---

[14] Griffis, *Three Homes*, 176.

absence of any funeral service, as he speaks of the body as simply "thrown overboard." He viewed this death as a "special work of God's providence," giving assurance to the passengers that God was taking particular care of them in a memorable and unusual way. Today's death, of a crew member, was the first of many on this journey.

SATURDAY, 3 OCTOBER 1620

A sharp change

Equinoctial weather, followed by stormy westerly gales; "encountered many times with cross winds and continued fierce storms with which the Ship was shrewdly [*in its original meaning of "sharply" or "severely"*] shaken and her upper works made very leaky; and one of the main beams in the midships was bowed and cracked." Some of the crew feared that the ship would not be able to complete the voyage. Bradford wrote, "The chief of the company perceiving the mariners to fear the sufficiency of the ship (as appeared by their mutterings) they entered into serious consultation with the Master and other officers of the ship, to consider, in time, of the danger, and rather to return than to cast themselves into a desperate and inevitable peril. There was great distraction and difference of opinion amongst the mariners themselves. Fain would they do what would be done for their wages' sake, being now near half the seas over; on the other hand, they were loath to hazard their lives too desperately." After breaking open the hold and examining the hull by candlelight, "the Master and others affirmed they knew the ship to be strong and firm under water, and for the buckling bending or bowing of the main beam, there was a great iron scrue the passengers brought out of Holland which would raise the beam into its place. The which being done, the carpenter and Master affirmed that a post put under it, set firm in the lower deck, and otherwise bound, would make it sufficient. As for the decks and upper works, they would caulk them as well as they could; and though with the working of the ship they would not long keep staunch [*meaning "watertight"*], yet there would otherwise be no great danger if they did not overpress her with sails. So they resolved to proceed." While there were much later (early twentieth century) stories that the "great iron scrue" was in fact part of a printing press that the

Pilgrims were bringing to America, Jeremy Bangs has shown that it was probably a house jack used by carpenters for construction.[15]

SUNDAY, 4 OCTOBER 1620

Storm continues

Bradford continued, "In sundry of these stormes, the winds were so fierce and the seas so high, as the ship could not bear a knot of sail, but was forced to hull drift under bare poles for divers days together." Nathaniel Philbrick, however, adds this description of the voyage of the *Mayflower II* in 1957: "At times, the motion in the high aft poop cabin became so violent that Captain Alan Villiers—one of the most experienced blue-water sailors in the world—feared that he might be flung out of his bunk. What this ship would do in survival conditions was a matter of deep concern to Villiers and his men. Toward the end of the voyage, a storm set in, forcing Villiers to do as Master Jones had done 337 years before. As the motion of the ship in the giant waves became intolerable, he decided he had no option but to lie ahull. The sails were furled, and everything on deck was tied down. Then, with considerable trepidation, Villiers ordered that the helm be secured to leeward. 'This was the crucial test,' Villiers wrote. 'Would she lie that way, more or less quietly, with the windage of the high poop keeping her shoulder to the sea? Or would she just wallow hopelessly in the great troughs, threatening to roll her masts out? We didn't know. No one had tried the maneuver in a ship like that for maybe two centuries.' As soon as the ship's bow swung into the wind, a remarkable change came over the *Mayflower II*. Even though she was under bare poles in a howling gale, her slablike topsides functioned as a kind of wooden storm sail, magically steadying the ship's motion. Almost perfectly balanced, the *Mayflower II* sat like a contented duck amid the uproar of the storm. After being pounded unmercifully by the waves, the ship was finally at peace. 'I reflected that the Pilgrim Fathers, who tossed through many such a wild night in Atlantic storms, at least knew tranquility in great gales,' Villiers wrote."[16] Villiers' quotations are from "How we sailed the New *Mayflower* to America," *National Geographic* v. 112, n. 5 (November 1957), 667.

---

[15] Bangs, *Strangers and Pilgrims*, 608-610
[16] Philbrick, *Mayflower*, 31-32

John Howland falls overboard and is saved

A succession of strong westerly gales. In one of the heaviest storms, while lying at hull, Bradford writes that "a lusty young man called John Howland," an indentured servant of John Carver, apparently grew restless down below. After almost two months as a passenger ship, the *Mayflower* was no longer "sweet smelling," and Howland wanted some air. He climbed the ladder "above the gratings [*the latticed covers to the hatches*] and was with the seele [*i.e., roll*] of the ship thrown into the sea; but it pleased God that he caught hold of the topsail halliards which hung overboard and ran out at length; yet he held his hold, though he was sundry fathoms under water, till he was hauled up by the same rope to the brim of the water, and then with a boathook and other means got into the ship again and his life saved. He was something ill with it." When Bradford wrote about the incident of "the boy who fell off the *Mayflower*," over ten years had passed, John had married Elizabeth Tilley (also a passenger), and they were well on their way to producing ten children and an astonishing eighty-eight grandchildren. The narrator of Ric Burns' PBS film *The Pilgrims* speaks eloquently: "John Howland's survival was as fortuitous and random as his near fatal plunge. In the New World he would thrive, work off his indenture, become a cornerstone of the colony, and marry a pretty young woman named Elizabeth Tilley ... from whom over the next four centuries an estimated two million Americans would descend, including Ralph Waldo Emerson, Joseph Smith, Franklin Roosevelt, Humphrey Bogart, Chevy Chase, and both George Bushes, father and son," William Jennings Bryan, both of President Theodore Roosevelt's wives, Henry Cabot Lodge, Cecil B. DeMille, Dr. Benjamin Spock, Ted Danson, Christopher Lloyd, John Lithgow, the Baldwin brothers, Samuel J. Ervin (the US Senator [Jr.][17] and the NC judges [III and IV]) ...

---

[17] Senator Samuel J. Ervin, Jr., perhaps best known as the Chairman of the Senate Select Committee on Presidential Campaign Activities (the "Watergate Committee"), served as Governor of the North Carolina Mayflower Society for one term, and as Counselor for a number of years. He never missed a meeting, even while serving in the United States Senate. See Becket Soule, *Centennial History of the Society of Mayflower Descendants in the State of North Carolina 1924-2024* (Berwyn Heights, MD: Heritage Books, 2024), 35-37.

and myself. As I continually point out, such is the role of contingency in history -- we cannot even imagine history -- or America -- without these people.

TUESDAY, 6 OCTOBER 1620

First Birth

Elizabeth (Fisher) Hopkins, one of the three pregnant women who boarded the *Mayflower* over a month ago, the wife of Stephen Hopkins, was delivered of a son, who, on account of the circumstances of his birth, was named Oceanus. This was the first birth aboard the ship during the voyage, and the only birth on the high seas. Giving a child a unique name like Oceanus was not unheard of, even in the 17th century when most names were either inherited, Biblical, or came from a king or queen. The White family named their son, born on board the *Mayflower* shortly after its arrival in the New World, Peregrine, meaning "traveller" or, significantly, "pilgrim." When Stephen Hopkins was a castaway in Bermuda in 1609, the two children born there were named Bermudas (a boy, son of Edward Eason) and Bermuda (a girl, daughter of John Rolfe and Sarah Hacker, who died -- both mother and daughter -- several months later). We have no further record of Oceanus Hopkins, and must conclude that he died before May 1627, because he is not included in the division of cattle of that month. On board the *Mayflower*, Oceanus joined his brother Giles (13) and sister Constance (14), the children of Stephen Hopkins by his first wife Mary, and Damaris (2), by his second wife Elizabeth. Stephen and Mary had an additional daughter Elizabeth (b. c. 1604), but William Bradford in his list of passengers names only two children by this couple who came on the *Mayflower*, and there is no record of Elizabeth after 1613. Only Constance and Giles reached adulthood and had issue; Stephen Hopkins and Elizabeth Fisher had five more children in Plymouth, of whom two reached adulthood and had children of their own. The Damaris Hopkins who came on the *Mayflower* must have died before about 1628, because Stephen and Elizabeth Hopkins named their daughter born in that year Damaris, indicating that the elder daughter of that name had already died. Of Stephen Hopkins' ten children by his two wives, only four are known to have reached adulthood and now have descendants, giving Stephen and his wives thirty-four grandchildren, in contrast to the more prolific Howlands' eighty-eight.

The verifiers at the GSMD Library in Plymouth keep a running list of the most astonishing given names they run across, and the competition for the most unusual name of the week is fairly stiff. I won the prize one week when I discovered a man named "Henchman Soule" (perhaps the modification of a Dutch name, but still rather humorous to modern ears). Longtime Harvard chaplain Peter Gomes enjoyed collecting these sorts of surprising (or at least ambiguous) names, and frequently pointed out that the not unusual seventeenth century girl's name "Experience" (indicating that her parents hoped she would have an experience of God's presence and providence) would mean something rather different in the late twentieth century.

WEDNESDAY, 7 OCTOBER 1620

Storm continues; Food

William Bradford is the authority for the statement that with the "governor" of the ship's company were chosen "two or three assistants . . . to order [*i.e., regulate*] the people by the way [*i.e., on the passage*] and see to the disposition of the provisions." The latter duty must have been a difficult and wearisome one. From what we have seen of the poverty of the ship's cooking facilities (especially for so large a company), it would be hopeless to expect to cook food in any quantity, except when all conditions were favourable, and then only slowly and with much difficulty. From the fact that so many would require food at practically the same hours of the day, it is clear that there must have been distribution of food (principally uncooked) to groups or families, who, with the aid of servants (when available), must each have prepared their own meals, cooking as occasion and opportunity permitted, after the manner of the "steerage passengers" in later days. There appears to have been only one cook for the officers and crew of the ship, and his hands were doubtless full with their demands. His service to the passengers must have been very slight. That "the cook" is named as one of the ship's crew who died in Plymouth harbour (New England) is all the knowledge we have concerning him. The use of and dependence upon tea and coffee, now so universal, and at sea so seemingly indispensable, was then unknown, beer supplying their places, and this happily did not have to be prepared with fire. "Strong waters" (Holland gin) and to some extent "aqua vitae" (brandy) were relied upon for the (supposed) maintenance of warmth. Our Pilgrims were by no

36

means total abstainers, and sadly bewailed being deprived of their beer when the supply failed. They also made general and habitual (moderate) use of wine and spirits, though they sharply interdicted and promptly punished their abuse.

THURSDAY, 8 OCTOBER 1620

Food (continued)

"Equinoctial Distrubances" continued. In the absence of cooking facilities, it became necessary to rely chiefly upon food that did not require to be prepared by heat, such as biscuit (hard bread), butter, cheese ("Holland cheese" was a chief staple with the Pilgrims), "haberdyne" (or dried salt codfish), smoked herring, smoked ("cured") ham and bacon, "dried neat's tongues," preserved and "potted" meats (a very limited list in that day), fruits, etc. Mush, oatmeal, pease-puddings, pickled eggs, sausage meats, salt beef and pork, bacon, "spiced beef," such few vegetables as they had (chiefly cabbages, turnips, and onions—there were no potatoes in that day), etc., could be cooked in quantity, when the weather permitted, and would then be eaten cold. Except as dried or preserved fruits, vegetables (notably onions), limes, lemon juice, and the free use of vinegar counteracted (rather feebly), their food was a distinctive stimulant of scorbutic disease and tuberculosis, which constant exposure to cold and wet and the overcrowded state of the ship could but increase and aggravate. More about diseases tomorrow.

FRIDAY, 9 OCTOBER 1620

Disease

It is remarkable that, totally unused to any such conditions, wet, cold, poorly fed, overcrowded, storm-tossed, bruised and beaten, anxious, and with no homes to welcome them, exposed to new hardships and dangers on landing, worn and exhausted, *any* of the *Mayflower's* company survived. It certainly cannot be accounted strange that infectious diseases, once started among them, should have run through their ranks like fire, taking both old and young. Nor is it strange that—though more inured to hardship and the conditions of sea life—with the extreme and unusual exposure of boat service on the New England coast in mid-winter, often wading in the icy water and living aboard ship in a highly infected atmosphere, the crew of seamen should have succumbed to disease in almost equal numbers with the colonists.

Edward Thompson, Jasper More, and James Chilton died within a month of the arrival at Cape Cod (and while the ship lay in that harbour), and following the axiom of vital statistics that "for each death two are constantly sick," there must have been some little (though not to say general) sickness on the *Mayflower* when she arrived at Cape Cod. It would, in view of the hardship of the voyage, have been very remarkable if this had not been the case. It would have been still more remarkable if the ill-conditioned, thin-blooded, town-bred "servants" and apprentices had not suffered first and most. It is significant that eight out of nine of the male servants died in the first four months. It was impossible that scurvy should not have been prevalent with both passengers and crew.

SATURDAY, 10 OCTOBER 1620

Passengers' Ages and Occupations [Part Two]

A full analysis of vocations (trades, etc.) represented by the *Mayflower* company is difficult. They were, since they intended to found a colony, of considerable variety, though it should be understood that the vocations given were the callings these individuals followed before boarding the ship. Several are known to have been engaged in other pursuits either before their residence in Holland or during their earlier years there. Bradford tells us that most of the Leyden congregation (or that portion of it which came from England in 1608) were agricultural people. These were mostly obliged to acquire other occupations. A few, *e.g.* Allerton, Brewster, Bradford, Carver, Cooke, and Winslow, possessed some means, while others had pursued occupations for which there was no demand in the Low Countries. Standish, bred to arms, apparently followed his profession nearly to the time of departure, and resumed it in the colony. Of the "arts, crafts or trades" of the colonists from London and neighbouring English localities, little has been gleaned. They were mostly people of some means, tradesmen rather than artisans, and at least two (Martin and Mullins) were evidently also of the Merchant Adventurers. Their marital status has not been determined in every case; though it is of course possible that some were married, but there is no surviving record, especially among the seamen. The passengers of the *Mayflower* on her departure from England appear to be grouped as follows:.

38

Adult males (hired men and servants of age included)	44
Adult females	19
Youths, male children, and male servants (minors)	29
Young women, female children	10
	102

Married males	26
Married females	18
Single (adult) males (and young men)	25
Single (adult) female (Mrs Carver's maid)	1

Besides these occupations, it is known that several were skilled in other callings, and were at some time teachers, accountants, linguists, writers, etc., while some had formerly practised certain crafts; Dr. Fuller, *e.g.* having formerly been a "silk-worker," Bradford (on the authority of Belknap) a "silk-dyer," and others "fustian-workers." Hopkins had apparently sometime before dropped his character of "lay-reader," and was a pretty efficient man of affairs, but his vocation at the time of the exodus is not known. The former occupations of fourteen of the adult colonists (Brown, Billington, Britteridge, Cooke, Chilton, Clarke, Crackstone, Goodman, Gardiner, Rogers, Rigdale, Turner, Warren, and Williams) are not certainly known. There is evidence suggesting that Brown was a mechanic; Billington and Cooke had been trained to husbandry; Chilton had been a small tradesman; Edward Tilley had been, like his brother, a silk-worker; Turner was a tradesman, and Warren a farmer; it is certain that Cooke, Rogers, and Warren had been men of some means. The women of the Mayflower will be discussed tomorrow.

SUNDAY, 11 OCTOBER 1620

Women of the Mayflower

Three significant resources on the women passengers of the *Mayflower* are Caleb Johnson's *The Mayflower and her Passengers*, on which I rely heavily, Robert Charles Anderson, *The Mayflower Migration: Immigrants to Plymouth, 1620*, as well as his other works in the Great Migration Project (particularly *The Pilgrim Migration*, 2004, for which *The Mayflower Migration* is an updating), and Sue Allan, *In the Shadow of Men: the Lives of Separatist Women*, a well written collection of biographical sketches which fills in quite a bit of the English social, historical and religious background both for women who came and those who stayed in England.

Prior to the *Mayflower*, very few English women had made the voyage across the ocean. Sir Walter Raleigh's Roanoke colony was founded in 1587, and among the 120 colonists there were 17 women: a baby girl, Virginia Dare, was born after arrival. When re-supply ships came from England, the colony had mysteriously disappeared and was never seen again. Jamestown was founded in 1607, but few women made that voyage until 1619.

As the *Mayflower* left for America, there were 19 adult women on-board. Three of them, Elizabeth Hopkins, Susanna White, and Mary Allerton, were actually in their last trimester of pregnancy. All the adult women on the *Mayflower* were married, with the exception of Mrs. Carver's maid, Dorothy (who became Francis Eaton's second wife[18]); there were a few teenage girls nearing marriageable age. While no women would die during the *Mayflower*'s voyage, 78% of the women would die the first winter, a far higher percentage than for men or children. Dorothy Bradford was the first woman to die, in December: more about the debate over whether her death was suicide when the time comes. Most of the women's death dates were not recorded (nor were most of the men's dates, for that matter), but we do know that Rose Standish died on January 29, Mary Allerton died on February 25, and Elizabeth Winslow died on March 24. Most women died in February and March.

Only five women survived the first winter. Katherine Carver died in May of a "broken heart," her husband John having died of sunstroke a month earlier. By the time of the famous "Thanksgiving," there were only four women left to care for the Colony's fifty surviving men and children (and Massasoit with 90 native warriors as "guests"): Eleanor Billington, Elizabeth Hopkins, Mary Brewster, and Susanna (White) Winslow. Of the wives who had been left behind, four came on the *Anne* in 1623, had additional children, and raised their families at Plymouth.

---

[18] See Caleb Johnson's careful and fascinating reconstruction of the record in *Mayflower Passengers*, 263-265

Teenaged Boys

As mentioned earlier, the most numerous age group of passengers were teenaged boys (perhaps 24 boys between 10 and 18, out of 102 passengers). This, as you might expect, caused some problems both on board and on shore. Francis Billington nearly caused a disaster onboard the *Mayflower* shortly after arrival in Plymouth Harbour, when he shot off his father's gun inside a cabin, sending sparks towards an open barrel of gunpowder. After he came ashore, he climbed up a tree and claimed to have spotted a "great sea" in the distance: a small pond that still carries the name "Billington's Sea" even today. The affidavit of Francis Billington,[19] dated 1674, in which he declared himself sixty-eight years old, would indicate that he was born in 1606, and hence must have been about fourteen years of age when he (almost) blew up the *Mayflower*. John Billington, who was perhaps two years older than his brother Francis, was lost in the wood and, "living on berries and what he could find" for several days, was returned to Plymouth from Nauset (Eastham) where he had been safeguarded by the Indians on Cape Cod. I have seen comments online suggesting that the Billingtons were Roman Catholic recusants, but no documentation for this seems to be offered. If this is true, it would explain quite a bit of the friction between the family and the rest of the community. The Billingtons were the only household to come through the epidemic of the first winter unscathed, which rather mystified (and perhaps annoyed) the Saints. Francis Billington's descendants include President James A. Garfield and (perhaps appropriately) Taylor Swift and three of the Beach Boys.

The early eighteenth century notes of Thomas Prince describe an incident of 18 June 1621 when the first duel ("upon a challenge at single combat with sword and dagger") was fought in New England between two servants of Stephen Hopkins, Edward Doty (probably in his early twenties) and Edward Leister (of a similar age): they were the last two men to sign the Mayflower Compact, which has led some to speculate they may have been originally unwilling to sign and required some, um, er, "persuasion." The duel ended with one being wounded in the hand and one in the thigh. Their punishment was to be tied head

---

[19] Plymouth County Deeds, v. 1, 81

and feet together for twenty-four hours without meat or drink. But soon their master Stephen Hopkins, apparently taking pity on their "great pains", made a "humble request, upon promise of a better carriage" and they were released. Leister eventually moved to Virginia, but Doty (spelled in a variety of ways) remained in Plymouth, married at least twice, and raised a numerous family.

TUESDAY, 13 OCTOBER 1620

Children on the Mayflower

"Strong October gales" persist, and the Mayflower continues to be blown off course. Caleb Johnson notes that most of the Pilgrim parents decided to leave the girls behind in England or Holland, and sent for them later once everything was built and more comfortable: William Brewster brought his sons Love and Wrestling, but left his daughters Patience and Fear behind; Thomas Rogers brought his son Joseph, but left his daughters Elizabeth and Margaret; Francis Cooke brought his son John, but left his daughters Jane and Hester; Richard Warren had five daughters, Mary, Ann, Sarah, Elizabeth and Abigail, ranging in ages from 2-10 years old, but he left them in England with his wife Elizabeth; Degory Priest left behind his daughters Mary and Sarah.

Eleven girls, however, ranging in ages from 1 through 17, did make the voyage on the Mayflower with their families. And perhaps more surprisingly, young girls proved to have the strongest bodies of all: the first winter, 78% of the women died, 50% of the men died, 36% of the boys died, but only two girls (18%) died. There were fewer deaths among the children than among the adults that first winter, which ultimately increased the chances of survival for the struggling colony. Children on the Mayflower who left descendants, with their approximate ages:

Priscilla Mullins (17)
Joseph Rogers (17)
Constance Hopkins (14)
Francis Billington (14)
Love Brewster (13)
Mary Chilton (13)
John Cooke (13)
Elizabeth Tilley (13)
Samuel Fuller (12), son of Edward Fuller
Giles Hopkins (12)
Bartholomew Allerton (7)

Richard More (6)

Remember Allerton (5)

Resolved White (5)

Mary Allerton (3), the last surviving passenger of the
Mayflower, died in 1699

Samuel Eaton (1)

Peregrine White (born aboard)

WEDNESDAY, 14 OCTOBER 1620

"after many difficulties in boisterous storms"

In 1603, James VI of Scotland was crowned James I of England. The Scots, in their pride that they had given a king to England, soon began to contend that the cross of St. Andrew should take precedence over the cross of St. George, that ships bearing the flag of the latter should salute that of St. Andrew. To allay the contention, the King issued the following Order in Council on 12 April 1606, "By the King: Whereas, some differences hath arisen between Our subjects of South and North Britaine travelling by Seas, about the bearing of their Flagges: For the avoiding of all contentions hereafter. We have, with the advice of our Council, ordered: That from henceforth all our Subjects of this Isle and Kingdome of Great Britaine, and all our members thereof, shall beare in their main-toppe the Red Crosse, commonly called St. George's Crosse, and the White Crosse, commonly called St. Andrew's Crosse, joyned together according to the forme made by our heralds, and sent by Us to our Admerall to be published to our Subjects: and in their fore-toppe our Subjects of South Britaine shall weare the Red Crosse onely as they were wont, and our Subjects of North Britaine in their fore-toppe the White Crosse onely as they were accustomed," and all vessels were forbidden to wear any other flag at their peril.

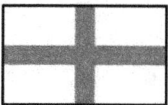

The new flag thus designed by the heralds and proclaimed by this order was called the "King's Colours." For a long period the red cross had been the flag of English navigators, as well as the badge of English soldiery. No permanent English settlement in America was made until after the adoption of the "King's Colours." Jamestown, Plymouth, Salem, and Boston were settled under the new flag. The ships bringing over settlers, being English vessels, also carried the red cross as permitted.

The "King's Colours" became the national flag, and not simply the naval ensign, after the Act of Union in 1707, until the union with Ireland in 1801, when the present national flag was adopted.

THURSDAY, 15 OCTOBER 1620

Dating and Calendars

Confusion about the dates is caused by the fact that the Pilgrims used the Julian calendar, while we use the Gregorian calendar. The principal, but not the only, difference between the two is when they have leap days. Technically, the two calendars do "agree" for 1 March AD 200 through 28 February AD 300, but those dates really do not occur in *Mayflower* history.

The Julian calendar has one leap day every four years. Thus, the average length of a Julian year is 365¼ days. The difference with the actual length of a tropical year is small and not immediately noticeable, but it does add up over the centuries, making the Julian calendar slowly drift relative to the seasons. The Gregorian calendar fixes the drift issue, through a more complex leap day rule, to better match the actual length of a year. The leap year rule is this: years that are multiples of four are leap years, except that years that are multiples of 100 are not, and years that are multiples of 400 are leap years. The Julian calendar is named after Julius Caesar, who introduced it as a reform of the Roman calendar. The Gregorian calendar was instituted by the papal bull *Inter gravissimas* (24 February 1582) of Pope Gregory XIII, after whom the calendar is named, because he noticed Easter shifting relative to the seasons. At that time, the accumulated error of the Julian calendar was ten leap days. To correct for this drift, it was decided to simply skip ten calendar days; Thursday 4 October 1582 on the Julian calendar was followed by Friday 15 October 1582 on the Gregorian calendar. Parts of the Low Countries (Brabant, Zeeland, the County of Holland, and the States General of the Netherlands) adopted the Gregorian calendar in 1582, while other parts of the Low Countries (Frisia, Overjissel, Utrecht) switched in 1700; Great Britain and its colonies kept using the Julian calendar till 1751. While living in Leiden, the Pilgrims must have used the Gregorian calendar, because others around them did so, but they certainly did not approve of what was seen as papal usurpation of a civil prerogative, namely, the determination of a calendar. William Bradford's journal, *Of Plimoth Plantation* uses the Julian calendar throughout.

One year is 365.24219 days, so 400 years is 146,096.876 days. If you want to commemorate something 400 years after it happened, you should do so 146,097 days later. That number happens to be a multiple of seven, so you'll actually end up **on the same day of the week [!!]**, which is a nice bonus. It does not matter in which calendar you add the 146,097 days; if you start with the same day in one calendar, you end up with the same day in that same calendar. Four hundred years after 5 October 1620 on the Julian calendar is 2 October 2020 on the Julian calendar (5 October 2020 minus three days: see below). Four hundred years after 15 October 1620 on the Gregorian calendar is 15 October 2020 on the Gregorian calendar. Back in 1620, the difference between the two calendars was ten days; it has since grown to thirteen days. The dates 2 October 2020 [Julian calendar] and 15 October 2020 [Gregorian calendar] are the *same day*. But Thursday, 15 October 2020 is *exactly* 400 years since Thursday, 15 October 1620 (both Gregorian calendar).

To make this slightly more confusing, the first day of the new year was 25 March each year, since this was the anniversary of the Incarnation of Christ. Thus, although we start the new year on 1 January, for the Pilgrims, the new year did not begin for almost another three months. William Mullins died on 3 March **1621** (Gregorian calendar), but 21 February **1620** in the Julian calendar. The Calendar (New Style) Act 1750 (24 Geo II c.23; also known as Chesterfield's Act after Philip Stanhope, 4th Earl of Chesterfield), an Act of the Parliament of Great Britain, had two parts: first, it reformed the calendar of England and the British Dominions so that the new legal year began on 1 January, rather than 25 March (Lady Day); and, second, Great Britain and its Dominions adopted (in effect) the Gregorian calendar, as already used in most of western Europe.

- - - - -

The opening line of the Calendar (New Style) Act 1750 must be close to a record for the longest sentence in an English official document, at 716 words: "In and throughout all his Majesty's dominions and countries in Europe, Asia, Africa, and America, belonging or subject to the crown of Great Britain, the said supputation, according to which the year of our Lord beginneth on the twenty-fifth day of March, shall not be made use of from and after the last day of December one thousand seven hundred and fifty-one; and that the first day of January next following the said last day of December shall be reckoned, taken, deemed, and accounted to be the first of the year of our Lord one thousand seven hundred and fifty-two; and the first day of January which shall happen next after the said first day of January one thousand seven hundred and fifty-two shall be reckoned, taken, deemed, and accounted to be the first day of the year of our Lord one thousand seven hundred and fifty-three; and so on from time to time the first day of January in every year which shall happen in time to come shall be reckoned, taken, deemed, and accounted to be the first day of the year, and that each new year shall accordingly commence and begin to be reckoned from the first day of every such month of January next preceding the twenty-fifth day of March on which such year would according to the present supputation have begun or commenced; and that from and after the said first day of January one thousand seven hundred and fifty-two the several days of each month shall go on, and be reckoned and numbered in the same order, and the feast of Easter and other moveable feasts thereon depending shall be ascertained according to the same method, as they now are, until the second day of September in the said year one thousand seven hundred and fifty-two inclusive; and that the natural day next immediately following the said second day of September shall be called, reckoned, and accounted to be the fourteenth day of September, omitting for that time only the eleven intermediate nominal days of the common calendar; and that the several natural days which shall follow and succeed next after the said fourteenth day of September shall be respectively called, reckoned, and numbered forwards in numerical order from the said fourteenth day of September, according to the order and succession of days now used in the present calendar; and that all acts, deeds, writings, notes, and other instruments, of what nature or kind soever, whether ecclesiastical or civil, publick or private, which shall be made, executed, or signed upon or after the said first day of January one thousand seven hundred and fifty-two, shall bear date according to the said new method of supputation; and that the two fixed terms of Saint Hilary and Saint Michael, in England, and the courts of great sessions in the counties palatine and in Wales, and also the courts of general quarter sessions and general sessions of the peace, and all other courts, of what nature or kind soever, whether civil, criminal, or ecclesiastical, and all meetings and assemblies of any bodies politick or corporate, either for the election of any officers or members thereof, or for any such officers entering upon the execution of their respective offices, or for any other purpose whatsoever, which by any law, statute, charter, custom, or usage within this kingdom, or within any other the dominions or countries subject or belonging to the crown of Great Britain, are to be holden and kept on any fixed or certain day of any month, or on any day depending upon the beginning or any certain day of any month (except such courts as are usually holden or kept with any fairs or marts), shall from time to time, from and after the said second day of September, be holden and kept upon or according to the same respective nominal days and times whereon or according to which the same are now to be holden, but which shall be computed according to the said new method of numbering and reckoning the days of the calendar as aforesaid, that is to say, eleven days sooner than the respective days whereon the same are now holden and kept, any law, statute, charter, custom, or usage to the contrary thereof in anywise notwithstanding."

FRIDAY, 16 OCTOBER 1620

Who were the Saints?

George Willison set the categories for discussion of the divisions of the Plymouth Colony for the next several generations. His writing was vivid, but his purpose, to debunk the Pilgrims, or, in the words of a reviewer, "to rescue [the Pilgrims] from their friends who have praised them too highly" led him into far too many extreme positions and absurd conclusions. Genealogists, in particular, have to use this work with care, because Willison overlooked many recent discoveries in the research which had not yet made their way into the general works in the field; the numerous works that have appeared in the seventy-five years that have passed since its first publication have laid bare scores of additional errors. All of Willison's pictures are black and white -- Saints or Strangers. In his repeated stress on the "guile of the Saints" he gives an unjustifiably bad picture of them. By dwelling at great length on the sexual irregularities among them he overemphasises that side of their lives. These misinterpretations

47

and most of the factual errors in the book arise from the unscholarly criteria which Willison chose to follow. In his bibliography he places the three asterisks of highest approval only against secondary works which he describes as "altogether interesting and relevant"; that the books should be historically sound and based on modern scholarship he does not consider important.

But Willison's dichotomy between Saints and Strangers seems to have lasted, as numerous editorials published last month for the 400th anniversary of the *Mayflower*'s departure show -- it even gave a name to a recent National Geographic film. The "standard" or "schoolbook" depiction of the *Mayflower* passengers (mostly merchant adventurers with a few religious zealots) owes quite a bit to Willison's technique of implied slander. I will address what I call "the numbers game" in a couple of days, but pause here to make some basic comments: Willison divides the 104 passengers on the *Mayflower* into 41 Saints, 40 Strangers, 5 hired hands, and 18 servants. Some, indeed many, of these identifications have been revisited and rejected. Willison's bias against the Saints may very well have led him to underestimate that category.

It is also important to realise that there is not a single litmus test to determine whether one is a Saint or a Stranger, although it is easy to determine that the Brewsters are firmly in the camp of the Saints, and the Billingtons are definitely Strangers. While membership in the Leiden congregation is a good indication of religious affiliation, absence from that list does not necessarily mean that a passenger was not a Saint. But even among the "Saints," there is something of a spectrum, as there is in any congregation. Trying to make too clean a split between Separatists and Puritans. Saints and Strangers, overlooks the fact that the religious issues changed over time, and people moved between groups. It is also vital to pay attention to English origins and family connections -- work that has been done by Robert Charles Anderson and Sue Allan in recent years -- which can identify passengers who, even if they are not "hot Protestants" (in Michael Winship's term) were definitely more than simply "fellow travellers." There was a certain homogeneity in the Plymouth Colony, which contributed to its failure: it is significant that the Colony was woefully unable to attract clergymen of their own stripe to minister to them -- Robinson stayed in Holland, and died without ever coming to the New World. Almost all of the clergy who came to the colony were from Massachusetts, many were Harvard trained, and of a far more "establishment" mindset than the Pilgrims.

SATURDAY, 17 OCTOBER 1620

Who were the Strangers?

Willison's dichotomy, mentioned yesterday, in which the Saints and Strangers were fairly evenly balanced, was forcefully challenged by Jeremy Bangs in *Strangers and Pilgrims, Travellers and Sojourners: Leiden and the Foundations of Plymouth Plantation*. Bangs pointed out not only Willison's bias against "the original Leiden religious fanatics" (as Willison considered the "Saints"), as well as his characterisation of the whole group recruited in London as "Strangers." Willison understood the Saints to be mostly members of the Scrooby community, and assumed most of those who came from London, and almost all of the servants, would be either hostile to or indifferent to the separatists' goals. Bangs made his own calculations, and came up with a new estimate of the London contingent: "the total number of *Mayflower* passengers who can be identified as having joined from London is seventeen, plus the four Moore children and John Alden. ... [This] leaves 80 of the 102 passengers who were either from Leiden or of uncertain origin but likely to have been from Leiden." Caleb Johnson in 2005 published an article[20] analysing the structure of Bradford's 1651 list of passengers, and argued that those who came from Leiden and those who did not were organised into different groupings. This article has received a good deal of respect, although a growing consensus has removed Miles Standish from the category of "Leading 'Strangers'," noting Standish's close relationship with John Robinson prior to 1620 and the possibility that he was actually living in Leiden before the voyage. Robert Charles Anderson has also done research on the servants, and has noted that in most cases we know nothing about the English origins of many of them (John Howland being a significant exception), so we cannot tell where or when they became associated with the Leiden families. Anderson, Johnson,

---

[20] *"New Light on William Bradford's Passenger List of the Mayflower,"* TAG 80 [2005] 94-99

Sue Allen and Simon Neal have all done extensive research about the English origins of the *Mayflower* passengers, both those from Leiden and those who came directly from England, providing a much fuller picture.

Few of the passengers had absolutely no connection at all with the Leiden community, which would only make sense -- if they had no knowledge of it, how would they have found out about the proposed journey in the first place? Nothing is known for sure of the religious inclinations of John Billington and his wife, but, as Anderson states, "the persistent antisocial behavior of this family once they arrived in New England suggests they did not share the religious beliefs of most of the other Mayflower passengers." Nothing is known about the English origins or religious beliefs of John Alden or seven other single men (Britteridge, Clarke, English, Ely, Gardiner, Margesson and Trevor). The four More children (aged between four and eight) presumably did not have any firm religious convictions of their own at that time, but Samuel More's father Richard More of Linley was a man of "firm, if not radical, puritan sympathies," suggesting that "religious considerations influenced the Mores in choosing this particular way of disposing of the children,"[21] (). Although Christopher Martin was frequently at loggerheads with the Leiden community, in 1612 and 1620 he was presented to church courts for activities that indicate he held puritan views.

Finally, to reiterate my comments of yesterday, the religious views of the passengers likely were on a spectrum, rather than a strict "either/or." Anderson concludes, "the boundary between puritan and separatist was quite porous. A person who remained nominally within the Church of England but who also frequently attended private puritan meetings might differ little in practice and belief from another person who had made the decision to leave the Church of England." The picture that appears from Anderson's *Puritan Pedigrees: The Deep Roots of the Great Migration to New England* is that of a siren call amalgamating separatists and puritans and non-conformists from many corners of England, united by religion, family ties and acquaintanceship. Identifying the "Strangers" is further

---

[21] MD 44:113-116 -- "being the offspring of scandal and sin, [the children] were to be given the opportunity of a new life in a righteous community"

complicated by the fact that while "Saints" can be classified using several beliefs held in common or traits that were in evidence, there is no one characteristic that makes a "Stranger."

- - - - -

In dozens of books, articles, and editorials written over the last year and referencing the 400th anniversary of the *Mayflower's* voyage, writers (and native activists) have raged -- at length -- against the errors of "what everyone was taught at school." Having read many of these, I can only conclude that no two of these people went to the same school, and none of them went to any school that I ever attended. The story presented when I was in grammar school (in the 1960s), accurate in part and erroneous in part, was that the passengers on the *Mayflower* were mostly in search of wealth, like Jamestown, except they had some religious fanatics on board; they were blown off course to New England, where most of them died until they were saved by the Indians, whom they invited to a three day Thanksgiving dinner. In a thoroughly unscientific survey I made of about a dozen young men and women who are currently in grammar school or high school in seven states, I discovered that only one had ever heard mention of the Pilgrims or the *Mayflower* in school. When another of them, a *Mayflower* descendant, went to the post office to get the new *Mayflower* stamps, the postmaster responded to him, "What's the Mayflower?" For the most part, schools are not propagating errors. They are simply ignoring history.

SUNDAY, 18 OCTOBER 1620

The Numbers Game

Disclaimer: A completely accurate identification of "Saints" and "Strangers" is well-nigh impossible, because of the state of our knowledge and the imprecision of the task. You have been warned.

George F. Willison in *Saints and Strangers* provides the following breakdown of passengers of the *Mayflower*: "Saints" 41 (17 men, 10 women, 14 children); "Strangers" 40 (17 men, 9 women, 14 children); hired hands 5 (all men); servants 18 (11 men, 1 woman, 6 children); yielding a total of 104 (50 men, 20 women, 34 children) ().[22] We have previously noted his bias against the Leiden community and his restriction of true

---

[22]Willison, *Saints and Strangers*, 395

51

"Saint"hood to the Scrooby community, so it can easily be assumed that this would be the lowest possible number of separatists on this voyage. The number of members of the Scrooby community who sailed on the *Mayflower* was a small minority of the total number of passengers. Further research in the last seventy-five years has modified or disproved many of his identifications: George Soule, for example, was probably not from Eckington in Worcestershire, and had nine and not seven children (Bradford states that "His [*i.e., Winslow's*] man, George Soule, is still living and hath eight children" -- Benjamin Soule probably had not yet been born when the 1651 list was compiled); Willison's classification of him as Edward Winslow's servant is correct.

Jeremy Bangs in *Strangers and Pilgrims* estimates that the "total number of Mayflower passengers who can be identified as having joined from London is seventeen, plus the four Moore children and John Alden." This "leaves 80 of the 102 passengers who were either from Leiden or of uncertain origin but likely to have been from Leiden" (614). Bangs also argues (reasonably so) that any men or women who sailed on the *Mayflower* as servants to one of the Leiden families should be counted as having been in Leiden in the 1610s. This is probably the upper limit of calculation for the separatist Saints.

Caleb Johnson's 2005 article in *The American Genealogist*, mentioned yesterday, suggested that Bradford's list, our main source of information about the *Mayflower* passengers, "was not just listing the passengers on paper as he remembered them in some kind of stream of consciousness. In fact, it is now possible to see that he was listing the passengers in a very specific order ... organized into five sections: the leading Leiden church members, followed by the leading 'Strangers,' followed by the remaining Leiden church members, then the remaining 'Strangers,' and last the hired seamen" (94). Johnson only listed heads of households and single men in his list (wives, children and servants were not). The totals for leading Leiden Church Members is 7; Leading 'Strangers' 7; Remaining Leiden Church Members 14; Remaining 'Strangers' 6; Hired seamen 5 (98-99). This yields a total of 39, which is significantly less than half, but has the advantage of relying on contemporary sources to make distinctions. Many of these identifications have since been challenged, principally Myles Standish. As mentioned yesterday, strong (even radical) puritan sympathies can be found in Christopher Martin, classified as a leading 'Stranger,' and the father of the More children (thus providing a plausible reason for their presence on board). There is also research into possible puritan sympathies for Richard Warren as well.

Robert Charles Anderson in his 2020 *The Mayflower Migration* has broken the passengers down by point of origin. Anderson counts sixty nine passengers who had some definable relationship with Leiden, and thirty-five who did not (a ⅔-⅓ split). Nevertheless, even the "London" contingent had significant puritan sympathies: some, such as the Mullins family and Peter Brown, from Dorking in Surrey, came from a significant centre of nonconformist activity; Christopher Martin had been charged with puritan views; Richard Warren had puritan family connections; the More children have been mentioned already, and Stephen Hopkins "had puritan tendencies at least." These would account for 23 of the 35 people in that contingent, which, when added to the 69 of the Leiden contingent, tops Bangs' number by a full dozen (92 out of 104). Of the remainder, nothing is known of John Alden's religious inclinations, and there remain seven single men about whom little can be said (either about their religion or their origins). Only the Billingtons stand out of this crowd, which suggests that they were stunningly isolated from the other passengers. One wonders why they were on the ship in the first place, if they were so different from the rest.

Anderson notes that one of the most significant new discoveries of recent decades "is the information elicited about the premigration religious activities of some members of the non-Leiden group, which, although they did not necessarily extend to separatism, in some cases exhibited something approaching radical puritanism" (14). Future research will undoubtedly change these totals, but it is significant that the number of "saints" has progressively increased with the increase of new evidence.

MONDAY, 19 OCTOBER 1620

Halfway

Today is the halfway point in the *Mayflower*'s trans-Atlantic journey. From the entrance to the English Channel at Plymouth (England) Harbour to Cape Cod, it is 2,750 miles. Allowing another 250 miles for zig-zagging against contrary winds, this yields a total of 3,000 miles from origin to destination. It took the Mayflower sixty-five days to make it (departure from Plymouth, England on Wednesday, 6 September 1620 until sighting Cape Cod on Thursday, 9 November 1620 [o.s.]), thus averaging 45 miles a day, or slightly less than two miles an hour. "She was deep loaded, her bottom must have been extremely foul with grass and barnacles from being in the water all through the hot months, during the last half of the western passage Captain Jones had to ease up on her every time the wind breezed up, and she struck right into the season of roaring westerlies."[23] Although it was unknown to any of the mariners or passengers at the time, the ship was also running against the Gulf Stream, and this probably impeded the progress further. Although first observed in 1513 by Ponce de Leon, the Gulf Stream was not charted until the early 1770s by Benjamin Franklin. In 1843, the United States Coast Survey set out to study the Gulf Stream in more detail, more than two centuries after the Pilgrims. Today, northbound ships choose the maximum velocity stream current while southbound ships hug the outer edges to conserve fuel. One problem is that the stream does not have definitive banks and meanders back and forth as well as varying in width as it proceeds north. The maximum current off the coast of Florida ranges from two to four knots, although speeds of eight knots have been reported. Its width varies, but generally is 40 to 50 miles in width. Its volume through the Florida Straits is about 30 million cubic meters per second - that is a lot of sea water! For a comparison, the combined volume of *all* the rivers that empty into the Atlantic Ocean is about 0.6 million cubic meters per second. This current was what the *Mayflower* was running *against*. "All in all, it is a wonder that she ever got here."

TUESDAY, 20 OCTOBER 1620

More about Food (and Drink)

This is the last post about food -- I promise. At least until the Pilgrims get to Plymouth in December.

Vinegar in hogsheads was named on the food-list of every ship of the Pilgrim era. It was one of their best antiscorbutics, and was of course a prime factor in their use of "sour krout," pickling, etc. The fruits (natural, dried, and preserved) were probably, in that day, in rather small supply. Apples, limes, lemons, prunes, olives, rice,

---

[23] Nickerson, *Land Ho! 1620*, 28

etc., were among the luxuries of a voyage, while dried or preserved fruits and small fruits were not yet in common use. Winslow urges that "your casks for beer ... be iron bound, at least for the first [*i.e.*, *end*] tyre [*i.e.*, *hoop*]". Cushman states that they had ample supplies of beer offered them both in Kent and Amsterdam. The passengers' supply seems to have failed, however, soon after the company landed, and they were obliged to rely upon the whim of the Captain of the *Mayflower* for their needs, the ship's supply being apparently separate from that of the passengers, and lasting longer. It was evidently a stipulation of the charter-party that the ship should, in part at least, provision her crew for the voyage — and certainly furnish their beer. This is rendered certain by Bradford's difficulty (as stated by himself) with Captain Jones showing that the ship had her own supply of beer, separate from that of the colonists, and that it was intended for the seamen as well as the officers.

Bradford mentions "aqua vitae" (brandy) as a constituent of their lunch on the exploring party of November 15. "Strong waters" (or Holland gin) are mentioned as a part of the entertainment given Massasoit on his first visit, and they find frequent mention otherwise. Wine finds no mention. Bradford states, "Neither ever had they any supply of foode from them [the Adventurers] but what they first brought with them;" and again, "They never had any supply of vitales more afterwards (but what the Lord gave them otherwise), for all ye company [the Adventurers] sent at any time was allways too short for those people that came with it."

WEDNESDAY, 21 OCTOBER 1620

Intellectual Baggage

In this connection it is of interest to note what freight the *Mayflower* carried for the intellectual needs of the Pilgrims. Of Bibles, as the "book of books," we may be sure — even without the evidence of the inventories of the early dead — there was no lack, and there is reason to believe that they existed in several tongues, *viz.* in English, Dutch, and possibly French (the Walloon contribution from the Huguenots), while there is little doubt that, as both publishers and as "students of the Word," Brewster, Bradford, and Winslow, at least, were possessed of, and more or less familiar with, both the Latin and Greek Testaments. It is altogether probable, however, that Governor Bradford's well attested study of "the oracles of God in the original" Hebrew, and his possession of the essential Hebrew Bible, grammar, and lexicon, were of a later day. The Holland voyagers had with them some few copies of the earliest hymnals ("psalme-bookes") — then very limited in number — in the singing of their parting hymns at Leyden and Delfshaven, as mentioned by Winslow and in the earlier inventories: These metrical versions of the Psalms constituted at the time, practically, the only hymnody permitted in the worship of the separatists. Given the other demands on their space during this journey, these books must have been precious.

Jeremy Bangs tried to organise a major exhibition at the Leiden Municipal Museum on the "world of ideas" that surrounded the Pilgrims. While the exhibition unfortunately did not come to fruition, the Leiden American Pilgrim Museum produced a profusely illustrated catalogue of what "could have been" in the exhibit, cleverly named *Intellectual Baggage*. The introductory essays, and particularly Bangs' own consideration of the place of printing in the Pilgrim's project, provide a largely overlooked context for the Pilgrims' story. The whole "catalogue" (for an exhibit that did not take place) is well worth a careful read. The one book on the Pilgrims which I have not read (as it is somewhat difficult to find on this side of the Atlantic), but which I want more than any other to read, is Bangs' *Plymouth Colony's Private Libraries* -- it provides insights gained by looking at the books they owned and read and seeing what literature they valued.

THURSDAY, 22 OCTOBER 1620

Armament

The arms and accoutrements (besides ordnance) of the *Mayflower* Pilgrims, known on the authority of Bradford and Winslow to have been brought by them, included muskets ("matchlocks"), "snaphances" (flintlocks), armor ("corslets," "cuirasses," "helmets," "bandoliers," etc.), swords, "curtlaxes" (cutlasses), "daggers," powder, "mould-shot," "match" (slow-match for guns), "flints," belts, "knapsacks," "drum," "trumpet," "manacles," "leg-irons," etc., etc. "Pistols" (brass) appear in early inventories, but their absence in the early hand-to-hand encounter at Wessagusset suggests that none were then available, or that they were not trusted. It is evident from the statement of Bradford that every one of the sixteen men who went out (under command of Standish) on the "first exploration" at Cape Cod had his "musket, sword, and corslet;" that they relied much on their armor, and hence, doubtless, took all possible with them on the ship. They probably did not long retain its use. In the letter written to the Adventurers from Southampton, the leaders complain of "wanting many muskets, much armour, &c." Bradford states that they used their "curtlaxes" (cutlasses) to dig the frozen ground to get at the Indians' corn, "having forgotten to bring spade or mattock." "Daggers" are mentioned as used in their celebrated duel by Doty and Leister, servants of Stephen Hopkins. Bradford narrates that on one of their exploring tours on the Cape the length of guard duty performed at night by each "relief" was determined by the inches of slow-match burned ("every one standing when his turn came while five or six inches of match was burning"), clearly indicating that they had no watches with them. The "drum" and "trumpet" are both mentioned in *Mourt's Relation* in the account given of Massasoit's reception, the latter as eliciting the special attention of his men, and their efforts at blowing it.

FRIDAY, 23 OCTOBER 1620

Smoother sailing

The equinoctial disturbances over and the strong October gales, the milder, warmer weather of late October followed. The *Mayflower* did not encounter any more ferocious storms on this journey, but it was also significantly off course and much further north than had been intended.

SATURDAY, 24 OCTOBER 1620

Indenture

An indentured servant or indentured labourer is an employee (indenturee) who is bound by a signed contract (indenture) to work without pay for the owner of the indenture for a period of time. The contract often let the employer sell the labour of an indenturee to a third party. Indenturees usually entered into an indenture for a specific payment or other benefit (such as transportation to a new place), or to meet a legal obligation, such as debt. On completion of the contract, indentured servants were given their freedom, and occasionally land. Indentured servitude was often brutal, with a high percentage of servants dying prior to the expiration of their indentures. In many countries, systems of indentured labour have now been outlawed, and are (currently) banned by the Universal

Declaration of Human Rights. Until the late 18th century, indentured servitude was very common in British North America; it was often a way for poor Europeans to immigrate to the American colonies: they signed an indenture in return for a costly passage they could not otherwise afford. After their indenture expired, the immigrants were free to work for themselves or another employer. Between one-half and two-thirds of European immigrants to the American colonies between the 1630s and American Revolution came under indentures. However, while over half of the European immigrants to the Thirteen Colonies were indentured servants, at any one time they were outnumbered by workers who had never been indentured or whose indenture had expired, and thus free wage labour was more prevalent for Europeans in the colonies.[24] In the 17th century, most indentured servants were of English origin and migrated to the Chesapeake and West Indies. Of the 120,000 emigrants to the Chesapeake during this era, roughly 90,000 arrived as bound labourers. Another 50,000 to 75,000 white indentured servants went to the islands, although these numbers included many Irish servants, political prisoners, and convict labourers. A few indentured servants, or *engagés*, appeared in the French colonies, but the institution was much more common in the British colonies. After the American Revolution, however, the system virtually disappeared in the United States. Document collections concerning the history of indentured servitude are particularly rich in Chesapeake material, but very little has been written about indentured servitude specifically in New England. Tomorrow I will look at the numbers and characteristics of indenture for New England, and the day after at the indentured servants on the *Mayflower*.

SUNDAY, 25 OCTOBER 1620

Indentured servants (continued)

Indentured servants could not marry without the permission of their master, were sometimes subject to physical punishment and did not receive legal favour from the courts. Of the European arrivals who came voluntarily, Tomlins estimates

---

[24]see John Donoghue, "Indentured Servitude in the 17th Century English Atlantic: A Brief Survey of the Literature," *History Compass* 11 [2013]: 893–902

that 48% were indentured.[25]   About 75% of these were under the age of 25. The age of adulthood for men was 24 years (not 21); those over 24 generally came on contracts lasting about 3 years.[26] Regarding the children who came, Gary Nash reports that "many of the servants were actually nephews, nieces, cousins and children of friends of emigrating Englishmen, who paid their passage in return for their labor once in America."[27]   In the case of New England, servants were clearly present among the approximately 20,000 migrants who entered Massachusetts Bay during the decade after 1630, but not in great numbers. Tomlins notes that, "there is little evidence of an organized trade in servants to New England of any significance (there is some scattered evidence in the early 18th century of unsuccessful efforts to encourage one -- see, for example, Province Laws, 1708-9, ch. 11, 'An Act to Encourage the Importation of White Servants'), and most migrant servants appear to have been recruited directly by migrant heads of household through family and community networks.   Scholars' estimates of the numbers of servants in the migrant stream have concentrated on the male population, varying in incidence from 1 in 3 to 1 in 6 of male migrants.   Given that roughly 60% of migrants were males and (again roughly) that male servants outnumbered female by 3 to 1, this suggests that servants constituted no fewer than 12.5% and no more than 25% of the Great Migration."[28]   Richard S. Dunn argues that 15% of 1630s migrants to New England were servants and that these servants

---

[25]Christopher Tomlins, "Reconsidering Indentured Servitude: European Migration and the Early American Labor Force, 1600–1775," *Labor History* 42 (2001): 5–43, at p. 9 and n. 11 -- Tomlins revises downward earlier estimates for the total number of indentured servants in the American colonies and argues that the institution may not have been as important as many other scholars have argued.

[26] Tomlins at fnn. 31, 42, 66.

[27] Gary Nash, *The Urban Crucible: The Northern Seaports and the Origins of the American Revolution* (Cambridge, MA: Harvard University Press, 1979) 15.

[28]"Reconsidering Indentured Servitude," 8 n. 8. For the sources of these estimates, see also David Hackett Fischer's controversial *Albion's Seed: Four British Folkways in America* (New York: Oxford University Press, 1989), 16, 27-28; Roger Thompson, *Mobility and Migration: East Anglian Founders of New England, 1629-1640* (Amherst, MA: University of Massachusetts Press, 1994), 122-23.

represented 33% of "the initial work force," but does not define work force.[29] On 19 indentured servants on the *Mayflower*, wait until tomorrow.

MONDAY, 26 OCTOBER 1620

Indentured servants on the Mayflower

Taken from Bradford's 1651 list of passengers, the following can be classified as servants or indentured to other passengers. All are identified by Bradford as being servants or apprentices of specific households, rather than placed in the section of the passenger list for free adults or hired hands (such as John Alden). Those four who have known descendants (21% of the *Mayflower*'s indentured servants) are given in **boldface**. Ages are difficult to estimate, although the dates of baptism for the four More children are known, and William Latham gave his age in a 1641 deposition. Eleven died in the first year (58% of the servants), and are marked with a dagger (†). Four signed the *Mayflower* Compact and are listed with an asterisk (*), which may help establish their approximate ages, although none would appear to have been over 25:

1. William Button (†) - servant of Samuel Fuller. Died before landfall in Cape Cod.
2. Robert Carter - servant of William Mullins. In his will, William Mullins asked his overseers to "have a special eye to my man Robert which hath not so approved himself as I would he should have done."[30]
3. **Edward Doty*** - servant to Stephen Hopkins. Married (twice) and had nine children by his second wife. Fought a duel with Edward Leister (below), the colony's second criminal offense, and was probably close to the end of his indenture at that time.
4. William Holbeck (†) - servant of William White. "Died soon after landing."
5. John Hooke (†) - "servant boy" of Isaac Allerton. Died first winter. Jeremy Bangs published John's apprenticeship record,[31]

---

[29]"Servants and Slaves: The Recruitment and Employment of Labor," in Jack P. Greene and J.R. Pole, eds., *Colonial British America: Essays in the New History of the Early Modern Era* (Baltimore: Johns Hopkins Press, 1984), 157-94, at 160.
[30]MQ 34:10; MD 1:230-232.
[31]NEHGR 143:207-8

Caleb Johnson published the marriage record of his parents,[32] and Sue Allan published his baptismal record.[33]

6. John Howland* - "manservant" to John Carver. "The boy who fell off the *Mayflower*" married Elizabeth Tilley (also a passenger) and had ten children. The statement in the *Plymouth Colony Records*[34] that he was "above eighty years" on his death on 23 February 1672/3 is "almost certainly exaggerated."[35]

7. John Langmore (†) - servant of Christopher Martin. "died in the first infection"

8. William Latham - "a boy" in the household of John Carver (b. about 1609); when John and Katherine Carver died, young William probably transferred into Governor Bradford's household. Robert Wakefield suggests that he was in William Brewster's household.[36] He became free of his indenture by 1633 (he is taxed in the lowest bracket in that year), and moved to Duxbury by 1638, where he was fined 40 shillings for the "entertaining of John Phillips into his house contrary to the act of the Court."[37] In 1639, after indictments for drunkenness, he sold his house and moved to Marblehead; he transferred to Marshfield by 1643. Latham's wife Mary was "a proper young woman about 18 years of age"; "being rejected by a young man whom she had an affection unto, vowed she would marry the next that came to her," and that turned out to be William Latham, "an ancient man who had neither honesty nor ability" -- being 35 at the time, William was significantly older than Mary. She then began to associate with "diverse young men who solicited her chastity, and drawing her into bad company, and giving her wine and other gifts, easily prevailed with her." One of these was James Britton of Weymouth; James and Mary were convicted of adultery by the Massachusetts Bay Court of Assistants and were hanged at Boston on 21 March 1643/4.[38] After the execution of his abusive teenaged wife (for more details, see Caleb Johnson's 2009 *Mayflower Quarterly* article), William and Roger Cooke were

---

[32]TAG 80:101

[33]NEHGR 173:204-5

[34] PCR 8:34.

[35] MM, p. 110; Johnson, *Mayflower Passengers*, 287 fn. 188.

[36] MQ 40:9.

[37] PCR 1:87.

[38] MQ 75 [2009]: 49-53; quotations from Governor Winthrop's *Journal*

living together in 1645 when they charged Ann Barker with burning down their house (two unmarried men living together was "a domestic arrangement not generally approved of by the colony authorities").[39] Latham returned to England in 1646, and then was part of a colonisation attempt in the Bahamas, where, after being shipwrecked on Eleuthera Island, he died of starvation and exposure in 1647. No known children.

9. Edward Leister* - servant to Stephen Hopkins. Died in Virginia after 1623.

10. Ellen (Helen) More (†) - "a little girl was put to [Edward Winslow] called Ellen, the sister of Richard More. ... Died soon after the ship's arrival." She was baptised in 1612.

11. Jasper More (†) - "a child that was put to [John Carver]. ... [Jasper] died before [the Carvers] of the common infection." He was baptised in 1613.

12. Mary More (†) - "Richard More's brother died the first winter." More about this confusion, and the story of these four children, later. She was baptised in 1616.

13. Richard More - Bradford records that "a boy was put to [William Brewster] called Richard More, and another of his brothers." He was baptised in 1614. Married twice, and had seven children.

14. Solomon Prower (†) - servant of Christopher Martin, who was probably his stepfather. He was born about 1597, and died 24 December 1620 -- "the last who died this [December]."

15. George Soule* - servant to Edward Winslow. Married Mary Becket (passenger on the *Anne*) and had nine children (Bradford records eight, suggesting that the ninth and youngest child, Benjamin, was born after the list was compiled. Benjamin Soule was killed on 26 March 1676 in "Captain [Michael] Peirse's Fight" during King Philip's War).

16. Elias Story (†) - servant to Edward Winslow; died early in 1621.

17. Edward Thompson (†) - servant of William White. "Died soon after their landing."

18. Roger Wilder (†) - "manservant" to John Carver, died "before either of [the Carvers] of the common infection."

---

[39] PCR 7:41

19. Dorothy (unknown surname) - "a maidservant" in the household of John Carver; married Francis Eaton as his second wife. Died between 1622 and 1626.

TUESDAY, 27 OCTOBER 1620
"A succession of fine days, with favouring winds"

Most of the passengers have now been on board a ship for over three months. While time above deck was certainly welcome in the fresh air, it has been a *very* long time since anyone has done laundry. Given the fierceness of the storms, everything must have become wet, even the clothing that was packed away. Edward Winslow, in his 1621 advice to future travellers, suggested that they take "a good store of clothes and bedding." After the ferocious storms of the beginning of the month, this "succession of fine days" must have been particularly welcome. Because of the cracked beam, however, the captain was not able to put out full sail, and had to ease up whenever the wind became strong to avoid further strain on the fractured main beam. Westward progress is slow.

WEDNESDAY, 28 OCTOBER 1620
Edward Winslow's birthday!

Edward Winslow, the son of Edward Winslow and Magdalene Oliver, was born on 18 October 1595 (o.s.) and was baptised at Saint Peter's Church in Droitwich, Worcestershire (England) on 20 October 1595. That would mean that today was his twenty-fifth birthday (what a place to celebrate -- in the middle of the Atlantic Ocean!). Young Edward attended The King's School at Worcester Cathedral from April 1606 to April 1611 (aged 10 to 15); he may (or may not) have then gone to Cambridge -- there is no documentation to that effect, which does not rule it out. He would certainly have learned Latin and Greek at the Worcester Cathedral School -- he may or may not have been a chorister. Edward next appeared in 1613 in London, as apprentice to John Beale, "citizen and stationer." Beale was imprisoned in 1614 for accepting Winslow as an apprentice ("against the orders of this house [i.e., the Company of Stationers]"), but Winslow re-enlisted as an apprentice in 1615 for a period of eight years after Beale paid a fine. In 1618, Winslow showed up in Leiden, having left his apprenticeship before it was over, as assistant to the Pilgrims' lay leader William Brewster along with John Reynolds.

Edward Winslow married Elizabeth Barker in Leiden in May 1618: his occupation on the marriage register was "printer"; he would have been 22 years old. The documentation on Edward Winslow in Leiden, what there is of it, is reviewed by Jeremy Bangs in *NEHGR* 154 (2000): 109-118, and in his later *Pilgrim Edward Winslow: New England's First International Diplomat*. By the *Mayflower*'s voyage, Winslow had become one of the acknowledged leaders of the group. His brother Gilbert accompanied him on the *Mayflower*, while his three remaining brothers all came to New England later (John Winslow on the *Fortune* in 1621, Josiah Winslow and Kenelm Winslow in 1631).

He came on the *Mayflower* with his wife, who died the first winter, and three indentured servants. There are hints that his wife Elizabeth had come into a substantial inheritance in England, and this was disposed of before the *Mayflower*'s departure. He would thus have been relatively flush with cash, which may account for the number of indentures, and was safely Puritan, which would account for eight year old Ellen More being entrusted to him. Winslow's wife Elizabeth, Ellen More, and one of the servants (Elias Story) all died the first winter. Only George Soule, the other of Winslow's male servants, survived, and, indeed, thrived. It would appear that all of the *Mayflower*'s indentured servants had some previous connection with the households to which they were attached, and this would suggest that George Soule was indentured to Winslow either through connections in Leiden or in London -- servants did not simply show up at a jobs centre looking for a ticket to America. The connection with the household to which they were indentured is usually the key to many other parts of the story. A surprising part of this is that George Soule, who signed the *Mayflower* Compact and thus was either over or almost 21 in November 1620, would not have been more than a few years younger than Edward Winslow himself -- this personal relationship may not have been exclusively "master-servant." If Soule had been associated with the Leiden congregation, or was a part of a separatist conventicle in or around London, this might explain why he was able to take advantage of Winslow's new wealth, particularly if, as a young, single man, he was not able to afford the journey himself and Winslow was generous in helping others he knew to make the trip. While the standard length of an indenture was seven, or even eight, years, other periods were possible (three and five years were not uncommon); since George Soule married between 1623 and 1626 (Mary Becket arrived on the *Anne* in 1623 and she was unmarried at the time of the land allotment; their eldest son Zachariah was born in 1627) and he would have been out of his indenture by then, the usual birth date given for him of 1599, based on his signature on the Compact and age at marriage, might be correct, although he may also have been only four or five years younger than Winslow. Soule went to Duxbury before 1637 and Winslow moved to Marshfield by 1643, so there was not necessarily any continuing connection: George Soule appears more closely connected to the Warren family after they arrive, being included with them in several divisions, than to Winslow's new family after Edward remarried.

THURSDAY, 29 OCTOBER 1620

Captain Jones and the Beer Wars

That Christopher Jones, Master of the *Mayflower*, was a man of large experience and fully competent in his profession is beyond dispute. His disposition, character, attitudes and deeds have been the subject of much discussion. By most writers he is held to have been a man of coarse, "unsympathetic" nature, "a rough sea-dog," capable of good feeling and kindly impulses at times, but neither governed by them -- nor by principle. An early twentieth century author stated, "that he was a 'highwayman of the seas,' a buccaneer and pirate, guilty of blood for gold, there can be no doubt." Bradford himself — whose authority in the matter will not be doubted — says: "As this calamitie, the general sickness, fell among ye passengers that were to be left here to plant, and were basted ashore and made to drinke water, that the seamen might have ye more bear [*beer*] and one in his sickness desiring but a small can of beare it was answered that if he were their own father he should have none." Bradford later claims that Captain Jones displayed excessive rapacity, when in command of the *Discovery*, with his extortionate demands upon the Plymouth planters, notwithstanding their necessities; this, however, was Thomas Jones, and not Christopher Jones. It must be freely admitted that if it were not for Jones, the Pilgrims would never have reached the New World. Christopher Jones' health was so impaired by the 1620-1621 voyage that, having sold the *Mayflower* within months of his return, he died not long thereafter

(March 1622). Over the next few days I will try to look at the charges and the evidence for Jones' (alleged) attempt to sabotage the voyage.

FRIDAY, 30 OCTOBER 1620

Where were they headed, exactly?

The specific statements of Bradford and others leave no room for doubt that the *Mayflower* Pilgrims fully intended to make their settlement somewhere in the region of the mouth of "Hudson's River." Morton states clearly that Captain Jones' "engagement was to Hudson's River." Presumably, the stipulation of his charter party required that he should complete his outward voyage in that general locality. The northern limits of the patents granted in the Pilgrim interest, whether that of John Wincob (or Wincop) sealed 9 June 1619, but never used, or the first one to John Pierce, of 2 February 1620, were brought within the limits of the First (London) Virginia Company's charter, which embraced the territory between the parallels of 34° and 41° N. latitude. The most northerly of these parallels runs about twenty miles north of the mouth of "Hudson's River." It is certain that the Pilgrims, after the great expense, labour, and pains of three years, to secure the protection of these Patents, would not willingly or deliberately have planted themselves outside that protection, upon territory where they had none, and where they might reasonably expect trouble as interlopers.

Henry Hudson, an Englishman who worked for the Dutch East India Company, had mapped the area. Barely a decade before the arrival of the *Mayflower*, Hudson came across Manhattan Island and the native people living there in 1609, and continued up the river that would later bear his name until he arrived at the site of present-day Albany. Although fur traders set up (temporary) trading posts after 1613, a permanent European presence in New Netherland only began in 1624, with the founding of a Dutch fur trading settlement on Governors Island. In 1625, construction was started on the citadel of Fort Amsterdam on Manhattan Island, later called New Amsterdam, in what is now Lower Manhattan. But in late 1620, there was no European settlement in what is now New York City. Imagine what it would have been like if the Pilgrims had been the first New Yorkers!

66

A Dutch Destination?

There was no reason why, if the Pilgrims had so desired, they should not have gone to "Hudson's River" or its vicinity, unless it was that they had once seemed to recognize the States General of Holland as the rightful owners of that territory, by making petition to them, through the New Netherland Company, for their authority and protection in settling there. But it appears certain that, whatever the cause, they themselves broke off their negotiations with the Dutch — whether on account of the inducements offered by Thomas Weston, or because of a doubt of the ability of the Dutch to maintain their claim to that region, and to protect them. The States General — whether with knowledge that the Leiden community had ended negotiations or from their own doubts about their ability to maintain their claim on the Hudson region — rejected the petition made to them on the Pilgrims' behalf. It is probable that the latter was the real reason, from the fact that the petition was twice rejected.

It also appears from the petition itself, made by the New Netherland Company (to which the Leiden leaders had looked, doubtless on account of its pretensions, for the authority and protection of the States General, as they afterward did to the English Virginia Company for British protection), that this Company had lost its own charter by expiration, and hence had absolutely nothing to offer the Leiden community beyond the personal influence of its members, and the prestige of a name that had once been potent. In fact, the New Netherland Company was using the Leiden congregation as leverage to pry for itself from the States General new advantages, larger than those that it had previously enjoyed.

Moreover it appears by the evidence of both the petition of the Directors of the New Netherland Company to the Prince of Orange (2/12 February 1619/20), and the letters of Sir Dudley Carleton, the British ambassador at The Hague, to the English Privy Council, dated 5/15 February 1621/22, that, up to this latter date the Dutch had established no colony on the territory claimed by them at the Hudson, and had no other representation there than the trading-post of a commercial company whose charter had expired. There can be no doubt that the Leyden leaders knew, from their dealings with the New Netherland Company, and the study of the whole problem which they evidently made, that this region was open to them or any other parties for habitation and trade, so far as any prior grants or charters under the Dutch were concerned, but they required more than this.[40]

To Englishmen, the English claim to the territory at "Hudson's River" was valid, by virtue of discovery by the Cabots, under the law of nations as then recognized, notwithstanding Hudson's more particular explorations of those parts in 1609, in the service of Holland, especially as no colony or permanent occupancy of the region by the Dutch had been made. So we can rule out an hesitation on the part of the Pilgrims from going to the mouth of the Hudson River because it was claimed by Holland. But the conversations of the previous two years show that they had definitely considered what is now New York Harbour as the principal destination for their journey, and for some time.

---

[40] See Sir Dudley Carleton's Letters. "They have certain Factors there, continually resident, trading with savages ... but I cannot learn of any colony, either I already planted there by these people, or so much as intended." British State Papers, Holland, Bundle 165.

NOVEMBER 1620

An English Destination?

Although the Pilgrims had discussed -- at length -- the area around the mouth of the Hudson River as the place for their permanent settlement, there were other options. "In the final chaotic months before their departure from England," Nathaniel Philbrick writes, "[Thomas] Weston and others had begun to insist that a more northern site in New England -- which was the new name for what are now the states of Massachusetts, Connecticut, Rhode Island, Maine, New Hampshire, and Vermont -- was a better place to settle." The waters off the coast were already known to be a profitable fishery, and trading posts had begun to pop up along the Maine shores for commerce with the Indians and fur trapping. But at the time that the *Mayflower* left England (almost two months ago), it had not been possible to obtain a patent, or permission to establish a permanent settlement, for that region, since King James had not yet chartered the group called the "Council for New England": this was established on 3 November 1620, so more about that in a few days. As far as anyone on the *Mayflower* knew, there was no English authority north of the 34th parallel. They did know, however, that Captain John Smith had completed a thorough survey of the Atlantic side of New England in 1614 (and he was the one who named it that) -- he was also the one who named what is now Plymouth, Massachusetts "Plymouth" (hence the British comedian Eddie Izzard's joke, "[The Pilgrims] set off from Plymouth and landed in Plymouth -- how lucky is that?!"). In 1605, Champlain had named it "Port St. Louis." In the winter of 1616, Richard Vines stayed off the Maine coast and discovered that a plague was decimating the native inhabitants. Although no one had yet established a permanent settlement, and no one was even sure who had the right to settle there, there was some information already known about the area called New England, and there were significant financial and political leaders who *very much* wanted the Pilgrims to settle *there*, and not at the mouth of the Hudson River.

MONDAY, 2 NOVEMBER 1620
Reasons for Dropping Pilgrims in New England (Economic)

There would seem to be three main reasons for dropping the Pilgrims off in New England. While it has become usual to view the Plymouth settlers through modern prisms, and declare that they came to the New World for "religious freedom," that phrase would probably have been meaningless to them, much less one that they would have agreed with. The far more common goals that the Pilgrim writers themselves stated were (a) the spread of the Gospel, and (b) the establishment of a godly order in a new plantation. The economic values were never far from the surface, but in a number of ways the colonists were somewhat naïve. I will eventually return to the first goal, but the second (colonisation in a godly order) had never been tried by English settlers in precisely this way before, and thus there was no precedent to which the Pilgrims could look in organising their settlement. They had brought what they thought they would need, but the disorganised way in which it was attempted, to which must be added numerous delays (foreseen and unforeseen), meant that they were not at all prepared for life 3,000 miles from England, in a place where resupply was simply not available, and where much of the minimum they had planned to bring had to be left behind when the two ships were combined into one. It remains to be seen what the colonists thought they were going to do once they got to the New World, and how they were going to provide a profit for their backers, the merchant adventurers.

That group, in trying very hard to steer the Pilgrims to New England, were not necessarily hostile or deceitful. They naturally wanted a return on their investment, and believed that this could best be achieved in an area rich in natural resources (particularly fish, fur, and lumber, to say nothing of what could be obtained by commerce with the natives). The merchant adventurers had tried to make this opportunity as available as they could, but this had fallen on somewhat deaf ears. It is not beyond the realm of possibility that, having failed in convincing the *Mayflower* passengers by reason and argument to settle in New England, where there was a greater possibility of immediate profit than the northern reaches of Virginia, they may have entered into a separate, perhaps clandestine, arrangement with Master Christopher Jones (through persuasion, or perhaps bribery) to deposit the Pilgrims further north than they thought they were going, so that they would be constrained by force of circumstances to become a part of the economic project of the merchant adventurers.

TUESDAY, 3 NOVEMBER 1620

Reasons for Dropping Pilgrims in New England (Political)

The second set of reasons for dropping the Pilgrims off in New England was political. As Jeremy Bangs pointed out in a comment on yesterday's post, the area between Florida (Spanish) and Quebec (French) claimed by England was called "Virginia," and thus in a broad sense it was certainly correct that they aimed to land in Virginia, and they in fact did land in that part of Virginia called New England. However, there is also the matter of the area granted to the Virginia Companies, which was more carefully circumscribed than simply "Virginia." The Pilgrims recognized the need of a strong power behind them, under whose aegis they might safely plant, and by virtue of whose might and right they could hope to keep their lives and possessions, and thus they needed to land in an area that was not simply claimed by England, but had been granted to specific individuals or a group that could ensure its survival.

In 1606, James I issued a royal charter to "adventurers" (a term that referred to both investors and settlers) in the Virginia Company of London, a joint-stock company, "to make habitation, plantation, and to deduce a colony of sundry of our people into that part of America commonly called Virginia." The Virginia Company actually consisted of two groups of investors: the Virginia Company of Plymouth and the Virginia Company of London. The king authorized the latter to settle on the American coast between 34° and 40° N. latitude, while the Plymouth investors were directed to lands to the north. The Virginia Company of Plymouth planted a colony at Sagadahoc in present-day Maine in August 1607, but it was abandoned the following spring. "In 1607," says Goodwin, "Gorges and the cruel Judge Popham planted a colony at Phillipsburg (or Sagadahoc, as is supposed), by the mouth of the Kennebec. Two ships came, *The Gift of God* and the *Mary and John*, bringing a hundred persons. Through August they found all delightful, but when the ships went back in December, fifty five of the number returned to England, weary of their experience and fearful of the cold ... With spring the ships returned from England;

'but by this time the remainder were ready to leave,' so every soul returned with Gilbert [the Admiral] ... For thirty years Gorges continued to push exploration and emigration to that region, but his ambition and liberality ever resulted in disappointment and loss." The annals of the time show that not a few of the Sagadahoc colonists were convicts, released from the English jails to people this colony. The differences, and indeed the similarities, between this attempt and the Plymouth colony are instructive.

The King by letter (15 December 1621) to Sir Dudley Carleton, his ambassador at the Hague, expressly claimed his rights in the New Netherland territory and instructed him to impress upon the government of the States General his Majesty's claim, "who, *jure prime occupationis* hath good and sufficient title to these parts." There appears to have been no legal bar to the Pilgrims' intention to settle in the vicinity of "Hudson's River," if they so chose. Despite the allegations of the truthful but not always reliable Morton, his charges of intrigue between the Dutch and Master Jones of the *Mayflower* to prevent settlement at "Hudson's River," may well be doubted. Writing in *New England's Memorial* in 1669, Morton says: "But some of the Dutch, having notice of their intentions, and having thoughts about the same time of erecting a plantation there likewise, they fraudulently hired the said Jones, by delays while they were in England, and now under pretence of the shoals the dangers of the Monomoy Shoals off Cape Cod to disappoint them in going thither. ... Of this plot between the Dutch and Mr. Jones, I have had late and certain intelligence." If this "intelligence" was no more reliable than his assertion concerning the responsibility of Jones for the "delays while they were in England," it may well be discredited, as not the faintest evidence appears to make Jones responsible for those delays, and they are amply accounted for without him. Without questioning the veracity of Morton (while noting his many errors, and that the lapse of time made it easy to misinterpret even apparently certain facts), it must be remembered that Morton is the originator of the charge of Dutch intrigue with Jones, and was its sole support for many years. All other writers who have accepted and endorsed his views are of later date, and simply follow him, while Bradford and Winslow, who were victims of this Dutch "conspiracy," if it ever existed, were entirely silent in their writings upon the matter, which we may be sure they would not have been, had they suspected the Dutch as prime movers in the treachery. But there are other, English, candidates for conspirators, as we shall see tomorrow.

WEDNESDAY, 4 NOVEMBER 1620
Political Conspiracy Theory -- Enter Ferdinando Gorges

But there was a party who had ample motive, and with whom Master Jones was already in close contact, and had been for years. Singularly enough, the motive governing this party was exactly the reverse of that attributed to the Dutch. In the case of the latter, the alleged animus was a desire to keep the Pilgrims away from their "Hudson's River" domain. In the case of the English "conspirators," the purpose was to secure these planters as colonists for, and bring them to, the more northern territory owned by them. Sir Ferdinando Gorges was the leading spirit of the Virginia Company of Plymouth, as he also became (with the Earl of Warwick a close second) of The Council of New England, of which both men were made Governors next week, when the Council superseded the "Second Virginia Company."

Although not its official head, Sir Ferdinando Gorges was the leading man. This was largely from his superior acquaintance with, and long and varied experience in, New England affairs. The Plymouth Company, holding — by the division of territory made under the original charter-grants — a strip of territory one hundred miles wide, on the North American coast between the parallels of 41° and 45° N. latitude, had not prospered, and its efforts at colonization (on what is now the Maine coast) in 1607 and later had proved abortive, largely through the character of its "settlers," who had been in good degree a somewhat notable mixture of two difficult elements of society — convicts and broken-down "gentlemen."

No one knew better than the shrewd Gorges the value of such a colony as the Leiden brethren would be, to plant, populate, and develop his Company's great holdings. None were more facile than himself and the buccaneering Earl of Warwick, to plan and execute the bold, but — as it proved — easy coup, by which the Pilgrim colony was to be "stolen" bodily; for the benefit of the Second Virginia (or Plymouth) Company and its successor, the Council for New England, from the First (or London) Company, under whose patent (to John Pierce) and patronage they sailed. They apparently did not take their patent with them — it would

73

have been worthless if they had — and they were destined to have no small trouble with Pierce, before they were established in their rights under the new patent granted (in the interest of the Adventurers and themselves), by the Council for New England.

THURSDAY, 5 NOVEMBER 1620

Reasons for Dropping Pilgrims in New England (Natural)

To the economic and political reasons for landing and staying in New England must be added what we might call the "natural" reasons. The full force of the Gulf Stream kept the *Mayflower*'s crossing further north than the more direct route; to this must be added the storms which disrupted the ship's forward progress. Steering was done by a stick called a whip-staff that was moved back and forth to move the tiller, which in turn moved the rudder: there was no large "steering wheel." The mathematical calculations of location were fairly accurate for latitude, so the sailors could tell with a moderate degree of accuracy how far north they were, but there was very little that could be done to calculate longitude with the same degree of accuracy. Dead reckoning (calculating the ship's position by the distance run and the course steered) was the common method, and that was rather the same as good guessing, particularly when compared to modern chronometers (or satnav/GPS). If the *Mayflower* and the *Speedwell* had departed when they were originally supposed to, the Pilgrims would have arrived in what is now New York well before the middle of October. Fresh provisions were a thing of the past. The supplies that they had on board were stretched to the limit, and beyond, by delays in leaving, so that a significant amount was consumed in the trips out and back to England before the ultimate departure. Supplies were also attenuated by the lengthy trans-Atlantic crossing, followed by having little or no food available once they arrived. Fresh water was so low that laundry could not be done; firewood was out, as well. To this must be added the difficult and continued enclosure of many of the passengers between decks for four to six months once the *Mayflower* arrived, since accommodations on shore were only constructed bit by bit. The prevalence of disease and sickness, particularly scurvy, which must have begun during the journey, was made worse by the unaccustomed cold. It seemed as though "the stars in their courses fought against" them.

FRIDAY, 6 NOVEMBER 1620

Captain Jones (part one)

The known facts favour the belief that Gorges' thoughts on colonial matters — especially as stimulated by his plottings in relation to the Leiden community — led to his project of the grant and charter for the new Council for New England, designed and constituted to supplant, or override, all others. It is probable that this grand scheme (duly embellished) being unfolded to Weston, with suggestions of great opportunities for Weston himself, warmed and drew him, and brought him to zealous cooperation in all Gorges' plans, and that from this time, as Bradford states, he "begane to incline" toward, and to suggest to the Pilgrims, association with Gorges and the new Council. Not daring openly to declare this change, he undertook, apparently at first by suggestions "not to place too much dependence on the London Company, but to rely on himself and friends;" that "the fishing of New England was good," etc.; and thus making no headway, then by a policy of delay, fault finding, etc., to breed dissatisfaction on the Pilgrims' part with the Adventurers, the patent of Wincob, etc., with the hope of bringing about "a new deal" in the Gorges interest. The same delays in sailing, that have been adduced as proof of Jones' complicity with the Dutch, would have been of equal advantage to these noble schemers, and if he had any hand in them — which does not appear — it would have been far more likely in the interest of his long-time patron, the Earl of Warwick, and of his friends, than of any Dutch conspirators. Once the colonists were landed upon American soil, especially if late in the season, they would not be likely, it doubtless was argued, to remove; while by a liberal policy on the part of the Council for New England toward them — when they discovered that they were upon its territory — they could probably be retained.

SATURDAY, 7 NOVEMBER 1620

Captain Jones (part two)

Once the colonists were landed upon American soil, especially if late in the season, they would not be likely, it doubtless was argued, to remove; by a liberal policy on the part of the Council for New England toward them — when they discovered that they were on its territory — they could probably be retained. That just such a policy was, at once and eagerly, adopted as soon as occasion permitted, supports the idea that the scheme was thoroughly matured from the start. The record of the action of the "Council for New England" — which had become the successor of the Second Virginia Company before intelligence was received that the Pilgrims had landed on its domain — is available and has not survived, but it appears by the record of the London Company of Monday, 16 July 1621, that the Council for New England had promptly made itself agreeable to the colonist : "It was moved, seeing that Master John Pierce had taken a Patent of Sir Ferdinando Gorges, and thereupon seated his Company [the Pilgrims] within the limits of the Northern Plantations, as by some was supposed ..." From this it is plain that, on receipt by Pierce of the news that the colony was landed within the limits of the Council for New England, he had, as instructed, applied for, and been given (1 June 1621), the (first) Council patent for the colony. See also the minutes of the Council for New England of 25 March 1623, and the fulsome letter of Robert Cushman returning thanks in behalf of the Planters (through John Pierce), to Gorges, for his prompt response to their request for a patent and for his general complacency toward them. James Phinney Baxter, Gorges' biographer, says: "We can imagine with what alacrity he [Sir Ferdinando] hastened to give to Pierce a patent in their behalf. ... The warm desire of Sir Ferdinando Gorges to see a permanent colony founded within the domain of the Plymouth [or Second] Virginia Company was to be realized in a manner of which he had never dreamed [sic!] and by a people with whom he had but little sympathized, although we know that he favored their settlement within the territorial limits of the Plymouth [Second] Company." He had indeed "favored their settlement" with all the skill of which he was master, and greeted their expected and duly arranged advent with all the jubilant open-handedness with which the hunter treats the wild horse he has coralled, and hopes to domesticate.

In summary, everything favoured the conspirators. The deflection north-ward from the normal course of the ship as it approached the coast, bound for the latitude of the Hudson, needed only to be so trifling that the best sailor of the Pilgrim leaders would not be likely to note or criticise it, and it was by no means uncommon to make Cape Cod as the first landfall on Virginia voyages. The lateness of the arrival on the coast, and the difficulties attendant on doubling Cape Cod, would increase the anxiety for almost any landing-place, and render it easy to retain the sea-worn and weary colonists when once on shore. The grand advantage, however, over and above all else, was the entire ease and certainty with which the cooperation of the one man essential to the success of the undertaking could be secured, without need of any other, that is, the Master of the *Mayflower*, Captain Christopher Jones. While proof is, four hundred years later, impossible, there was opportunity, motive, and execution.

SUNDAY, 8 NOVEMBER 1620

Thomas Weston (1584-c.1647)

In response to a comment on the first of the posts on Captain Jones, perhaps something should be said about Thomas Weston, who was the villain (if any there was) of Bradford's *Of Plimoth Plantation*. In 1615 Weston, through his uncle, William Greene, "a man of much wealth," prevailed upon Edward Pickering, "then a shop keeper in Cheapside of mean estate," to become his agent in Holland. According to Weston's evidence, Pickering "professed himself to be so farre of the opinion with the Brownists such as that his conscience would not permit him to conf[orm to] the Church of England nor to allow of the Rites and Ceremonies thereby required and therein used, and that for his non Conformity to the same he was called in question and in danger and to undergoe the Censure of the Ch[urch] .... goe to Amsterdam in Holland where he might live in peace and enjoy the freedome of his Conscience, but for that the said Pickering had not acquaintance there nor meanes to get his liveing." Together Weston and Pickering began to import a variety of seditious (nonconformist) religious tracts into England. By 1619 he was implicated in a shady venture whereby one of his agents, Philemon Powell, imported 30 tons of alum and unloaded it secretly at night to avoid customs duties; he was observed and reported by a vigilant customs official. He and some of his associate Merchant Adventurers had been brought before the Privy Council and ordered to cease unlimited trade in the Netherlands. Soon after, he left England and travelled to Leiden, where his agent Pickering had married a woman belonging to the Separatists.

What became the Plymouth colony was financed and begun under Thomas Weston's direction, but he quit the enterprise in 1622. As agent for the merchant adventurers'

77

investment in the *Mayflower* voyage, Weston played a part in the transportation of the More children of Shropshire, who had been taken in 1616 in a dispute arising from their mother's supposed adultery; the children had been held incommunicado in Shropshire for four years and were then taken to Weston and held at Weston's home in Aldgate, London, for some weeks until the *Mayflower* was to sail. They were then given over (or indentured) to three Pilgrims for the voyage to the New World. Three of the four children died the first winter in Plymouth: only Richard More survived.

In early 1622, Thomas Weston began the colony of Wessagusset (Weymouth) which failed by March 1623; he left New England for Virginia, and by 1640, Maryland. Phineas Pratt later wrote an account of the company's experience in Wessagusset. Weston's activities in the Plymouth colony are detailed in Bradford's journal and Robert Cushman's letters. He was a Merchant Adventurer, promoter and capitalist, and a citizen and ironmonger of London. One derogatory comment recorded in records of the time summarises the rest: "He was eager to reap quick profits from the New World, and not very scrupulous about the means." On 1 March 1622, Weston obtained an export license from the Privy Council to send cannon (thirty pieces of ordnance, the big guns weighing nearly two tons) to New England, intended for the use of the Plymouth Colony; the consignment came from the royal arsenal at the Tower of London, but it never reached America. Weston sold it instead and pocketed the money: the ordnance was indeed taken aboard in England by Andrew Weston (Thomas' brother), but "was sold abroad to Turkish pirates ... for extraordinary and excessive gain," or, as less hostile witnesses put it, "sold in some foreign part by Weston's direction, although the same was sold in a countrie both in peace and freindshippe to this Kingdome." The discovery of this capital offence, for which Thomas Weston appears never to have been pardoned, was his downfall. On 31 May 1622, the Council for New England ordered the immediate forfeiture of Weston's ships. An inquisition was taken at the London Guildhall on 28 July 1622, and Weston's assets, including Pickering's bond for £1500 and his own for £800 to the King, were ordered forfeit and Weston was declared an outlaw from the Crown. When he arrived in New England in 1622, Thomas Weston was penniless and wearing borrowed clothes, and he was soon expelled. His activities and movements thereafter remain obscure, but by 1641 he was again visiting England and, so it would appear, still being sought by authority for his old misdemeanours. Thomas Weston's residence during his last years was the 1250 acre Westbury Manor on the east side of St. George's Creek in Saint Mary's County, Maryland, laid out for him on 10 January 1642/3. According to Charles Andrews: "Weston, after squeezing all he could out of the Pilgrims, became a planter and burgess in Virginia, where he made trading and fishing voyages to the Maine coast. After being arrested more than once for breaking the Colony's laws, he went to Maryland, acquired new property, and returned to England;" he died in London of the plague between 5 May 1647 and 29 November 1648.[41]

MONDAY, 9 NOVEMBER 1620

Navigation

Ships of the *Mayflower*'s day had a very simple array of navigating instruments. The compass, the cross-staff or the astrolabe, the log-line with its accompanying "sand glass" (hour glass), parallel rulers and dividers, and a spyglass (telescope) were all that was usually available for offshore or deep water navigation. To this should be added the leadline for soundings when the ship was near enough to the coast to be within a depth of one hundred fathoms (six hundred feet).

The compass was similar to its modern counterpart. The local variations of the magnetic needle from true north (as indicated by the North Star or the meridian altitude of the sun) were known and a source of some anxiety. Whether the *Mayflower* had a cross-staff or an astrolabe is unknown. The astrolabe had been in use for a century or more, but it was expensive, complicated, and delicate. Samuel de Champlain used one onboard ship and on shore for making astronomical observations, but his expedition was well financed and outfitted. As an aside, in May 1613, to avoid the rapids of the Ottawa River, Champlain chose a course through a number of small lakes near Cobden, Ontario; he and his men were forced to portage and to climb over and under fallen logs at one particularly difficult point by Green Lake (now also known as Astrolabe Lake). It was here

---

[41]Charles Andrews, *The Colonial Period of American History* [New Haven, CT: Yale University Press; 1934-38] 3:184

79

that Champlain lost his astrolabe. The astrolabe remained where it had fallen for 254 years: eventually a 14 year old farm boy named Edward Lee found it in 1867 while helping his father clear trees. It is probable that Captain Jones, being only a merchant captain and not being as well funded, relied on the cross-staff, which yielded accurate results with much less trouble.

The cross-staff was about three feet long, across which (at right angles) was attached a sliding bar about two feet long. On one end of the staff and on both ends of the bar were sights, so that the observer, holding the sighted end to his eye, could slide the bar along in a vertical position until the horizon could be seen through the sight at the lower end of the bar, while the star or planet being observed showed through the sight at the upper end. This provided the angle between the horizon and the heavenly body. Occasionally the North Star was used, but the sun could also serve. As mentioned in a posting several days ago, Captain Jones probably knew within a few miles what degree of north latitude he was on, but could not possibly have known his longitude within several hundred miles. No doubt he recognised and made allowance for this.

TUESDAY, 10 NOVEMBER 1620

Speed Calculation

"The log-line and log-glass were the ship's speedometer. The log was originally just that, a log of wood with a line made fast midway of its length, so that, when dropped over the stern of a moving vessel, it immediately took up a position practically stationary in the water, broadside to the course of the ship, causing the line to pay out over the taffrail [*the handrail around the open deck area toward the stern of a ship*] as the ship ran on away from it. In the *Mayflower's* day the log had evolved into a quadrant of wood, weighted on one side, having a log line one hundred and fifty fathoms [*900 feet*] long and graduated into lengths by short pieces of knotted marline inserted through its strands. Each length, or 'knot,' bore the same relation to the nautical mile of about six thousand and eighty feet as the log glass did to the conventional hour glass, and the number of knots run out while the sands of the glass were running through determined miles, or knots, per hour the ship was logging. Like the old hog-yoke [*cross-*

staff], it was pretty good in fair weather, but in heavy weather and head winds there was considerable slip."[42]

Charts

The last set of navigation tools to look at would be charts and calculation tools, such as dividers and parallel rulers. Captain John Smith wrote about what was available before his 1614 voyage to New England, that the charts available to him "of those Northern parts" were "so unlike each to other; and most so differing from any true proportion, or resemblance of the Countrey, as they did mee no more good, then so much waste paper, though they cost me more." Smith and his foolhardy band of sailors, nonetheless, covered 350 miles, from the Bay of Fundy down to Cape Cod, in an open boat probably no more than 30 feet long. And, with a humble set of surveying tools — a crude compass, astrolabe, sextant, a lead line to measure depth, a quill pen and paper — they gathered notes for their very own map of what Smith named for the first time "New England." The official map was published alongside Smith's book, *A Description of New England*, in 1616. Smith was actually the first to call the site where the Pilgrims finally settled "New Plimouth" on his map four years earlier. In fact, in *A Description of New England*, Smith astutely noted that Plymouth was "an excellent good harbor, good land; and now want of any thing, but industrious people." It is unlikely that the *Mayflower* carried either the charts of Champlain or Lescarbot; Captain Jones definitely had John Smith's published description and map of his 1614 voyage, but the map as originally published had no description of the back side of Cape Cod -- Smith only sailed as far south as the tip of Cape Cod, and he took the word of the Indians for what lay further south (see the 1616 map below -- the Pilgrims were sailing into *terra incognita*). The old Dutch trade route from Holland to the trading post on Manhattan had skirted the shoals of Cape Cod for years, but they had not published any information about these (perhaps trying to guard their "trade secrets"). The Pilgrims may have gained some information about the Atlantic Coast from their Dutch acquaintances, and perhaps even obtained Dutch charts for the area for which they were headed. It was not until the beginning of the nineteenth century

---

[42] Nickerson, *Land Ho! 1620*, 31.

that the area around the shoals was mapped with any degree of accuracy.

THURSDAY, 12 NOVEMBER 1620

The Shoals

When we look carefully at Captain John Smith's map, it is startling to see that it is blank in the area known as "the back side of Cape Cod." Heading south from the northern tip of Cape Cod (named "Cape James" by Captain Smith after the reigning monarch) on the eastern side of the peninsula, no ship would meet any serious obstacle until passing what is now Chatham. At that point, sailors met a barrier of shifting, barely submerged sandbars lying easterly off Monomoy Point, and almost blocking the entrance to Nantucket Sound. They begin about seven or eight miles southeast of Chatham. These sandbars were dumped on top of clay beds by retreating glaciers during the last ice age, and were constantly shifting because of the actions of winds and sea. Smith notes what the Indians told him about the shoals lying south and southwest of Cape Cod, but he himself in his 1614 voyage did not go much further south than Peaked Hill at the Head of the Cape. He says that he took the Indians' word for it that the "shoales beginne from the main at Pawmet, to the Ile of Nausit, and so extends beyond their knowledge into the sea." The description aligns with Point Care (observed by Bartholomew Gosnold in 1602) and Malle-barre (so named by Champlain in 1605 and called "a very dangerous place" on his return in 1606). Although the shoals were not on the more recent maps, previous explorers such as Gosnold and Champlain had left notice of their shifting shape and their dangerous currents.

Bartholomew Gosnold obtained backing to found an English colony in the New World and in 1602 he sailed from Falmouth in Cornwall with thirty-two men, intending to establish a colony in New England. Gosnold pioneered a direct sailing route due west from the Azores to what later became New England, arriving in May 1602 at Cape Elizabeth in Maine. On 15 May 1602, he sailed into Provincetown Harbour, where he is credited with naming Cape Cod for the abundant fish. Continuing down the Atlantic coast of Cape Cod, pivoting on Gilbert's Point, they coasted westward, observing numerous natives on shore, many running after them to gaze. Following the coastline for several days, he discovered Martha's Vineyard which they explored but

82

found seemingly uninhabited. Gosnold named it after his deceased daughter, Martha, and the wild grapes that covered much of the land. An attempt was made to settle on Cuttyhunk Island (the outermost of a chain of small islands extending southwest from the southern coast of Cape Cod at the outer edge of Buzzards Bay), where the colonists harvested sassafras. The post was abandoned in June after a month when settlers decided to return to England since they feared they had insufficient provisions to carry them through the winter.

FRIDAY, 13 NOVEMBER 1620

The Council of New England

The Council of New England was established on this day four hundred years ago (3 November 1620, o.s.), and was disbanded (although with no apparent changes in land titles) in 1635. It provided for the establishment of the Plymouth Colony, the Colony (and eventual State) of New Hampshire, the Massachusetts Bay Colony, the New Haven Colony, and the eventual State of Maine. It was largely the creation of Sir Ferdinando Gorges. Some of the persons involved had previously received a charter in 1606 as the Plymouth Company and had founded the short-lived Popham Colony within the territory of northern Virginia (actually in present-day Maine). The company had fallen into disuse following the abandonment of the 1607 colony. In the new 1620 charter granted by James I, the company was given rights of settlement in the area now designated as New England, which was the land previously part of the Virginia Colony north of the 40th parallel, and extending to the 48th parallel. The Council would have full legal rights of governance and administration over the colonial plantation, and the members of the Council would elect a President to oversee administrative affairs. Although this explicitly covered the land that the Pilgrims would land on and settle, they were ignorant of this grant because they had now been at sea for more than two months when the charter was issued. They only found out about it when the *Fortune* arrived in November 1621, over a year from now.

SATURDAY, 14 NOVEMBER 1620

Charter of the Council of New England

"JAMES, by the Grace of God, King of England, Scotland, France and Ireland, Defender of the Faith, &c. to all whom these Presents shall come, Greeting, Whereas, upon the humble Petition of divers of our well disposed Subjects, that intended to make several Plantations in the Parts of America, between the Degrees of thirty-ffoure and ffourty-five; We according to our princely Inclination, favouring much their worthy Disposition, in Hope thereby to advance the in Largement of Christian Religion, to the Glory of God Almighty, as also by that Meanes to streatch out the Bounds of our Dominions, and to replenish those Deserts with People governed by Lawes and Magistrates, for the peaceable Commerce of all, that in time to come shall have occasion to traffique into those Territoryes, ... And lastly, because the principall Effect which we can desire or expect of this Action, is the Conversion and Reduction of the People in those Parts unto the true Worship of God and Christian Religion, in which Respect, Wee would be loath that any Person should be permitted to pass that Wee suspected to affect the Superstition of the Ch[urch] of Rome, Wee do hereby declare that it is our Will and Pleasure that none be permitted to pass, in any Voyage from time to time to be made into the said Country, but such as shall first have taken the Oathe of Supremacy; for which Purpose, Wee do by these Presents give full Power and Authority to the President of the said Councill, to tender and exhibit the said Oath to all such Persons as shall at any time be sent and imployed in the said Voyage."

Note three things:

(1) the purpose of the grant is for the conversion of "the people in those parts" and the furtherance of the Gospel;

(2) not only Roman Catholics, who were treasonous, but also anyone who refused to accept the King's supremacy over the English Church were excluded (and thus, presumably, the Separatists, who denied not only the Royal Supremacy but also the legitimacy of the English Church as a whole);

(3) the territory overlapped in its southern and western region with the northern region of the (first) Virginia Company. The land on which the Pilgrims landed thus was covered by a royal charter at the time of their arrival, but they had been at sea for so long that they were unaware of that grant.

SUNDAY, 15 NOVEMBER 1620

Popham/Sagadahoc Colony

The Popham Colony—also known as the Sagadahoc Colony—was a short-lived English colonial settlement in New

England which in many ways provides an instructive contrast with the much less well organised Pilgrim voyage. It was established in 1607 by the proprietary Virginia Company of Plymouth and was located in the present-day town of Phippsburg, Maine, near the mouth of the Kennebec River. The Popham Colony was the second colony in the region: the first was St. Croix Island, near what is now the town of Robbinston. (St. Croix Island was settled in June 1604, and subsequently abandoned).

About 120 colonists (all men and boys) left Plymouth (England) on 31 May 1607, in two ships. They intended to trade precious metals, spices, furs, and show that the local forests could be used to build English ships. The ship's log and diary from the voyage and first 6 weeks of the colony is the main contemporary source of the information about the colony; it was called "Popham" after its principal financial backer, Sir John Popham. Late summer arrival meant that there was no time to grow food. With inadequate supplies, half of the colonists returned to England in December 1607 aboard the *Gift of God* and almost starved on the return trip and had to sell their cargo in the Azores. Others faced a cold winter during which the Kennebec River froze. Records indicate that fire destroyed parts of the storehouse and its provisions, but archaeological excavations indicate that other buildings were burned and not the storehouse. George Popham died on 5 February 1608; he is the only colonist known to have died (in contrast to Jamestown which lost half its population that year) although the Abenaki claim that they killed eleven colonists and set fire to the site. The first ocean-going ship built by the English in the New World was completed during the year of the Popham Colony and was sailed back to England. The pinnace, named *Virginia of Sagadahoc*, was apparently quite seaworthy, and crossed the Atlantic again successfully in 1609 as part of Sir Christopher Newport's nine-vessel Third Supply mission to Jamestown. The small *Virginia* survived a powerful three-day storm en route which was thought to have been a hurricane and which wrecked the mission's large new flagship *Sea Venture* on Bermuda. In May 1608 a supply ship brought a message that Sir John Popham had died. The supply ship returned to England with a cargo. When *Mary and John* returned in September 1608, it brought news that John Gilbert, the elder brother of Raleigh Gilbert's (originally second in command of the expedition, son of

Sir Humphrey Gilbert and half-nephew of Sir Walter Raleigh) had died; he decided to return to England and as no other leader was found, the colony disbanded and the remaining colonists sailed home in *Mary and John* and *Virginia*. The Popham colony was abandoned after only 14 months, apparently more due to the death of patrons and the first colony president than lack of success - this may have been on the minds of the Plymouth settlers as they drafted the *Mayflower* Compact..

The exact site of the Popham Colony was lost until 1888 when a plan for the site was found in the General Archives in Simancas, Spain. This plan exactly matches the location at Sabino Head near Popham Beach State Park. Later archaeology in 1994 confirmed the location and the accuracy of the plan.

MONDAY, 16 NOVEMBER 1620

First Death of a Passenger

"In all this voyage there died but one of the passengers, which was William Butten, a youth [born perhaps in 1605], servant to Samuel Fuller." Today marks the 400th anniversary of the death of the first of the passengers to die on this voyage. Caleb Johnson notes a William Butten, son of John Butten, baptised at Worksop, Nottinghamshire, on 13 March 1605 as possibly being this passenger. Worksop was not all that far from Scrooby and briefly had a Separatist gathering in 1607. Some members of the Worksop congregation had joined with members of the Scrooby separatist congregation in the migration to Holland in 1608 and soon thereafter. There is at least one other possible William Butten in the area, but his birth date is too early for him to qualify as a "youth" in 1620. Nothing else is known about this passenger, his cause of death or his origins.

The fact that the first passenger to die was the servant to the physician does not fill us with great confidence about how well everyone else will be.

TUESDAY, 17 NOVEMBER 1620

Birds sighted

The body of William Butten was committed to the deep. This was the first burial at sea of a passenger on this voyage; a crew member (the name of the first casualty is unknown) was buried at sea on 2 October, over a month ago.

Sailors often see seagulls flying more than a hundred miles from the nearest shore, so the fact that birds were sighted today, while very encouraging, does not necessarily mean that the voyage is almost over.

WEDNESDAY, 18 NOVEMBER 1620
Signs of land. Closing in with the land at nightfall.

It is usually supposed that the *Mayflower* hit on Cape Cod by accident, but the fact that the Pilgrims felt reasonably sure that the land that they saw at daybreak tomorrow morning was Cape Cod is proof enough that they knew what land it ought to be. They were neither sailors nor navigators, and outside of one or two of them, none of them had ever seen North America before. Two of the ship's officers had been in that locality previously, but it would take something more definite than that to account for the Pilgrims believing it was Cape Cod until they were close enough to make it out clearly. The logical answer is that when they sighted land Captain Christopher Jones knew that he was close to the 42nd parallel of north latitude, and was heading toward Cape Cod. It was usual for early navigators to strike out for the parallel they wanted to reach, and then keep to that parallel. Jones was not in a hurry to reach Cape Cod in particular, but circumstances beyond his control were getting so out of hand that he must have been quite anxious to get to land somewhere, *anywhere*, and **soon**. They had been held back by all kinds of bad weather, and winter was closing in. There was a broken main beam, and the ship was in no condition to handle heavy weather. Fresh water was getting scarce, fresh provisions were getting low, they were out of all firewood. Scurvy was breaking out among crew and passengers, and the stork was due to come on board again for the second time almost any day now. Any decent captain would head for the nearest land he could reach with whatever wind and weather he could manage.

The *Mayflower* had enjoyed clear northwest winds for a day or two now; with a good noon sight of the sun yesterday and today, Jones' cross staff would tell him he was on the 42nd parallel of latitude, which he undoubtedly knew would lead him in to Cape Cod if he followed it. He would probably not have known his longitudinal position, having no way to check up on it since leaving England. But he could be sure of his latitude.

He must have known by the change in the colour of the sea water and by the general appearance of the western clouds that land was not far off, and it is more than likely that he had caught the earthy smell of the land in an offshore breeze. Bradford states distinctly that the weather was clear and crisp, and that there was a northwesterly breeze off the land, when daylight broke on Thursday. The sun rose on the back side of Cape Cod tomorrow morning at 6:55 AM. The moon, which was nine days after full, was a waning crescent in mid-sky, too thin to help. Daybreak, when the Pilgrims say they "espied" the land, was twenty or thirty minutes before sunrise; they thus caught their first glance of Cape Cod over the bow of the *Mayflower* at about half past six in the morning tomorrow.

THURSDAY, 19 NOVEMBER 1620

Sighted land at daybreak.

The landfall was made out to be the bluffs of Cape Cod in what is now the town of Truro, Mass. After a conference between the Master of the ship and the chief colonists, tacked about and stood for the southward. Wind and weather fair. Made course SSW, proposing to go to Hudson's River, ten leagues south of the Cape. After sailing that course about half the day, between 12 noon and 1:00 pm the ship fell amongst dangerous shoals and foaming breakers [the shoals off Monomoy]. The *Mayflower* got out of them before nightfall and, the wind being contrary, put round again for the Bay of Cape Cod. Captain Jones abandoned efforts to go further south and abruptly announced this to passengers at sunset. No one will question that Jones' assertion of inability to proceed, and his announced determination to return to Cape Cod harbour probably fell upon many acquiescent ears, for, as Winslow says: "Winter was come; the seas were dangerous; the season was cold; the winds were high, and the region being well furnished for a plantation, we entered upon discovery." Tossed for sixty-seven days on the north Atlantic at that season of the year, their food and fire wood well spent, cold, homesick, and gravely ill, the mere thought of once again setting foot on *any* land, *wherever* it might be, must have been an allurement that lent Jones some potential aid in his high-handed course.

On course for Cape Cod harbour, along the coast

       Disaffection appeared among the colonists, on account of abandonment of their destination. Bradford (in *Mourt's Relation*) says: "This day before we come to harbor, observing some not well affected to unity and concord, but gave some appearance of faction, it was thought good there should be an Association and Agreement that we should combine together in one body; and to submit to such Government and Governors as we should, by common consent, agree to make and choose, and set our hands to this that follows word for word." Then follows the text of the *Mayflower* Compact. Bradford is even more explicit in his *Of Plimoth Plantation*, where he says: "I shall a little returne backe and begin with a combination made by them before they came ashore, being ye first foundation of their governments in this place; occasioned partly by ye discontent & mutinous speeches that some of the strangers amongst them [*i.e. not any of the Leiden contingent*] had let fall from them in ye ship—That when they came ashore they would use their owne libertie: for none had power to command them, the patents they had being for Virginia, and not for New-England which belonged to another Government, with which ye London [*or First Virginia*] Company had nothing to doe, and partly that such an acte by them done ... might be as firm as any patent, and in some respects more sure." Bradford speaks only of Billington and his family as those "shuffled into their company," and while he was not improbably one of the agitators (with Hopkins) who were the proximate causes of the drawing up of the Compact, he was not, in this case, the responsible leader. It is evident from the foregoing that the "appearance of faction" did not show itself until the *Mayflower* was turned back toward Cape Cod Harbor, and it became apparent that the effort to locate "near Hudson's River" was to be abandoned, and a location found north of 41° N. latitude, which would leave them without charter rights or authority of any kind. Stephen Hopkins,—then "a lay-reader" for Chaplain Buck,—on Sir Thomas Gates' expedition to Virginia, had, when some of them were shipwrecked on the Bermudas, advocated just such sentiments—on the same basis—as were now raised on the *Mayflower*, and it could hardly have been only a coincidence that the same were repeated here. That Hopkins fomented the discord is almost certain. His attitudes and actions caused him to receive a sentence of death for insubordination, at the hands of Sir Thomas Gates, in the first instance, from which his pardon was with much difficulty procured by his friends. The placing of Hopkins' two servants at the very end of the signatories of the Compact has also been noted, suggesting that they were not in full agreement with either the course of action or the mechanism of the Compact.

* * * * *

Two final comments on the "factionalisation" of the passengers:

1. The more research is done, the more religious connections are discovered between the Leiden congregation and the other passengers. The only real members of the "stranger" group appear to be those in the Billington household, with the Hopkins household keeping itself apart from the main body as well. It is thus extremely disappointing to see so many writers in this past year, including Nathaniel Philbrick (who really should know better) in his conversation sponsored by the Massachusetts State Library earlier this month, ignoring the substantial research of the last thirty years on the numerous and manifold connections between passengers (particularly the women) and separatist communities, and simply parroting the discredited dialectic of George Willison's *Saints and Strangers*. Willison, a Marxist, was explicitly trying to enlarge the divisions and reduce the size of the separatist community, and he either did not know about or intentionally overlooked the connections. Willison, in effect, doubled or trebled the size of the "strangers," and way too many commentators have followed him in the intervening 70 years.

2. Bradford's descriptions of the Leiden congregation, and (to a lesser extent) those of Edward Winslow, echo the somewhat idealised description of the early Christian church in the Acts of the Apostles -- they held all things in common, they were of one heart and mind, they sacrificed for the common good. As many commentators have noted over the last few years, this strikes us now as incredibly naïve; the failure of this project makes the second half of *Of Plimoth Plantation* much darker than the first. But against this background of this vision for the community, *any* division or dissension, however small, stands in stark contrast. We are in danger of overestimating the size of the "muntinous speeches" because Bradford gives them so much attention -- but Bradford does so not because the treasonous group of mutineers

90

was so large, but because it was so counter in every respect to the project of the colony, which was to establish a godly community based on Gospel principles. Saying that the Pilgrims came to the New World for "freedom of religion" (a concept they would not have understood) or to "worship as they pleased" (which addresses only a small part of their project) seriously restricts the breadth of their envisioned purpose.

SATURDAY, 21 NOVEMBER 1620

Comes in with light, fair wind. Signing of the Mayflower Compact

[This is a long post -- you may want to get a really hot cup of tea.]

There is good reason to believe that "sickness" would not have prevented the obtaining of the signatures (by "mark," if need be, since it is probable that some were illiterate) of the nine men who did not subscribe, if they were considered eligible. Two whom we know did not sign were Ely and William Trevor (Ely -- whose first name is unknown -- returned to England before 1623, because he is not included in the 1623 division of land, and William Trevor returned to England in 1621 on the *Fortune*). The fact seems rather to be that age—not social status—was the determining factor as to those eligible.

If the intention to land south of the 41st parallel had persisted, there would have been no occasion for the Compact, as the patent from the London Virginia Company would have been in force. The Compact became a necessity, therefore, only when they turned northward to make settlement above 41° N. latitude. Hence it is plain that no opportunity for "faction"—and so no occasion for any "Association and Agreement"—existed till the *Mayflower* turned northward late yesterday afternoon. The Compact was not drawn up and presented for signature until Saturday morning. Bradford's language, "This day, before we came into harbour," leaves no room for doubt that it was rather hurriedly drafted—and also signed—before noon today. That they had time on this winter Saturday—hardly three weeks from the shortest day in the year—to reach and encircle the harbour; secure anchorage; get out boats; arm, equip, and land two companies of men; make a considerable march inland; cut firewood; and get all aboard again, indicates that they must have made the harbour not far from noon. These facts also correct another common and current error of traditional Pilgrim history, that the Compact was signed "in the harbour of Cape Cod." The instrument itself simply says, "Cape Cod," not "Cape Cod harbour" (writers add "harbour" specifically to later descriptions of actions, but not here). The leaders clearly did not mean to drop anchor until there was a form of law and authority.

Five short comments, in order not to drag this out too long:

1. The original copy of the *Mayflower* Compact, with the signatures, has been lost. A copy was made in Bradford's handwritten journal, *Of Plimoth Plantation*, about 1630 (and now in the State Library of Massachusetts). Reproductions with "original" signatures at the bottom are the result of later "cut and paste" activity from other sources.

2. The text was first published in London in 1622 in *A Relation or Journal of the Beginning and Proceeding of the English Plantation Settled at Plymouth in New England*. Nathaniel Morton, secretary for Plymouth Colony, published it in 1669, along with the earliest known list of the signers, in his history, *New England's Memoriall*. The *Mayflower* Compact was an attempt to establish a temporary but binding form of control until such time as they could get formal permission from England. This formal permission came in the form of the Pierce Patent of 1621, which superseded the Compact.

3. The Compact was signed on 11 November (old style), which is in our current calendar 21 November. *Today* is thus the 400th anniversary of the signing of the *Mayflower* Compact, and not 11 November (which would be 399 years and 354 days afterwards), the GSMD press release and the angry protestations of Richard Pickering from Plimoth Plantation to the contrary notwithstanding. Both of them really should know better.

4. Most of the language of the Compact is taken verbatim from John Calvin's *Sermons* (1 Sam. 11: 6–10) and *Institutes of the Christian Religion* (4.11.1; 4.20.2–3), both of which existed in English translations in the early seventeenth century and were undoubtedly well known to the passengers. Note also that "civil" (as in "civil body politick") was normally used in this period as distinct from "ecclesiastical" (on the one hand) and "military" (on the other hand). "civil" was not used to mean "secular," a concept which did not yet exist in its modern form. Ecclesiastical and military organisation were the only two other forms which could provide authority and control, because the passengers were outside

of the reach of government: since there were no clergy on the *Mayflower*, and they were not organised in a military unit, mutual agreement, particularly one which had religious roots and language, would be the only way to preserve order.

5. There is no reason to believe that those who drafted either the Declaration of Independence or the Constitution of the United States based it on the *Mayflower* Compact. The Compact itself, as well as Bradford's *Of Plimoth Plantation*, had disappeared by the late eighteenth century (with Bradford's book reappearing in the nineteenth century, after both the Declaration and the Constitution had been written). The Compact is not referenced in either document, either by name or by quotation (or even paraphrase). The connection with these documents can be traced to Daniel Webster's famous address on Forefathers' Day in 1820 -- passages from which were memorised by schoolchildren for generations -- but two hundred years after the Compact, and over 40 years after the Declaration of Independence. To see how views of the *Mayflower* Compact have changed, frequently radically, over the last four hundred years, see John Seelye, *Memory's Nation: The Place of Plymouth Rock*[43] -- this long and detailed work shows that statements about the *Mayflower* Compact, Plymouth Rock, and the Pilgrims almost always and inevitably say more about the speakers than they do about the events of 1620.

In other events of this day:

John Carver was "confirmed" as governor -- the use of that term suggests that he had been elected previously, probably in Plymouth before departure from England, and once the Compact was signed that choice was re-affirmed.

The *Mayflower* bore up for the Cape, and by short tacks made the Cape [Paomet, now Provincetown] Harbour, coming to an anchorage a furlong within the point. The bay was so circular that before coming to anchor, the ship boxed the compass [i.e., went clear around all points of it]. The ship let go anchors three quarters of a mile off shore, because of shallow water, 67 days from Plymouth (England), 81 days from Dartmouth, 99 days from Southampton, and 120 days (four months!) from London. Got out the long-boat and set ashore an armed party of fifteen or sixteen in armour, and some to fetch wood (having none left), landing them

---

[43] Chapel Hill, NC: University of North Carolina Press, 1998

on the long point toward the sea. Those going ashore were forced to wade a bow-shot or two in getting to dry land. The party sent ashore returned at night, having seen no person or habitation, and having filled the boat with juniper wood.

SUNDAY, 22 NOVEMBER 1620

At anchor in Cape Cod harbour

All hands piped to service; first Sunday in New England -- this must have been a welcome day of rest. Weather mild.

MONDAY, 23 NOVEMBER 1620

At anchor in Cape Cod harbour

Unshipped the shallop and drew it on to land to mend and repair it. Bradford says: "Having brought a large shallop with them out of England, stowed in quarters in ye ship they now gott her out and sett their carpenters to worke to trime her up but being much brused and shatered in ye ship with foule weather, they saw she sould be longe in mending." In *Mourt's Relation* he says: "Monday, the 13th of November, we unshipped our shallop and drew her on land to mend and repair her, having been forced to cut her down, in bestowing her betwixt the decks, and she was much opened, with the peoples lying in her, which kept us long there: for it was sixteen or seventeen days before the Carpenter had finished her." Goodwin says she was "a sloop-rigged craft of twelve or fifteen tons." There is an intimation by Bradford that she was "about thirty feet long." It is evident from Bradford's account of her stormy entrance to Plymouth harbour next month that the shallop had only one mast, as he says "But herewith they broake their mast in 3 pieces and their saill fell overboard in a very grown sea."

Many passengers went ashore to refresh themselves, and the women to wash (since this was the first day after the Lord's Day). It has been suggested, perhaps jokingly, that this is why Monday has been considered laundry day ever since. But this would be the first clean clothes in four months.

TUESDAY, 24 NOVEMBER 1620

Lying at anchor in Provincetown Harbour

The carpenter at work on the shallop. Arms and accoutrements being got ready for an exploring party inland to leave first thing tomorrow: sixteen men are chosen, under the

94

command of Myles Standish. William Bradford, Stephen Hopkins, and Edward Tilley join him for a council.

WEDNESDAY, 25 NOVEMBER 1620

Lying at anchor in harbour

The Master and boat's crew went ashore, followed in the afternoon by an armed party of sixteen men under the command of Myles Standish: the party was supposed to be gone from the ship for a day or two. The weather was mild and the ground not frozen, but it was still a long, *very* cold wade to the beach from the boat, weighted down with armour, weapons, and supplies. The Pilgrims had originally approached Captain John Smith (of Jamestown fame) to be the military muscle of their journey, and certainly no one knew more about New England than he did, but they eventually settled on the more amenable and complaisant Standish (whose short stature earned him the nickname "Captain Shrimp") -- who knew absolutely nothing about the area. Standish immediately had the men march single file down the beach. Having marched for about a mile, the party saw six men and a dog. While they initially assumed it was Captain Jones and the crew, they soon realised that these were not Englishmen at all, but were the first natives they had seen. "The Indians paused to whistle for the dog, and the group disappeared into the trees," Philbrick narrates. "[Captain Standish and his party] followed at a trot, hoping to make contact. But as soon as the Indians saw that they were being pursued, they made a run for it. ... Standish and his party did their best to chase them, but it was slow going in ankle-deep sand, and after several months aboard ship, they were in no shape for a long sprint across a beach. ... They followed the Indians' footprints in the sand. From the tracks they could tell that the Indians would bound up each hill and then pause to look back to see whether they were still being pursued. After what the Pilgrims judged to be ten miles (but which was probably closer to seven), they stopped for the night. With three sentinels on guard at a time, they gathered around a log fire and tried to get some sleep."[44]

---

[44]*Mayflower*, p. 60

THURSDAY, 26 NOVEMBER 1620

Lying at anchor in harbour

The exploring party was still absent from ship. Weather continued open; the incessant exposure to damp increased the coughs and colds they were already subject to from their long time at sea.

Meanwhile ... on the mainland ...

Awaking early this morning, the exploration party continued following the Indian tracks, but "fell into such thickets as were ready to tear their clothes and armour into pieces." They found plentiful water, however, at about ten o'clock in the morning in a grassy meadow (the place is now called Pilgrim Spring) and drank it without any ill effect. All that the party had up to that point was some horribly dry and hard ship's biscuit, and old Dutch cheese -- and not much of either of those -- and the only thing they had to drink was some aquavit (brandy), which must have left them even more thirsty. The water was "the first New England water they drunk of, and was now, in great thirst, as pleasant unto them as wine or beer had been in foretimes." That must have been some water, to taste as good as beer! They then marched back to the shore, where they could see the *Mayflower* about four miles away across the bay. They made camp, and that night built a large log fire on the beach, which was the prearranged signal to let those on the *Mayflower* know that they were safe and were ready to come back.

One of the major results of the day's reconnaissance was that it became clear that this area (present day Provincetown) was completely unsuitable for a permanent settlement because it was too small, too sandy, and too exposed. They needed fields to grow grain, and fresh running water (the area had ponds, but no springs). They also needed a good harbour: boats could not get very close to the beach because of a shallow bar and a long shelf reaching out from the shore to the boats so that the *Mayflower* had to anchor quite a ways away, and passengers, after transferring to smaller boats, had to wade to the land because of the shallow depth of the water (there was no dock, after all), soaking their clothes, which added to their health problems.

FRIDAY, 27 NOVEMBER 1620

At anchor, Cape Cod harbour

Weather open. Master Jones, Governor Carver, and many of the company went ashore in the afternoon, and met the exploring party there. Hearing their signal-guns before they arrived at the shore, they sent the long-boat to fetch them.

While back on the mainland ...

When the exploration party had awakened, they moved further south and found what appeared to be a cornfield. A small path led them to what appeared to be a grave site: mounds of sand covered with decayed reed mats. In one of the mounds was a bow and several badly decayed arrows. They decided that "it would be odious unto [the Indians] to ransack their sepulchres," and so they buried the contents and replaced the covering on the mound. They continued south and found an iron kettle, probably from a French shipwreck of 1615. Near the mouth of a small saltwater creek (the Pamet River in modern Truro) they found the remains of Martin Pring's 1603 fort.

Nearby, they discovered an area in which the sand had been recently smoothed out. This was clearly different from the grave mounds seen earlier in the day. Philbrick elaborates: "As three of them dug, the others gathered around in a defensive ring with their muskets ready. Not far down they found a basket made of woven reeds filled with approximately four bushels of dried Indian corn -- so much corn, in fact, that two men could barely lift it. Nearby they found a basket containing corn that was still on the cob, 'some yellow and some red, and others mixed with blue.' One of the more remarkable characteristics of Indian corn or maize is that, if kept dry, the kernels can be stored indefinitely. ... Due to the woeful state of their provisions, as well as the lateness of the season, they knew they were in a survival situation. ... Without a plan they were willing to try just about anything if it meant they might survive. They decided that they had no choice but to take the corn. The place where they found the buried seed is still called Corn Hill. The decision to [take] the corn was not without considerable risks. They were, after all, taking something of obvious value from a people who had done their best, so far, to avoid them. The Pilgrims might have opted to wait until they had the chance to speak with the Indians before they took the corn, but the last thing they possessed was time."[45] While the Pilgrims had brought wheat, barley, and peas with them aboard the *Mayflower* to plant in the spring, they were running dangerously low on provisions and might be forced to eat some of these over the winter. Few, if any, of them were farmers by trade, and they were not sure whether their European seeds would grow in American soil. In Bradford's telling, beneath the corn, they also discovered two corpses, one of a "European man with yellow hair" and the other of a young Indian boy. They decided to compensate the Indians for the corn -- as soon as they could find any Indians -- and put it into the kettle (which they suspended from a staff carried between two men), and started back to the *Mayflower*.

By dusk it was raining, and they became lost in the woods. Stephen Hopkins discovered an Indian deer trap (a young sapling bent to the ground where a rope noose encircled some acorns). Not paying attention to where he was going, William Bradford stepped into the trap and was ensnared. He marvelled that this was a "very pretty device, made with a rope of their own making, and having a noose as artificially made as any roper in England can make." They took the noose, and continued to the shore line, where they set off their guns and waited to be ferried back to the ship, "and thus we came both weary and welcome home."

SATURDAY, 28 NOVEMBER 1620

At anchor, Cape Cod harbour

The passengers started helving tools; the carpenter was at work on the shallop, which was taking a lot more time and labour than had been anticipated. It was somewhat worse for wear after the journey, having been split into four pieces and used as a cabin and a place to sleep during the journey. The weather was still moderate. Those not otherwise occupied fetched wood and water.

SUNDAY, 29 NOVEMBER 1620

At anchor, Cape Cod harbour

Second Sunday in harbour. Services aboard ship. Seamen ashore. There was a change in weather, and temperatures became significantly colder. Britain is warmed by the Gulf Stream (there are even palm trees in Cornwall at Lands End!), and New

---

[45] *Mayflower*, pp. 61-62

England was coming out of what climatologists call the "little ice age" (which lasted in to the eighteenth century), a period of exceptional cold. The Pilgrims were really not prepared for the fact that the winters were much colder and the summers were much hotter than they were in England.

MONDAY, 30 NOVEMBER 1620

At anchor, Cape Cod harbour

The carpenter and others were still at work on shallop, getting out stock for a new shallop, helving tools, making articles needed, etc. There was growing impatience on the part of the captain and the crew with the lack of any plan about what to do and where to go. The dip in temperatures and increasing illness among the passengers is compounded by the risk of supplies running out (for the Pilgrims, and also for the crew, who needed to have sufficient stores to cover their return voyage to England), the isolation and the lack of any possible help, coupled with the danger of hostile natives. While this certainly must have taken a toll on the passengers, the crew undoubtedly wanted to get back as soon as they could: several men had signed on to remain in America for a year, but such an undertaking had not been given by the whole crew, who did not want to stay in such a precarious situation any longer than necessary. As it turned out, they were gone for the better part of a year, and any delay rankled.

DECEMBER 1620

At anchor in harbour

The passengers and crew have found it very difficult to go ashore: they can only go and come at peak high tide except by wading for several yards, sometimes up to the knees, from which many have become ill (and taken coughs and colds). Fetching wood and water has become laborious, dragging it to the beach, and then (bit by bit) wading to the long boat to go back to the ship.

WEDNESDAY, 2 DECEMBER 1620

At anchor in harbour

Weather cold and stormy, having changed suddenly. Cross winds batter the ship at anchor. The *Mayflower* was anchored at Long Point, a peninsula at the extreme tip of Cape Cod, as it curls back in on itself to create Provincetown (or Cape Cod) Harbour. The Long Point Light was built on this point in 1827; the lighthouse once shared this peninsula with a settlement of fishermen. This village grew and thrived from 1818 until the late 1850s. When the settlers decided to leave Long Point, they took most of their houses with them – about 30 structures in all – by floating them across the harbour. Today, Long Point is a ghost village – nothing remains, except for the lighthouse and an earthen mound, the last remnant from the earlier Civil War military post known as "Fort Useless" and "Fort Ridiculous" by the local residents.

THURSDAY, 3 DECEMBER 1620

At anchor in harbour

Cold and stormy. Work progressing on shallop. The geography of Provincetown as a whole made for an isolating existence throughout most of its history, as the town was essentially cut off, not just from the mainland, but in many ways, even from neighbouring towns on Cape Cod. The town was surrounded by water in every direction: the Atlantic Ocean to the north; Massachusetts Bay to the northwest; Cape Cod Bay to the west and southwest; Provincetown Harbour to the south and southeast; East Harbour and a salt marsh to the east. Until late in the 19th century, there was not a single road leading in or out of Provincetown – the only way to travel by land to the rest of Cape

Cod was to first head north, traversing a series of tall, rolling sand dunes, and to then follow the thin strip of beach along the northern shore line, known as the "backshore".

FRIDAY, 4 DECEMBER 1620

At anchor in harbour

Continues cold and stormy. While Long Point provides a natural barrier to protect Provincetown and its harbour from many storm hazards, the point bears the brunt of such a storm when it does so: this sickle of sand which encloses the harbour was so narrow that encroaching storms played havoc with it and threatened at one time to sweep the narrow point away. More discussions among the passengers, trying to formulate a plan to settle. As the Semisonic song (and plenty of other references) repeats: "You don't have to go home, but you can't ... stay ... here."

SATURDAY, 5 DECEMBER 1620

At anchor in harbour

Weather the same. Work on shallop pretty well finished and it can now be used, although more remains to be done. Another exploration party is getting ready for Monday. Master Jones and crew have become quite anxious to unlade and return to England, and the Pilgrims do not seem (to them) to be in a hurry to get off the ship. Fetched wood and water.

SUNDAY, 6 DECEMBER 1620

At anchor, Cape Cod harbour

Third Sunday here. Master Jones notified the passengers in no uncertain terms that they **must** find a permanent location and that he **must and would** keep sufficient supplies for his ship's company and their return voyage. It is not clear how the ship's and the colonists' provisions were divided and held. It is difficult, however, to understand how the Master "must and would" retain provisions with his small force against the larger, if it came to an issue of strength between Jones and Standish.

MONDAY, 7 DECEMBER 1620

Second Exploration Party; "First Child of New England"

Rough weather and cross winds. The Pilgrims determined, after Christopher Jones' ultimatum of yesterday, to send out a strong exploring party, and invited Jones to join them and go as leader, which he agreed to and offered nine of the crew

101

and the long-boat. One of the mates was left in charge of the ship. Of the colonists there were twenty four, making the party in all thirty four (or double the size of the previous exploration party). The wind proved so strong that, setting out from the ship, the shallop and long-boat were obliged to row to the nearest shore, and the men to wade above the knees to land; the shallop had to harbour where she landed, in an inlet that is now part of Pilgrim Lake, and here all of the men spent the night: their wet shoes and stockings began to freeze. "Some of our people that are dead," Bradford wrote, "took the original of their death here." The wind blew fiercely and it snowed all day and at night, and froze.

Susannah White was delivered of a son, who was named "Peregrine" (meaning "Pilgrim"). This was the second child born on the voyage, and the first in this harbour: he is called "the first child of New England" in the Marshfield church record of May 1696 (at age 75). Peregrine joined William and Susannah White and an older brother Resolved. He survived the first winter, and around 1649 married Sarah Bassett (b. c. 1628, daughter of William and Elizabeth Bassett, who both came on the *Fortune* in 1621). Bradford's list said that Peregrine White had two children at that time (1651); he had five more in the next twenty years. One was killed in Captain Pierse's Fight during King Philip's War (along with Benjamin Soule, son of the pilgrim George Soule,[46] while all of the others have descendants. At least three autographs of Peregrine White have been identified,[47] but he signed his will with the initials "PW" and his mark; he was over 83 years old at the time. He died in Marshfield on 20 July 1704.

TUESDAY, 8 DECEMBER 1620

At anchor, Cape Cod harbour

Cold. Master Jones and the exploring party were absent on shore with the long-boat and the colonists' shallop. Six inches of snow fell yesterday and last night. The crew was hard at work clearing snow from the ship.

The shallop, which beached yesterday in a strong wind and harboured there last night, got under way this morning and sailed up the harbour, following the course taken by the long-boat yesterday, with the wind favouring. By the time they reached

---

[46] see *Mayflower Descendant* 45 [Jan 1995]:53
[47] all pictured in *Mayflower Descendant* 13 [Jan 1911]: frontispiece, 1-2

Pamet Harbour (in present day Truro) they were so frostbitten and numb that they named it "Cold Harbour." Jones explored the northern and larger of the two creeks by land, but gave up after "marching up and down the steep hills, and deep valleys, which lay half a foot thick with snow." Some of the Pilgrims wanted to continue, but Jones insisted that it was time to make camp under some large pine trees. They feasted on six ducks and three geese "with soldiers' stomachs for we had eaten little all day." Cold Harbour was too shallow to support a permanent settlement ("no harbour for ships but only for boats"), so they would have to continue searching tomorrow.

WEDNESDAY, 9 DECEMBER 1620

At anchor, Cape Cod harbour

Very cold. Foul weather threatening.

On shore, the exploratory party went looking for the place where they had discovered the corn two weeks ago ("Corn Hill"); the snow made it difficult to find the exact location again, but after brushing away the snow and hacking at the frozen topsoil with their cutlasses (they had not brought spades or shovels), they located the original bag of seed, and an additional ten bushels "of their corn & of their beans of various colours." [This seems to be the first mention of beans in Pilgrim literature. They have held an important place in the New England diet ever since.] "And sure it was God's good providence that we found this Corn, for else we know not how we should have done, for we knew not how we should find or meet with any of the *Indians*, except it be to do us a mischief." Master Jones then returned towards night to the (relative) warmth of the *Mayflower* with corn and beans and several men who were too sick to go on (eighteen men remaining ashore).

THURSDAY, 10 DECEMBER 1620

At anchor in harbour

Master Jones sent the shallop to the head of the harbour with mattocks and spades, as desired by those ashore; the seamen took their muskets, also.

Myles Standish was in charge of those eighteen who had been left on shore, and they went in search of Indians. They were ignorant of the normal Indian migration pattern (staying inland in the winter and near the water in the summer), and, in any event,

103

found no one. On the way back, they found "a place like a grave, but it was much bigger and longer than any we had yet seen." The arrangement was different from anything they had previously seen, including the Indian graves, so they "resolved to dig it up." They found quite a few boards, one of which was "finely carved and painted, with three tines, or broaches on the top, like a crown" (probably Neptune's trident); further down they "came to a fair new mat, and under that two bundles, the one bigger, the other less." "We opened the greater [bundle] and found in it a great quantity of fine and perfect red powder [red ochre] ... the red powder was a kind of [embalming], and yielded a strong, but [not offensive] smell; it was fine as any flower." They also found the skull of a man with "fine yellow hair still on it, and some of the flesh unconsumed." With the skull was a sailor's canvas bag containing a knife and sewing needle. Then they turned to the smaller bundle: inside were the skull and bones of a small child, along with a tiny wooden bow "and some other odd knacks." Even if they had not been frightened beforehand, they must have been now. They were clearly not the first Europeans here, and they must have had many, many questions: who was the man, and who was the child? Did either or both die a natural death? Or had they been killed? Why were they buried with special care by the Indians? How recent was this? How did the blond haired man get here? Despite the fact that the Pilgrims had not seen any other humans for the last three months other than their fellow passengers and six spectre-like Indians far away on the beach two weeks ago, who had run away before contact was made, this must have been startling and brought home that they were not the first or the only people here. I have to admit that this discovery fills me, even at the distance of four centuries, with dread and foreboding like no other part of this story.

The exploration party then discovered some Indian houses not far away. There were several deer heads, one of which was quite fresh, and a piece of broiled herring, suggesting that the occupants had -- very recently -- left in quite a hurry. The Pilgrims decided to leave behind some beads and other trade goods and tokens for the Indians "in sign of peace ... purposing to give them full satisfaction when they should meet with any of them (as about some 6 months afterwards they did, to their great content)." While they were still trying their level best to make contact with

Indians, the Indians were quite successful in avoiding any such contact. It was now getting dark. The shallop collected the party and came alongside the *Mayflower* at nightfall with the rest of the explorers — the tide being out — bringing "some of the best things," baskets, pottery, wicker-ware, etc., with them. They reported that the ground was frozen a foot deep.

FRIDAY, 11 DECEMBER 2020

At anchor, Cape Cod harbour

The carpenter was finishing work and repair on the shallop. The colonists continued discussing locations visited as places for settlement, but no place yet seen was entirely suitable. Edward Winslow (in *Mourt's Relation*) suggested four reasons for staying near where they were: "First, ... there was a convenient harbour for boats, though not for ships. Secondly, good corn-ground ready to our hands, as we saw by experience in the goodly corn it yielded, which would agree with the ground, and be natural seed for the same. Thirdly, Cape Cod was like to be a place of good fishing ...; Fourthly, the place was likely to be healthful, secure, and defensible. But the last and especial reason was, that now the heart of winter and unseasonable weather was come upon us, so that we could not go upon coasting and discovery without danger of losing men and boat, upon which would follow the overthrow of all, especially considering what variable winds and sudden storms do there arise. Also, cold and wet lodging had so tainted our people, for scarce any of us were free from vehement coughs, as if they should continue long in that estate it would endanger the lives of many, and breed diseases and infection amongst us. Again, we had yet some beer, butter, flesh, and other such victuals left, which would quickly be all gone, and then we should have nothing to comfort us in the great labour and toil we were like to undergo at the first. It was also conceived, whilst we had competent [*sufficient*] victuals, that the ship would stay with us, but when that grew low, they would be gone and let us shift as we could."

SATURDAY, 12 DECEMBER 1620

At anchor in harbour

Much discussion among colonists as to settlement, with the Master insisting on a speedy determination. Whales were playing about the ship in considerable numbers: "one, when the sun shone warm, came and lay above water as if she had been dead, for a good while together, within half a musket shot of the ship, at which two were prepared to shoot to see whether she would stir or no. He that gave fire first, his musket flew to pieces, both stock and barrel, yet, thanks be to God, neither he nor any man else was hurt with it, though many were there about. But when the whale saw her time, she gave a snuff, and away." Passengers fetched wood and water.

SUNDAY, 13 DECEMBER 1620

At anchor in Cape Cod harbour

The fourth Sunday here. Weather very variable. Discussions continued about settlement, with a variety of reasons being advanced for **not** staying where they were: "Others again, urged greatly the going to Anguum, or Angoum [*modern Ipswich, Massachusetts, north of Cape Ann*], a place twenty leagues off to the northwards, which they had heard to be an excellent harbour for ships, better ground, and better fishing. Secondly, for anything we knew, there might be hard by us a far better seat, and it should be a great hindrance to seat where we should remove again. Thirdly, the water was but in ponds, and it was thought there would be none in the summer, or very little. Fourthly, the water there must be fetched up a steep hill. But to omit many reasons and replies used hereabouts, it was in the end concluded to make some discovery within the bay, but in no case so far as Anguum."

MONDAY, 14 DECEMBER 1620

At anchor in Cape Cod harbour; First death since arrival

Carpenter completing repairs on shallop. Much discussion of plans for settlement: "Robert Coppin, our pilot, made relation of a great navigable river and good harbor in the other headland of this bay, almost right over against Cape Cod, being in a right line not much above eight leagues [*24 miles*] distant, in which he had been once; and because that one of the wild men with whom they had some trucking stole a harping iron [*harpoon*] from them, they called it Thievish Harbour [*probably modern Boston, Massachusetts - you may draw whatever conclusions you wish from Boston's original name being "Thievish" -- although Boston is 49 miles west of Provincetown, but Coppin's memory was certainly hazy*]. And beyond that place they were enjoined not to go, whereupon a company was chosen to go out upon a third discovery." Master Jones urged that the settlers should explore with their shallop at some distance; he refused, given the season, to stir from the present anchorage until a safe harbour had been discovered where they would settle permanently, and where the *Mayflower* might go without danger.

Edward Thompson, an indentured servant of William White, died today, the first to die aboard the ship since it anchored in the harbour. Jeremy Bangs notes that the servants of Pilgrims known to have lived in Leiden (such as the Whites) may also be counted as from Leiden, because their apprenticeships or similar terms of service must have been contracted there (and not in England.[48] Caleb Johnson indicates that Edward was not yet 21, since he did not sign the *Mayflower* Compact: it is possible, however, that he could not sign because his health was so poor. He might have been over 21 (as Bradford calls him a "servant" and not a "lad") and was one of the men who did not sign (comprising as much as 20% of the adult male passengers). I have frequently wondered about the dynamic in the community of having more than three quarters of the adult male passengers signing (whether all signatures were voluntary, or some were coerced, cannot now be determined), yet a substantial number of adult male passengers did not sign (for reasons that cannot now be known). The fact that he was indentured to William White would suggest that his not signing was not for religious reasons or from a desire to bolt once it became clear that the group was not headed to the Hudson River; at this distance it is impossible to tell for certain. Thom(p)son is a common enough name, and "it is unlikely anything conclusive can be determined [*about his English origins*] unless he can be tied with an association to his master William White (whose English origins are also unknown)."[49] Winslow and Bradford both give as a reason for speeding up a choice of a permanent settlement, the fact that people were now dying onboard the *Mayflower*; this must have added significant pressure to come to a quick determination.

TUESDAY, 15 DECEMBER 1620

At anchor in harbour

Weather cold and foul. Francis Billington, the young son of one of the passengers, put the ship and all in great jeopardy, by shooting off a fowling-piece in his father's cabin between decks

---

[48] see *Strangers and Pilgrims*, pp. 446f.
[49] *Mayflower Passengers*, p. 233

where there was a small barrel of gunpowder open, and many people about the fire close by. None were hurt. Ten settlers were chosen to make a third, and more extensive, exploration of sites for a permanent settlement: "Captain Standish, Master Carver, William Bradford, Edward Winslow, John Tilley, Edward Tilley, John Howland, and three of London, Richard Warren, Stephen Hopkins, and Edward Doty, and two of our seamen, John Allerton and Thomas English. Of the ship's company there went two of the master's mates, Master Clarke and Master Coppin, the master gunner, and three sailors."

WEDNESDAY, 16 DECEMBER 1620

Second death in the harbour; Third discovery party departs

Very cold, bad weather. Today Jasper More died, a seven year old bound to John Carver: this was the second death in the harbour. Jasper was the second of four children, all below the age of ten, who were placed with leading members of the Leiden congregation: three of the four died within the first few months, and only Richard More, aged six, survived, reached adulthood and married, and had children. The (exceptionally) complicated story began well over one hundred years earlier when William More of Larden in Shropshire (England) had two sons, Edward and Thomas, one of whom inherited the Larden estate and the other of whom became an officer of Henry VIII and received a lease on a valuable and substantial (former) abbey at the time of the dissolution of the monasteries. Fast forwarding to the seventeenth century, the sole heiress to the Larden estate was Katherine More; the family was concerned that when Katherine married, as both of her brothers had died by 1608, the estate would fall out of the family's hands. Katherine was therefore married to her second cousin Samuel More (Katherine was 25, Samuel was 17), thus reuniting the two branches and estates of the family. Katherine, however, had established, ahem, um, er, a "friendship" with Jacob Blakeway (aged 27 at the time of Katherine's marriage), a tenant on one of her father's farms. Four children were born and baptised in Shipton, Shropshire between 1612 and 1616: Jasper was baptised on 8 August 1613; four days after the baptism of the youngest, Samuel More (now 21) cut the children off from their rights to inherit the Larden estate, and Samuel's father made similar moves to protect the other estate -- in this period property was almost always inherited solely along blood lines, and thus since it appeared that the children were not in fact Samuel's, steps had to be taken to preserve the property in the family. "Samuel ... had come to the realization that these were not his children after all; in fact, most of them appeared to resemble Jacob Blakeway."[50] Numerous suits and counter suits followed over the next two years; Samuel stopped short of actually declaring the children bastards, and was careful to have them entrusted to staunch Puritan families to be cared for (to keep them in his own home might have been interpreted as admitting paternity, and would have interfered with his desire to start a family of his own): Samuel purchased a double share in the Plymouth Company for each of the children plus an additional investment of £20, with the contractual obligation that each child was to be given 50 acres of land after seven years, and handed them over to Robert Cushman and Thomas Weston. The children lived in Weston's house in London before the *Mayflower*'s departure.[51] Of the three children who died within the first few months of arrival in America, we only have a precise date for Jasper's death. I will have more to say about the More children if I have time and space later on.

Mourt's Relation provides a narration of the discovery party "penned by one of the company." The third exploring party got away from the ship in the afternoon in the shallop: "we set out, being very cold and hard weather. We were a long while after we launched from the ship before we could get clear of a sandy point which lay within less than a furlong of the same. ... Two were very sick, and Edward Tilley had like to have sounded [swooned] with cold; the gunner also was sick unto death, (but hope of trucking made him to go), and so remained all that day and the next night.

---

[50] Caleb Johnson, *Mayflower Passengers*, p. 190

[51] For more information on this story (and there is *a lot* more), see Anthony Richard Wagner's accurate account in *NEHGRegister* 114 (1960):163-168 [includes transcripts of the original documents], 124 (1970):85-87, and Donald Harris, "The More Children of the *Mayflower*," *Mayflower Descendant* 43 (1993):123-132, 44 (1994):11-20, 109-118. Wagner also published an outline of various royal descents (Malcolm III of Scotland and Edward I of England) for the More children in *NEHGRegister* 124 (1970):85-87. David Lindsay's biography of Richard More, *Mayflower Bastard: A Stranger among the Pilgrims* (New York: St Martin's Press, 2002) has been characterised as "readable ... but rather speculative."

At length we got clear of the sandy point and got up our sails, and within an hour or two we got under the weather shore, and then had smoother water and better sailing, but it was very cold, for the water froze on our clothes and made them many times like coats of iron. We sailed six or seven leagues by the shore, but saw neither river nor creek; at length we met with a tongue of land, being flat off from the shore, with a sandy point. ... As we drew near to the shore, we espied some ten or twelve Indians very busy about a black thing — what it was we could not tell — till afterwards they saw us, and ran to and fro as if they had been carrying something away. We landed a league or two from them, and had much ado to put ashore anywhere, it lay so full of flat sands. When we came to shore, we made us a barricade, and got firewood, and set out our sentinels, and betook us to our lodging, such as it was. We saw the smoke of the fire which the savages made that night, about four or five miles from us." The "black thing" was probably (as recorded in *Mourt's Relation* for tomorrow) a grampus, the genus that includes Risso's dolphin as its only species; it is also a common name for the orca (killer whale) and pilot whale.

THURSDAY, 17 DECEMBER 1620

Third death: death of first woman passenger

Dorothy May Bradford, wife of William Bradford, who was away with the exploring party to the westward, fell over board and was drowned. Sue Allan has done substantial work on Dorothy's English origins, and has connected her to the White family -- so that it appears probable that Susannah White, wife of William White and mother of newborn Peregrine White, was Dorothy's aunt. Dorothy was born in 1597 and came from Wisbech in Cambridgeshire.[52] In 1869, Jane Goodwin Austin's short story, "William Bradford's Love Life" in *Harper's New Monthly Magazine* suggested that Dorothy Bradford had jumped overboard as a suicide because of unrequited love for Captain Christopher Jones. Although this is clearly fiction, this is the first time (two hundred and fifty years after the fact) that suicide while of unsound mind had been given as the cause of death. It has since, unaccountably, been taken as established fact by a number of

---

[52] For further information, the result of old-fashioned traditional research, see Sue Allan, *In the Shadow of Men: The Lives of Separatist Women* (Burgess Hill: Domtom Publishing, 2020), 59-69.

writers. Given the fact that the *Mayflower*'s decks were slippery and coated with ice and snow, Dorothy was undoubtedly wearing (several layers of) heavy woollen garments and her shoes had flat, smooth leather soles, and that once she hit the freezing sea water death would have happened in minutes, there is no reason to conclude that this was necessarily suicide. While it is not impossible, there is nothing to suggest this in the facts of this case.

Meanwhile, back on shore:

The exploration party looked for a possible place for permanent settlement around present day Wellfleet: some took the shallop and went down the coast, while others struck inland. Those on land found plenty of graves, more numerous than before, but when they determined that they were Indian graves, they left them alone. They also found abandoned Indian houses, with some of them appearing to have been recently abandoned; here again, they left them alone. Neither the shallop nor the shore party found any place for a settlement or for an anchorage. When the two parties were reunited at dusk at what is now called Herring River, a small tidal creek, they gathered tree trunks and branches into a circular barricade, stationed guards at the small opening in the makeshift palisade, and tried to get some sleep.

FRIDAY, 18 DECEMBER 1620

First Encounter; first death of a head of a family (fifth death on the journey)

A strong south-east gale with heavy rain, turning to snow and growing cold toward night, as it cleared. This day James Chilton died aboard the ship; he was the third passenger, and the first head of a family; to die in this harbour. James was born about 1556 in Canterbury, Kent, and was therefore about sixty-four years old at the time of his death -- easily the oldest passenger on the *Mayflower*. He was referred to in English records as a tailor, and married about 1586 -- the name of his wife has not yet been discovered. She was excommunicated in June 1609, along with Thomas Bartlett and Moses Fletcher, for "privately burying a child ... which some of them seem now to dissent by calling into question the lawfulness of the king's constitutions in this and other behalfs, affirming these things [*viz.*, *burial rites*] to be popish ceremonies and of no other force." James' own brush with fame, or at least with the public records, came in April 1619, when he made a statement in court about being pelted with stones by a gang of about twenty boys, who shouted anti-Arminian slurs. (Caleb Johnson notes that since the Pilgrims themselves, being good Calvinists, were staunchly opposed to the teaching of Jacob Arminius, "in a sense James was hit by 'friendly fire'"[53]). James' wife and thirteen year old daughter Mary accompanied him on the *Mayflower*; daughters Isabella and Ingle were left behind in Leiden.

Meanwhile, on shore ...

After midnight, the encamped discovery party heard strange noises; although they grabbed their weapons, nothing happened, and one of the party said that he had heard similar noises from wolves in Newfoundland. At about 5:00 AM, the group stirred and joined in morning prayer. As part of the group were taking some of their armament down to the boat, they heard another strange call, followed by flying arrows. "Captain Miles Standish, having a snaphance [*an early version of the flintlock*] ready, made a shot, and after him another. After they two had shot, other two of us were ready, but he wished us not to shoot till we could take aim [*the equivalent of 'Don't fire until you can see the whites of their eyes'*], for we knew not what need we should have, and there were four only of us which had their arms there ready, and stood before the open side of our barricade, which was first assaulted. They thought it best to defend it, lest the enemy should take it and our stuff, and so have the more vantage against us." Standish did not know how many Indians were in the woods, and they might need every shot they could take. The group was divided, with some at the barricade, and others at the shallop -- but those at the shallop, although they had weapons, had no fire to light them. "Our care was no less for the shallop, but we hoped all the rest would defend it; we called unto them to know how it was with them, and they answered, 'Well! Well!' every one and, 'Be of good courage!' We heard three of their pieces go off, and the rest called for a firebrand to light their matches. One took a log out of the fire on his shoulder and went and carried it unto them," an act of bravery or foolhardiness which "was thought did not a little discourage our enemies. The cry of our enemies was dreadful, especially when our men ran out to recover their arms; their note was after this manner, 'Woach woach ha ha hach woach.'" The Pilgrims estimated that their attackers were at least thirty or forty,

---

[53] *Mayflower Passengers*, p. 116

and perhaps more; the discovery party were backlit by their campfires, and thus made very easy targets. "There was a lusty man and no whit less valiant, who was thought to be their captain, stood behind a tree within half a musket shot of us, and there let his arrows fly at us. He was seen to shoot three arrows, which were all avoided, for he at whom the first arrow was aimed, saw it, and stooped down and it flew over him; the rest were avoided also. He stood three shots of a musket. At length one took, as he said, full aim at him, and after which he gave extraordinary cry and away they all went. We followed them about a quarter of a mile, but we left six to keep our shallop, for we were careful about our business. Then we shouted all together two several times, and shot off a couple of muskets and so returned; this we did that they might see we were not afraid of them nor discouraged. Thus it pleased God to vanquish our enemies and give us deliverance." The clothes that the group left hanging on the barricade were riddled with arrows, but none of the men suffered even a scratch. They collected eighteen arrows, which they sent back to England with Captain Jones; most were over a yard long, "some whereof were headed with brass, others with harts' horn, and others with eagles' claws." They named site of this battle First Encounter Beach, as it is still called in modern Eastham. This put an end to any lingering idea of having a permanent settlement on this part of Cape Cod.

The party loaded up the shallop and headed along the southern edge of Cape Cod Bay. The wind picked up, and with the temperature just at about freezing, horizontal sleet along with salt spray hit them full in the face. They were somewhere near Manomet Bluff when a wave dislocated the rudder. "The seas were grown so great that we were much troubled and in great danger, and night grew on. Anon Master Coppin bade us be of good cheer; he saw the harbour. As we drew near, the gale being stiff and we bearing great sail to get in, split our mast in three pieces, and were like to have cast away our shallop." They gathered up the pieces of the broken mast, took up their oars and started to row for their lives. Coppin then realised that this was not Thievish Harbour, but a dangerous beach on which they were about to be flung. Rowing hard, they passed Saquish Head, and found themselves on the lee of what they later discovered to be an island. It was a windy night, and deepening darkness, and they discussed what to do. Some suggested staying on board the shallop in case of another Indian attack, but more were afraid of freezing to death, and went ashore and built a large fire. "Yet still the Lord kept us, ... it pleased the Divine Providence that we fell upon a place of sandy ground, where our shallop did ride safe and secure all that night, and coming upon a strange island kept our watch all night in the rain upon that island."

Quite a day, all around ...

SATURDAY, 19 DECEMBER 1620

At anchor in harbour

"A fair, sunshining day." Burying-party sent ashore to bury James Chilton. Passengers continued to fetch wood and water.

And on the other side of the Bay ...

The exploration party now realised they were not, in fact, at Thievish Harbour, but on a heavily wooded island, and since John Clark, one of the *Mayflower's* crew, had been the first to set foot on it, they named the island after him. "We marched about it and found no inhabitants at all, and here we made our rendezvous all that day," drying their clothes and doing what they could to repair the shallop after yesterday's disastrous events.

SUNDAY, 20 DECEMBER 1620

At anchor in Cape Cod harbour

The fifth Sunday in this harbour. Four deaths, one by drowning; very severe weather; the ship's narrow escape from being blown up; and the absence of so many of the principal men, made it a hard, gloomy week.

The exploring party was still absent on the other side of the Bay, on Clark's Island, but they recorded that "on the Sabbath day we rested."

MONDAY, 21 DECEMBER 1620

At anchor in harbour; Discovery party reaches Plymouth

Clear weather.

The discovery party, having made necessary repairs to the shallop, took soundings in the harbour "and found it a very good harbour for our shipping." Philbrick continues the story: "They ventured on land, but nowhere in either *Of Plimoth Plantation* or *Mourt's Relation* ... is there any mention of a Pilgrim stepping on a rock. Like Cape Cod to the southeast, the shore of Plymouth Bay is nondescript and sandy. But at the foot of a high hill, just to the north of a brook, was a rock that must have been impossible to miss. More than twice as big as the mangled chunk of stone that is revered today as Plymouth Rock, this two-hundred-ton granite boulder loomed above the low shoreline like a recumbent elephant. ... At half tide and above, a small boat could have sailed right up alongside the rock. For these explorers, who were suffering from chills and coughs after several weeks of wading up and down the frigid flats of Cape Cod, the ease of access offered by the rock must have been difficult to resist."[54]

Today's first landing at Plymouth was enshrined as Forefathers' Day, although the earlier celebrations miscalculated the difference between the Julian and the Gregorian calendars and added eleven days instead of ten, and thus observed the landing a day later until the middle of the nineteenth century. By 1769, Plymouth inhabitants had created an Old Colony Club; meeting annually on the (erroneous, it turns out) anniversary of the Pilgrims' landing, club members ate a meal that supposedly re-enacted the plain foodways of the Forefathers and toasted ancestors and contemporaries. Quickly, members settled into a yearly ritual that added a military parade followed by an address celebrating the ideals and suffering of the small band. Just as quickly, the Old Colony Club disbanded; by 1773, the majority of members were Loyalists, and the few "patriots" among them left. It thus is highly ironic (if not comical) that nineteenth century orators have associated the Pilgrims and the *Mayflower* Compact with the Declaration of Independence and the United States Constitution. John Seelye's expansive (with 700 pages of text, it is not for the faint of heart -- it took me two months to plough through it) *Memory's Nation: The Place of Plymouth Rock* notes that commemorations of the landing started about one hundred and fifty years after the original, and these events most often imagined or, perhaps, re-imagined the Pilgrims in the light of the present: during the American Revolution, the Pilgrims were the original secessionists, while fifty years later they became the paradigm of anti-secessionists, and not long afterwards they were distinguished from the Puritans to avoid being tarred with the brush of being persecutors, and then fifty years after that they were strongly pro-immigration or anti-immigration, depending on who

---

[54] *Mayflower*, p. 75

was talking. Various theologians claimed the rock to defend doctrines ebbing or emerging: Congregationalists, new and old, on the one hand, Unitarians on the other, debated the Separatists' beliefs -- and thereby defended their own theological legitimacy. I have been alternately amused and horrified by the duelling signs on the two churches across Leiden Street from each other in Plymouth, *both* of which claim, or, since the demise of one of the congregations, claimed to be *the* Church of the Pilgrims. What the Pilgrims themselves would have thought about the United States and its founding documents, the cataclysm of the War Between the States, or the political activism of the twentieth and twenty-first centuries, is anyone's guess, as they seem to have been remade in different images by every speaker, depending on whether the speaker's goal is to praise or to attack the Pilgrims. James W. Baker's fascinating new book, *Plymouth Rock's Own Story* distinguishes between the story of the physical rock itself (and its "travels," remarkable for a multi-ton large boulder) and the story of the story of the rock, or the meaning that has been attached to it.[55] Unlike Plymouth Rock, the Pilgrims are not completely mute, but also unlike the Rock, they have proven to be completely malleable.

Bradford continued, "We marched also into the land, and found divers cornfields, and little running brooks, a place very good for situation." The presence of several freshwater springs close to the shore was a very important consideration: by now the passengers were forced to ration their beer, and one of the reasons why the Provincetown area was deemed unsuitable was because the water had to be lugged up and down dunes and hills, and its sufficiency was unknown (particularly in summer). The fact that the land had already been cleared was also a benefit, although it was also recognised that there were no recent Native settlements anywhere in evidence. Samuel de Champlain's map of 1613 dots the harbour with wigwams (some with cute plumes of smoke coming out of them), and shows fields of corn, beans and squash growing all around. The bay was filled with bluefish and striped bass, and the lobsters, it was said, were so numerous that the Indians plucked them from the shallows of the harbour by hand. The human habitation came to an end from 1616 to 1619 because of an epidemic; the disease returned the following decade, when Roger Williams wrote, "I have seen a poor house left alone in the

---

[55] Plymouth: Pilgrim Society, 2020

wild woods ... all being fled, the living not able to bury the dead. So terrible is the apprehension of an infectious disease, that not only persons, but the houses and the whole town, take flight." There were no native dwellings in Plymouth in the winter of 1620, "a very sad spectacle to behold," Bradford wrote. The explorers found not only no inhabitants, but no sign of recent occupation. Other than the "encounter" of last Friday morning, and occasional distant sightings of what they thought were Indians, the group had not been able to establish (despite their best efforts) any contact, friendly or otherwise, with anyone. This emptiness was seen as an instance of God's dreadful providence, blessing, and sovereignty.

Where the party spent the night is unknown (whether on the mainland or back at Clark's Island), but, being gone for a week, it was clearly time to return.

TUESDAY, 22 DECEMBER 1620

At anchor in harbour

Exploration party still absent.

"This harbour is a bay greater than Cape Cod, compassed with a goodly land, and in the bay, two fine islands uninhabited, wherein are nothing but wood, oaks, pines, walnuts, beech, sassafras, vines, and other trees which we know not. This bay is a most hopeful place, innumerable store of fowl, and excellent good, and cannot but be of fish in their season; skote, cod, turbot, and herring, we have tasted of, abundance of mussels the greatest and best that ever we saw; crabs and lobsters, in their time infinite. It is in fashion like a sickle or fish-hook." Plymouth is unique to the South Shore as from its hills, one can gaze across almost the entire inner coast of Cape Cod -- from Sandwich to Provincetown. Much of the harbour, as large as it was, was too shallow for ships as large as the *Mayflower*: this ship drew twelve feet of water, and that meant that it would have to anchor about a mile from the shore, making the transfer of cargo and personnel slow and laborious. The harbour also did not connect to a navigable river to permit transportation or exploration into the interior. There were no native settlements nearby, but it was certainly possible that an attack could be launched with little or no warning, as was done the previous week at First Encounter Beach. Many of the passengers (and some of the crew) were ill, and although the exploratory party did not yet know that four had died in their absence, they certainly must have known that they were very much living on borrowed time, and they must establish a settlement quickly, as they were in what Bradford called "the heart of winter." They had been exploring for a full month, time was running out, and it was unlikely that any other, better option would appear soon. So the party returned to the *Mayflower* to report back.

WEDNESDAY, 23 DECEMBER 1620

At anchor in harbour

Much sad intelligence met the discovery party (especially Bradford, as to his wife's drowning) on their return to the *Mayflower*. But the report from the explorers brought "good news to the rest of our people, which did much comfort their hearts."

THURSDAY, 24 DECEMBER 1620

At anchor, Cape Cod harbour

The colonists determined to make settlement at the harbour the exploratory party visited, and which is apparently, by Captain John Smith's chart of 1616, none other than the place he calls "Plimoth." Fetched wood and water, and prepared to weigh anchor.

FRIDAY, 25 DECEMBER 1620

Weighed anchor to go to Plimoth

Course west, after leaving harbour, with the shallop in company. Coming within two leagues (six miles) of Plymouth Harbour, the wind coming northwest, the ship was unable to enter the harbour, and had to turn around and return to Cape Cod. They made their old anchorage at night, the thirty-fifth night they have lain at anchor here. The shallop returned with the ship. I find this return to be one of the most frustrating of the many discouraging events of this voyage.

SATURDAY, 26 DECEMBER 1620

Comes in with fair wind for Plymouth.

Weighed anchor and put to sea again and made harbour safely this time, the shallop in company. "But it pleased God that the next day, being Saturday the 16th day [*old style*], the wind came fair and we put to sea again, and came safely into a safe harbour; and within half an hour the wind changed, so as if we had been letted [*i.e., hindered*] but a little, we had gone back to Cape Cod." Let go anchors just within a long spur of beach a mile or more from shore. This is the end of the *Mayflower's* outward voyage: one hundred and two days from Plymouth (England) to Plimoth (New England), one hundred and fifty-five days from London.

SUNDAY, 27 DECEMBER 1620

At anchor in Plymouth harbour

Services on board ship; first Sunday in Plymouth harbour. Rested on the Sabbath.

MONDAY, 28 DECEMBER 1620

At anchor, Plymouth harbour

The Master of the ship, with three or four of the sailors and several of the Pilgrims, went on land: "We marched along the coast in the woods some seven or eight miles, but saw not an Indian nor an Indian house; only we found where formerly had been some inhabitants, and where they had planted their corn." Bradford noted that the Indians' "skulls and bones were found in many places lying still upon the ground," since there had not been sufficient people to bury them when they had died several years earlier; they were now eerie, bleached testimony to the epidemic -- the sight must have been chilling. "We found not any navigable river, but four or five small running brooks of very sweet fresh water, that all run into the sea. The land for the crust of the earth is a spit's depth, excellent black mould, and fat in some places, two or three great oaks but not very thick, pines, walnuts, beech, ash, birch, hazel, holly, asp, sassafras in abundance, and vines everywhere, cherry trees, plum trees, and many other which we know not. Many kinds of herbs we found here in winter, as strawberry leaves innumerable, sorrel, yarrow, carvel, brooklime, liverwort, watercresses, great store of leeks and onions, and an excellent strong kind of flax and hemp. Here is sand, gravel, and excellent clay, no better in the world, excellent for pots, and will wash like soap, and great store of stone, though somewhat soft, and the best water that ever we drank, and the brooks now begin to be full of fish." The party came aboard at night, "many being weary with marching."

119

TUESDAY, 29 DECEMBER 1620

At anchor, Plymouth harbour

A party from the ship went ashore to explore, some going by land and some keeping to the shallop. A creek was found leading inland to a settlement site near the (modern) town of Kingston: "We found a creek, and went up three English miles. A very pleasant river, at full sea a bark of thirty tons may go up, but at low water scarce our shallop could pass. This place we had a great liking to plant in, but that it was so far from our fishing, our principal profit, and so encompassed with woods that we should be in much danger of the savages, and our number being so little, and so much ground to clear, so as we thought good to quit and clear [*i.e.*, leave] that place till we were of more strength." It was given the name of "Jones River" in compliment to the captain of the *Mayflower*. "Some of us having a good mind for safety to plant in the greater isle," i.e., Clark's Island, where the exploration party had spent two days the previous week after almost being shipwrecked during a storm, "we crossed the bay which is there five or six miles over, and found the isle about a mile and a half or two miles about, all wooded, and no fresh water but two or three pits, that we doubted of fresh water in summer, and so full of wood as we could hardly clear so much as to serve us for corn. Besides, we judged it cold for our corn, and some part very rocky, yet divers thought of it as a place defensible, and of great security" -- this would certainly have been a safe spot to defend in case of an Indian attack. All came aboard at night with resolution to fix, tomorrow, which of the several places examined they would settle upon: the options were (1) making a settlement inland near modern day Kingston, although this was the least acceptable, and was probably not even considered in the final choice; (2) returning to the defensible and wooded but water-poor Clark's Island; (3) the top of a 165-foot hill that had been cleared by the Indians (although none were in evidence) and from which the surrounding coastline could be seen for miles, near several fresh water springs, a salt marsh, and an anchorage for small boats.

WEDNESDAY, 30 DECEMBER 1620

At anchor, Plymouth harbour, many ill

After service the colonists decided to go ashore this morning and determine upon one of two places which were thought most fitting for their habitation. "After we had called on God for direction, we came to this resolution: to go presently ashore again, and to take a better view of two places, which we thought most fitting for us, for we could not now take time for further search or consideration, our victuals being much spent, especially our beer. After our landing and viewing of the places, so well as we could we came to a conclusion, by most voices, to set on the mainland, on the first place, on a high ground, where there is a great deal of land cleared, and hath been planted with corn three or four years ago, and there is a very sweet brook runs under the hillside, and many delicate springs of as good water as can be drunk, and where we may harbour our shallops and boats exceedingly well, and in this brook much good fish in their seasons; on the further side of the river also much corn-ground cleared. In one field is a great hill on which we point to make a platform and plant our ordnance, which will command all round about. From thence we may see into the bay, and far into the sea, and we may see thence Cape Cod." It is interesting to note the "voice vote" -- probably calling out names and asking for a choice (as opposed to a written ballot), rather than using the equivalent of an applause meter. The site known as Plimoth, and Cole's Hill in particular, was chosen. A considerable party went ashore and left twenty of their number there on the hill to make a rendezvous, the rest returning to the *Mayflower* at night, "resolving in the morning to come all ashore and to build houses." "Our greatest labour will be fetching of our wood, which is half a quarter of an English mile, but there is enough so far off. What people inhabit here we yet know not, for as yet we have seen none."

THURSDAY, 31 DECEMBER 1620
At anchor, Plymouth harbour

Wet and stormy, so the Pilgrims could not go ashore as planned; the *Mayflower* had to set out another anchor in the gale-force winds. It was exceptionally uncomfortable for the party on shore, who were soaked, freezing, and starving: they "were wet, not having daylight enough to make them a sufficient court of guard to keep them dry. All that night it blew and rained extremely; it was so tempestuous that the shallop could not go on land so soon as was meet, for they had no victuals on land. About eleven o'clock the shallop went off with much ado with provision, but could not return; it blew so strong and was such foul weather

121

that we were forced to let fall our anchor and ride with three anchors ahead."

This day Richard Britteridge died aboard the ship, the first to die in this harbour. Richard was a signer of the *Mayflower* Compact, and was listed in Bradford's list of passengers with other adult, unmarried males (as opposed to indentured servants or children). Richard's exact date of death is recorded in Thomas Prince's *Chronological History of New England* (1736), which relied in part on William Bradford's "Register of Births and Deaths" (which no longer exists, having disappeared in the chaos of the American Revolution). Caleb Johnson has identified a Richard Brightridge (not a very common surname), son of Anthony Brightridge, who was baptised in Crowhurst, Sussex, on 31 December 1581, which, if he is one and the same as the passenger, would make him 39 at his death.[56] This is, however, only a possibility. There is no record of any marriage or children for him.

---

[56] Johnson, *Mayflower Passengers,* 101

JANUARY [1620]/1621

FRIDAY, 1 JANUARY [1620]/21

At anchor, Plymouth harbour

The storm continues, so that no one could go ashore, or those on land come aboard.

This morning goodwife Allerton was delivered of a son, but still-born. He was the third child born on board the ship since leaving England (all boys!) — the first in this harbour.

Note that although we start the new year on 1 January, the Julian calendar still used by the Pilgrims did not start the new calendar year until 25 March (the anniversary of Jesus' Incarnation). Thus the year from today through the end of March would be 1620 to the Pilgrims and the English, but 1621 to most of the rest of the world and to us, who follow the Gregorian calendar. Years in this blog will accordingly be "double dated." This change is in addition to the addition of ten days that occurred with the transition to the Gregorian calendar (so that while 1 January 1621 would be exactly 400 years ago in the Gregorian calendar, the date would be 22 December 1620 in the Julian calendar).

SATURDAY, 2 JANUARY [1620]/21

At anchor in Plymouth harbour

Sent body of Richard Britteridge ashore for burial, the storm having prevented taking it before, and also a large party of colonists to fell timber and begin construction of houses. Left a large number on shore at the rendezvous. Fetched wood and water.

SUNDAY, 3 JANUARY [1620]/21

At anchor, Plymouth harbour

Second Sunday here. "Our people on shore heard a cry of some savages (as they thought) which caused an alarm, and to stand on their guard, expecting an assault, but all was quiet."

This day Solomon Prower died, son of Mary and step-son of Christopher Martin. Solomon's death was the sixth this month, and the second in this harbour: the passengers are now well below one hundred. A burying-party went ashore with Prower's body, despite it being the Sabbath.

123

Caleb Johnson notes that Solomon did not sign the *Mayflower* Compact, and concluded that he was not yet 21 (putting his birth somewhere between 1600 and 1606, when his widowed mother married Christopher Martin).[57] Solomon, like his stepfather, was charged with ecclesiastical offenses while in Great Burstead, Essex: he was presented to the Archdeacon's Court for "refusing to answer me at all unless I would ask him some question in some other catechism" (i.e., in some catechism other than the *Book of Common Prayer*, which the Puritans rejected). Johnson, however, later placed his birth in 1597, as the son of Edward and Mary Prower, since "Solomon Prower, singleman," was on night watch duty in Billericay on 15 September 1619, and must therefore have been at least 21 at the time.[58] If this is correct, then Solomon is a tenth adult male who did not sign the *Mayflower* Compact, bringing the non-signers to 20% of the adult male passengers.

Caleb Johnson notes in "Mary (Prower) Martin: A new *Mayflower* ancestor" that since Mary Prower (her maiden name is unknown) was a *Mayflower* passenger, all of her children by her first marriage (five are known) would be *Mayflower* descendants. Edward, the eldest, was born around 1594, and was probably named for his father; Solomon, the second son, was born around 1596. Two of the children died in infancy, and Solomon died (unmarried) in Plymouth Harbour, so if there are any descendants of Mary Prower living today, they would be descendants of either Edward Prower or Mary Prower (baptised 21 June 1601, and presumably named after her mother -- nothing further is known about her).

"News of Solomon Prower's death in America," Johnson continues, "would have returned to the families in England with the *Mayflower*, which arrived back in May 1621. Three months later, Edward Prower and his wife Dorothy registered the baptism of their first child at Great Burstead, naming him Solomon Prower. There seems little doubt that Edward named his son after his recently deceased brother Solomon. The young infant Solomon Prower did not survive very long ... So important was the family name that Edward and Dorothy named their next child Solomon as well, baptised 22 November 1622." Why was the name Solomon

---

[57] Johnson, *Mayflower Passengers*, 199
[58] MQ 76 [2010]:242-246

so important to this family? Is this a clue for some other relative's name who has not been previously identified? Edward and Dorothy Prower (Solomon's older brother and sister-in-law) also had a daughter (Martha Prower), and there is no burial record in the parish for either Solomon or Martha, so it is entirely possible that they survived to adulthood, married, and left behind descendants. Caleb Johnson, in the same article, has also turned up a son of Mary (Prower) and Christopher Martin named Nathaniel, who was in trouble with ecclesiastical authorities in March 1619 for "answering [the vicar] crosslie," perhaps during catechism instruction. So if there are any descendants of Nathaniel Martin, they, too, would be *Mayflower* descendants.
* * * * *

The issue about answering questions that was brought to the Archdeacon's court has to do with the catechism of the *Book of Common Prayer*. In the "Instruction to be learned of every person before he be brought to be Confirmed by the Bishop," the first two questions are: **Q:** "What is your name?" **Answer:** *N. or N.N.* **Q:** "Who gave you this name?" **Answer:** *My Godfathers and Godmothers in my Baptism; wherein I was made a member of Christ, the child of God, and an inheritor of the kingdom of heaven.* Solomon Prower (and probably Nathaniel Martin), following their parents, refused to answer these questions because they were associated with baptismal ceremonies that were not contained in Scripture, and were part of the preparation for Confirmation, a sacrament rejected by the Puritans. Actually, smart-mouthed Solomon Prower is recorded (11 April 1620) to have answered "Mr. Pease the vicar when he asked him who gave him his name: he answered him he did not knowe because his father was dead and he did not knowe his godfathers."[59] I have often been amused by the difference in the opening questions of various catechisms: the Baltimore Catechism of the Roman Catholic Church starts out: "Who made you?"; the Westminster Catechism of the Reformed tradition starts out "What is the chief end of man?" The *Book of Common Prayer* catechism (Anglican) sets the bar **much** lower with "What is your name?"

---

[59] MQ 76 [2010]: 243, from the Essex Record Office, Archdeaconry Records D/AEA 31 folio 279d

MONDAY, 4 JANUARY [1620]/21

At anchor in Plymouth harbour

"We went on shore, some to fell timber, some to saw, some to rive (*i.e., to split wood or stone*), and some to carry, so no man rested all that day. But towards night some, as they were at work, heard a noise of some Indians, which caused us all to go to our muskets, but we heard no further. .... That night we had a sore storm of wind and rain." They began to frame the first house about twenty feet square for their common use, to receive them and their goods: there was no foundation to it, since they had neither the manpower, the time, nor the equipment for that kind of construction. All but twenty of the passengers came back aboard at night, leaving the rest to keep guard on shore.

In the Julian calendar, today was 25 December [Christmas Day], but it was not observed by these colonists, being opposed to all saints' days as a profanation of the pure Word of God; "we began to drink water aboard, but at night the master caused us to have some beer, and so on board we had divers times now and then some beer, but on shore none at all." Philbrick eloquently describes the setting: "Ahead of them was an unknown wilderness that they could not help but inhabit with all their fears. Behind them was the harbour and the distant *Mayflower*, lights beginning to twinkle through her cabin windows, a smudge of smoke rising from the galley stove in the forecastle. What would have astounded a modern sensibility ... was the absolute quiet of the scene. Save for the gurgling of Town Brook, the lap of waves against the shore, and the wind in the bare winter branches, everything was silent as they listened and waited."[60] Silent Night, indeed.

TUESDAY, 5 JANUARY [1620]/21

At anchor in Plymouth harbour

A violent storm of wind and rain. The weather so foul this morning that none could go ashore. Only a small amount of work could be done, but those on land refused to be deterred by the weather. The walls of the house were made of hewn tree trunks, interwoven with branches and twigs that were covered with clay. This "wattle and daub" construction was surmounted

---

[60] Philbrick, *Mayflower*, 81

by a thatched roof (which they would have been a familiar construction from England). There may or may not have been a chimney -- it is possible that there was just a hole in the roof, through which the smoke from the open fire on the dirt floor escaped. There was probably no window covering, at least immediately: eventually there would have been parchment coated with linseed oil used to cover the openings, which would have been semi-opaque. There was no glass. The common house would thus have been very dark and very smoky, and the floor was soon covered with bedding (wall to wall) as this was initially the only shelter on land.

WEDNESDAY, 6 JANUARY [1620]/21

At anchor in harbour

Sent working party ashore. All but the guard came back to the *Mayflower* at night; the common house by now has partial walls and a roof, with the thatch made from reeds and cattails from the nearby marsh.

THURSDAY, 7 JANUARY [1620]/21

At anchor

All who were able went ashore this morning to work on a platform for ordnance on the hill to the back of the settlement: "so many as could, went to work on the hill where we purposed to build our platform for our ordnance, and which doth command all the plain and the bay, and from whence we may see far into the sea, and might be easier impaled, having two rows of houses and a fair street. So in the afternoon we went to measure out the grounds, and first we took notice of how many families there were, willing all single men that had no wives to join with some family, as they thought fit, that so we might build fewer houses, which was done, and we reduced them to nineteen families." This was the initial plan, but the death toll later caused them radically to revise their expectations downward. Instead of nineteen, only seven houses were built during the first year, along with four common use buildings, including the "rendezvous," which served as fort, church, storehouse, common area, and gathering place. "To greater families we allotted larger plots, to every person half a pole in breadth, and three in length, and so lots were cast where every man should lie, which was done, and staked out. We thought this proportion was large enough at the first for houses and gardens, to

127

impale them round, considering the weakness of our people, many of them growing ill with cold, for our former discoveries in frost and storms, and the wading at Cape Cod had brought much weakness amongst us, which increased so every day more and more, and after was the cause of many of their deaths." All but the guard returned to the ship at night, about a mile and a half away.

FRIDAY, 8 JANUARY [1620]/21

At anchor in harbour

The weather wet and cold; no working-party went on shore. The colonists were assembling and fitting tools for their work. The centre street of the settlement (although at this time there were really not enough buildings to merit that title) is now underneath Leyden Street in modern day Plymouth. The two rows of houses planned on either side of the main street (which were not completed until a couple of years later) were arranged according to Dutch fortification plans, probably learned by Myles Standish during his time in Leiden. The main (at this point, the only) street was capped by the artillery platform at the top of the hill, and intersected by a path going down to Town Brook, ending at the shore of the harbour.

SATURDAY, 9 JANUARY [1620]/21

At anchor in harbour

Very stormy and cold. The second day in a row on which no working party was sent on shore; the settlers were assembling tools. Great smoke of fires visible from the ship, six or seven miles away, probably made by Indians.

SUNDAY, 10 JANUARY [1620]/21

At anchor in harbour

The third Sunday in this harbour; Sunday service on board ship. Sailors given leave to go ashore. Many colonists ill.

MONDAY, 11 JANUARY [1620]/21

At anchor in Plymouth harbour

A large party went ashore early to work. Much time lost ferrying passengers, the ship drawing so much water that it could only anchor a mile and a half off shore. The working-party came back aboard at nightfall. Fetched wood and water.

Today Degory Priest, a hatter who was part of the Leiden congregation, died aboard the ship. His English origins are unknown, although his wife was Isaac Allerton's sister and he was probably a little over 40 years old at the time of his death (calculated from his statement in a 1619 deposition in Leiden). He married Sarah Allerton, widow of Jan (John) Vincent, on 4 November 1611 -- the same day and at the same office that Isaac Allerton married Mary Norris (a double wedding?). The couple's two children were born in Leiden in the years immediately after their marriage; the children came to America on the *Anne* in 1623 with their mother and her (third) husband, the improbably named Godbert Godbertson (sometimes written as "Cuthbert Cuthbertson" -- another hatmaker!). Godbert was previously married (to Elizabeth Kendall, d. 1621), and married Sarah in Leiden in November 1621; Robert Charles Anderson notes that according to both his marriage records, Godbert Godbertson was of "'Eastland,' meaning presumably that region around Danzig, now part of Poland."[61] The elder daughter, Mary Priest, married Phineas Pratt, who was part of the ill-fated settlement at Wessagusset, and had eight children (all of whom had children); Sarah Priest married John Coombs in Plymouth about 1630. Sarah went to England in 1645 (where she had never lived previously), leaving her two children in America in the custody of William Spooner, and apparently never returned; John Coombs had apparently died by this time. Speculation is that Sarah died either on the journey to England or not long afterwards, for she is never heard from again. In 1648, the Plymouth court ordered William Spooner to "keep the children of Mis Combe and not dispose of them without further order." Both John Coombs and Francis Coombs grew to adulthood and had children (some of whom married into the Eaton, Howland, and Cushman families). Thus, even though neither Sarah nor her two daughters were *Mayflower* passengers, their descendants are *Mayflower* descendants because their husband and father Degory Priest was a passenger. No indication of any other Priest children has been found; Sarah (Allerton) (Vincent) (Priest) Godbertson and her husband Godbert (or Cuthbert) had a son Samuel, but neither he nor any of his descendants would be *Mayflower* descendants. It is unclear whether Samuel ever married or had children (although "Samuell Cutbird aged about 42 years," according to a 1699 death record in Middleborough, would have been born at the right time to be

---

[61] GM1 II:778

Samuel's son). According to the 1623 Plymouth land division, "Cudbart Cudbartsone" received six acres as a 1623 passenger on the *Anne*, for himself, his wife Sarah, , their son Samuel, Sarah's deceased husband Degory Priest, and Sarah's two Priest daughters.

As mentioned several times before, today would have been 1 January in the Julian calendar, but it would not have been the beginning of a "new year," and the settlers and crew would have considered that it was still 1620 until 25 March; only then would the calendar have turned over to 1621.

TUESDAY, 12 JANUARY [1620]/21

At anchor in harbour

Sent burying-party ashore with Priest's body. Weather good. Working-party went on shore and returned to the ship at night.

WEDNESDAY, 13 JANUARY [1620]/21

At anchor in harbour

"Some of our people being abroad to get and gather thatch, they saw great fires of the Indians, and were at their corn-fields, yet saw none of the savages, nor had seen any of them since we came to this bay." For centuries, the Indians had been burning the landscape on a seasonal basis as a form of land management; this created open forests, without significant underbrush. Philbrick notes that, "the constant burning created stands of huge white pine trees that commonly grew to over 100 feet tall, with some trees reaching 250 feet in height and as much as 5 feet in diameter. ... In swampy areas, where standing water protected the trees from fire, grew white oaks, alders, willows, and red maples. But there were large portions of southern New England that were completely devoid of trees. ... Come summer, this ... blackened ground would resemble, to a remarkable degree, the wide and rolling fields of their native England."[62]

THURSDAY, 14 JANUARY [1620]/21

At anchor in Plymouth harbour

The colonists had seen the odd Indian "skulking about them," but they always ran away when they were approached. Captain Standish went out today, with four or five more men, to see if they could "meet with any of the savages in that place where

---

[62] Philbrick, *Mayflower*, 87

the fires were made. They went to some of their houses, but not lately inhabited, yet could they not meet with any. As they came home, they shot at an eagle and killed her, which was excellent meat; it was hardly to be discerned from mutton." (Tastes like chicken?)

FRIDAY, 15 JANUARY [1620]/21

At anchor in Plymouth harbour

Working-party went on shore early. "One of the sailors found alive upon the shore a herring, which the master had to his supper, which put us in hope of fish, but as yet we had got but one cod; we wanted [i.e., lacked] small hooks." A recent article in the *Virginia Magazine of History & Biography*, the quarterly journal of the Virginia Historical Society, has suggested that one of the main hopes of the Virginia Company investors for the Pilgrim settlement was that they could provide large quantities of fish for the Jamestown settlement, which was starving, as well as for other parts of the Virginia colony, in addition to commerce with England. If they were able to catch only two fish (one of which was simply found lying on the shore) in the space of as many months, that did not bode well for their fishing opportunities. The fact that they had absolutely no equipment to catch the fish, much less keep or process them, didn't help.

SATURDAY, 16 JANUARY [1620]/21

At anchor in harbour

Fetched wood and water. In the judgment of Brewster, Bradford, and others, Christopher Martin, the colonists' first governor and current treasurer, was so hopelessly ill that Governor Carver, who had taken up his quarters on land, was sent for to come aboard to speak with him. The colonists had to quiz the dying businessman about their accounts with the Merchant Adventurers and about the bills for their provisions before he died.

SUNDAY, 17 JANUARY [1620]/21

At anchor in harbour

Fourth Sunday here. Governor Carver came aboard to talk with Christopher Martin, "who was very sick, and, to our judgement, [with] no hope of life."

We have met Christopher Martin back in September, when he was making himself disagreeable to the Leiden congregation. We have also seen him a week or so ago as the step father of Solomon Prower, recalling when he was cited by the Archdeaconry Court of the Diocese of Chelmsford for "suffering his son to answer ... that his father gave him his name,"[63] and in 1612 he was accused of refusing to kneel for Holy Communion. In 1982, R. J. Carpenter published a twelve-page pamphlet that thoroughly traces what is known of Christopher Martin in English court and ecclesiastical records.[64] Martin was living on board ship at this point because the women, children, and ill (those unable to do "heavy lifting" in the construction of the settlement) were all confined to the *Mayflower*: this was about three quarters of the surviving passengers.

MONDAY, 18 JANUARY [1620]/21

At anchor in Plymouth harbour

A very fair day. The working-party went on land early. The Master sent the shallop for fish. They had a great storm at sea and were in some danger, which seemed to happen almost every time the shallop set out. They returned to the ship at night, with three great seals they had shot, and an excellent great cod.

Christopher Martin died today, as Bradford wrote, "in the first infection."

Today Francis Billington, the same tyke who almost blew up the *Mayflower* by setting off a musket next to a powder keg in a small cabin last month, "having the week before seen from the top of a tree on a high hill a great sea as he thought," went with one of the master's mates to see it. They went three miles and then came to, not the Pacific Ocean, but "a great water," divided into two great lakes. The larger of them was five or six miles in circuit (originally called "Fresh Lake" and now known as Billington's Sea), the source of Town Brook that flowed past the tiny settlement, "and in it an isle of a cable length square; the other [was] three miles in compass" and is now known as "Little Pond." In their estimation, they are the source of fine fresh water, full of fish, and fowl; "it will be an excellent help for us in time." They found seven or eight Indian houses, but not lately inhabited. When they saw the houses, they were scared, since they were only

---

[63] NEHGR 21:77
[64] *Christopher Martin, Great Burstead and The Mayflower* [Chelmsford, Essex: Barstable Book, 1982].

two people with but one musket, and one shot. They found the same eerie, unexplained situation as had been found in each other discovery -- numerous Indian habitations, but no Indians or inhabitants of any sort in evidence anywhere.

TUESDAY, 19 JANUARY [1620]/21

At anchor in harbour

A remarkable fair day. Sent burying-party ashore with the body of Christopher Martin. A summary of the past few weeks is contained in *Mourt's Relation*: "We went to labour that day in the building of our town, in two rows of houses for more safety. We divided by lot the plot of ground whereon to build our town. After the proportion formerly allotted, we agreed that every man should build his own house, thinking by that course men would make more haste than working in common. The common house, in which for the first we made our rendezvous, being near finished wanted only covering, it being about twenty feet square. Some should make mortar, and some gather thatch, so that in four days half of it was thatched. Frost and foul weather hindered us much, this time of the year seldom could we work half the week."

WEDNESDAY, 20 JANUARY [1620]/21

At anchor in harbour

Frosty. Working party went on land from ship. In addition to the problems with construction mentioned in yesterday's post, the small number of healthy men also slowed the project. At times there were only six or seven men able to work at any one time; while the settlers tried to keep about twenty men in the settlement as a guard at all times, at this point not all of those were able bodied.

The common house had bedding laid from wall to wall, but this was also the sole place of storage on land as well. Weapons, ammunition, and powder were kept there, as well as all of the tools needed in construction. Tools left outside the main area of the settlement would occasionally "disappear," particularly when there was an Indian scare. In addition to the twenty or so on guard, working parties had to be ferried from the *Mayflower*, anchored a mile and a half away -- although this became impossible if the weather was bad, stranding the guard on shore and leaving both groups without a means of ready communication with each other.

THURSDAY, 21 JANUARY [1620]/21
At anchor in harbour; William Bradford becomes ill

A fair day. "William Bradford being at work ... was vehemently taken with a grief and pain, and so shot to his huckle-bone [*hip bone*]. It was doubted [*thought*] that he would have instantly died; he got cold in the former discoveries, especially the last, and felt some pain in his ankles by times, but he grew a little better towards night and in time, though God's mercy in the use of means, recovered." Bradford, as a boy in Austerfield, had been too weak and ill for farm work; even with the searing pain of today, he was one of the few people whose health had not broken down completely. Many were ill aboard the ship, which had become something of a hospital. Bradford later noted that the only two passengers who did not get sick or die during the first year were Myles Standish and William Brewster. Those who were strong enough to work not only had to build, but also had to fetch wood, prepare food, tend the sick (both on shore and on the ship), draw water, make and tend fires, care for the beds, and change the "loathsome clothese. In a word," Bradford concluded, "they did all the homely and necessary offices for them which dainty and queasy stomachs cannot endure to hear named." They also had to bury the dead, an increasingly onerous duty.

FRIDAY, 22 JANUARY [1620]/21
At anchor in harbour; two passengers get lost

Began to rain at noon and stopped all work. Froze and snowed at night. The first snow for a month: an extremely cold night.

John Goodman and Peter Brown, two of the colonists, were cutting thatch about a mile and a half from the settlement; they had with them the two dogs (a small spaniel and a very large mastiff), which were used a guard dogs to protect them from wild animals and Indians. When it started to rain, the two men stopped for lunch by a lake, leaving behind two companions to bundle up the thatch that had been cut; they then saw a large deer - - which the dogs immediately chased after. By the time Goodman and Brown caught up with the dogs, they were completely lost: "they wandered all that afternoon being wet, and at night it did freeze and snow, they were slenderly apparelled and had no weapons but each one his sickle." They had hoped to find an (abandoned) Indian village or house to take shelter from the rain and snow, but they were forced "to make the earth their bed, and the element their covering." They heard what they took to be "two lions roaring exceedingly for a long time together" (it was possibly an eastern cougar), and the two were undoubtedly terrified and climbed a tree, only to discover that it was much colder aloft. They paced back and forth underneath a tree all night, trying to keep warm in the sub-freezing weather. They had sickles with which they had been cutting thatch, but this was their only means of defence. In addition to keeping watch and trying to keep warm, they also had to restrain the mastiff, a very large dog, by its collar whenever it was roused by whatever was out in the woods that was making the lion-like sounds. "But it pleased God so to dispose that the wild beasts came not." When the work party returned to the Mayflower that afternoon, they announced that Goodman and Brown were missing, and the settlers entertained fears that they may have been taken by Indians.

SATURDAY, 23 JANUARY [1620]/21

At anchor in harbour

The Governor sent out an armed party of ten or twelve to look for the missing men, but they returned without seeing or hearing anything at all of them. Those on shipboard "much grieved, as deeming them lost." Fetched wood and water.

At daybreak, Goodman and Brown set out in search of the settlement. After passing several streams and ponds, they came upon a five mile section of blackened earth that the Indians had recently set fire to. In the middle of the afternoon, they climbed a hill that gave them a view of the harbour -- they were thus able to get their bearings when they saw two islands (Clark's Island being one of them), and headed back. They arrived late at night, and Bradford wrote that they were "ready to faint with travail and want of victuals, and almost famished with cold." Goodman's feet were frostbitten and swollen, so that he "was fain to have his shoes cut off his feet ... and it was a long while ere he was able to" walk. Goodman's adventures are not over -- we will catch up with him again next week.

SUNDAY, 24 JANUARY [1620]/21

At anchor in harbour; common house on fire

Fifth Sunday in this harbor. In the morning about 6:00 AM, the wind being very great, those on shipboard saw their new common house on fire, "which was to them a new discomfort, fearing because of the supposed loss of men, that the savages had fired them." They could not go on shore to them immediately, because the tide was out and the harbour was too shallow for the boats to approach. Yet after three quarters of an hour they went; they had intended to keep the Sabbath services on shore for the first time today, because this was now where the greatest number of (healthy) people were, but the fire, tide, and other difficulties prevented them from doing so. "At their landing they heard good tidings of the return of the two men, and that the house was fired occasionally [*i.e., accidentally*] by a spark that flew into the thatch, which instantly burnt it all up but the roof stood and little hurt. The most loss was Master Carver's and William Bradford's, who then lay sick in bed, and if they had not risen with good speed, had been blown up with powder, but, through God's mercy, they had no harm. The house was as full of beds as they could lie one by another, and their muskets charged [*i.e., were loaded*], but, blessed be God, there was no harm done." Some of those sick in the common-house decided to return aboard the *Mayflower* for shelter.

MONDAY, 25 JANUARY [1620]/21

At anchor in Plymouth harbour

Rained much all day. Those on board the ship could not go ashore, nor could they on shore do any labour, but were all wet.

Some more comments on frostbitten John Goodman: Robert Charles Anderson notes that, "For a man who generated so few records, John Goodman has left behind a remarkable number of unresolved problems."[65] Both his origins and the circumstances of his departure or death are unknown. Based on his analysis of Bradford's list of *Mayflower* passengers, Caleb Johnson concluded that Goodman was a member of the Leiden congregation, but Jeremy Bangs has not included him in his list of Leiden church members.[66] Bradford stated that he died "soon after arrival in the

---

[65] MM 97
[66] *TAG* 80 [2005]: 99; Johnson, *Mayflower Passengers* 154; Bangs, *Strangers and Pilgrims* 706

general sickness that befell," which would probably indicate that he died during this first winter, but John Goodman also received a grant (presumably one acre) as a passenger on the *Mayflower* in the 1623 land division. He had certainly died or departed by 1627, because he is not included in the division of cattle. There are no clear indications of where he came from or where he went, and other than getting lost in the woods and his (almost) encounters with wild animals, we know very little.

TUESDAY, 26 JANUARY [1620]/21

At anchorage

A fine, sunshining day "like April." Party went on shore; the common house almost completed (and repaired). Many passengers and crew are ill both on ship and on shore.

The other of the wanderers from last weekend was Peter Browne (with or without the final "e": there was really no standardised spelling even of surnames in the seventeenth century -- for different spelling, just check with the Soule/Soule/Sowle/Sole/Sowles/Sewell family). He was baptised on 26 January 1594/5 in Dorking, Surrey, the same home town as the Mullins family (also *Mayflower* passengers). Peter Browne was the son of William Browne, who died when Peter was 10; he had two older siblings (Jane and Thomas) and three younger brothers (Samuel, John and James). There are a number of family connections between the Browne and the Mullins families in Dorking, detailed rather fully in Caleb Johnson's article;[67] Peter Browne was probably out of any indenture or apprenticeship before he boarded the Mayflower (he would have been about 26 or perhaps a little bit older), and signed the *Mayflower* Compact. The 1620 sketch of Plymouth house locations shows that Peter Browne and John Goodman were neighbours, with Peter's house being closest to the bay on the south side of the street; he received one acre of land in the 1623 division, "on the south side of the brook to the baywards." Shortly after the division of land, Peter married the widow Martha Ford, who arrived on the *Fortune* in November 1621. Martha's husband apparently died on the voyage, or shortly

---

[67]"The Probable English Origin of *Mayflower* Passenger Peter Browne, and His Association with *Mayflower* Passenger William Mullins," *TAG* 79 [July 2004]: 161-178; see also Barbara Merrick, "Some New Information about Pilgrim Peter Brown," *MQ* 53 [Feb 1987]: 10-13.

after arrival, and Martha gave birth the day after arriving in Plymouth (!). By the 1627 division of cattle, Peter and Martha had a child of their own (Mary, who married Ephraim Tinkham), and Martha was pregnant with another daughter (Priscilla, who married William Allen). Also in the household were Peter's stepchildren, John and Martha Ford. Peter's wife Martha died around 1630, and he remarried to a woman named Mary (whose maiden name and parents have not been discovered) and had two additional children by her (one of whom died before reaching adulthood; the other, Rebecca, married William Snow). Peter died in the early autumn of 1633. Peter only had daughters survive, marry and have descendants, and thus there are no Browne descendants with a direct male line. Among his more famous descendants are Dick Van Dyke and the three Wilson brothers from the Beach Boys.

WEDNESDAY, 27 JANUARY [1620]/21

At anchorage

Another fine, sunshining day. Working-party went out early, and set on shore some of the passengers' goods. Bradford states that they were hindered in getting goods ashore by "want of boats," as well as sickness. Mention is made only of the "long-boat" and shallop; it is possible there were no others, except the Master's skiff.

THURSDAY, 28 JANUARY [1620]/21

At anchorage

Another fine, bright day. Some of the common goods (i.e., goods belonging to the group) set on shore, and a shed was started to receive and store the goods being brought to the settlement, and relieve some of the overcrowding in the common house. Transferring stores from the ship to the shore is excruciatingly slow. This also is a problem for those on the ship, since these stores had been a substantial part of the ship's ballast, and the higher the *Mayflower* rode in the water, the less stable it was.

FRIDAY, 29 JANUARY [1620]/21

At anchorage

Rained at noon but cleared toward night. John Goodman went out to exercise his frozen feet, "that were pitifully ill with the cold he had got, having a little spaniel with him. A little way from the plantation two great wolves ran after the dog; the dog ran to him and betwixt his legs for succor. He had nothing in his hand but took up a stick, and threw at one of them and hit him, and they presently ran both away, but came again; he got a pale-board in his hand, and they sat both on their tails, grinning at him a good while, and went their way and left him." I wonder what they were grinning at.

SATURDAY, 30 JANUARY [1620]/21

At anchorage

Shed for goods from the ship completed and made ready to receive the remainder of the stores. Fetched wood and water.

SUNDAY, 31 JANUARY [1620]/21

At anchor in Plymouth harbour

Sixth Sunday in this harbour. Many ill. The settlers kept their Sunday services on land today for the first time, in the common-house. This is the first time worship has taken place on dry land since the Pilgrims left Leiden in canal boats on 31 July, exactly six months ago.

FEBRUARY [1620]/1621

MONDAY, 1 FEBRUARY [1620]/21

At anchorage

Fair day. Hogsheads of meal sent on shore from ship and put in storehouse.

TUESDAY, 2 FEBRUARY [1620]/21

At anchorage

The general sickness increases, both on shipboard and on land. William Bradford kept a register of all births, marriages and deaths for the first few years of Plymouth's existence, distinct from his famous journal *Of Plimmoth Plantation*, and Thomas Prince used it in his history, but he did not include all of the deaths or their dates. Bradford's register has since disappeared (along with the *Mayflower* Compact), probably around the time of the American Revolution. By this point in the winter there were probably fewer than 90 passengers left alive, and on a good day no more than a dozen able bodied men available for work. The *Mayflower* had become something of a hospital ship.

WEDNESDAY, 3 FEBRUARY [1620]/21

At anchor in harbour

Fair weather. Working party on shore from ship and returned at night: "We wrought on our houses, and in the afternoon carried up our hogshead of meal to our common storehouse. The rest of the week we followed our business likewise."

THURSDAY, 4 FEBRUARY [1620]/21

At anchorage

Weather good. Working party set ashore and came aboard at night.

FRIDAY, 5 FEBRUARY [1620]/21

At anchorage

Weather good. Working party set ashore. The sickness increases; details are scarce. Although the deaths of several more prominent passengers are recorded over the next couple of months, Bradford's journal and *Mourt's Relation* stop listing each death, probably because there were so many of them in February and

140

March: at times daily, and faster than burial parties could bury them (particularly during freezes and massive storms).

SATURDAY, 6 FEBRUARY [1620]/21

At anchorage

Weather fair. Good working weather all the week, but many sick -- including some of the ship's crew. Fetched wood and water.

SUNDAY, 7 FEBRUARY [1620]/21

At anchorage, Plymouth harbour

Seventh Sunday in this harbour. Worship service held on shore. Those of the settlers on board who were able, and some of the ship's company, went ashore, and came back after service.

MONDAY, 8 FEBRUARY [1620]/21

At anchor, Plymouth harbour

Morning cold, with frost and sleet, but afterward reasonably fair. Both long-boat and shallop carried goods on shore.

Rose Standish, wife of Captain Standish, died today, the eighth passenger to die this month. Only her first name, married name, and date of death are known from the records. There are no known children of Rose and Myles, and thus she left no known descendants. The notice of this death is taken from the first volume of the Rev. Thomas Prince's *Chronological History of New-England in the Form of Annals* (not to be confused with Thomas Prence, governor of the Plymouth colony). This Thomas Prince was the minister (from 1718 to 1758 -- quite a long tenure) of Boston's Third Church, later called the Old South Church. The first volume was published in 1736, bringing the history down to September 1630. This work has preserved a number of records of deaths (and births and marriages) for which no other authority has been discovered; it is unfortunate that he printed only a part of those he found in the original documents to which he had access. Prince here consulted "Governor Bradford's Pocket Book," which contained a "Register of Deeds, &c." from 6 November 1620 to the end of March 1621. Prince's record reads: "Jan. 29 [o.s.]. Dies

Rose, the Wife of Capt. Standish. [under January 1620/1:] N.B. This Month, 8 of our Number Die" (pp. 97-8).[68]

TUESDAY, 9 FEBRUARY [1620]/21

At anchorage

Cold, frosty weather, so no working-party went on shore from ship. "In the morning the master and others saw two savages that had been on the island near our ship [Clarke's Island]. What they came for we could not tell; they were going so far back again before they were descried, that we could not speak with them." These were the first natives actually seen since the "first" encounter on Cape Cod two months ago. The settlers on the shore, and the crew and the sick on the *Mayflower*, knew that the native inhabitants were watching them closely, but so far the Indians had refused to come forward or make any contact. The smoke from large fires was visible as the Indians cleared land up and down the coast, and several large attempts were made to find the natives to initiate trade, or even basic communication, but all in vain. The natives must have known that many had died, and even though the Pilgrims carried out their burials under cover of darkness, it must have been clear that the settlers were incapable of mounting any effective resistance in the event of an attack.

WEDNESDAY, 10 FEBRUARY [1620]/21

At anchor in harbour

Still cold and frosty, with sleet. No party went on shore.

Returning, for a moment, to Thomas Prince's *Chronological History of New-England in the Form of Annals*: this work probably strikes most moderns as quite curious, since very few histories of New England now start with the Great Flood of Genesis ("now generally reckoned ... [to be in] the year of the world 1656," or 2348 BC, following Archbishop Ussher's chronology). Despite the title, there is no actual mention of New England (with Martin Pring's 1603 expedition) until chapter 5! While Prince uses many of the now familiar printed sources (*Mourt's Relation*, Bradford's *Of Plimmoth Plantation*, Winslow's *Good Newes from New England*), it is valuable for the other

---

[68] See George Ernest Bowman's article about Prince's work in MD 30 (Jan 1932): 1-5.

unpublished sources cited (such as Bradford's "register") which have since been lost.

THURSDAY, 11 FEBRUARY [1620]/21

At anchor in harbour

Weather better, and some of those on board the ship went on shore to work, but many ill. There were two doctors in the company: the *Mayflower*'s doctor, Giles Heale, and Samuel Fuller, a weaver while in Leyden who functioned as the Pilgrims' "surgeon and physician." Fuller, said Bradford, was a tender-hearted man and "a great help and comfort to them." During the General Sickness, however, neither doctor was mentioned. Perhaps they, like Bradford, were among those stricken. More about Dr. Fuller next week.

FRIDAY, 12 FEBRUARY [1620]/21

At anchorage

In addition to the strain that came from disease and death, and the steady and heavy work needed from the fewer and fewer able-bodied men, there was the mounting fear of Indian attack. Philbrick notes: "Whenever the alarm was sounded, the sick were pulled from their beds and propped up against trees with muskets in their hands. They would do little good in the case of an actual attack, but at least they were out there to be counted. The Pilgrims also tried to conceal the fact that so many of them had died. They did such a diligent job of hiding their loved ones' remains that it was not until more than a hundred years later, when the runoff from a violent rainstorm unearthed some human bones, that the location of these ancient, hastily dug graves was finally revealed."[69]

SATURDAY, 13 FEBRUARY [1620]/21

At anchorage

Weather threatening. Fetched wood and water. A nagging question that arises is why the *Mayflower* stayed as long as it did with the settlers: it was in Provincetown and Plymouth for five months, and no one had anticipated that long of a layover. The initial intention was to drop the passengers off and return, but it was now considered inexpedient to send the *Mayflower* back to

---

[69] Philbrick, *Mayflower*, 90

England until both the settlers and the crew were in better health, as Bradford writes: "The reason on their part why she stayed so long was the necessity and danger that lay upon them, for it was well towards the end of December before she could land anything here, or they able to receive anything ashore. Afterwards, the 14th of January the house which they had made for a general randevoze [*rendezvous/meeting house*] by casualty fell afire, and some were fain to retire aboard for shelter. Then the sickness began to fall sore amongst them, and the weather so bad as they could not make much sooner any dispatch. Again, the Governor and chief of them, seeing so many die, and fall down sick daily, thought it no wisdom to send away the ship, their condition considered, and the danger they stood in from the Indians, till they could procure some shelter; and therefore thought it better to draw some more charge upon themselves and friends, than hazard all. The master and seamen likewise, though before they hasted the passengers ashore to be gone, now many of their men being dead, and of the ablest of them (as is before noted) and of the rest many lay sick and weak, the master durst [*dared*] not put to sea, till he saw his men begin to recover, and the heart of winter over."

SUNDAY, 14 FEBRUARY [1620]/21

At anchor, Plymouth harbour

The eighth Sunday in this harbour.

Very wet and rainy. The February weather, starting "with the greatest gusts of wind that ever we had since we came forth," continued severe. "Though we ride in a very good harbour, yet we were in danger" since the *Mayflower* was lightened now because of goods that had been brought ashore, and the ship had become unballasted. The storm today was so fierce that the buildings began to fall apart: "it caused much daubing of our houses to fall down." It must have been horrific to see their hard work literally dissolve.

MONDAY, 15 FEBRUARY [1620]/21

At anchor in harbour

Clearing weather. Many comments to these postings have asked what disease or condition the passengers and crew were suffering. Accounts are far from specific as to the name or proper treatment for the dreadful sickness engulfing the community. Medical techniques of that day were so primitive that they could have brought more harm than cure to patients unquestionably suffering from improper diet, anxiety, overexertion, and exposure to damp and cold. Bradford ascribed the affliction to "the scurvy and other diseases which this long voyage and their inaccomodate condition had brought upon them." The other diseases could have been pneumonia or ship fever, a form of typhus.

TUESDAY, 16 FEBRUARY [1620]/21

At anchor in harbour

Cold and clear. More on the Plymouth colony's first physician: Samuel Fuller's inventory upon his death in 1633 included "a surgeon's chest with the things belonging to it" valued at £5. His surviving correspondence show an educated man, although the details of where and when he studied are unknown.[70] His inventory also included about thirty books valued at £3 2s 6d; they were mostly Bibles and other religious works, but there were also "physic books" and other practical reference works.[71] Baptised in Redenhall, Norfolk, on 20 February 1580/81, the son of Robert Fuller,[72] he was a deacon of the Leiden congregation, where he worked as a say [wool] weaver. At 40, he must have been one of the older men on the voyage. While Bradford described him as "a man godly and forward to do good, being much missed after his death," this estimation was not universally shared. Thomas Morton, Anglican lawyer and all around wiseguy,[73] thought little of Fuller's medical skills, described him as a quack and called him "Doctor Noddy."[74] Fuller married three times (Alice Glascock [d. 1613]; Agnes Carpenter [d. 1615]; Bridget Lee [marr. 27 May 1617, d. 1667] joined him in Plymouth later). Samuel Fuller was the younger brother of Edward Fuller, also a *Mayflower* passenger, and through his second wife was related to

---

[70] *Bradford's Letter Book* 56-59

[71] See Bangs, *Plymouth Libraries* 24-30 for a list of the titles

[72] MQ 86 [2020]: 35

[73] See my review of Peter C. Mancall, *The Trials of Thomas Morton: An Anglican Lawyer, His Puritan Foes, and the Battle for a New England.* MQ 87, n. 1 (Spring 2021): 37 - 38.

[74] *New England Canaan* 297-299, 309: this is the same author who referred to Myles Standish as "Captain Shrimp"

William Bradford, William White and others in the Carpenter family.[75] More on his brother Edward next week.

WEDNESDAY, 17 FEBRUARY [1620]/21

At anchor in harbour

Much colder. As noted before, there was as much puzzlement about those who did not get sick as there was about those who did get sick. William Brewster and Myles Standish both were identified by *Mourt's Relation* as passengers who did not get sick during the first winter, and spent their time ministering to those who had succumbed. I have never seen an explanation for why these two were spared any contagion, despite their sharing the common life of the passengers and crew, while *everyone* else got sick or died. Also, there were no deaths in the Billington family, which caused a certain wonderment among the more religious passengers, since almost every other family lost at least one member to the General Sickness -- and it absolutely wasn't their piety that kept them from the illness.

THURSDAY, 18 FEBRUARY [1620]/21

At anchorage

Hard, cold weather. Little work possible.

FRIDAY, 19 FEBRUARY [1620]/21

At anchorage

Cold weather continues. The common house for the sick on shore took fire this afternoon, by a spark that kindled in the roof. No great harm done. Master Jones going ashore, killed five geese, which he distributed among the sick. "He found also a good deer killed; the savages had cut off the horns, and a wolf was eating of him; how he came there we could not conceive."

SATURDAY, 20 FEBRUARY [1620]/21

At anchor in harbour

Transferring goods to shore, but sickness makes both passengers and crew shorthanded. The numbers affected continue to increase. Fetched wood and water.

---

[75]See PM 93-95, 524 and Sue Allan, *In the Shadow of Men* 69-76

SUNDAY, 21 FEBRUARY [1620]/21

At anchor in Plymouth harbour

Ninth Sunday in this harbour. It is not possible to tell whether there was any activity on this Sabbath, or where, as the number of able bodied was now fewer than a dozen.

MONDAY, 22 FEBRUARY [1620]/21

At anchorage

Getting goods on shore.

We looked last week at Samuel Fuller, the physician. His older brother, Edward Fuller, was also a passenger. While Samuel survived until 1633, Edward and his wife (whose name remains unknown) died "soon after they came ashore," according to Bradford's 1651 list. Caleb Johnson's analysis of that list places Edward Fuller as a member of John Robinson's Leiden congregation prior to 1620.[76] In 1985, Jeremy Bangs published a Leiden record that was thought to indicate Edward Fuller,[77] but Donald Blauvelt demonstrated that this "Eduwaert Fauwler, Englishman" was still alive in 1622, a year after our Edward Fuller died.[78] Edward was born at Redenhall, Norfolk, in 1575 (bapt. 4 September 1575, the son of Robert Fuller).[79] He married by about 1605; his wife's name is unknown, and she also died about February 1620/21.[80]

His son Samuel (easily confused with his brother Samuel, although Edward's son is regularly mentioned as "Samuel Fuller Junior") received three acres in the 1623 division of land (for himself, and for his mother and father who died the first winter.[81] After being orphaned shortly after arriving in Plymouth with his parents on the *Mayflower*, Samuel was raised by his uncle, Samuel Fuller (are you confused yet?). Samuel (Jr.) moved to Scituate in 1635, where he married Jane Lothrop (daughter of the Rev. John Lothrop and his first wife Hannah Howes), and later moved to Barnstable on Cape Cod, where he died in 1683 at about the age of 80. He was the only *Mayflower* passenger to settle permanently in

---

[76] *TAG* 80 [2005]: 99
[77] MQ 51 [1985]: 58
[78] MQ 86 [2020]: 32-33
[79] NEHGR 55 [1901]: 192, 410-416
[80] MQ 86 [2020]: 34-35
[81] PCR 12:4; MD 40:12

Barnstable. He and Jane had nine children, so there are many descendants today (including myself).

Matthew Fuller, a physician, came to Plymouth in 1640, and extensive research has led to the conclusion that Matthew was an elder son of Edward Fuller (,[82] and yes, I am descended from Matthew Fuller, too). Matthew was one of the first physicians to settle in Barnstable; he took a public stand on the side of the unpopular Quakers and was fined for it. He died a wealthy man (for the times) in 1678. He and his wife Frances (maiden surname unknown) had five children: the fourth daughter (Anne Fuller, b. c. 1640, probably in England but perhaps in Plymouth) married Samuel Fuller (bapt. 11 Feb 1637/38,[83] the son of, er, um, Samuel Fuller (the *Mayflower* passenger), thus marrying her first cousin.

TUESDAY, 23 FEBRUARY [1620]/21

At anchorage

Rainy. The sickness and mortality had rapidly increased and was now at its height.

It is interesting to survey some of the passengers who died during the Great Sickness but whose later descendants (if any) have not been identified, and I will try to look at several over the next few weeks.

John Crackston was a member of the Leiden congregation. Based on the date of his marriage, he was probably at least 50 at the time of the Mayflower's journey, and he died between the arrival in Plymouth and the departure of the *Mayflower*. John married Katherine Bates at Stratford St Mary's in Suffolk on 9 May 1594;[84] his wife did not accompany him on the *Mayflower*, and it may be concluded that she probably had died before 1620, and perhaps earlier. We know that John signed the Mayflower Compact, but almost nothing else.

John Crackston's son John Crackston accompanied his father on this voyage, and survived the first winter. He did not

---

[82] Bruce MacGunigle, Robert Sherman, Robert Wakefield, "Was Matthew Fuller of Plymouth Colony a Son of Pilgrim Edward Fuller" *TAG* 61 [1986]: 194-199. More recent research, however, has caused this conclusion to be re=evaluated.

[83] *Scituate Vital Records* 1:159

[84] Caleb Johnson has published the marriage record in *TAG* 80 [2005]: 100

sign the Mayflower Compact (only one John Crackstone did, which must have been his father), and this would suggest that his year of birth was 1601 at the earliest. In the 1623 land division, John Crackstone received an allotment as a passenger on the *Mayflower* (perhaps two acres, one for himself and one for his father).[85] He is mentioned in the 22 May 1627 cattle division (still, apparently, unmarried); Bradford notes that "about five or six years after [the death of his father] his son died, having lost himself in the woods; his feet became frozen, which put him into a fever of which he died." This would probably have been in the winter of 1627/28, in his mid-twenties. Isaac Allerton was part of the Suffolk Separatist community, and John Crackston (Jr.) was included in Allerton's company in the 1627 division of cattle, so there may be some connections to be discovered both in England and in Leiden.

An intriguing person in all of this is John Crackston's daughter Anna. On 22 December 1618 [n.s.], when the marriage banns for Thomas Smith, a wool comber from Bury St Edmunds, and Anna Crackston were entered in Leiden, the bride was described as "spinster, from Colchester in England."[86] Her witness was Patience Brewster.[87] She would have been born about 1598. In 1974, Robert Wakefield gathered all the evidence then available for John Crackston (*MQ* 40 [1974]: 117-119); none of the children for any Thomas Smith after 1618 appear to have been born to Anna Crackston.[88] This does not mean that Anna had no children, however, and if there are any who left descendants, these, too, would be *Mayflower* descendants -- although none have ever proved a lineage, and since the name is, well, Smith, this would be the proverbial needle in a haystack. John and Katherine (Bates) Crackston may have also had other children than John and Anna, and *Mayflower* descent could be claimed through them, as well.

---

[85]PCR 12:4

[86] MQ 40 [1974]: 117; Dexter, *The England and Holland of the Pilgrims*, 634; Tammel, *The Pilgrims ... in Leiden 1576-1640*, 54, 96, 163, 247

[87] Bangs, *Strangers and Pilgrims*, 294, 719

[88] see also Caleb Johnson, "Undiscovered *Mayflower* Lineages," *New England Ancestors* 11 [2010]: 37

At anchorage

More sickness on ship and on shore than at any time before, and more deaths. Rainy, clearing.

Bradford's 1651 list named John Rigsdale and his wife Alice among the passengers, and John definitely signed the Mayflower Compact, but left behind no other record. According to Bradford, "Thomas Tinker and his wife and son all died in the first sickness [*more about them tomorrow*]. And so did John Rigsdale and his wife."

Caleb Johnson notes that Bradford "grouped John and Alice Rigsdale in a list that included other Leiden residents."[89] Jeremy Bangs, however, does not include them in his list of members of the Leiden congregation,[90] and they are not mentioned in any Dutch records. Johnson also reports a marriage of John Rigsdale and Alice Gallard in Weston, Lincolnshire, on 17 November 1577; this could possibly be the *Mayflower* passenger, although they would have been in their mid-sixties during the voyage, and would have been one of the oldest passengers (Robert Charles Anderson declares that "they would be quite old to undertake such a voyage." *Mayflower Migration*, 145). The Rigsdale family of St Mary Weston appears to be related to the Rigsdale family of Spalding (also in Lincolnshire), a parish associated with the Billingtons. A letter from Edward Winslow to his wife's uncle Robert Jackson of Spalding (dated 30 October 1623) may be another hint. If this Lincolnshire couple are the *Mayflower* passengers, they might have had children who were adults and on their own in 1620. Further research may uncover these (possible) children, and their descendants would thus have *Mayflower* ancestors. Caleb Johnson also notes the possibilities for a married couple with no children on the *Mayflower*: (1) they were so recently married that they had not yet had any children; (2) they were unable to have children; (3) they left their children in England to be sent for later; (4) their children were grown and so did not accompany them.[91] Given the lack of any documentation, there is no way of telling for sure which of these would apply to the

---

[89] *TAG* 80 [2005] 99; Johnson, *Mayflower Passengers*, 200
[90] Bangs, *Strangers and Pilgrims*, 709
[91] *New England Ancestors* 11 [2010]:36

Rigsdales, although the relatively unusual surname does enable document searches to be more focussed.

THURSDAY, 25 FEBRUARY [1620]/21

At anchorage

A fair day; northerly wind and frost.

Bradford notes that "Thomas Tinker and his wife and son all died in the first sickness"; the 1651 list does not mention the names of either Tinker's wife or son. Thomas Tinker's name occurs in Leiden records when he became a citizen on 6 January 1617 [n.s.] (guaranteed by Abraham Gray and John Keble); his occupation was listed as a wool sawyer. Caleb Johnson suggests that he may be the same as Thomas Tinker, carpenter, who married Jane White on 25 June 1609 in Thurne, Norfolk.[92] The maiden name White is an intriguing connection, but nothing has been found to support any possibilities. This is one of the families that was wiped out completely by the sickness, and about which little, if anything, is known.

FRIDAY, 26 FEBRUARY [1620]/21

At anchorage

A fair day, but the northerly wind continued, which continued the frost. This day after noon one of the Pilgrims was hidden in the reeds of a salt creek, "about a mile and a half from our plantation," hunting ducks, when "there came by him twelve Indians marching towards our plantation, and in the woods he heard the noise of many more. He lay close till they were passed, and then with what speed he could he went home and gave the alarm, so the people abroad in the woods returned and armed themselves, but saw none of them." Miles Standish and Francis Cook were at work in the woods when they heard the signal, and hurrying down the hill, they left their tools behind them. The men armed themselves, but the Indians never appeared. Later, when Standish and Cook returned to retrieve their tools, they discovered that they "were taken away by the savages. This coming of the savages gave us occasion to keep more strict watch, and to make our pieces and furniture ready, which by the moisture and rain were out of temper." That evening, a great fire was seen from the ship, about where the duck hunter had seen the Indians.

---

[92] Johnson, *Mayflower Passengers*, 239

SATURDAY, 27 FEBRUARY [1620]/21

At anchorage

Fetched wood and water. All the colonists on the ship able to go on shore went this morning to attend the meeting "for the establishment of military orders among ourselves." They chose Myles Standish as their captain, and gave him "authority of command in affairs."

In the middle of this meeting, someone noticed that there were two Indians standing on the top of what later was called Watson's Hill, on the other side of Town Brook from the settlement, about a quarter of a mile to the south. The meeting was immediately adjourned and the men hurried to grab their muskets. When the newly organised militia assembled, the two natives were still standing on the hill.

The two groups stared at each other for a while, and then the Indians made signs for the settlers to come to them. "All armed and stood ready, and sent two towards them, Captain Standish and Master Hopkins," with only one musket between them. The two crossed Town Brook, and before they started up the hill, they laid the musket down on the ground "in sign of peace." The natives then ran off, "to the shouts of a great many more" who were concealed on the other side of the hill. The Pilgrims feared an immediate attack, "but no more came in fight. It was determined to plant the great ordnance in convenient places at once."

* * * * *

As an aside, the action on this day provided an organisation in the third way a community could organise. The three forms were ecclesiastical, civil, and military: each had its own hierarchy, officers, duties, qualifications and roles. Some, but not all, of the Pilgrims, both men and women, had organised as an ecclesiastical body in Leiden, and this membership continued when they arrived in Plymouth - it was the only one to include women. Some, but not all, of the men had organised as a "civil body politic" upon arrival at Cape Cod. Today some, but probably not all, of the men organised as a military body by electing officers and "establishing military orders."

Although there is no reason to think that there is a direct causal connection here, it is intriguing that the Bill of Rights (the first ten amendments of the United States Constitution) adopted exactly the same divisions: the first amendment prohibited Congress from establishing or regulating the body of citizens when they were organised as an ecclesiastical body; the second amendment prohibited limiting the right to bear arms of the militia (i.e., the body of citizens when they were organised as a military body); the fifth and sixth amendments referred to juries (i.e., the body of citizens when they were organised as a political or judicial body). In this neither the Pilgrims nor the first Congress were original or ground breaking: we still use, almost instinctively, the word civil as opposed to and distinct from ecclesiastical (on the one hand) and military (on the other hand) -- these are the three forms of law, a mediaeval division.

SUNDAY, 28 FEBRUARY [1620]/21

At anchor in Plymouth harbour

The tenth Sunday in this harbour. Many sick, both on board the ship and on shore.

The third family wiped out by the general sickness (the first two being those of John Rigsdale and Thomas Tinker) was that of John Turner, a long-time member of the Leiden congregation. He is mentioned as a merchant in a Leiden record of 1610. Caleb Johnson believes he was related to the Turner families of Great Yarmouth, Norfolk;[93] based on the date of his Leiden citizenship, he must have been born by 1589 (and thus be at least in his early thirties, and perhaps older). He could have been born much earlier, especially if he underwent an extensive apprenticeship before becoming a merchant. Turner was used as a messenger between the Leiden community and agents in England: on 10 June 1620 he delivered correspondence to Robert Cushman in London, and returned to Holland a few days later with letters; Cushman alerted his correspondents to information which "you shall hear distinctly by John Turner, who I think shall come hence on Tuesday night" (Bradford, *Of Plimmoth Plantation*). It is unknown whether he acted in this capacity on other occasions. According to Bradford's 1651 list, John Turner came on the *Mayflower* with two sons, whose names are not given. Since John signed the Mayflower Compact but neither of his sons did, they were surely under the age of twenty-one. All three died during this winter of 1620.

---

[93] Johnson, *Mayflower Passengers*, 243

Nothing is known about his wife. She did not come over on the *Mayflower* in 1620, and she must have died before 1622, when her daughter is listed as an orphan. We do not know whether John married his wife in England before he (or they) came to Holland, or whether they married in Leiden.

Bradford, however, does add in 1651 that Turner had "a daughter still living in Salem, well married and approved of." Robert Wakefield noted that a "Lysbet Turner," orphan from England, was found on the Leiden poll tax of 1622, residing in the household of Anthony Clement (*TAG* 52 [1976]:110-113). In October 1635, an Elizabeth Turner witnessed a property deed between William Lord and John Woolcott of Salem, Massachusetts, and later (28 December 1637) Elizabeth Turner joined the Salem church. Christopher Child examined the Salem church records, however, and concluded that this Elizabeth Turner was not the daughter of the *Mayflower* passenger ().[94] Who Elizabeth Turner married in Salem remains unknown, as well as whether she had any children, but Child's careful annotations may provide clues for her eventual identification. Elizabeth's children, and their descendants would, of course, be *Mayflower* descendants, even though Elizabeth herself apparently came over later.

---

[94] *MD* 64 [2016]: 151-173

MARCH [1620]/1621

MONDAY, 1 MARCH [1620]/21

At anchorage

It was determined, given the "close encounters" with Indians over the past few weeks, that heavy artillery was needed, rather than the damp and rusty muskets that were available to the guard on shore. The Pilgrims brought the first one of the great guns on shore today. This took all day. The settlers were short handed, and the guns were large; there was also no machinery (or even animals) to assist with moving the larger guns, so when they were moved up the hill, it was all manpower. A gun platform had been erected at the top of the hill (now within Burial Hill cemetery), but the settlers had been unable to mount any guns there until now.

TUESDAY, 2 MARCH [1620]/21

At anchorage

Getting cannon ashore and mounted. Master Jones, with some crewmen, brought ashore a minion—a cannon with a 3½-inch bore. This, along with a larger bore cannon called a "saker" that had been left by the shore, were lugged to the platform on top of Burial Hill. They were mounted there with two smaller cannon, called "bases," which had a 1½-inch bore. A hard day's work. "He [Jones] brought with him a very fat goose to eat with us, and we had a fat crane, and a mallard, and a dried neat's tongue [*ox tongue*], and so we were kindly and friendly together." When Jones went on shore, he sent for Governor Carver to take the directions of William Mullins regarding his property, as Mullins was one of those lying near to death.

WEDNESDAY, 3 MARCH [1620]/21

At anchorage

William Mullins dictated his will to the Governor, which Carver wrote down, and Giles Heale, the ship's surgeon, and Christopher Jones, the *Mayflower*'s captain, witnessed, "they being left aboard to care for the sick, and keep the ship." Mullins and William White both died this day, as did two others who were not named (William Mullins and his family will be discussed tomorrow).[95] The work party completed bringing the ordnance up the hill and the men returned aboard about nightfall.

William White has appeared in this narrative several times over the past six months, but, as Caleb Johnson mentioned, "throughout the years, William White has proven to be a very difficult passenger to research. ... Unfortunately, William White is such a common name in England that it is extremely difficult to identify the correct man."[96]

There were at least two William Whites in Leiden, one a wool comber and the other a tobacco merchant, "but both appear to still be living in Leiden after the *Mayflower* departed." Johnson notes that Bradford's 1651 list of passengers places William White in the section listing the London merchants (Martin, Mullins, Hopkins, Warren and Billington), and not in the section listing the members of the Leiden congregation (Carver, Brewster, Winslow, Bradford, Allerton, Fuller and Crackston).

Sue Allan, Caleb Johnson, and Simon Neal published the evidence that establishes William White's origin in Wisbech, Cambridgeshire and his connection with the May family.[97] William was baptised at Wisbech on 25 January 1586/7, born into a family which had been involved with the proscribed sect known as the "Family of Love" or the "Familists." By May 1608 he had moved to Amsterdam and joined the Ancient Church, an English separatist congregation which had been organised there in the 1590s. By about 1615, he married Susanna Jackson, daughter of Richard Jackson of Scrooby, Nottinghamshire, although no record has been found of the Jackson family ever living in Amsterdam or Leiden. Richard had been a member of the separatist congregation in Scrooby, and was probably not residing in England at the time of the marriage.[98] Note again here that just

---

[95] Prince, *Chronological History*, 184
[96] Johnson, *Mayflower Passengers*, 246.
[97] *TAG* 89 [2017]: 81-94, 168-88
[98] see Allan, Neal and Johnson, "The Origin of Mayflower Passenger Susanna (Jackson) (White) Winslow," *TAG* 89 [2017]: 241-264, which relates in some detail previous attempts to establish Susanna's identity; see also Sue Allan's description of the Family of Love and the Mays of Wisbech in *In the Shadow of Men*, 61-64, 98f., and, of course, her *In Search of Mayflower Pilgrim Susanna White-Winslow* [Burgess Hill, West Sussex: Domtom Publications, 2018]

because someone was a merchant adventurer does not mean that he was not connected to or at least in sympathy with the Separatists and Puritans: the portrayal of the "Strangers" as imposed or forced upon unwilling "Saints" is not the picture that emerges from a close reading of the sources and research.

William White and his pregnant wife Susanna boarded the *Mayflower* with their five year old son Resolved. Susanna gave birth to their son Peregrine on board the *Mayflower*, while her husband was out exploring for a place to settle. After William's death, four hundred years ago today, Susanna remarried Edward Winslow on 12 May 1621 (o.s.) -- the first marriage to take place at Plymouth. In the 1623 Plymouth division of land, the now deceased William White received five acres as a passenger on the *Mayflower*.[99] Robert Wakefield argued that these five acres were the shares of the late William White, his two sons Resolved and Peregrine, and his two servants. The acre for his widow Susanna is included in the grant to her second husband, Edward Winslow.

William White's two servants, William Holbeck and Edward Thompson, both predeceased him. Thompson died on 14 December 1620 (n.s.) in Provincetown harbour, the first death after arrival; the date of Holbeck's death is unknown.

THURSDAY, 4 MARCH [1620]/21

At anchorage

Large burial-party went ashore with bodies of Mullins and White, and, joined with those on shore, made the largest burial thus far.

William Mullins, who died yesterday and was buried today, was one of the chief subscribing Adventurers, "a man pious and well-deserving, endowed also with a considerable outward Estate; and had it been the will of God that he had survived, might have proved an useful Instrument in his place, with several others who deceased in this great and common affliction, whom I might take notice of to the like effect."[100] He was born in England (probably at Dorking in Surrey) about 1572, the son of John and Joan (Bridger) Mullins. His father died in February 1583/84; Caleb Johnson concluded that his mother remarried to Vincent

---

[99] PCR 12:4; MQ 40:12
[100] Nathaniel Morton, *New England Memoriall*, 37

Benham on 1 November 1585,[101] but Alicia Crane Williams in the Alden silver book listed her as John Mullins' sister, and thus William Mullins' aunt.[102] William served an apprenticeship as a shoemaker during the later 1580s[103] and later moved to Stoke-next-Guildford (also in Surrey), where he had one of his children baptised in 1598.[104] Returning to Dorking by 1604, he operated a fairly prosperous shoemaking business; William sold his real estate for £280 in Dorking in May 1619, perhaps in preparation for emigration.[105]

The last will and testament of William Mullins is the only surviving will of anyone who died that first winter. This will was drawn up in Plymouth (then considered part of Virginia, otherwise the words "also if my son William will come to Virginia" would not make as much sense), and was nuncupative, i.e., declared orally and written down at the time. The date of 2 April 1621 at the top of the document is evidently the day on which the copy was made to be carried back to England on the *Mayflower*'s return. This date is of particular interest, because it establishes that the *Mayflower* did not leave Plymouth on its return voyage until 2 April (o.s.) or 12 April (n.s.) 1621, or later. The probate record in England was made on 23 July 1621, and proves that William Mullins' former residence was at Dorking, and that he left behind in England a married daughter, Sarah (Mullins) Blunden, who was appointed administratrix by the court. We learn from the will that William's wife's given name was Alice, and his eldest son, also named William, was in England at the time as well. William's widow Alice and his son Joseph must have been alive at the time the *Mayflower* sailed, otherwise John Carver, in forwarding the copy of the will to be probated, would have included a statement about the death of two of the legatees.[106]

---

[101] Johnson, *Mayflower Passengers*, 193

[102] MF 16 pt. 1 [2002]: 16

[103] MD 61 [2012]:19

[104] MD 61 [2012]:20

[105] MD 61 [2012]: 24-25, 62 [2013]: 78-87; £280 in 1619 might be worth £55,640 now, following the Retail Price Index [RPI]

[106] The full transcript of the will can be seen in MQ 34 [1967]:9-10; NEHGR 42 [1888]: 62-64; MD 1 [1899]: 230-232; MF 16 pt. 1 (2002): 14-15; Atherton and Horne, *The Weaver, the Shoemaker and the Mother*

Mullins apparently had five children (William, b. 1593; Elizabeth, bapt. 11 Nov 1598; Sarah, b. c. 1600; Priscilla, b. c. 1602; and Joseph, b. c. 1604). Caleb Johnson has thoroughly researched the association of William Mullins with several other Dorking families, showing potential relationships with Peter Brown and with others who later came to New England.[107] More on the family, and questions about how many times William married, tomorrow.

FRIDAY, 5 MARCH [1620]/21

At anchorage

Party from the ship went on shore to help finish work on the ordnance.

While quite a bit of attention has been paid to the Mullins family, mostly because of Priscilla, there remain a significant number of questions.

Starting with who was Priscilla's mother. If it were not for William Mullins' will, we would not know the first name of his wife: Bradford's list of increasings simply says that William's "wife and son and servant died the first winter";[108] in his 1651 list of passengers, he names Joseph Mullins as William's son, but does not give the name of William's wife. William names his wife Alice in his will, so that much is established. Alice's maiden name is unknown: claims that her maiden name was Atwood or Poretiers are unsubstantiated, if not erroneous. Because we have no marriage date for William and Alice, and no baptismal dates for the children, we cannot prove that Alice was the mother of any (much less all) of William's children. This is a not unlikely assumption, but it remains an assumption nonetheless.

Caleb Johnson speculates that William Mullins had two wives: (1) Elizabeth Wood, daughter of John and Joan (Taylor) Wood of Dorking; and (2) Alice, the widow of William or Thomas Browne. If that is correct, the Mullins family might have a

---

of a Nation [Cockerel Press: Dorking, 2020] 62-63, with a picture of the clerk's copy of the will on p. 36.
[107] TAG 79 [2004]: 161-178; MQ 78 [2012]: 44-57; MD 61 [2012]: 17-27, 64 [2016]: 37-39
[108] MD 1 [1899]: 13

close relationship to Peter Brown of the *Mayflower*: Alice Mullins might be his aunt.[109]

There is significant speculation about William Mullins' religious views. If he were on the Puritan or Separatist end of the spectrum, this might account for why there is no record of marriage for him and Alice, or of baptism for his children. In the latter case, this was not because the Puritans rejected infant baptism, but because of their pious horror at the use of the sign of the cross in the baptismal ceremony of the *Book of Common Prayer*. There is a baptismal record of one of William's daughters, Elizabeth Mullins (Holy Trinity, Guildford, Surrey, 11 November 1598: see *MQ* 78 [March 2012]: 45). There is no further record for Elizabeth, so she may have died young.

William Mullins had four children who are attested in his will:

1. William Mullins (b. c. 1593) was his eldest son, born probably at Dorking, Surrey, and came to the Plymouth Colony to lay claim to the inheritance left to him by his father's will: the earliest reference to him in Plymouth documents is in 1637 in Duxbury (near his sister Priscilla). He returned to England at least once, and was one of the founders of the Society for the Propagation of the Gospel in New England (1649). He later removed to Braintree, where he died in 1672. He had three children baptised in Dorking between 1618 and 1622: his older children stayed in England. The youngest, Sarah Mullins (bapt. 5 May 1622) joined her father in coming to America, and married three times before dying in Braintree before 1697. Because her will made bequests of all of her possessions to named individuals and "my nearest relations," it is presumed that Sarah (Mullins) (Gannett) (Savill) Faxon had no surviving children.[110]

2. Sarah Mullins' (b. c. 1600) married name is known to be Blunden from her father's will, and she was the administratrix of his estate in England, but no more is known of her. She is the only one of William Mullins' children who never travelled to America.

[109] *TAG* 79 [July 2004]: 161-178, "The Probable English Origins of *Mayflower* Passenger Peter Browne, and his Associations with Mayflower Passenger William Mullins"; *MQ* 78 [March 2012]: 44-57, "Investigating the Origins of Alice Mullins"

[110] *MD* 7 [1906]: 37-48, 179-183

3. Joseph Mullins (b. c. 1604) accompanied William and Alice Mullins on the Mayflower, but, according to Bradford, he died the first winter, although this must have been after 2 April 1621 when his father's will was copied.

4. And last, but certainly not least, was the fabled Priscilla, my ninth great grandmother. No birth or baptismal record exists for her, and no recorded age has been found for her. She was probably not married until 1623: the delay in marriage may have been either because of a period of mourning for her parents' deaths or a reflection of her youth at the time of the voyage. Although she has recently been portrayed as an outrageously outspoken proto-feminist, she has left almost no traces behind. As we do not know the date of her birth (probably between 1600 and 1605), so also we don't know the date of her death (probably after 1650, since she is on Bradford's list of increasings).

SATURDAY, 6 MARCH [1620]/21

At anchorage

Fetched wood and water. "The spring now approaching," said Bradford, "it pleased God the mortality began to cease amongst them, and the sick and the lame recovered apace, which put as it were new life into them, and contentedness as I think any people could do. But it was the Lord which upheld them..."

When the General Sickness had finally run its course, half of all of *Mayflower*'s passengers had perished. The loss among the wives was the heaviest. Among the eighteen couples aboard, eight of the men (Isaac Allerton, John Billington, William Bradford, William Brewster, Edward Fuller, Stephen Hopkins, Miles Standish, Edward Winslow) but only four of the women survived (Eleanor Billington, Elizabeth Hopkins, Mary Brewster, and Susanna White). Four families were wiped out completely, and only in three families did all the members survive (Billington, Brewster, Hopkins). Six children lost one parent and five lost both. Children fared comparatively well, with twenty-five of thirty-two surviving; of the eleven young women, only one died.

SUNDAY, 7 MARCH [1620]/21

At anchorage in Plymouth harbour

Eleventh Sunday in this harbour. Mary (Norris) Allerton, wife of Isaac Allerton, died on board this day, not having mended well since the birth of her child, stillborn about two

161

months ago. Isaac Allerton and his sister the widow Sarah (Allerton) Vincent had a double wedding in Leiden on 4 November 1611; both Isaac and Sarah were identified as being "of London": Sarah married Degory Priest, and Isaac married Mary Norris of Newbury, Berkshire (the marriage record is pictured, transcribed and translated in MD 7 [1905]: 129-130: Mary's witnesses were Anne Fuller and Dille [Priscilla?] Carpenter). Caleb Johnson, in his extensive survey of the Allerton family, writes: "No Mary Norris of Newbury has been identified, but five miles northwest of Newbury is the town of Welford, where a Mary Norris was baptized on 9 March 1592, daughter of John. This would seem to be a reasonable match, though perhaps a tad younger than would be expected. Additional research is definitely needed in identifying the origin of Mary."[111] Mary was a witness for Elizabeth Barker at her wedding to Edward Winslow in Leiden (27 April 1618).   In 5 February 1620 (n.s.), Isaac and Mary buried a child (name not recorded, probably an infant) at Saint Peter's in Leiden.[112]   The couple brought three of their children on the *Mayflower* voyage (Bartholomew [age 7], Remember [5], and Mary [3]); Mary was in her final trimester of pregnancy. She gave birth to a stillborn son during a winter storm on 1 January (n.s.): see my post on that date. Her death today left Isaac to care for their three young children. More on them tomorrow. I find this intriguing that, given the many passengers dying, daily, this one is mentioned by name on this date while the others are not.   I suspect that the reason is her husband's prominence in the community -- Rose Standish was also mentioned on the date of her death, for example.

MONDAY, 8 MARCH [1620]/21

At anchor in harbour

Burying-party went ashore to bury Mary Allerton.

Isaac and Mary (Norris) Allerton had a total of five children. Bradford records: "Mr. Allerton his wife dyed with the first, and his servant, John Hooke. His sone Bartle is maried in England, but I know not how many children he hath. His doughter Remember is maried at Salem, & hath 3. or 4. children living. And his doughter Mary is maried here, & hath 4. children.

---

[111] Johnson, *Mayflower Passengers*, 59
[112] Dexter and Dexter, *The England and Holland of the Pilgrims*, 601

Him selfe maried againe with ye doughter of Mr. Brewster, & hath one sone living by her, but she is long since dead. And he is maried againe, and hath left this place long agoe. So I account his increase to be 8. besids his sons in England."

1. Bartholomew Allerton (b. in Leiden, Holland c. 1613) came to America with his parents on the *Mayflower*. He survived the first winter, and appears in the Division of Cattle in 1627 as part of Isaac Allerton's group, when Bart would have been fourteen or fifteen. This is his last appearance in any Plymouth Colony records. He probably returned to England after 1630, perhaps with his father, who made numerous trips back and forth on personal and colony business. This introduces the cast of those *Mayflower* passengers who returned to England, even though none of them did so on the *Mayflower*'s return voyage (in addition to Bartholomew Allerton, we know of Humility Cooper, Desire Minter, Richard Gardiner, William Latham and Gilbert Winslow). He was ordained in the Church of England, and thus must have attended university (even if he did not graduate) - so much for his Separatist roots. He was serving in the Church of Ireland (in Knocktemple and Liscarroll in Cork) from 1641 to 1644, and as vicar of Bramfield, Suffolk, from 1644 to his death in 1658.[113] Bartholomew married twice and had at least four children. Descendants of Bartholomew Allerton would obviously be *Mayflower* descendants, but "[n]o one has yet been able to connect Bartholomew's lineage with any of the Allertons who lived in Suffolk during the late seventeenth and early eighteenth centuries, but those efforts continue with the hope that DNA and additional research will link Isaac Allerton's New World Allertons with Bartholomew Allerton's Suffolk family."[114]

2. Remember Allerton (b. in Leiden c. 1615) married Moses Maverick by May 1635, when Moses is listed as the son-in-law of Isaac Allerton in Massachusetts Bay Colony records. Moses came to America on the *Mary and John* in 1630 along with his father. Remember and Moses had seven children together; descendants are known from four of them. Remember died somewhere between September 1652 (the baptism of their youngest child) and October 1656 (Moses Maverick's second marriage).

---

[113]See David Furlow's complete review of the evidence and marvellous presentation of the background in *MJ* 3 [2018]: n. 1: 63-79, n. 2: 24-50
[114] *MJ* 3 [2018]: n. 2: 49

3. Mary Allerton (my tenth great grandmother; b. in Leiden c. 1617) around 1636 married Thomas Cushman, son of Robert Cushman and passenger on the *Fortune* with his father in 1621. Thomas was elder of the Plymouth Church from April 1649 until his death in December 1691 (quite a long tenure!). Thomas and Mary had eight children, seven of whom have known descendants. Mary herself died in Plymouth on 28 November 1699, "the last survivor of those who came on the *Mayflower*" (depending on how you classify Peregrine White, who made most of the voyage *in utero*).

Isaac and Mary Allerton had two other children: a son who was buried from the Pieterskerk in Leiden on 5 February 1620 (n.s. -- just about a year before Mary's death), probably as an infant, and a son stillborn aboard the *Mayflower* in Plymouth harbour during a storm on 1 January 1621 (n.s.).

More on Isaac Allerton and his many adventures when I have more time. Much more time.

TUESDAY, 9 MARCH [1620]/21

At anchorage

The sickness and deaths of the colonists on shore have steadily increased, and have extended to the ship, which has lost several of its petty officers, including the master gunner, three quarter-masters, the cook, and a third of the crew, many from scurvy.

WEDNESDAY, 10 MARCH [1620]/21

At anchorage

The last day of the month of February (in the Julian calendar). The settlers have lost seventeen this month, their highest mortality;[115] their total number is now a bit more than seventy. The fifty-third day the ship has lain in this harbour, and from the present rate of sickness and death aboard, no present capacity or prospect of getting away, those recovering still being weak.

THURSDAY, 11 MARCH [1620]/21

At anchorage

Blustering but milder weather.

---

[115] Prince, p. 98

164

Like the Mullins family, the Tilley families lost every member except for a younger child. Also like the Mullins family, the daughter of John and Joan Tilley went on to marry another passenger. But there were on this voyage two Tilley families: Edward Tilley, the younger brother of John Tilley, was also on board with his wife Agnes (or Ann) Cooper and Ann's sixteen year old nephew Henry Samson and her one year old niece Humility Cooper. A look at Edward's group today and tomorrow will lead us to John's group next week.

Edward Tilley (bapt. 27 May 1588, son of Robert and Elizabeth Tilley) and Ann (or Agnes) Cooper (bapt. 7 November 1585, daughter of Edmund Cooper) were married in Henlow, Bedfordshire on 20 June 1614.[116] It was certainly unusual for men to marry older women in this period, and the Pilgrims' pastor John Robinson specifically warned that this was not a good idea in "Of Marriage" of his *Observations Divine and Moral*. Edward and Ann appear in Leiden records in 1616, so they must have moved not long after they married; they are not known to have had any children. His occupation was listed as a serge weaver.[117] Edward, 32 on this voyage, was a part of most of the early explorations in search of a place to settle, and Bradford notes that he became very sick, "and like to have sounded [*swooned*] with cold." He died in January or February, most likely of pneumonia, perhaps caught from wading through too many frozen waters. His wife Ann died soon after.

* * * * *

Robinson wrote: "After goodness, fitness in marriage is most to be regarded: and that so much that, as for a pair of gloves or yoke of oxen, two alike, though meaner, both are them are fitter and better for use, than if the one were more excellent; so in this marriage pair and yoke, the woman best qualified is not always the best wife for every man; nor every man the best qualified, the fittest husband for every woman: but two more alike, though both meaner, sort better usually. And according to this, Pittacus, being demanded by a friend what kind of wife he should marry,

---

[116] For more information on the manifold connections with other passengers, see Robert Leigh Ward, "English Ancestry of Seven *Mayflower* Passengers: Tilley, Sampson and Cooper," *TAG* 52 (1976): 198-208.

[117] *NEHGR* 143 [1989]: 208

answered: one fit for him [Laertius]. Fitness of years is requisite, that an old head be not set upon young shoulders; nor the contrary, which is worse: fitness in estate, lest the excelling person despise the other, or draw him to a course above his reach: fitness for course of life and disposition unto it, the dislike whereof, in either by other, breeds many discontentments."

FRIDAY, 12 MARCH [1620]/21

At anchorage

Another blustery day.

The two children that were part of the (Edward) Tilley household are interesting subjects by themselves. Humility Cooper, one of the youngest *Mayflower* passengers, was the niece of Agnes (Cooper) Tilley, the wife of Edward Tilley. She was born in Leiden by about 1619, the daughter of Robert Cooper, Ann's brother, and Joan (Gresham) Cooper.[118] Robert Charles Anderson notes that Humility "was no more than a year old at the time the *Mayflower* sailed";[119] there is a possibility that she was orphaned in Holland, which would explain her presence in the Tilley household. Edward and Agnes Tilley died the first winter, as we saw yesterday, and Humility received one acre as a passenger of the *Mayflower* in the 1623 Plymouth land division (*Plymouth Colony Records* 12:4). She was a part of the 1627 cattle division as the last person in the fifth company,[120] and this is the last record for her on this side of the Atlantic. She reappears when she is baptised as an adult at Holy Trinity in Minories, London on 17 March 1638/39; the record states that she was nineteen years old and was born in Holland (*TG* 6 [1985]:166). Bradford writes in his 1651 list of increasings that "the girl Humility, their [viz., Edward and Agnes Tilley's] cousin, was sent for into England and died there." She must therefore have died between 1639 and 1651, although the exact date of her death is not now known. There is no record of any marriage or of any children. She is thus the second person we have seen permanently to return to England (we have already met Bartholomew Allerton).

---

[118] *TG* 6 [Fall, 1985]: 166

[119] MM 69

[120] In the William Brewster group, suggesting that the Brewster family was taking care of her: *Plymouth Colony Records* 12:10

Henry Samson was the nephew of Agnes Tilley, being the son of James Samson and Agnes (Cooper) Tilley's sister, Martha (Cooper) Samson. He was sixteen at the time of the voyage, having been baptised in Henlow, Bedfordshire on 15 January 1603/04; Henry's parents and other siblings remained behind in Henlow. Henry may have been apprenticed to his uncle, but the circumstances of how he came on the *Mayflower* are unclear. His aunt and uncle both died the first winter, as did John and Joan Tilley (his uncle's older brother and wife), leaving behind Henry and his two female relatives: Humility Cooper and Elizabeth Tilley. It is probable that he (and his cousin Humility) were taken care of by the Brewster family, since they are included in that group in the 1627 division of cattle; he received an acre in the 1623 land division, next to Humility on "the north side of the town next adjoining to their gardens which came in the *Fortune*." He married Anne Plummer (who arrived in Plymouth in 1635); they lived mostly in Duxbury and had nine children.[121] Henry died in 1684/85 in Duxbury.

My particular interest in Henry arises from my descent from Abraham Sampson (don't obsess about distinctions between the "p" and "non-p" Sam(p)sons); there is evidence that Abraham and Henry were cousins, but connecting the dots is not easy. Abraham, called "of Duxbarrow," first shows up in Plymouth Colony Records on 4 December 1638, when he was "presented for striking and abusing John Washbourne, the younger, in the meetinghouse [!] on the Lord's Day [!!]" (1:107). Until Robert Leigh Ward's discovery of the origin of Henry Samson of the *Mayflower*, it was generally assumed that Henry and Abraham Sam(p)son were brothers, since they both lived in Duxbury.[122] Henry, however, did not have a brother named Abraham. In a later article, Ward showed that Henry had a first cousin Abraham, baptised at Campton, Bedfordshire, on 14 August 1614, son of Lawrence Sampson, who may have been the Lawrence Samson who married Mary Sharbery at Cranfield, Bedfordshire on 2 June 1602.[123] This Abraham Sampson may be the immigrant; further

---

[121] Anderson laments, "There are few chronological clues to help us in arranging the children of Henry Samson" PM 404
[122] *TAG* 52 [1976]: 198-208
[123] *TAG* 56 [1980]: 141-143

evidence is needed to prove or disprove this hypothesis.[124] The *Descendants of Abraham Sampson* is a 13 Generation Report [!!!] based on the Pilgrim Henry Samson Kindred's "Abraham Sampson Database of Sources"; because there are no recent publications similar to the Mayflower Society's Five Generation Project specifically for non-Pilgrim Abraham, the database was assembled to help prospective members find sources to help prove their lines to Abraham. It is a work in progress that currently consists of more than 27,500 individuals.[125]

SATURDAY, 13 MARCH [1620]/21

At anchorage

Fetched wood and water. The wind was south, the morning misty, "but towards noon warm and fair; the birds sang in the woods most pleasantly. At one of the clock it thundered, which was the first we heard in that country; it was strong and great claps, but short, but after an hour it rained very sadly till midnight."

SUNDAY, 14 MARCH [1620]/21

At anchor in Plymouth harbour

The twelfth Sunday in this harbour. Cooler. Clear weather. The *Mayflower*'s crew remain too ill to contemplate a return to England any time soon.

MONDAY, 15 MARCH [1620]/21

At anchorage

Rough weather.

Now for the other Tilleys. John Tilley of Henlow, Bedfordshire (bapt. 19 December 1571, and thus about fifty years old at the time of the voyage) was the elder brother of fellow *Mayflower* passenger Edward Tilley. He was the eldest son of Robert and Elizabeth (maiden name unknown) Tilley; John married Joan (Hurst) Rogers on 20 September 1596. While kid brother Edward shows up in Leiden records (once), no records have yet been found to indicate that either John or Joan were living

---

[124] see Robert Wakefield, "The Daughters of Abraham Samson (born 1614?) of Duxbury MA" [*TAG* 63 [1988]: 207-210

[125] The production of a comprehensive genealogy of The Descendants of Abraham Sampson, to the ninth generation, called "The Crimson Book," is in progress.

in Holland before the *Mayflower's* departure. This does not, of course, prove that they were *not* living there, but very little is known about this family. John signed the Mayflower Compact, and participated in the early explorations of Cape Cod and the Plymouth area. He died during the first winter.

Joan (Hurst) Tilley died the first winter as well. Joan was the youngest daughter of William and Rose (Marsh) Hurst, and was baptised in Henlow on 13 March 1567/68, making her several years older than her husband (is this a pattern with the Tilley men marrying older women?). Remarkable work has been done in establishing the Hurst ancestry in Bedfordshire by Randy West,[126] Eugene Cole Zubrinsky,[127] and Caleb Johnson.[128] She married Thomas Rogers (no relation to the *Mayflower* passenger of the same name) and had a daughter Joan (bapt. 26 May 1594); Thomas died not long afterwards, and Joan [Hurst] Rogers married John Tilley a year or two later. Joan Rogers (daughter of Thomas Rogers and Joan [Hurst] Rogers) married Edward Hawkins, brother of her half-brother Robert's wife (confused yet?). John Tilley and Joan [Hurst] had five children, all baptised in the parish in Henlow between 1597 and 1607:[129] Rose (who died young), John, Rose (another), Robert, and Elizabeth (more on her tomorrow). The fate of John and Rose (the younger) is not known; Robert married Mary Hawkins at Saint Paul's Church in Bedford, Bedfordshire on 1 November 1632.[130] Any children of Robert and Mary (Hawkins) Tilley would also be *Mayflower* descendants, even though there is no sign that Robert or Mary ever came to America; there is, however, no record of any children for this couple that has yet been discovered.

TUESDAY, 16 MARCH [1620]/21

At anchorage

Another rough and stormy day.

Elizabeth Tilley (bapt. in Henlow on 30 August 1607) came on the *Mayflower* with her parents. She was about thirteen

---

[126] *MD* 66 [Winter 2018]: 10-13
[127] *TAG* 85 [2011]: 1-8
[128] Particularly the manorial records of Henlow Grey in *MQ* 76 [2010]: 125-134
[129] see *TAG* 52 [1976]: 198
[130] *MQ* 65 [1999]: 322-325

years old, and is the only member of this family to survive the first winter in America. At about seventeen years old, she married fellow *Mayflower* passenger John Howland (who was probably at least nine or ten years older than Elizabeth). John and Elizabeth Howland had ten children and 88 grandchildren (!!). John Howland died in 1672, and Elizabeth lived as a widow for an additional fourteen years, dying on 22 December 1687 in Swansea. I would point out that Elizabeth was known as Elizabeth Tilley for only seventeen years, but was known as Elizabeth Howland for sixty-three years. Her will is extant, and she notably bequeathed books to her heirs, including John Robinson's *Observations Divine and Moral.*

WEDNESDAY, 17 MARCH [1620]/21

At anchor in harbour

Wind full east, cold but fair. Today John Carver with five others went "to the great pond" discovered by one of the ship's mates and Francis Billington, "which seem to be excellent fishing places; all the way they went they found it exceedingly beaten and haunted with deer, but they saw none. Amongst other fowl, they saw one a milk-white fowl, with a very black head." This day some garden seeds were sown: the first planting.

THURSDAY, 18 MARCH [1620]/21

At anchor in harbour

Rough easterly weather.

We have seen John Carver several times in the past six months, so perhaps now is a good time to look at him more closely. John was born at Great Bealings, Suffolk in 1581, so he was just shy of 40 on this voyage. He appeared -- frequently - in the manorial records of Seckford Hall (in Great Bealings), but he sold off all of his holdings there between 1605 and 1608, and disappeared from English records thereafter. Carver and his family appear in Leiden by 1615, when he became deacon of Pastor John Robinson's congregation (*Plymouth Church Records* 1:51; Sue Allan, Caleb Johnson, and Simon Neal have published the evidence for Carver's English origins in *NEHGR* 174 [2020]: 5-20). Carver became one of the principal negotiators and agents for the Leiden community with the merchant adventurers, along with Robert Cushman, over the next few years. He married twice: first in England to Martha Rose, daughter of William Rose of

Tuddenham St. Martin in Suffolk (she died by 1608 or thereabouts); second to the widow Katherine (White) Leggatt, daughter of Alexander White. Katherine came on the *Mayflower* with her husband, and survived him, but not for very long, dying in the summer of 1621. Carver's household in Plymouth also included Desire Minter, two servants (John Howland and Roger Wilder), William Latham, "a maidservant," and "a child that was put to him, Jasper More." More about these people tomorrow.

John Carver and his first wife had a daughter, Margaret, who was baptised in Great Bealings on 26 April 1603; she was named in her grandfather's will in November 1604, but there is no record of her after that. John Carver thus has no known descendants.

It would appear that Carver was elected Governor at the end of August, before the colonists left England: this was the point at which Christopher Martin was dropped as leader and Carver, who had been his assistant, was elevated in his place. Upon arrival at Cape Cod, Bradford says that Carver's election as Governor was "confirmed," suggesting that he had been elected previously. He was active in many of the early exploratory parties, and oversaw both the colony's operations and its finances. Caleb Johnson describes the colony's situation in early March as follows: "With half of the colonists sick or dead, with all the winter weather that hampered construction, with the accidental fires -- what more could possibly go wrong? On February 16[/26], some tools mysteriously disappeared from the woods; and the next day, some Indians stood on a hill overlooking the new settlement, waving and making signals. When the Pilgrims sent some armed men to investigate, they heard 'a great noise of many others,' but the Indians went into hiding and could not be located."[131] By this point in March, the settlers were (finally!) starting to recover their health, although almost half of them were now dead. Carver remained reluctant to send away the *Mayflower*, because he felt that the colonists needed the security of a ship that could return them home, at least until their health was more assured, and their safety from the Indians was more secure. But, as many modern commentators seem to forget, the *Mayflower*'s presence was not free of charge: the colonists were paying for the ship, the crew, and the master by the day (!); and each day was costing the already

---

[131] Johnson, *Mayflower Passengers*, 112

broke company more and more money. So their main problem was not (only) that they had run out of beer.

FRIDAY, 19 MARCH [2020]/21

At anchorage

Rough easterly weather. Many still sick aboard.

There are six other people in the household of John Carver mentioned in Bradford's list of passengers, in addition to John' wife Katherine:

1) **John Howland:** John Howland was born about 1599 to Henry and Margaret Howland of Fenstanton, Huntingdonshire. The Howland family appears to have had connections with Randall Thickens, John Carver's brother-in-law, which may help explain why he was placed in this household. Howland signed the Mayflower Compact, and took part in several of the exploratory trips before settling in Plymouth. Both John and Katherine Carver died in the spring and summer of 1621, and Howland's indenture must have been close to ending in any event, as he married Elizabeth Tilley (see last Tuesday's post) not long before the 1623 division of land. Their first daughter, Desire, was born about 1624, and some have speculated that she was named after Desire Minter, who was probably a close contemporary of Elizabeth and may have recently died (see below), and who was one of John's fellow servants in the Carver household. The Howlands' second child was born in 1626. In the 1627 division of cattle, John and Elizabeth were in the only lot that did not contain two female goats. He was also one of the surveyors for the 1627 division of land. Howland was active in the colony, and lived out his last years at his house in Rocky Nook, near Kingston. He made out his will on 29 May 1672, and died on 23 February 1672/73 "above eighty years."[132] All ten of John and Elizabeth's children survived to adulthood and had children of their own -- an unusual set of circumstances, which has led many to conclude that there are more descendants of John and Elizabeth Howland than there are of any other *Mayflower* passenger. There is much more to say about John Howland, particularly his activities in Maine; these are summarised by Caleb Johnson in *Mayflower Passengers*, 169-175.

---

[132] PCR 8: 34 -- there is general agreement that this age at death is almost certainly exaggerated

On the White and silver books (sorry, I couldn't resist), see tomorrow's post.

2) **William Latham**: see my posting of 26 October 1620 on the indentured servants on the Mayflower. Although William was not included by name in the 1623 division of land, he was included in the 1627 division of cattle in the group of William Bradford. He was born about 1609, moved to Duxbury, Marblehead and Marshfield before he returned to England in 1645, and then headed to the Bahamas, where he was abandoned on Eleuthera Island and starved to death in 1648. He married a woman by the name of Mary by 1643; she was hanged in Boston on 21 March 1643/44. Lots more stories where those care from (see my earlier post).

3) **Desire Minter**: Robert Charles Anderson notes that "although the precise connection is not yet clear, Desire Minter was related to John Carver in some way,[133] thus placing her in the Southeast Suffolk Separatist cluster of immigrants to Leiden." Her father, William Minter, had died by 1618 in Leiden; at that point her mother Sarah (Willet) Minter remarried to Roger Simons (or Simonson), and by 1622 Sarah had married a third time to Roger Eastman. Desire was born about 1610;[134] Bradford states that she "returned to her friend and proved not very well and died in England." The word "friend" in this period could also mean kinsman or guardian. Her mother made an arrangement for her support on 10 May 1622, which is the last mention of her in any extant document. There is no record of either a marriage or children for her.

4) **Jasper More**: see my posting of indentured servants of 26 October 1620, and on Jasper himself on 16 December 1620 (the date of his death). Jasper was baptised in 1613, the elder of the More sons, and died during this winter "of the common infection" at about the age of eight.

5) **Roger Wilder**: also died during this winter, according to Bradford. He presumably came with Carver from Leiden. Roger did not sign the Mayflower Compact, either because he was too young, or because he was one of eight or ten men who refused to do so. Caleb Johnson notes a Roger Wilder baptised at Rotherwicke in Hampshire on 28 December 1595 (*Mayflower*

---

[133] *NEHGR* 174 (2020): 5-20
[134] see *NEHGR* 143 [1999]: 209

Passengers, 249); Robert Charles Anderson comments that this Hampshire man, "although probably too old to be the Mayflower passenger, may provide a clue to discovering the correct origin."[135]

6) "**maidservant**": see my post of 11 October 1620. Bradford does not name this passenger, but I think it reasonable to identify her as "Mrs. Carver's maid." All the adult women on the Mayflower were married, with the exception of Mrs. Carver's maid, Dorothy (who became Francis Eaton's second wife -- see Caleb Johnson's careful and fascinating reconstruction of the complicated record in *Mayflower Passengers*, 263-265. Whether or not she was alive in 1623, one acre of land was granted to Francis Eaton in Dorothy's right in the land division of that year. Francis Eaton remarried (a third time) in 1626, so Dorothy must have died before then.

SATURDAY, 20 MARCH [1620]/21

At anchorage

Rough easterly weather. Fetched wood and water.

Between 1990 and 2008, Elizabeth Pearson White prepared four volumes covering the first five generations of the descendants of John Howland through his four oldest children: Desire (1990), John (1993), Hope (2008), and Elizabeth (2008). These were published by the Picton Press in Maine, independent of the silver books ("Mayflower Families through Five Generations") project. Robert Charles Anderson notes that these books need to be used with caution;[136] Martin Hollick in *MD* 58 (2009): 97-98 warns that Elizabeth Pearson White's long years of research on the Howland family may have caused her to lose a certain objectivity in evaluating new evidence, dismissing instead of investigating possibilities (in more than one case, getting the person's sex wrong). Elizabeth Pearson White died in 2011 (aged 96!), and Picton Press, alas, ceased publication in 2014. Thus the books, where they can be found, are out of print, out of stock, and hideously expensive (I have seen online prices well over $7,000 a volume -- which must mean that someone, somewhere, will pay that outrageous price for it); I am told that the White heirs appallingly continue to refuse to permit the books to be republished. While these books do have flaws, they are well done,

---

[135]MM 186.
[136] MM 113

up to modern standards, and indispensable to anyone working on these lines.

Beginning in 1959, the General Society of Mayflower Descendants sponsored the publication of a series of books originally called the "Five Generation Project," which sought to document all of the descendants of the passengers with known descendants for the first five generations. The aim of the project was to bridge the research gap between the Plymouth Colony's beginnings and Revolutionary times. Most of the Mayflower Families have been published as a single volume for each individual passenger; those covering Pilgrims with a large number of descendants have been published as multi-part sets. They soon became known as the "Silver Books" (because of the colour of the cover), and are an invaluable tool because of the meticulous research and documentation they contain. The more recent books have expanded to contain six generations, naming the seventh, and thus frequently reach into the early nineteenth century.

One of the earliest volumes to appear (vol. 3 [1981]) was the descendants of George Soule, and was the work of John E. Soule and Milton E. Terry. While it was a painstaking operation, it suffered from the change in genealogical standards that was occurring at just about that time; it very quickly became clear that this book was not adequate to substantiate the identities and families of George Soule's descendants, the purpose of the silver book series. Starting in the 1990s, other researchers began documenting the Soule lines with substantial further research, and published several soft cover volumes officially called Mayflower Families in Progress (MFIP), but more colloquially known as "Pink Books" because their covers are the hue of the "may flower." Other family organizations have produced these interim books, as well, and then combined and revised them for publication in the final, definitive silver book: the most recent volume to go from pink to silver is William Brewster, and a series of (green) books have been published on the descendants of Phillip Delano, a passenger on the *Fortune* (1621), but whose children married into many Pilgrim families. The Soule family, which counts at least 40,000 descendants and spouses in the first six generations, is the largest family without a more than provisional publication of its *Mayflower* descendants, but I remain hopeful that the new Soule silver book can be published in the next three years. Soule

Kindred in America is sponsoring a revision and completion of the Soule pink books with the ultimate goal of producing a final silver book, thus fulfilling the project begun by John Soule and Milton Terry over half a century ago.

Mayflower silver book researchers continued with the subsequent children of John and Elizabeth Howland not covered in Elizabeth Pearson White's four volumes; the organization of these new silver book volumes, however, was slightly changed, and this makes consulting them somewhat confusing. Volume 23, Part 1 (2006) covers the first four generations of the remaining six children (Lydia, Hannah, Joseph, Jabez, Ruth, and Isaac). Part 2 (2010) then goes on to the fifth generation of his daughters, Lydia and Hannah. Part 3 (2012) goes to the fifth generation of his sons Joseph and Jabez. The fifth generation descendants of Ruth and Isaac remain to be published (just my luck, since I am descended from Isaac); I hope it is not far off. At some point the four volumes previously done by Elizabeth Pearson White will be revised in order to coordinate them with the silver books that have been published.

SUNDAY, 21 MARCH [1620]/21

At anchorage, Plymouth harbour

The thirteenth Sunday the ship has been in this harbour. Many of *Mayflower* crew still sick, including the boatswain. Those on shore beginning to recover.

MONDAY, 22 MARCH [1620]/21

At anchorage

Easterly weather.

More has probably been written, with fewer solid conclusions, about George Soule, an indentured servant to Edward Winslow and signer of the Mayflower Compact, than about any other passenger on the *Mayflower*. Speculation has been rampant about his origins (English? Dutch? French?) and has ranged from agnosticism to wildly imaginative speculation (that he was a Sephardic Jew from Spain, who came to Leiden via Africa), with none of it -- absolutely none of it -- resting on even a single document that has his name. As it happens, the very first document on which George Soule's name appears is the Mayflower Compact. It may be valuable, or at least entertaining, to look at the various theories for his origins:

1. A generation ago it was generally agreed that George Soule of the *Mayflower* came from Eckington, a small village in Worcestershire. There *was* a George Soule there in the early seventeenth century, but this identification is too problematic to be a prime answer in the search. The facts that argue in its favour have to do with connections of the Winslow family to the area; arguing against it is that the Soules in that area (and there are still some) do not share any DNA connection with George or his descendants, and no documentation clearly shows any local George Soule of the right age or occupation, or one with Separatist sympathies. The Eckington origin, however, is still the story that is used in the Plimoth Plantation playbook for the actors who portray George.

2. About twenty years ago, several researchers, particularly Louise Throop, pointed to a couple of Dutch Reformed refugees named Jan Sol (or Soltz or Solis or Sols) and Mayken Labis (or Labus). They married in London at the old Austin Friars Church in 1586, and had seven children, who were baptised in Haarlem in Holland. While the name sounds a lot like "Soule," the problem with this identification is that the record of their children's baptisms appears to be complete into the seventeenth century, and *none* of their children are named George (or any variation of that). Another John Soule (Jan Sol, Johannes Sol) was a Leiden book printer, thus putting him in the right place at the right time, but his marriage was in 1616, making it impossible for him to be *this* George Soule's father.[137] There has, thus far, been no documentation to either prove or disprove George Soule's Dutch origins. Overheated speculations on DNA results have been inconclusive as well.

3. With the discovery of Elizabeth (Barker) Winslow's family connections a couple of years ago, a new place of research has opened up. She was the daughter of Samuel Barker of East Bergholt and Chattisham in Suffolk,[138] and it is clear that both Edward and Elizabeth went back in 1619 to sell off property she inherited from her parents. They purchased shares in the merchant group financing the *Mayflower* voyage, and this recent sale would have made Edward and Elizabeth two of the wealthier people in the community. I have speculated in these posts several times before that it is possible that the Winslows were thus in a

---

[137]See Bangs, *Strangers and Pilgrims*, 299f. n. 135
[138]See the work of the intrepid trio of Sue Allan, Caleb Johnson, and Simon Neal in *NEHGR* 173 [2019]: 5-17

position, being newly flush with cash, to pay for the passage of others of like mind; the fact that George Soule and Edward Winslow were roughly contemporaries is also intriguing, as well as the fact that George did not have any particular trade that would have made his presence necessary or valuable to the settlers (such as John Alden, who was a cooper). There were Soules in this area of Suffolk, and it is possible that the Winslows picked up George Soule while they were back there making arrangements for the Barker estate. This is, however, the proverbial needle in a haystack, but researchers are looking to see if there are any candidates for a George Soule in Suffolk, where it is known that there were influential Separatist conventicles. Nothing has yet shown up to prove or disprove this possibility, either.

4. Edward Winslow's relationship to John Beale, a London printer, is also a possible connection to look at. Winslow was apprenticed to Beale, "citizen [of London] and stationer, for the term of eight years," on 19 August 1613, but left England in 1617, before his apprenticeship ended (Bangs, *Edward Winslow*, 3-4). No penalties were imposed on him when he returned in 1635, which they would have been if he has been a runaway. This suggests that Winslow's relationship with Beale was not merely master-servant. The facts will bear the interpretation that Beale was a distributor of the Puritan and Separatist tracts produced in Leiden, and if George Soule were from London and could be connected with Beale's circle, whether as a courier or in some other capacity, it would be easy to connect him to Edward Winslow (by occupation and religious preference) before the *Mayflower* sailed. In some ways this is the most difficult of the possibilities, since Winslow's printing activity was illegal in England, and there is not likely to be a very obvious paper trail connecting George with anyone involved in seditious activity.

There may be other possibilities, as well, but these all (except for the Eckington connection) are currently live options. Stay tuned ...

TUESDAY, 23 MARCH [1620]/21

At anchorage

The sickness and mortality on ship and on shore continue.

Whenever I have to talk about George Soule, there is one question that is asked *far more* frequently than where did he come

178

from and what were his origins. That is, "How do you pronounce the name Soule?" This is closely connected to the question of how it was spelled. Note that spelling was not standardised in this period, and would have been closer to pronunciation (as people would have been spelling in accord with how it sounded more frequently than they would have been spelling from how it appeared in print or writing).

We have an original signature from George the Pilgrim, as a witness on the will of John Barnes (6 March 1667[/68]). A close examination of this document clearly shows that the surname was spelled "Soule," with the addition of "Senr" after it, to show that this was the Pilgrim and not his son George Soule. There is no indication that the name of this branch was ever written with an accent ("Soulé") or pronounced "Soo-lay" in the French fashion (where it means, er, um, uh, "drunk"). George Ernest Bowman reported in his article on the pronunciation of the name in the *Mayflower Descendant* that after reviewing numerous documents not found in print, he had discovered six ways of spelling the surname: Soule, Soull, Soul, Sole, Soal, and Sowle.[139] The earliest contemporary written use of the name is in the record of the division of land in 1623: it is there written as Soule.[140] In Bradford's list of *Mayflower* passengers (1651), he uses the form "Sowle," but in the same list he states "aboute a hundred sowles came over in the first ship," showing that he pronounced the surname as if it rhymed with coal. The frequent occurrences in the original records of the forms Soule, Soul, Soale, Soal, and Sole, with the numerous autograph signatures in the forms Soule, Soul, and Sole, furnish conclusive evidence that for the first century in America (at least), the name was pronounced to rhyme with "coal" (and hole, bowl, troll, etc.) rather than with "fool."

WEDNESDAY, 24 MARCH [1620]/21

At anchorage

A group of my parishioners are going to plant a large bed of Mayflowers in the garden behind my house, but I have to admit that I really didn't know what one looked like for real and can't say that I could identify it if I saw it in the wild.

---

[139]All of which can be pronounced to rhyme with coal: *MD* 14 [1912]: 129-130
[140]PCR12:4; *MD* 1 [1899]:228

The mayflower plant, also called "trailing arbutus" (*Epigaea repens*) is a trailing plant with fuzzy stems and clusters of sweet-smelling pink or white blooms about half an inch across when expanded, and borne in clusters at the ends of the branches. It is found from Newfoundland to Florida, west to Kentucky and the Northwest Territories. This unusual wildflower grows from a specific type of fungus that nourishes the roots. The seeds of the plant are dispersed by ants, but the plant rarely produces fruit and trailing arbutus wildflowers are nearly impossible to transplant. Due to the plant's particular growing requirements and destruction of its habitat, mayflower trailing arbutus wildflowers have become very rare. If you are lucky enough to see a mayflower plant growing in the wild, do not attempt to remove it. The species is protected by law in many states, and removal is prohibited. Once trailing arbutus disappears from an area, it will probably never return. Mayflower trailing arbutus requires moist soil and partial or full shade. Like most woodland plants growing under tall conifers and deciduous trees, the Mayflower plant performs well in acidic (humus-rich) soil. Mayflower arbutus grows where many plants fail to thrive: I hope that the Great Smoky Mountains qualify.

The mayflower is the official flower of the Province of Nova Scotia and the Commonwealth of Massachusetts [digging up one in Massachusetts is punishable with a $50 fine].

When I went to the nursery last week to talk about getting more, the horticulturalist confessed that he had never, in almost forty years, been asked to obtain one. So keep your fingers crossed that it will flourish, like the Pilgrims -- with lots of moisture and in partial or full shade. I have decided to put up two flagpoles: one will, of course, have the King's Colours; I think that the other one should have the new flag of the Canadian Society of Mayflower Descendants.

THURSDAY, 25 MARCH [1620]/21

At anchorage

The Allerton household was hit by more than Mary (Norris) Allerton's death. Isaac Allerton's servant, John Hooke, died at about this time, as did Isaac's brother, John Allerton.

John Allerton had intended to spend only that first winter in America, helping his brother's family, and then return to his wife. He was hired as help for the colony, and is identified by

Bradford as a seaman -- he signed the Mayflower Compact, between two others identified as seamen: Richard Gardinar and Thomas English. He was on several of the exploratory expeditions, was at the "First Encounter" with the Nauset Indians, and was with the group when it explored Plymouth Harbour for the first time. We know nothing about his wife or any of his children. If there were any, and they had descendants, they would be Mayflower descendants.

John Hooke was born about 1607 in Norwich, Norfolk, making him about thirteen at the time the Mayflower set sail. At some point the Hooke family moved to Leiden, where their former pastor John Robinson led the congregation. John Hooke's father (also named John) died in Leiden and his mother remarried to Henry Gallant. Henry and Alice apprenticed young John on 8 January 1619 to Isaac Allerton of Leiden, a tailor, for a period of twelve years; John only survived a bit more than two.

Friday, 26 March [1620]/21

At anchorage

A fair, warm day, towards noon.

Master Jones and others went ashore to the general military meeting. It was planned that there would be drill after the meeting. Oddly enough, *whenever* the Pilgrims gathered for drill or other meetings, they were *always* interrupted by Indians.

This morning the same thing happened, although there was only one of them this time. Unlike the previous times, "a tall, straight man, the hair of his head black, long behind, only short before, none on his face at all" appeared at the top of Watson's hill, and then walked straight into the settlement, and down the main street (such as it was) toward the meeting house, where the women and children had been assembled in case of attack. He showed no hesitation or fear, although he was "stark naked, only a leather about his waist, with a fringe about a span [*i.e., about nine inches*] long or little more." When a cold breeze came up, the settlers threw "a horseman's coat" over him to keep him warm. He was armed with "a bow and two arrows, the one headed, the other unheaded." No special significance was attached to this at the time, but they may have been signs of the alternatives of war and peace. Some of the men came out of the meeting house and blocked the entrance. This strange visitor "saluted us in English" and with great enthusiasm spoke the now famous words:

181

"Welcome, Englishmen!"

Bradford wrote that the Pilgrims offered him something to eat, and he immediately asked for beer. Since their beer had run out, the settlers offered him some "strong water" (probably the aqua vitae [brandy]) along with some "biscuit, and butter, and cheese, and pudding, and a piece of mallard, all of which he liked well" (*Mourt's Relation*).

"He introduced himself as Samoset -- at least that is how the Pilgrims heard it -- but he may actually have been telling them his English name, Somerset. He was not, he explained in broken English, from this part of New England. He was a sachem from Pemaquid Point in Maine, near Monhegan Island, a region frequented by English fishermen. It was from these fishermen, many of whom he named, that he'd learned to speak English."[141] He saw the *Mayflower* in the harbour, from a distance, and supposed it to be a fishing vessel. He told the Governor that the plantation was formerly called "Patuxet" [or Apaum], "and that about four years ago all the inhabitants died of an extraordinary plague, and there is neither man, woman, nor child remaining, as indeed we have found none, so as there is none to hinder our possession, or to lay claim unto it. All the afternoon was spent in communication with him; we would gladly have been rid of him at night, but he was not willing to go this night." Governor Carver purposed sending him aboard the ship at night, "and he was well content to go and went aboard the shallop to come to the ship, but the wind was high and water scant [*low*], that [the shallop] could not return back. We lodged him that night at Stephen Hopkins's house, and watched him" (*Mourt's Relation*).

SATURDAY, 27 MARCH [1620]/21

At anchor in harbour

A reasonably fair day. Fetched wood and water.

Samoset was a Wabanaki Indian from the Maine coast, who had survived both the epidemic that swept the coast as well as attacks from neighbouring tribes (such as the Tarrantines). His presence with the Wampanoags suggests that there was extensive communication and coastal trade between the various tribes in New England, which did not end with the spread of disease. Samoset told the settlers about opportunities for trade along the

---

[141] Philbrick, *Mayflower*, 93-94

Maine coast, before he returned there permanently a year or two later, where he was encountered by the English explorer Christopher Leverett, who wrote about his meeting with "Somersett [Samoset], a Sagamore, one that hath been found very faithful to the English, and hath saved the lives of many of our nation" ().[142] Today, Samoset "went away back to the Massasoits, from whence he said he came, who are our next bordering neighbours. They are sixty strong, as he saith. The Nausets are as near southeast of them, and are a hundred strong, and those were they of whom our people were encountered, as we before related. They are much incensed and provoked against the English, and about eight months ago slew three Englishmen, and two more hardly escaped by flight to Monchiggon; they were Sir Ferdinando Gorges his men, as this savage told us, as he did likewise of the huggery, that is, fight, that our discoverers had with the Nausets, and of our tools that were taken out of the woods, which we willed him should be brought again, otherwise, we would right ourselves. These people are ill affected towards the English, by reason of one Hunt, a master of a ship, who deceived the people, and got them under color of trucking with them, twenty out of this very place where we inhabit, and seven men from Nauset, and carried them away [in 1614], and sold them for slaves like a wretched man (for twenty pound a man) that cares not what mischief he doth for his profit" (Mourt's Relation). Samoset also mentioned that there was another Indian at "the Massasoits" (a place called Pokanoket, forty miles to the southwest at the head of Narragansett Bay) named Squanto, who spoke even better English than he did.

"In the morning we dismissed the savage, and gave him a knife, a bracelet, and a ring; he promised within a night or two to come again, and to bring with him some of the Massasoits, our neighbors, with such beavers' skins as they had to truck with us" (Mourt's Relation). "To truck" means to trade: all early and modern lexicographers give the word, which, though now obsolete, was in common use in parts of New England just over a century ago.

---

[142]A Voyage into New England begun in 1622 [London: William Jones, 1624], 9

SUNDAY, 28 MARCH [1620]/21

At anchor in Plymouth harbour

The fourteenth Sunday the ship has lain at this anchorage. A fair day. The sickness stayed a little. Many went on shore to the meeting in the common-house.

"On this day came again the savage, and brought with him five other tall proper men; they had every man a deer's skin on him, and the principal of them had a wild cat's skin, or such like on the one arm. They had most of them long hosen up to their groins, close made; and above their groins to their waist another leather, they were altogether like the Irish-trousers. They are of a complexion like our English gypsies, no hair or very little on their faces, on the heads long hair to their shoulders, only cut before, some trussed up before with a feather, broad-wise, like a fan, another a fox tail hanging out. These left (according to our charge given him before) their bows and arrows a quarter of a mile from our town." This Sunday visit was doubtless very much to the dislike of our good brethren, but policy dictated every possible forbearance. Their consciences drew the line at trade, however, and they got rid of their untimely visitors as soon as possible without giving offense. Massasoit's men seem to have shown, by leaving their pelts with them, a confidence in their new English neighbours that is remarkable in view of the brevity of their friendship. "We gave them entertainment as we thought was fitting them; they did eat liberally of our English victuals. They made semblance unto us of friendship and amity; they sang and danced after their manner, like antics [*i.e., clowns*]. They brought with them in a thing like a bow-case (which the principal of them had about his waist) a little of their corn pounded to powder, which, put to a little water, they eat. He had a little tobacco in a bag, but none of them drank [*i.e., smoked*] but when he listed. Some of them had their faces painted black, from the forehead to the chin, four or five fingers broad; others after other fashions, as they liked. They brought three or four skins, but we would not truck with them at all that day, but wished them to bring more, and we would truck for all, which they promised within a night or two, and would leave these behind them, though we were not willing they should, and they brought us all our tools again which were taken in the woods, in our men's absence. So because of the day we dismissed them so soon as we could. But Samoset, our first acquaintance, either was sick, or feigned himself so, and would not go with them, and stayed with us till Wednesday morning. The Sabbath day, when we sent them from us, we gave every one of them some trifles, especially the principal of them. We carried them along with our arms to the place where they left their bows and arrows, whereat they were amazed, and two of them began to slink away, but that the other called them. When they took their arrows, we bade them farewell, and they were glad, and so with many thanks given us they departed, with promise they would come again" (*Mourt's Relation*).

MONDAY, 29 MARCH [1620]/21

At anchorage

A fair day. The settlers digging and sowing seeds.

What was Massasoit thinking? It is inconceivable that the chief of a loose confederation of local villages and tribes, that would, several decades later, coalesce as the Wampanoag, did not know about Samoset's visit to Plymouth, or that Samoset came without Massasoit's approval. What most modern writers seem to be agreed on is that, when the Pilgrims arrived last November, the Indians were most startled by the fact that the settlers had women and children -- these would probably be the first European women and children that the Indians had ever seen. These new Englishmen also did not seem all that interested in trading, which had been the major preoccupation of all previous visitors -- although, to be fair, the Indians did make themselves very scarce for the first five months, making any trade impossible. All of the writers of the last century have also presented a constantly repeated catalogue of incidents that had taken place over the previous two decades, detailing the kidnapping of Indians by the Europeans, and the torture and killing of Europeans by the Indians. One of these incidents had occurred less than a year before the *Mayflower*'s arrival: the Nauset were "much incensed and provoked against the English," according to Bradford, and had tortured and killed three men the previous summer. When they saw the *Mayflower*, they assumed that retribution had arrived, and it is in this context that the "First Encounter" can be viewed: a "first strike" (or "anticipatory retaliation").

But the attack did not scare off the Pilgrims. The tribes then resorted to their shamans for an emergency curse: Bradford wrote that the settlers learned that the Indians had met for three days "in a horrid and devilish manner, to curse and execrate them [the settlers] with their conjurations, which assembly and service they held in a dark and dismal swamp." The Pilgrims were placed under the most fearsome curses imaginable -- three times -- but they were, unaccountably, still there. When an armed attack failed, and then witchcraft failed, Massasoit must have realised that his options were decreasing, one by one, and quickly. He was also being threatened by other larger, much more powerful tribes to his west and north. He did not need another enemy to his east, essentially surrounding him completely. The only way definitively to get rid of an enemy is to transform the enemy into a friend.

TUESDAY, 30 MARCH [1620]/21

At anchorage

A fine day. Digging and planting of gardens on shore. Those crew members who were sick are now on the mend.

There was another dynamic working in the Indians' plans: Squanto, the only surviving resident of the village which had, several years before, occupied the place where the Pilgrims were now constructing their plantation, but of which nothing remained. Kidnapped by Thomas Hunt and brought to Spain, he was almost sold into slavery before he was freed by Franciscan friars, who taught him the Catholic faith; he received baptism from them. I will pause while you contemplate that the ferocious anti-Catholics, who hated with a perfect hatred anything that even had a slight whiff of the Church of Rome, were ultimately saved by ... a *Catholic!* He was now dwelling at Pokanoket with Massasoit. The chief, however, did not trust Squanto, but his knowledge and connections were too valuable for Massasoit to ignore, and Squanto certainly made use of them all to get Massasoit's attention and bring him around to Squanto's way of thinking. He insisted that the worst thing that they could do would be to attack the settlers: they had not only cannons and guns, but they were the bringers of the plague, as well. Squanto began to insist that the Pilgrims could unleash the plague at will; this was by far the most fearsome weapon in their arsenal. And if Massasoit allied himself with the Pilgrims, then he would have access to this weapon as well, and he could unleash it (or get the Pilgrims to unleash it) on the relatively unscathed tribes of the Narragansett and the Massachusett Indians. Philbrick summarises: "It was a suggestion that played on Massasoit's worst fears. ... Reluctantly, Massasoit determined that he must 'make friendship' with the English. To do so, he must have an interpreter, and Squanto -- the only one fluent in both English and Massachusett, the language of Pokanoket -- assumed that he was the man for the job. Though he'd been swayed by Squanto's advice, Massasoit was loath to place his faith in the former captive, whom he regarded as a conniving cultural mongrel with dubious motives. So he first sent Samoset, a visiting sachem with only a rudimentary command of English, to the Pilgrim settlement. But now it was time for Massasoit to visit the English himself. He must turn to Squanto."[143]

WEDNESDAY, 31 MARCH [1620]/21

At anchorage

A fine warm day. Beginning to put ship in trim for return voyage. Bringing ballast on board.

The Pilgrims sent Samoset back to Pokanoket to see what was taking so long to arrange a meeting. He was given a hat, a pair of stockings and shoes, a shirt, and a piece of cloth to tie about his waist.

A general meeting of the settlers was held in the meeting house, to lay down laws and orders, and to confirm the military orders formerly proposed. The Pilgrims had tried to have this kind of a meeting twice before, and twice before it was broken off by the Indians appearing on the outskirts of the village. And today, as if on cue, it happened again. After the meeting had gone on for an hour or so, "two or three savages presented themselves, that made semblance of daring us, as we thought. So Captain Standish with another, with their muskets went over to them, with two of the master's mates that follow them without arms, having two muskets with them. They whetted and rubbed their arrows and strings, and made show of defiance, but when our men drew near them, they ran away; thus were we again interrupted by them."

It is almost as though the Indians had a mole in the Pilgrim number, who was able to signal them whenever the group was getting ready to gather. It is clear that the Indians had been watching the Pilgrims -- closely -- all winter, and they could have attacked at any point and probably obliterated the nascent colony. But they did not. The journalist Rebecca Fraser wrote, "The rapid depletion of settlers convinced Massasoit that they [*the Pilgrims*]

---

[143]Philbrick, *Mayflower*, 96

187

were not going to harm him and that some kind of treaty could be negotiated. In the past historians tended to believe the Indian populations were innocent dupes of the early English settlers. The development of ethnohistory has shown that the Indians had their own agendas to use powerful newcomers against other tribes." [144]

"This day with much ado we got our carpenter that had been long sick of the scurvy, to fit our shallop, to fetch all from aboard." They were finally removing all of their belongings from the *Mayflower*; the last group of Pilgrims were removed from the ship, and the whole company was now on shore.

---

[144] *The Mayflower, 68-69*

APRIL 1621

At anchorage

A very fair, warm day. At work on ship getting ready for sea, bringing ballast aboard. The last of the colonists on board the ship went ashore to remain to-day. *Mourt's Relation* gives a long description of the day's events, which I will attach here with a few comments:

"Another general meeting of the settlers was called for noon today. They had not even been an hour together when ... and you could see this coming by now, couldn't you? ... Samoset the Indian came again with "Tisquantum [Squanto], the only native of Patuxet, where we now inhabit, who was one of the twenty captives that by [Captain Thomas] Hunt were carried away, and had been in England, and dwelt in Cornhill [London] with Master John Slanie, a merchant, and could speak a little English, with three others, and they brought with them some few skins to truck, and some red herrings newly taken and dried, but not salted ... [They] signified that their great Sagamore, Masasoyt, was hard by, with Quadequina his brother, and all their men. They could not well express in English what they would, but after an hour the king came to the top of a hill over against us, and had in his train sixty men, that we could well behold them and they us. We were not willing to send our governor to them, and they unwilling to come to us, so Tisquantum went again unto him, who brought word that we should send one to parley with him, which we did, which was Edward Winslow, to know his mind, and to signify the mind and will of our governor, which was to have trading and peace with him. We sent to the king a pair of knives, and a copper chain with a jewel at it. To Quadequina we sent likewise a knife and a jewel to hang in his ear, and withal a pot of strong water, a good quantity of biscuit, and some butter, which were all willingly accepted." Edward Winslow gives us here another proof of his self-sacrifice and devotion to his work, and that splendid intrepidity which characterized his whole career. At this most critical moment, the fate of the little colony trembling in the balance, when there was evident fear of treachery and surprise on the part of both the English and the Indians; though his wife lay at the point of death (which came two days later); he went forward

189

alone, his life in his hands, to meet the great sachem surrounded by his whole tribe, as the calm, adroit diplomat, upon whom all must depend; and as the fearless hostage, to put himself in pawn to the chief.

Winslow "made a speech unto him, that King James saluted him with words of love and peace, and did accept of him as his friend and ally, and that our governor desired to see him and to truck with him, and to confirm a peace with him, as his next neighbor. He liked well of the speech and heard it attentively, though the interpreters did not well express it. After he had eaten and drunk himself, and given the rest to his company, he looked upon our messenger's sword and armor which he had on, with intimation of his desire to buy it, but on the other side, our messenger showed his unwillingness to part with it. In the end he left him in the custody of Quadequina his brother, and came over the brook, and some twenty men following him, leaving all their bows and arrows behind them. We kept six or seven as hostages for our messenger. Captain Standish and Master Williamson met the king at the brook, with half a dozen musketeers." It would seem from the frequent mention of the presence of some of the ship's company, Master Jones, the "Masters-mates," and now Williamson, the "ship's-merchant," that the *Mayflower* was daily well represented in the little settlement on shore. Williamson's presence on this occasion is perhaps easily accounted for: every other meeting with the Indians had been unexpected, the present one was anticipated, and somewhat eagerly, for almost everything depended on its successful outcome. By this time Standish had probably become aware that Tisquantum's command of English was very limited, and he desired all the aid the ship's interpreter could give. The guard of six was probably made small to leave the body of the colonists as strong a reserve force as possible to meet any surprise attack on the part of the Indians. The guard seems to have advanced to the hill ("Strawberry" or later "Watson's") to meet the sachem, instead of only to "the brook."

"They saluted him and he them, so one going over, the one on the one side, and the other on the other, conducted him to a house then in building, where we placed a green rug and three or four cushions. Then instantly came our governor with drum and trumpet after him, and some few musketeers. After salutations, our governor kissing his hand, the king kissed him, and so they sat

190

down. The governor called for some strong water, and drunk to him, and he drunk a great draught that made him sweat all the while after; he called for a little fresh meat, which the king did eat willingly, and did give his followers. Then they treated of peace" -- more on that tomorrow -- "all the while he sat by the governor he trembled for fear. In his person he is a very lusty man, in his best years, an able body, grave of countenance, and spare of speech. In his attire little or nothing differing from the rest of his followers, only in a great chain of white bone beads about his neck, and at it being his neck hangs a little bag of tobacco, which he drank and gave us to drink; his face was painted with a sad red like murry, and oiled both head and face, that he looked greasily. All his followers likewise, were in their faces, in part or in whole painted, some black, some red, some yellow, and some white, some with crosses, and other antic works; some had skins on them, and some naked, all strong, tall, all men in appearance. So after all was done, the governor conducted him to the brook, and there they embraced each other and he departed; we diligently keeping our hostages, we expected our messenger's coming, but anon, word was brought us that Quadequina was coming, and our messenger was stayed till his return, who presently came and a troop with him, so likewise we entertained him, and conveyed him to the place prepared. He was very fearful of our pieces, and made signs of dislike, that they should be carried away, whereupon commandment was given they should be laid away. He was a very proper tall young man, of a very modest and seemly countenance, and he did kindly like of our entertainment, so we conveyed him likewise as we did the king, but divers of their people stayed still. When he was returned, then they dismissed our messenger. Two of his people would have stayed all night, but we would not suffer it. One thing I forgot, the king had in his bosom, hanging in a string, a great long knife; he marveled much at our trumpet, and some of his men would sound it as well as they could. Samoset and Tisquantum, they stayed all night with us, and the king and all his men lay all night in the woods, not above half an English mile from us, and all their wives and women with them. They said that within eight or nine days they would come and set corn on the other side of the brook, and dwell there all summer, which is hard by us. That night we kept good watch, but there was no appearance of danger." Quite a day.

191

FRIDAY, 2 APRIL [1620]/21

At anchor

A fair day. Some of the ship's company went on shore. Making ready for sea, getting ballast, wood, and water from the shore, etc.

Yesterday, it was noted, Massasoit "drank a great draught" of brandy and broke out in a sweat. The sweat may not have been only because of the alcohol. He didn't say all that much, but it was clear not only to Bradford but also to others that Massasoit was trembling with fear. He was every bit as afraid of the Pilgrims as they were of him. Yet he was able to agree to a "treaty" of sorts, which held, remarkably (under the circumstances), for more than half a century: "1. That neither he nor any of his should injure or do hurt to any of our people.

2. And if any of his did hurt to any of ours, he should send the offender, that we might punish him.

3. That if any of our tools were taken away when our people are at work, he should cause them to be restored, and if ours did any harm to any of his, we would do the likewise to them.

4. If any did unjustly war against him, we would aid him; if any did war against us, he should aid us.

5. He should send to his neighbor confederates, to certify them of this, that they might not wrong us, but might be likewise comprised in the conditions of peace.

6. That when their men came to us, they should leave their bows and arrows behind them, as we should do our pieces when we came to them.

Lastly, that doing thus, King James would esteem of him as his friend and ally." The agreement had a definite downside for the English, however, because the Pokanoket were at war with the Narragansett, and Massasoit was definitely counting on the support of his new friends, who might very soon be dragged into a war between the two tribes, particularly if Massasoit decided to take advantage of the powerful new weaponry to take out the Narragansett in a decisive first strike.

This morning "divers of their people came over to us, hoping to get some victuals as we imagined; some of them told us the king would have some of us come see him. Captain Standish and Isaac Allerton went venturously, who were welcomed of him after their manner: he gave them three or four ground-nuts, and some tobacco." They came back safely; this was one of several good signs that the peace agreement was working. "We cannot yet conceive but that he is willing to have peace with us, for they have seen our people sometimes alone two or three in the woods at work and fowling, when as they offered them no harm as they might easily have done, and especially because he hath a potent adversary the Narragansets, that are at war with him, against whom he thinks we may be some strength to him, for our pieces are terrible unto them. This morning they stayed till ten or eleven of the clock, and our governor bid them send the king's kettle, and filled it full of peas, which pleased them well, and so they went their way."

The settlers held a meeting -- *finally* without being interrupted by Indians appearing -- and concluded both military orders and some laws, and chose as Governor, for the coming year, John Carver, who had been elected Governor in Plymouth (England) on the ship last August, and was confirmed in that office last November.

SATURDAY, 3 APRIL [1620]/21

At anchorage

The ship's company busy with preparations for the return voyage, bringing ballast, wood, and water from the shore, etc., the ship having no lading for the return.

Many still sick; more on the ship than on shore. This day Elizabeth (Barker) Winslow, wife of Edward Winslow, died on shore. They had been married not quite three years. Edward Winslow was still with the Indians as a hostage.

Only Samoset and Squanto spent the night; Massasoit and his people (including their wives and children) camped about half a mile away. The settlers kept watch all night, but the woods were silent.

SUNDAY, 4 APRIL 1621

At anchor in Plymouth harbour

HAPPY NEW YEAR!

The first day of the new year 1621 -- the calendar changed year on the Feast of the Annunciation, also known as Lady Day ("the Annunciation of the Lord to the Blessed Virgin Mary" occurring on 25 March), since it was the anniversary of the Incarnation. New Year's Day only changed to 1 January in

English speaking territories in 1752. 25 March in the Julian Calendar of 1621 would be 4 April in the Gregorian Calendar that we use.

In the ecclesiastical calendar of the Book of Common Prayer, this would have been the Sunday Before Easter -- from what I can tell from very complicated programs now online, Easter in 1621 was on 11 April (n.s.) or 1 April (o.s.).

The fifteenth Sunday in this port. Many of the crew dead and some still sick, but the sickness and mortality lessening: there were now days on which no one died. There was now enough housing for everyone to sleep indoors, even though some houses were not yet complete. The weather was warmer.

MONDAY, 5 APRIL 1621

At anchor

Bringing ballast from shore and getting ship in trim.

At some point not long after Carver was re-elected Governor and Standish was named commander of the military force, John Billington got into the first of a rapidly degenerating series of scrapes. He engaged in some kind of argument with Standish; Standish had called him to stand his turn at watch, a duty required of all men and especially important at this time when the Pilgrims were in such dire straits. Billington was charged "before the whole company for his contempt of the Captain's lawfull command with opprobrious speeches." This was while people were still suffering and dying around the settlement, and this is the first time since the *Mayflower* had arrived at Provincetown harbour that such an altercation had burst out into the open. The colony had never had to deal with such open disagreement before; apparently John Carver stepped in, as Governor, and called together a group of settlers to enquire into the circumstances and restore order. Billington was sentenced "to have his neck and heels tied together" in a public display of humiliation. Billington, "humbling himself and craving pardon," was eventually "forgiven," whether at the impassioned requests of his family or with his own promise of better behaviour. It was specifically recorded that this was a "first offense" -- both for Billington and for the new colony; John Billington was thus the first person to commit a crime in New England. Tensions were rising with the temperatures.

TUESDAY, 6 APRIL 1621

At anchorage

Getting ballast, overhauling rigging, getting wood, water, etc., from shore.

Christopher Jones had certainly not intended to spend the winter in New England: the *Mayflower*, of which he was part owner, had left England too late in the year, and then the settlers took too long to find a place to settle, and then they took too long to build a place to live and move their goods to shore, and then most of his crew got sick. Those who did not die were too sick to sail back across the ocean in the winter. If the Pilgrims had arrived when they were originally supposed to, they would have been able to grow at least a little produce to send back, along with any other commodities that they could have sent back for sale in England (such as furs) to pay back the Adventurers. The winter was cold, and no work was possible except for what was needed for immediate, hand-to-mouth necessities. Jones could have waited until the summer, and perhaps have brought back some things, but he clearly was not all that optimistic about what could be produced. The lack of cargo meant that the ship lacked ballast; it was probably loaded with stones from the beach, but stone was not really something of which England was in need. And they had run out of beer, so the crew would have to drink water. All the way back.

WEDNESDAY, 7 APRIL 1621

At anchorage

The Pilgrims really did not have a whole lot to show for the last six months. Forty-five dead out of one hundred and two, only a handful of buildings up -- and most of them were not finished, not a single fur-bearing animal trapped, and precisely one (1) single fish caught, and that was found on the shore so you can't really count it as "caught," but it more or less threw itself at them. With the *Speedwell* back in England, it was impossible to do any serious fishing. They needed fish nets, hooks, as well as gun powder and other supplies that could not be made on site. If the *Mayflower* left soon (and it showed all signs of doing so), it might be able to make it back quickly, and the Adventurers could stock up another ship with supplies and send it back, so that it might arrive by the beginning of September, if they were lucky. But if the

Adventurers were angry that there was no return -- absolutely none -- on their investment, it was impossible to tell when, or if, anything might come.

THURSDAY, 8 APRIL 1621

At anchorage

Getting in stores and ballast.

Master Jones offered to take back any of the colonists who wished to return to England, but none desired to go. There are a number of ways of interpreting this, and it was undoubtedly a combination rather than one single reason: a basic optimism may have led them to believe that the worst was over; a strong commitment to the project may have been in evidence; a desire to stay with the others, with whom they had suffered so much; or perhaps they really had no place to which they could return. Each passenger who stayed probably had a unique reason, but the only ones who left any written discussion of the colony's early history are Edward Winslow and William Bradford, and they quite consciously framed their work for a widespread public consideration. Famously, John Alden, who had been the ship's cooper, decided to remain and not to go back to England.

This was home now.

FRIDAY, 9 APRIL 1621

At anchorage

Hastening all preparations for sailing. Getting ballast, etc. Water butts filled.

In the past month, according to Bradford's calculations (as reported in Prince's *Annals*), the Pilgrims lost thirteen by death; this makes in total half of their number since November. With the rising temperatures and increasing sunshine, people are beginning to recover.

SATURDAY, 10 APRIL 1621

At anchorage

Setting up rigging, bending light sails; getting ballast and wood from the beach and island.

SUNDAY, 11 APRIL 1621

At anchor in Plymouth harbour

The sixteenth Sunday the ship has lain at anchor here, and the last, being nearly ready to sail. Most of the crew ashore on liberty. In the sixteen weeks the ship has lain here, half of her crew (but none of her officers) have died, and a few are still weak. Among the petty officers who have died have been the master gunner, boatswain, and three quartermasters, beside the cook, and more than a third of the sailors. An exceptionally bad voyage for the owner, Adventurers, ship, and crew. Bradford and *Mourt's Relation* mention few (or none) of the crew by name, but the toll above can be calculated from passing references and descriptions in those works. Given the audience of these two works, and the intention to describe God's Providence over the settlers in the early days of the colony, this is not all that surprising.

MONDAY, 12 APRIL 1621

Still at anchor, but making last preparations for voyage

Ship's officers made farewells on shore. Governor Carver copied out, and Giles Heale and Christopher Jones witnessed, William Mullins' will, to go to England.

TUESDAY, 13 APRIL 1621

Still at anchorage, but (nearly) ready to sail with a fair wind

Said goodbyes to Governor Carver and company. Master Williamson, the ship's merchant [purser], appointed by William Mullins an overseer of his will, takes a copy to England for probate, with many letters, keepsakes, and other communications to Adventurers and friends. Very little lading, chiefly skins and roots: the Pilgrims had hoped to load the *Mayflower* up with goods that could be sold in England. For the investment of thousands of pounds, all the Adventurers received in return was "a pile of ballast stones and a few native artifacts."[145] There was a distinct possibility that they might withdraw further financial support.

WEDNESDAY, 14 APRIL 1621

Still at anchor in Plymouth harbour

Sails loosened and all ready for departure except for the Governor's letters. Last visits of shore people to the ship. The *Mayflower* will sail with the morning tide, if the wind serves; it has been one hundred and ten days in this harbour.

---

[145] Philbrick, *Mayflower*, 103

THURSDAY, 15 APRIL 1621

Got anchors, and with fair wind got underway at full tide

Many wait on the shore to bid goodbye. *Mayflower* set colours and gave the Pilgrims a parting salute with the ensign and ordnance. Cleared the harbour without hindrance, and laid a general course ESE for England with a fine wind. Took departure from Cape Cod early in the day, shook off the land and got ship to rights before night. All sails set, with the ship logging her best.

And so the *Mayflower* began her speedy, uneventful homeward run, of only thirty-one days (!), arriving in England on 6/16 May 1621, having been absent on her "round-trip voyage" from her sailing port two hundred and ninety-six days.

FRIDAY, 16 APRIL 1621

Mort's Relation

Some brief comments on two of the sources for the voyage and the first year in New England: today, *Mourt's Relation*, and tomorrow Bradford's various writings.

The booklet *Mourt's Relation* (full title: *A Relation or Journal of the Beginning and Proceedings of the English Plantation Settled at Plimoth in New England*) was written primarily by Edward Winslow, although William Bradford appears to have written most of the first section: they are referred to in the third person throughout, and Bradford is sometimes cited as "one of the travellers." It was written between November 1620 and November 1621 and describes in detail what happened from the landing of the Pilgrims on Cape Cod in Provincetown Harbour through their explorations and eventual settlement in Plymouth. After the departure of the *Mayflower*, the book contains several separate sections on the settlers' relations with the surrounding Indian tribes, up to what is commonly called the first Thanksgiving and the arrival of the ship *Fortune* in November 1621.

Mourt's Relation was first published and sold by John Bellamy in London in 1622. The text probably was brought back to England on the *Fortune*, and survived the ransacking of that ship by French pirates on the way back to England. It was attributed early on to "George Morton, sometimes called George Mourt" (hence the name of the work). Morton, who had moved to Leyden with the congregation, stayed behind when the first settlers left for America. He continued to coordinate their business affairs in Europe and London, presumably arranging for the 1622 publication. In 1623 Morton himself emigrated on the *Anne* to Plymouth Colony with his wife Juliana Carpenter and her sister, Alice Southworth, who was to become William Bradford's second wife: Morton died soon afterward. The original booklet appeared to have been lost or forgotten by the eighteenth century. A copy was rediscovered in Philadelphia in 1820, with the first full reprinting in 1841. In a footnote, editor Alexander Young in his *Chronicles of the Pilgrim Fathers* (1841) was the first person to identify the description of a 1621 feast as "the first Thanksgiving." In 1921, a copy sold at auction for $3,800 (adjusted for inflation, that is about $510,000 now).

From December 1645 until his death, Morton's son Nathaniel was annually elected Secretary of the Plymouth Colony, and most of the colony records are in his handwriting. His careful maintenance of the records enabled him to compile *New England's Memoriall*, considered the first comprehensive history of the colony, published at Cambridge (Massachusetts) in 1669 -- this is widely considered the first book of history published in the United States. This work draws both from *Mourt's Relation* and from the writings of Nathaniel Morton's uncle, William Bradford. The passage in the *New England Memoriall* is the most frequently quoted description of the First Thanksgiving; Nathaniel Morton's *Memoriall* was also the first to record in 1669 the list of signers of the Mayflower Compact almost fifty years after it was written (the original has been lost, but it is unclear when that happened).

SATURDAY, 17 APRIL 1621

Bradford's Books (part one)

Alongside *Mourt's Relation* (see yesterday) are Bradford's books.

The most famous is his journal *Of Plimmoth Plantation* (on the first page, where Bradford gives the title, there is a small macron over the "m" which usually represents the doubling of the letter); the journal was written between 1630 and 1651 and describes the story of the Pilgrims from 1608, when they settled in Holland, through the 1620 *Mayflower* voyage, until 1647. The book ends with a list of *Mayflower* passengers (and what happened to them) written in 1651. It is in two parts; the first part contains the description of the preparations and the voyage, and the second part (much darker) describes the early history of the colony and begins in 1620 with the Mayflower Compact (although without the list of signers). Bradford apparently never made an effort to publish the manuscript during his lifetime, but he did intend it to be preserved and read by others. It is not a "diary" in the conventional sense, and appears to be in great part evangelistic: the first part showing how God led the Pilgrims to the New World, and the second showing their increasing faithlessness. While numerous people have wondered why Bradford did not include more personal details or reflections, particularly about the death of his wife, it is clear that this work, mostly written in the third person, was intended as a historical and theological record of the colony and its foundations rather than a description of the inner life of any particular individual.

Bradford's original manuscript was left in the tower of the Old South Meeting House in Boston during the Revolutionary War. British troops occupied the church during the war, and the manuscript disappeared and remained lost for the next century. Some scholars noted that Samuel Wilberforce quoted Bradford's work in *A History of the Protestant Episcopal Church in America* in 1844, and the missing manuscript was finally discovered in the Bishop of London's library at Fulham Palace; it was brought back into print in 1856. Americans made many formal proposals that the manuscript should be returned to New England, but to no avail. Massachusetts Senator George Frisbie Hoar started an initiative in 1897, supported by the Pilgrim Society, the American Antiquarian Society, and the New England Society of New York. Frederick Temple, then Bishop of London, learned of the importance of the book, and thought that it should be returned to America. But it was being held by the Church of England and the Archbishop of Canterbury needed to approve such a move—the Archbishop was the same Frederick Temple by the time that Hoar's request reached England. The bishop's Consistorial and Episcopal Court of London observed that nobody could say for certain exactly how the book arrived in London, but he argued that the marriage and birth registry which it contained should have been deposited with the Church in the first place, and thus the book was a church document and the Diocese of London had proper control of it. The court, however, observed that the Diocese of London was not the proper repository for that information at the time when the Thirteen Colonies declared independence in 1776. So the bishop's court ordered that a photographic copy of the records be made for the diocesan archives, and that the original be delivered to the Governor of Massachusetts.

The Bradford journal was presented to the Governor of the Commonwealth of Massachusetts during a joint session of the legislature on 26 May 1897. It is on deposit in the State Library of Massachusetts in the State House in Boston. In June 1897, the state legislature ordered publication of the history with copies of the documents associated with the return. In 1912, the Massachusetts Historical Society published a final authorized version of the text.

William Bradford's manuscript journal is a vellum-bound volume measuring 11½ by 7¾ inches. There are 270 pages numbered (sometimes inaccurately) by Bradford. The ink is slightly faded and has turned brown with age, but it is still completely legible. The pages are somewhat foxed, but otherwise the 400 year-old document is in remarkably good condition. Page 243 is missing, with a note from Prence that it was missing when he got the document; the front pages of the bound manuscript contain three documents describing how the book was transferred to the Commonwealth of Massachusetts, and a poem (of unknown authorship) about Alice (Carpenter) (Southworth) Bradford, William Bradford's second wife, written after William's death. A facsimile of the original manuscript was produced by the State Library of Massachusetts and Plimoth Plantation last year, and numerous transcriptions and editions (some with modernised spelling) have been produced in the last hundred years.

SUNDAY, 18 APRIL 1621

Bradford's Books (part two)

Although *Of Plimmoth Plantation* has come down to us (more or less) intact, and with *Mort's Relation* it is one of the two contemporary works that describe the early history of the colony in narrative fashion, there are two other works by Bradford which were used by other writers in fashioning their accounts, but which have either completely or in part been lost:

(a) The Rev. Thomas Prince assembled his *Chronological History of New England* (1736: see my entries for 8 and 10 February) relying on Bradford's "Pocket Book," in which Bradford recorded births, deaths, marriages, and a variety of other legal transactions (such as deeds). Prince used it extensively as a source, but did not copy it completely into his text: it is thanks to that work that we know the few actual death dates of Pilgrims who died in the first winter. This work has been lost.

(b) Bradford also had a "book of letters" of some 400 pages. These were letters to and from Bradford, who made his own annotations on them; this cache was an invaluable source of early colonial history: here men other than Bradford speak in their own words. This book of letters also went missing, but in 1793, about two decades after *Of Plimmoth Plantation* was lost, a "fragment" of the letter book of about fifty pages (perhaps 15% of the whole) was discovered in a Nova Scotia grocer's shop (!). The letters in this find are principally from 1624 to 1630, with a particularly full group from 1627. This fragment was published in 1794, one of the first publications of the new Massachusetts Historical Society, and was republished in 1905 in the *Mayflower Descendant*.[146] While the whereabouts of Bradford's *Of Plimmoth Plantation* has been closely observed since its rediscovery almost two centuries ago, I have been unable to find where Bradford's fragmentary cache of letters is now, which is odd, given their value. Bowman stated, "Unfortunately the fragment of the original manuscript rescued by Mr Clarke cannot now be found."[147]

The fate of these two sources raises some questions about how writings come down to us. While vital records that belong to towns are (usually) preserved in the town archives, what happened to the archives of the Colony of New Plymouth when that colony ceased to exist in 1691? The notes from the State Library of Massachusetts facsimile of *Of Plimoth Plantation* say that this work, along with the pocket book and letter collection, was handed down in the Bradford family (which begs the question of how they wound up in the tower of the Old South Church). Where, for example, is the colony's seal? Nathaniel Shurtleff and David Pulsifer published many of the records of the colony in twelve volumes (*Records of the colony of New Plymouth, in New England.* Boston: Press of W. White, 1855-61), but (apparently) less than half of their work was published. The publication was interrupted

---

[146] Available in *The Mayflower Reader*, 299-362; in 2001, another reprint was made by Applewood Press, with a tendentious and rather poor introduction by John C. Kemp

[147] *Mayflower Reader*, 299

by the War Between the States, leaving eleven volumes unpublished. Jeremy Bangs has done substantial work on several volumes, as well, both in his *Indian Deeds* (2008) and in *Records of the Colony of New Plymouth: deeds, &c. vol. II, 1651-1663* (2016) and *Records of the Colony of New Plymouth: deeds, &c. vol. III, 1664-1671* (2017). Occasional comments on the internet have suggested that neither the originals of the remaining documents nor Shurtleff and Pulsifer's proposed edition of the rest now remain intact.

MONDAY, 19 APRIL 1621

Planting

After this, Bradford's journal records, "we planted 20 Acres of Indian Corn wherein Squanto is a great Help; showing us how to set, fish, dress & tend it, of which we have a good Increase: we likewise sow 6 Acres of Barley and Pease; our Barley indifferent Good, but our Pease parched up with the Sun."

Modern (hybrid) corn sprouts only when the ground reaches a consistent 50 degrees, which may not happen in New England until the middle of May; "Indian corn" (maize) may have sprouted at cooler temperatures, but seed planted too soon will rot. For fields in bad soil, as Squanto explained, the planting of corn began with catching lots of fish for use as fertiliser. Here, again, the Pilgrims were up against a problem with their lack of equipment: they were complete failures as fishermen, and had neither a boat to fish in nor hooks to catch fish. But there was a better way ...

TUESDAY, 20 APRIL 1621

Fishing

It started the day after the *Mayflower* left: the fish came up Town Brook in enormous numbers, so quickly and with such energy that the dam built to corral them was breached. They leaped over it, sometimes tumbling on to the dry land. These were not cod, which the settlers would have needed hooks to catch, but alewives, perfect for fertiliser. The Pilgrims simply had to wade out into the brook, and grab as many as they could with their hands. Cousins to the herring and the shad, alewife were also good to eat, and were so fatty that they could be fried without grease. They could also be preserved by smoking.

Squanto showed them how to arrange the fish (three

alewives in each mound of corn, with their heads toward the centre); in the centre of the mound, a few kernels of corn or beans. The soil could be banked up against the stalk as it grew up; the same mound could be used the following year, even without putting in new fish.

WEDNESDAY, 21 APRIL 1621

Death of Governor Carver

Bradford continued, "While we are busy about our Seed, our Governor, Mr. Carver comes out of the Field very Sick, complains greatly of his Head, within a few Hours his Senses fail, so as He speaks no more, and in a few Days after Dies, to our great Lamentation and Heaviness. His Care and Pains were so great for the common Good, as therewith 'tis tho't He oppressed Himself and shortned his Days: of whose Loss we cannot sufficiently complain: and His Wife deceases about 5 or 6 Weeks after." Carver's reputation among the settlers was high, and he certainly sacrificed much for the success of the colony. Daniel Wilson, in his 1849 work *The Pilgrim Fathers*, wrote, "Of his integrity and disinterested zeal, the colony had received abundant proof. As he had borne so large a share in the cost of the plantation, and had taken so prominent a part in all the arrangements needful for carrying it into effect, the new settlers could not fail to have unbounded confidence in his honest zeal for the successful carrying out of their scheme of colonization, and therefore it is probable that the choice fell upon him as first Governor of New Plymouth, almost as a matter of course."[148]

THURSDAY, 22 APRIL 1621

Burial with Honours

Given John Carver's position, "He was buried in the best manner they could, with some volleys of shot by all that bore arms." The high estimation of Carver was not shared by all, however. When the *Fortune* arrived in November, it contained a number of angry letters from frustrated London investors -- directed at John Carver, who had been dead for six months by that time -- for what they perceived to be his mismanagement of the colony. Instead of furs, lumber, and fish, the investors' return was a virtually empty ship (a lot of ballast stones and some Indian

---

[148] Stowell and Wilson, *Puritans and Pilgrim Fathers*, 453.

artefacts). The company could not survive (or even resupply the colonists) without some profits from the New World.

But one of the changes that might be missed is the very funeral itself. Instead of burying their dead in the middle of the night for fear that the Indians might learn of their depleted numbers, the Pilgrims now buried in broad daylight with full honours. That they could do so was at least in part a tribute to Carver's skill in negotiation with the neighbouring tribe.

In Nathaniel Morton's *New England Memoriall* (1669), the following brief but most honourable tribute to Carver's memory occurs: "I may not omit to take notice of the sad loss the church and this infant commonwealth sustained by the death of Mr. John Carver, who was one of the deacons of the church in Leyden, but now had been and was their first Governor. This worthy gentleman was one of singular piety, and rare for humility, which appeared, as otherwise, so by his great condescendency, when as this miserable people were in great sickness. He shunned not to do very mean services for them, yea, the meanest of them. He bare a share likewise of their labour in his own person, according as their great necessity required. Who being one also of a considerable estate, spent the main part of it in this enterprise, and from first to last approved himself not only as their agent in the first transacting of things, but also all along to the period of his life, to be a pious, faithful, and very beneficial instrument. He deceased in the month of April in the year 1621, and is now reaping the fruit of his labour with the Lord."

FRIDAY, 23 APRIL 1621

Election of William Bradford as Governor

"Soon after [the death of John Carver], we chuse Mr. William Bradford our Governor, and Mr. Isaac Allerton his Assistant: who are by renewed Elections continued together sundry Years." The election of Isaac Allerton as Bradford's assistant is usually attributed to the fact that Bradford was "not recovered of his illness, in which he had been near the point of death." Bradford was re-elected as Governor of the Plymouth Colony **thirty one times** (!): every year until his death in 1657, with only five exceptions (1633-1634, 1636, 1638, and 1644). Caleb Johnson aptly points out that "As governor, Bradford's biography from this point on is, in a sense, a history of

Plymouth."[149] Bradford had left his son in Holland, and lost his wife in Provincetown Harbour, and now, as the ultimate decision maker in the Colony, must have felt very much alone.

SATURDAY, 24 APRIL 1621

Wolves

The aroma of rotting fish, used as fertilizer, would draw the wolves from the woods. If the fields were not guarded, day and night, the wolves would come to dig up the fish, and would scatter the seed that had been planted and ruin the harvest. The settlers really did not have enough manpower to spare someone to keep watch for two weeks (long enough to enable the fish to disintegrate) over the cornfields, particularly given that there were more than twenty acres of fields, but they did their best. Until their two dogs got in to the mounds. The Pilgrims responded by hobbling the dogs (tethering their legs to prevent them from straying). That meant that all they had to look out for was racoons, deer, rabbits, crow, and woodchucks, and keep this up for about three months, while weeding the fields often, and hope that it rained regularly.

SUNDAY, 25 APRIL 1621

Bradford's Books (part three)

Although William Brewster may have had the largest private library in the Plymouth Colony, approaching 400 volumes, William Bradford's inventory at his death was not inconsiderable.[150] The breadth of subjects is remarkable: in addition to theological works (Calvin's homilies on Acts, Luther's treatise on Galatians, Ainsworth's annotations on the Pentateuch) there were books on "physick", several polemical works against the Church of England and the Church of Rome, but also several patristic works. The books were in English, Latin, Dutch, and French (the French book, which is thought to have previously belonged to Myles Standish, is on "manners"). Recently, special attention has been paid to the Hebrew exercises Bradford included in the same manuscript as his journal *Of Plimmoth Plantation*. These eight pages are a rudimentary list of words, rather than a full scale elementary language course; a modern commentary has asked,

---

[149] Johnson, *Mayflower Passengers*, 83
[150] See Bangs, *Plymouth Private Libraries*, n. 87 [pp. 216-231]

"Why exactly Bradford selected the words he did (and not others) is hard to know. ... Since perhaps as early as Cotton Mather's *Magnalia*, there has been a tendency among scholars to characterize William Bradford's familiarity with Hebrew as greater than it actually was."[151] While the lists are filled with errors, it certainly bespeaks an inquisitive and probing mind, seeking to search the Word of God in its original idiom.

MONDAY, 26 APRIL 1621
Eels: Not for the squeamish

Squanto taught the Pilgrims to fertilise their crops with herring and alewife, but also showed them how to fish for eels. At this time of the year, the eels lay dormant in the mud; Squanto would wade out into the cold water of the nearby tidal creek (now named, aptly enough, "Eel River," near Plimoth Plantation). He would then use his feet to "trod them out." The first time he tried this "with his hands without any other instrument," he returned with so many eels that he could barely lift them. That night the Pilgrims said they were "fat and sweet." Timing is everything here: the sweet, fat eels swim upstream to spawn; on the return journey to the sea, they are bitter and thin.

TUESDAY, 27 APRIL 1621
Bradford's books (fourth and final part)

Although I mentioned the peregrinations of Bradford's journal over a week ago, I have not spoken of the work itself beyond giving lengthy quotations in previous posts. Bradford recorded the events of the first thirty years of the Plymouth Colony in a work that has been hailed as the first work of American literature. In a real sense, however, those phrases require heavy qualification.

Bradford began the work with the Pilgrims' departure for Holland in 1608, and ended the first half with the arrival in New England. The first part thus predates the foundation of the colony, and is the story of triumph over overwhelming odds -- political, cultural, and natural. It is also surprisingly upbeat and thankful: far more than simply a record of events, this is certainly a work of faith.

The second part, which begins with the Mayflower

---

[151] Eric Reymond "William Bradford's 'Some Hebrew Words Englished'," in *Of Plimoth Plantation - 400*, 552, 582, 588

Compact and ends with a list of the original settlers, what has become of them, and their increasings, goes to 1647 (with the list of settlers added in 1651), and it is markedly different. Bradford, who maintained a confident disposition despite his wife's death in Provincetown harbour in 1620, paints a dark picture indeed of the Plymouth Colony's fall from its original ideal, a long, long series of compromises and subservience to forces that were beyond the colony's control. I am always touched by Bradford's words in chapter 33: "And thus was this poor church left, like an ancient mother, grown old, and forsaken of her children, (though not in their affections,) yet in regard of their bodily presence and personal helpfulness. Her ancient members being most of them worn away by death; and these of later time being like children translated into other families, and she like a widow left only to trust in God [1 Tim 5.5]. Thus she that had made many rich became herself poor [2 Cor 6.10]."

There are numerous editions of this work available, and I find Samuel Eliot Morison's 1952 edition to be the most accessible to modern readers: the spelling and punctuation are modernised (and, 400 years later, that is important), the abbreviations are expanded, and the notes are few, necessary, and judicious. Copies published before that time either have no or few notes, or give only selections of the whole work. Copies published since are typically revisions of Morison's work. It is still readily available, having been through more than twenty printings.

It would take more time and space than I have to critique fully the much trumpeted "400th anniversary edition" published last year. It is a woefully inadequate display of 21st century politics, and while parts of the essays are useful presentations of the sixteenth and seventeenth century religious context, far too much of it is a heavy handed rewriting of Bradford's story. It tells us quite a bit about the writers and their ideas about what Bradford *should* have said, and precious little about Bradford, but that was undoubtedly its purpose. Pillorying the Pilgrims in the introductory essays, the work cries out for balance; the footnotes are helpful, but long and rambling. There are also more errors than an early Mets game: p. 202 n. 4 states "This was the marriage of Edward Winslow to Susannah White, whose husband had died in February 1621. Her daughter was Peregrine White." As I am sure the readers of this post will by now realise, Peregrine White was *nobody's* daughter; he was the *son* of William and Susannah (Jackson) White.

WEDNESDAY, 28 APRIL 1621

When is a Puritan not a Puritan?

When I was in graduate school, doing research on the English Reformation, one of my teachers said, "You know, you are going to have to go to England and continue this research: they actually still fight about this stuff there." I am nonetheless regularly surprised by the vehemence with which people (usually Americans) contend -- sometimes without, sometimes with threats and force -- that Puritans and Separatists are mutually exclusive. They usually know one, and *only* one, thing about each group: that one thing is normally membership in the Church of England -- the Puritans accepted membership in the Church of England, so the story goes, and the Separatists rejected it. That is, however, a distinction without a difference.

Andrew Cambers, in his 2011 study on *Godly Reading: Print, Manuscript and Puritanism in England, 1580-1720*, came up with this as a definition of Puritanism: "This book defines Puritanism as a way of characterising that strand of reformed Protestantism which is best known for its expression of dissatisfaction with the prevailing theological and ecclesiological state of the English church and for desiring its reform in line with the precepts of Calvinist theology. It argues that this desire for reform was rooted in a series of cultural practises which were used by the godly to deliberately set themselves apart from the majority of the population and to confirm them in their status as a persecuted minority."[152] This definition has the virtue of picking out doctrine (Calvinism), church government (arguments against episcopacy), and "cultural practises" (a strong desire for sermons, which included gadding after the sermons of preachers in other parishes; the refusal of some ministers to wear the surplice; taking communion standing; and so on) as signs of puritanism, even if all of them were not present in any one person at a given time. Unlike "puritan," an opprobrious term created by opponents, "godly" was a designation used by the godly themselves. This usage derived in part from the feeling that those so described could recognise one another just by their behaviour. So the Puritans did

---

[152] Cambers, *Godly Reading*, 13.

not really call themselves "Puritan."

As Robert Charles Anderson convincingly points out in *Puritan Pedigrees*, "Puritanism" was something of a spectrum: on the one end, there was the conforming Puritan, who might even wear vestments and use the sign of the cross at baptism (both hideous Popish monstrosities); then there were the Presbyterians, the backbone of Cromwell's movement, who rejected episcopacy but were happy for their own polity to manifest in the established church; then there were the "independents" or Congregationalists who gathered in single individual congregations; finally, at the other end, there were the fringe groups: the Family of Love, the Brownists, and the Separatists. These last groups certainly satisfy Cambers' definition of "Puritan" in doctrine, Church government and cultural practises. But the continuum of radical Protestantism is not simply an interpretative tool: it is a valuable way of seeing interconnections between various groups, geographically, theologically, and genealogically.

The distinction and division, at least the notional distinction, between the Puritans and Separatists seemed to arise in the United States. John Seelye's book,[153] which I managed to complete -- and it was pretty hard slogging in parts -- is a marvellous review of how the Pilgrims have been re-imaged and re-imagined in every generation. He points out that the strict division between the Puritans and the Pilgrims arose in the nineteenth century, as the Puritans were blamed for hanging witches, persecuting Quakers, attacking Indians, and generally making everyone miserable. In short, it was H. L. Menken's definition of Puritanism.[154] The Pilgrims, on the other hand, were the few, the happy few, who found religious liberty and freedom, and turkey with cranberry sauce, and lived in peace with everyone. Both are, of course, caricatures and neither is really accurate, except when viewed through nineteenth century lenses. But it is also clear that once shorn of nineteenth century (or even twenty-first century) intellectual baggage, the godly Pilgrims were *both* Puritans and Separatists, who came to America principally to be left alone.

---

[153] *Memory's Nation: The Place of Plymouth Rock.*
[154] "The haunting fear that someone, somewhere, may be happy": "Clinical Notes by H. L. Mencken and George Jean Nathan," *The American Mercury*, v. 4, n.13 [Jan 1925], p. 59

THURSDAY, 29 APRIL 1621

Daub

Another of the advantages of the warmer weather, in addition to the start of planting crops, was the thawing of the ground. During the winter, it was not possible to construct houses in the preferred fashion because it was not possible to dig clay. Walls were usually of a construction known as "wattle and daub" - - after vertical studs were put in, sticks were woven into a lattice called "wattle"; these wattles then were packed with a mud plaster (clay mixed with water). This form had been used in England for centuries and would become common in America for centuries afterward. This assumes that a roof has been put up first (so that rain would not wash the wet clay away, as happened at least once in the winter). Chimneys were also made in this way; before the chimney went in, there was simply a hole in the roof. Before the ground thawed, it was difficult and time consuming to extract enough clay to cover the wattle.

I was amused by two common phrases for this time of the year when I lived in New Hampshire: the first was "mud season" (when the upper layer of the ground had thawed, but the lower layer had not, causing water to be trapped in the upper layer); the second was the ubiquitous sign "Frost Heaves": I pondered whether either, or which, of those words was a verb.

FRIDAY, 30 APRIL 1621

Thatch

While settlers in New England would eventually roof their houses with shingles (assuming they could find a large enough cedar tree), that would have taken too much work to start out with. Each shingle would also need (at least) two nails, and all nails had to come from England and were thus a precious commodity. The easiest roofing material was thatch: large bundles of cattails or marsh reeds. Thatch or reed roofs needed no nails at all, were impervious to rain, and when they did leak, all one had to do was to put another bundle of reeds on top. Carefully done, a thatch or reed roof could last more than fifty years.

The roof was placed on top of four posts at the four corners, and the early houses had only a single room -- everyone (parents, children, servants) ate and slept in the one room, and at night sheets or curtains might be put up for privacy. In the next

211

generation, as houses became larger for fewer people, a second floor or a loft would be included. It is still astonishing to see the size of some of the first generation houses: the footprint of the original house of John and Priscilla Alden at the Alden First Site in Duxbury seems (by modern standards) to be tiny (10 x 38 feet) -- one can almost touch both opposite walls at the same time when standing in the centre of the building. And there were, at one time, not only John and Priscilla, but also their ten children.

MAY 1621

SATURDAY, 1 MAY 1621

Windows

One last set of comments on construction. There was probably no glass for windows, as that would have to be brought from England, and would have used up precious space in the cargo. The first homes would have simply had openings for windows and doors, with shutters to close off the windows. Eventually there would have been paper rubbed with linseed oil, as Edward Winslow suggested in his 1621 letter for prospective colonists regarding "what to bring." Rubbing paper with oil made it translucent, letting in light while keeping out wind and rain.

I have been thinking over the past few days about how much paper the Pilgrims brought with them -- not so much books, for we know that they brought quite a few of them, but just writing materials and for other purposes. It highlights the fact that everything -- *everything* -- had to be used, and there was only the tiniest margin for waste. At this point they were still discovering what worked and what didn't, but the nearest shop was over 3,000 miles away. The Indians provided significant know-how, and the seed corn that the exploration party had taken from the grave on Cape Cod grew well and was the margin between survival and starvation, while the seeds brought from England were not all that good (not really being suited for the New England soil), but the settlers' neighbours were not really sources for familiar goods. Adaptation, it seems, was not just the key to survival, but also to thriving.

And, of course, I mused while reading the current problems at Downing Street, there was no wallpaper.[155]

---

[155] In March 2021, the *Daily Mail* reported that Boris and Carrie Johnson had dramatically overspent the annual taxpayer-funded allowance permitted for refurbishing their flat above 11 Downing Street. The Prime Minister's despairing cry to Downing Street aides about the lavish new No. 10 décor was, "She's buying gold wallpaper. It's costing tens and tens of thousands [of pounds]. ... I can't afford it." *Daily Mail*, 27 April 2021.

What family doesn't have its problems?

This week I am going to jump several centuries and talk about famous and infamous descendants of the Pilgrims. I have mentioned famous descendants of the Howlands and several others, but perusing Gary Boyd Roberts' *The Mayflower 500* had me alternately giggling and gasping, so perhaps I can look at the descendants this week, grouped in different categories.

The first chuckle is that there are 585 descents in the book, not 500.

Howland and Alden have probably the two largest sets of Pilgrim descendants, and they have, not surprisingly, the largest number of American presidents linked to them: Alden has the Adamses (John and John Quincy) and Calvin Coolidge; Howland has Franklin Roosevelt and the Bushes (George H. W. and George W.). Richard Nixon and Gerald Ford both (!) descend from John Howland's brother Henry. The runner up is Isaac Allerton, who counts Zachary Taylor, Franklin Roosevelt, and Jefferson Davis' first wife (so that may count as two and a half).

Not surprisingly, Franklin Roosevelt has the most Pilgrim ancestors: the Tilleys, John and Elizabeth Howland, Isaac and Mary Allerton, Degory Priest, Richard Warren, and Francis and John Cooke (total of 10). The surprise here is that there does not appear to be any descent from John and Priscilla Alden -- the Delanos and the Aldens were next door neighbours in Duxbury for quite some time, and intermarried quite frequently, but not in the case of the line of Sara Delano, Franklin's mother (perhaps because Philip Delano [Philippe de la Noye]'s son Jonathan moved early on and became one of the original proprietors of Dartmouth, Massachusetts, while the Aldens tended to move to other places). Philip Delano was a passenger on the *Fortune*, which arrived in November of 1621 (the ship next after the *Mayflower*), although he may very well have been an original passenger on the *Mayflower* but got bumped when the *Speedwell* sprang a leak.

The Bushes come second (the Tilleys, John and Elizabeth Howland, and Francis Cooke, for a total of 5), and if you add in Barbara Bush (a descendant of Henry Samson), then George W. beats out his father.

John Billington, executed for murder, was an ancestor of the assassinated James A. Garfield, whose wife was a descendant of Mary Chilton.

Not to ignore those who steadfastly remained loyal to their allegiance to the Crown, Richard Warren's descendants include both a Canadian Prime Minister (Sir Charles Tupper) and the wife of a Canadian Prime Minister (Olive Evangeline Freeman, second wife of John Diefenbaker).

Almost half of the Supreme Court was connected to the *Mayflower* in the early 1990s -- William Rehnquist (William Bradford, natch), Byron White (Brewster, Allerton), Harry Blackmun (Standish), and the quintessential New Englander David Souter (Hopkins, Rogers, Brewster).

MONDAY, 3 MAY 2021

Let us entertain you

I was going to leave this until Thursday, but I got so many messages yesterday that I had to move this group up in the list.

Celebrities and entertainers make up a significant body of descendants, and many have several Mayflower lines. Comedian Richard Wayne ("Dick") van Dyke is not unusual in the number of lineages he has: he is descended from John and Priscilla Mullins, Myles Standish, George Soule, Francis Eaton, Peter Brown, Francis Cook, Edward Doty, and Degory Priest. Adding at least one Mullins parent, that yields a total of 10 passengers.

One of the most controversial lines is Hugh Hefner, founder of Playboy Enterprises. Perhaps the only thing about him that is not controversial is his descent from William Bradford. Numerous sources state that this line was formally disavowed by the Mayflower Society, although I don't see how it could be: if it was, it would have happened because of the activity of the descendant and not because there was any doubt about the lineage.

The rock musicians are the most fun: the lead singer of Metallica (James Hetfield) was descended from Degory Priest, Thomas Rogers, William and Susanna White, and Resolved White. Which certainly goes against the stereotype of *Mayflower* descendants all being old, staid and grey-headed. Also descended from Resolved White is singer-songwriter James Taylor ("You've Got a Friend") and George Hamilton. Mrs. Elvis Presley (nee Priscilla Ann Wagner) is descended from Stephen Hopkins (of course! "All Shook Up!") and William Brewster; Lisa Marie Presley (Mrs. Michael Jackson) would also share that lineage. And we couldn't possibly bypass Richard Wagstaff ("Dick") Clark, host

215

of *American Bandstand* for thirty years, who is a descendant of Edward Fuller; also descended from Edward Fuller and his son Samuel is Don Knotts -- not someone usually associated with Dick Clark -- and Burt Reynolds.

William Brewster was the ancestor of both Mrs. Spencer Tracy and Katherine Hepburn -- you just knew that Hepburn had to be a *Mayflower* descendant, didn't you? -- as well as Bing Crosby, Bette Davis, Chevy Chase (also a Howland), Richard Gere (also Warren, Cooke, Soule, Eaton, Billington, Samuel Fuller, Priest, and Hopkins -- that may be a record number)

And yes, Clint Eastwood *is* descended from William Bradford. So is Henry Fonda (and Jane and Peter, too), John Lithgow (also Howland and Billington), Sally Field (what would Bradford have thought about one of his granddaughters being a flying nun?), the Baldwin brothers (also Howlands), Ellen de Generes (also Alden), and Christopher Reeve.

Tomorrow I will deal with entertainers from the two big families (Alden and Howland), but I have to close today by saying that the one that always makes me laugh is the Wilson brothers (Brian, Dennis, and Carl) of the Beach Boys, who are descended from Francis Cooke, Peter Brown, and John and Francis Billington (the boy who almost blew up the *Mayflower*).

TUESDAY, 4 MAY 2021

"I'm ready for my close-up ..."

Beginning with the descendants of John and Elizabeth Howland (and thus also of John and Joan Tilley), we can highlight the film director Cecil B de Mille, who was a descendant of the Howlands on (at least) three separate lines. Although I don't know whether CB ever directed him, movie actor cousins would have included Humphrey Bogart.

More recently we can count Christopher Lloyd (also a Warren and Chilton descendant), Tuesday Weld (wife of Dudley Moore and Pinchas Zukerman; she is also a Warren cousin), Cornelius Crane ("Chevy") Chase (also a Brewster descendant), John Lithgow (also a Bradford and Billington descendant), Glenn Close, Ted Danson (Edward Bridge Danson III -- which sounds much more *Mayflower*-y -- he is also a Brewster descendant), William Macy, the Baldwin brothers (Alec, Daniel, Billy and Stephen) and Hailey Baldwin (Mrs. Justin Bieber!): these Baldwins are also Bradford descendants, and Matt Bomer

Movie actor descendants of John and Priscilla Alden include Orson Welles, Shirley Temple, Marilyn Monroe (neé Norma Jean Baker), Raquel Welch (also a Doty and Eaton descendant), Jodie Foster, James Brolin (and thus Josh Brolin, as well), and Zac Efron.

The surprise addition to the Alden cousins is Benedict Cumberbatch. While many of these have multiple *Mayflower* lines, for quite a few it is apparent that all one needs is *one single line* to become a *Mayflower* descendant!

WEDNESDAY, 5 MAY 1621

Inventors and explorers

The listing of inventors or, as Gary Boyd Roberts calls them, "product developers," is fascinating, both because of *Mayflower* connections as well as because in many cases I had not realised who the actual inventor was in the first place.

For example, Chilton descendant Eleanor Gannett married Clarence Birdseye, who developed a process for quickly freezing and packaging foods. Mary Chilton was also the ancestor of Nobel laureate and geneticist Barbara McClintock (who is also a descendant of the Aldens and Richard Warren). Vannevar Bush, computer pioneer and president of the Carnegie Institute, descended from Stephen Hopkins and William Brewster.

Bradford descendant George Eastman was the founder of Eastman Kodak; his camera and film led to amateur photography and movies -- he himself died unmarried, and has no known descendants.

The Wright Brothers were descendants of Richard Warren, as was Willis Carrier, the pioneer of air conditioning, and William and Charles Mayo, the founders of the Mayo Clinic. The famous, or infamous, paediatrician Dr. Benjamin Spock was a Howland descendant; the maligned "founder of progressive education," John Dewey, was a Brewster descendant, while his wife descended from the Howlands and Edward Fuller.

The inventor of television, Philo Taylor Farnsworth, was a descendant of George Soule. It is difficult for those of us below a certain age to think of an "inventor" of television -- hasn't it always just been there? -- even though I definitely remember black and white television, and when a particular Sunday night programme was called "Walt Disney's Wonderful World of Color," because colour television was so new and exciting.

217

I am currently finishing up my supplementary application for Edward Fuller, and I was startled to go down a pedigree listed in the book and discover exactly the same names, except for the last two generations, on two lines (Fuller and Warren) as in my applications. I was even more startled when I got to the end and saw that it was the pedigree of Amelia Earhart. Astronaut Alan Shepard is also a Warren (and Delano) cousin.

John Batterson Stetson developed the Stetson hat, and was a Brewster descendant, while the Remingtons (father Eliphalet and son Philo) developed the Remington rifle, and were major suppliers of arms to the Yankee army during the War between the States.

And Edward Fuller had a direct male descendant named Alfred Carl Fuller, who was the founder of the Fuller Brush Company (a pioneer in door to door sales).

THURSDAY, 6 MAY 1621

Other Descendants

I will deal with military figures tomorrow, but today's list of descendants is something of a grab bag.

Descendants of John and Priscilla Alden include Bishop Samuel Seabury, the first bishop of the Protestant Episcopal Church in the United States of America and hearty Loyalist, Martha Graham (the dancer and choreographer) and Phyllis Baker (Mrs. Fred Astaire, although not Fred himself, who was born Frederick Austerlitz).

Descendants of John and Elizabeth Tilley include William Sloane Coffin (social activist, chaplain of Yale University, and minister of Riverside Church in New York City -- he is also a Bradford), Joseph Smith (Mormon Prophet and founder of the Church of Jesus Christ of Latter Day Saints -- he is also a Fuller descendant) as well as his wife Emma Hale (also a Howland), and Emily Post (writer on etiquette).

Several famous people are descended not from *Mayflower* passengers but from those passengers' brothers. Chief among these is Winston Churchill (descended from Arthur Howland, brother of John -- the novelist John Steinbeck is also a descendant of Arthur Howland). Descendants of John Howland's other brother, Henry, include Richard Nixon, Gerald R Ford, Johnny Carson and Meryl Streep.

FRIDAY, 7 MAY 1621

Military

Given that the figure commonly set for the number of current living *Mayflower* descendants is 35 million (about 10% of the US population), the list of famous and semi-famous descendants could go on almost indefinitely. But I will end this week with a review of some famous military figures today and literary lights tomorrow.

Muriel Cushing's "Patriot to Passenger Project" has highlighted the hundreds of connections between those who fought for American independence and the passengers of the *Mayflower*. It is, of course, important to recognise that those who fought for independence were a minority of the population of the thirteen colonies (the usual number given is about one third of the total). A bit more than one third remained loyal to the Crown, although only a fraction of those were forced to go to what became Canada. The war between 1776 and 1783 was in a very real sense a civil war; I am currently attempting to parallel Muriel's work by trying to link Loyalists to *Mayflower* passengers -- I don't have as catchy a title, however, and I am certainly open to any suggestions. I would anticipate that there were just as many *Mayflower* descendants who fought for the Crown as who fought against it, if not more.

I was going to entitle this set "Military Men," until I realised that the first famous soldier was not a man: Deborah Sampson (oddly enough, not a descendant of Henry Samson, but rather of the Aldens and Myles Standish) fought in the American Revolution dressed as a man under the name of "Robert Shurtleff." John Adams, a significant figure in the war and the second US President, was a descendant of John and Priscilla Alden.

In the War of 1812, the "Hero of Lake Erie," Commodore Oliver Hazard Perry, was a George Soule descendant, as was his brother, Commodore Matthew Perry, famous for the opening of Japan. Oliver's grandson, John LaFarge, was a famous stained glass artist, and Oliver's wife was a descendant of John and Elizabeth Howland.

In the War Between the States, both the wife of Vice President of the United States (Ellen Vesta Emery, the wife of Hannibal Hamlin of Maine -- where I think almost everyone is a

Mayflower descendant of some sort -- was a descendant of John and Priscilla Alden) and the first commander of all the Union Armies, George McClellan (Bradford), were *Mayflower* descendants. McClellan was the 1864 Democratic candidate for President and later governor of New Jersey. General Grant was a Warren and Delano cousin. On the Confederate side, Jefferson Davis' first wife, Sarah Knox Taylor, was a descendant of the Allertons,[156] and while Robert E. Lee was not a *Mayflower* descendant, two of his uncles married descendants of William Brewster (Richard Henry Lee, signer of the Declaration of Independence and first senator from Virginia, and Charles Lee, second Attorney General and Aaron Burr's defense attorney -- both R H Lee and Charles Lee were grandparents of Supreme Court Justice Byron White, who always displayed the awesome totemic power of skinny bow ties).

Leonard Wood (leader of the "Rough Riders" in the Spanish-American War, military governor of Cuba, and governor of the Philippines) was descended from Richard Warren, Francis Cooke, and Stephen Hopkins. The wives of famous soldiers should not be ignored, either: Mrs. Chester Nimitz was descended from Peregrine White (and Richard Warren, Stephen Hopkins, Thomas Rogers, and William Brewster); Mrs. "Billy" Mitchell was descended from the Howlands, William Brewster, and Henry Samson; Mrs. John Pershing was descended from the Howlands

---

[156] Sarah's brother was Lieutenant General Richard Strother Taylor, the hero of the Red River Campaign; her nephew was John Taylor Wood, captain of the CSS *Tallahassee*, on the CSS *Virginia* during its fight with the USS *Monitor* in Hampton Roads – and also the man who blew the CSS *Virginia* up to keep it from being captured by the Yankees, and was with his uncle Jefferson Davis when he was captured in Irwinville, Georgia. While Davis did not escape, his nephew did; Wood met up with John C Breckenridge (former US Vice President and CS Secretary of War), escaped to Florida, captured a pirate ship, sailed through a hurricane to Cuba, and from there went to Halifax, Nova Scotia. He never returned to the United States. The other high ranking *Mayflower* descendants – both descendants of George Soule -- in Confederate service were Major General Matthew Calbraith Butler (nephew of the two Perrys mentioned above) and Lieutenant General Nathan Bedford Forrest., whom Robert E. Lee named as the greatest Confederate general of The War, and whom Shelby Foote called one of the two natural geniuses The War produced (the other being Abraham Lincoln).

on two lines; Mrs. George Armstrong Custer was also a Howland.

SATURDAY, 8 MAY 1621

Literary Lights

One last pass through the list of descendants, this time looking at the writers: it is somewhat amusing to look at all of the descendants grouped by their family -- there are many strange connections.

The Howlands lead off with Ralph Waldo Emerson; I smiled when I saw that Emerson's (great-great-)niece married Alistair Cooke (am I the only person left who remembers him as the host of *Masterpiece Theatre?*). Although Henry Wadsworth Longfellow made his fame as an Alden descendant, he was also descended from Howland, Brewster, Sampson and Warren. The Howlands can also claim Edward Everett (President of Harvard, US Senator and Secretary of State, and orator who gave the *other* address at Gettysburg in November 1863) and Phillips Brooks (Episcopal Bishop of Massachusetts and author of "O Little Town of Bethlehem").

Descended from Richard Warren are Henry David Thoreau and Ernest Hemingway (you never thought you would see those two in the same sentence, did you?), John Irving (*The World According to Garp,* whose world also includes the Allertons, Brewsters, Aldens and Sampsons, Hopkins and Cookes), Laura Ingalls Wilder, Erle Stanley Gardner (the creator of Perry Mason), and David McCullough (historian and biographer).

Tennessee Williams is descended from Stephen Hopkins, which sounds appropriate in its own way, as is the actor Ethan Hawke.

George Soule's line runs to the poet and translator Ezra Pound (as do the Howlands), and to the historian Charles Beard. William Bradford claims Noah Webster, although he can keep him.

I just have to start the list of Alden descendants out with Julia Child, even though her main claim to fame is not as a writer. You *know* that that voice has to be *Mayflower,* don't you? She is also descended from Francis Cooke, Richard Warren, William Bradford, and William Brewster.

And it is probably fitting that Samuel Eliot Morison, the editor of the most useful edition of Bradford's *Of Plimoth Plantation,* is descended from (deep breath): William Mullins, Priscilla Mullins,

John Alden (on three lines), William Bradford (on two lines), Thomas Rogers, Richard Warren (on two lines), William and Mary Brewster (on two lines), Love Brewster, Isaac Allerton, Mary (Norris) Allerton, and Francis Cooke (a total of twelve passengers).

SUNDAY, 9 MAY 1621

Bradford in England

For the next three days, I will be looking (very, very briefly) at William Bradford's life in England, in Holland, and in Plymouth. Unlike Edward Winslow, who has recently received a full scale, extensive and judicious biography,[157] biographies of Bradford have been sometimes fawning, or sometimes partial, though excellent.[158] "Bradford deserves a full, modern biography," Robert Anderson pleads.[159]

We have a baptism record for William Bradford, which commonly substitutes for a birth record in this period. William Bradford, the son of William and Alice (Hanson) Bradford, was baptised in Austerfield, Yorkshire, on 19 March 1589/90.[160] His father died when he was only a year old, and his mother when he was seven. After his mother's remarriage, he went (or was sent) to live with his paternal grandfather (also called William Bradford) until the latter's death in 1596, after which he was sent to live with his uncles Thomas and Robert Bradford. It is likely that while living with his uncles, he attended grammar school in Tickhill, Yorkshire.

When he was 12, young William had a profound religious experience and came within the circle of the (illegal) preacher Richard Clifton, who was then at Babworth, Nottinghamshire (about ten miles from Austerfield); the two became closer (geographically and personally) when Clifton began preaching in Bawtry, the parish next to Austerfield. William would have been sixteen or seventeen by that time. Bradford fled to Amsterdam, and eventually Leiden, in 1608, which is where his journal *Of Plimmoth Plantation* begins. While he was still a minor when he left, we know that Bradford did return to England in 1611,

---

[157]Bangs, *Pilgrim Edward Winslow.*
[158]The most significant one recently is surely Sue Allan's *In Search of Governor William Bradford of Austerfield.*
[159] MM 40
[160] MD 7:65-66; NEHGR 84:10-11

perhaps to claim the property to which he was entitled.

MONDAY, 10 MAY 1621

Bradford in Holland

Bradford was a part of the Scrooby congregation by the time they made the decision to flee to Holland. During the first attempt to leave in 1607, the group was deceived by the ship's captain, and they were returned to Boston (Lincolnshire), where they were imprisoned for about a month. Bradford was released early, perhaps because of his youth. He was part of the successful attempt to leave in 1608, although when he got to Amsterdam, he was imprisoned there because he lacked the necessary permission to leave England: he managed to talk his way out of that one, and took a job as an apprentice with a French silk merchant. He is listed as a fustian worker later on: fustian is a heavy fabric of cotton and flax, or of cotton and low-quality wool.

After a year in Amsterdam, the congregation led by John Robinson and William Brewster decided to leave (since the Ancient Brethren, a local English speaking congregation, seemed to be tilting toward Anabaptism and away from more orthodox Calvinism). Jeremy Bangs notes that theology "got in the way of employment. ... The Ancient Brethren had a reputation for contentiousness, although by 1608 a leading trouble-maker had died and calm had temporarily returned to the congregation. Peace lasted until the split of ... 1610."[161] The (former) Scrooby congregation moved to Leiden, about 25 miles away, which Bradford described as "a fair and beautiful city and of a sweet situation, but made more famous by the university wherewith it is adorned"; permission to come was granted by the City of Leiden in early 1609, and the move took place that April. Once Bradford turned 21, he gained control of his "comfortable inheritance": he was the only son of his parents, and his sister Alice had died just before he left for Holland. He turned it all in to cash, a move that he later regretted, since he spent it all quickly. He would later attribute this as a lesson from God teaching him to avoid vanity and pride.

Upon returning to Holland, he married (in Amsterdam) William White's niece Dorothy May, a sixteen year old girl from

---

[161] Bangs, *Strangers and Pilgrims*, 72-3

Wisbech in Cambridgeshire;[162] they had their first son, John, in 1617. Not long afterwards, the congregation decided to move forward with plans to settle in some "uninhabited" section of America, eventually determining to go to northern Virginia. Bradford sold his house in April 1619, and in 1620 he and his wife Dorothy boarded the *Speedwell* for Southampton, and then the *Mayflower* for the voyage across the Atlantic. Three year old John was left behind until it was safe for him to join them.

TUESDAY, 11 MAY 1621

Bradford in Plymouth

We have seen several references to William Bradford on the voyage over and the first landing on Cape Cod, which is not surprising since he was the author of the only two first-hand accounts we have of those events in his journal *Of Plimmoth Plantation* and in *Mourt's Relation*. He was one of the early signers of the Mayflower Compact, and was in at least two of the first exploring parties, including the one that found Plymouth Harbour. Upon his return to the *Mayflower*, he discovered that his wife had drowned. He lost his wife's uncle, William White during the following winter. Unlike many of the other Pilgrims, the Bradfords had no servants.

He was elected governor of Plymouth Colony in April 1621 upon the sudden death of John Carver (probably from heatstroke). He served as Governor for the rest of his life, with the exception of 1633-1634, 1636, 1638, and 1644, for a total of 31 terms as governor (Robert Anderson notes that this total is at odds with a number of secondary sources). Those years he was not Governor he was elected Assistant Governor, and was elected as Plymouth Commissioner to the United Colonies in 1647-49, 1652, and 1656 (and was elected President of that group for those last two years). He took part in all of the major events of the colony during those years, either in virtue of his office as magistrate or by common consent of the settlers.

His son John joined him in America, although (oddly enough) I can find no record of when he actually came across. William Bradford received three acres in the 1623 land division, presumably for himself, in the right of his first wife, and for his

---

[162] 10 December 1613 [n.s.]; see MD 9:115-17, 22:63-64; TAG 89:81-94, 186-88.

second wife, so it is evident that John had not yet come. In the division of cattle of 1627, the list included William Bradford followed by William Bradford, Jr. -- John Bradford is not named, and presumably was not yet in Plymouth. It is usually assumed that the last of the Leiden congregation that came to America travelled before 1629, and this is as good a guess as any about John's arrival: he would have been about twelve or thirteen years old at the time, and have spent the vast majority of his life without either parent. I have also not been able to find the family or families who took care of John in Holland: it could have been with his grandfather, Henry May. Both of the sons of Edward Southworth came from Holland (or perhaps England) where they had been left to complete their schooling; by this time they would have been John's step-brothers, so it is possible he travelled in their company: they would have been slightly older teenaged contemporaries. They may have remained with their Aunt, Juliana Carpenter, who was married to George Morton of *Mourt's Relation* fame. The boys (perhaps with, perhaps without John Bradford) came over to Plymouth with their aunt Juliana in 1628, possibly on the ship *White Angel*. John Bradford married Martha Bourne, the daughter of Thomas and Elizabeth Bourne, in 1650 or perhaps a little earlier. John died in Norwich, Connecticut before 1676, and so far as we know John and Martha Bradford left no children.

In the fourth wedding to take place in Plymouth, William Bradford married on 14 August 1623 Alice Carpenter, the widow of Edward Southworth. She had two sons, Constant and Thomas Southworth (both mentioned in the last paragraph), from her first husband. William and Alice had three children of their own: William Bradford [Jr.], Mercy Bradford, and Joseph Bradford. Mercy married Benjamin Vermayes (or Fearmayes) in 1648; they also left no children of which we know. Joseph Bradford (born in Plymouth in 1630) married Jael Hobart in 1664 (after Governor Bradford's death), and had three children, only one of whom was mentioned in his father's will and is known to have descendants.

William Bradford, Jr., however, had a whopping fifteen children with three wives, thus ensuring the survival of the Bradford name (and the future existence of many of us). He was born in Plymouth on 17 June 1624 and died there on 20 February 1703/4.

Governor William Bradford fell ill during the winter of

1656; his health had never been exactly vigorous, and he is recorded to have been quite sick several times in the winter of 1620/21 and the following years. The day before he died, Bradford reported that "the God of Heaven so filled his mind with ineffable consolations." He was hoping that his friend, and successor as Governor, Thomas Prence, would assist him in the writing of his will, but in the event he dictated a nuncupative will on the morning of the day of his death, 9 May 1657.

The colony of Plymouth only survived Bradford by about 35 years, and in a couple of cases, people were able to witness both its beginning and its end.

I will try to summarise over the next few days what I consider to be five main events (or even crises) of Bradford's time as governor: the arrival (and departure) of the *Fortune* and the financial problems of the colony and its investors, the John Lyford affair in 1623, the problems with the competing colony of Wessagusset, problems with John Morton, and the execution of John Billington in 1630. I will conclude by speculating on why Bradford was not re-elected in the six years he was not elected Governor, and on why he felt that the Plymouth Colony was a failure.

WEDNESDAY, 12 MAY 1621

Problems with Investors

The first crisis Bradford faced as Governor was the arrival of the *Fortune* in November 1621. By the beginning of November, the colony was all set after a very difficult year, and plenty of food and supplies was prepared for the winter and stored, when news came from Indians further down the coast that a sail had been sighted off of Provincetown. While there was fear that this was an hostile Spanish, French or Pirate ship (which might amount to the same thing), it turned out to be the *Fortune*, sent by the investors in England with ... more mouths to feed, and not much else. They had no food, only the clothes on their backs, and no supplies. Their addition to the community meant that what had appeared to be a comfortable winter was now going to be touch and go, with everyone on half rations. The *Fortune* also brought several exceptionally angry letters by the investors for Governor Carver, who had died in the meantime. As an aside, my current intention is to continue *Mayflower, Day by Day* until the 400th anniversary of the return of the *Fortune* (which was 13 December

1621 [o.s.], so the 400th anniversary of that will be 23 December 2021). I will have quite a bit more to say about the *Fortune* come next November.

The *Fortune* only stayed for about three weeks and was sent back to England with about £500 of supplies for sale (mostly clapboard and lumber, beaver and otter skins -- taking inflation into account, that would be about US$200,000 in 2020). Unfortunately, the *Fortune* (sorry, I couldn't resist) was intercepted by French pirates, and all of the cargo was confiscated or destroyed, so that it, like the *Mayflower*, returned to England empty. The problem was not what the London merchants accused the Pilgrims of (laziness and deceitfulness), but bad planning, and even worse luck.

Thomas Weston, one of the leading organisers and investors and a "friend" of the Pilgrims (that last characterisation is meant to be ironic), sold out and quit the company, and decided to start his own colony -- more about that later this week. This was just the tip of the iceberg as far as quarrels among the investors are concerned. As divisions grew over the next few years between the settlers in Plymouth and the company of investors in England, Bradford was able to negotiate a deal to organise a group of men to buy the company from the shareholders, a process that began in 1626: these were known as the "Purchasers, " and they acquired the rights to land distribution in the Plymouth Colony as a consequence of the agreement made between the London merchants and the Plymouth settlers: before that, everything in the colony was quite literally owned by the investors, and they were looking for a return on that investment. The Purchasers assumed responsibility for the colony's debts: what the colonists got in return was a monopoly on trade with the Indians for fur. This was, in a real sense, the beginning of private property in the new colony. In 1627 the debts and shares in the company were assigned to 8 Plymouth colony leaders and 4 Merchant Adventurers, all known as "Undertakers." The first crisis was thus averted by the judicious introduction of private property into the colony.

THURSDAY, 13 MAY 1621

Problems with John Lyford

The second crisis was less economic, and more domestic.
The *Charity*, which arrived in March 1624, brought three

heifers and a bull, the first of any cattle in the colony. It also brought the Reverend John Lyford, who joined the Plymouth church. He was the first clergyman to come to the colony, and was certainly a well-educated man (probably having attended Trinity College, Dublin); he was expected to minister to the congregation at Plymouth -- which he did, apparently, for a short period of time. He became a close friend and confidant of Governor Bradford "in their weightiest businesses." As time went on, however, Bradford and several others became suspicious of Lyford. In particular, Bradford noted that Lyford was writing a lot of letters back to England (there was really no need to send "domestic" letters to Plymouth), so Bradford went out to the ship which was preparing to leave, intercepted and read the letters. He "found about 20 of Lyford's letters, many of them large, and full of slanders and false accusations, tending not only to the prejudice [of the Pilgrims], but to their ruin and utter subversion." The governor made copies of them, and held a few of the more incriminating originals, passing along copies and rebuttals to the intended recipients in England. Bradford, however, waited for the right moment, rather than immediately confront Lyford with the letters: he wanted to know exactly who was involved in this cabal, and what their intentions were.

After weeks with no response to the letters, Lyford continued about his business, but then, with no warning, one day set up a separate church and began to carry out their designs (doing things such as, according to the dismay of the leaders, celebrating sacraments! He probably even wore vestments!). The Governor convoked the court and charged Lyford and another settler (John Oldham); he then began to read copies of some of the letters. "At this [Lyford] was struck mute"; Bradford asked him "if he thought they had done evil to open his letters; but he was silent, and would not say a word, well knowing what they might reply." Ultimately, "In conclusion, he was fully convicted, and burst out into tears, and confessed he feared he was a reprobate; his sins were so great that he doubted God would not pardon them; he was unsavory salt, etc.; and that he had so wronged them as he could never make them amends, confessing all he had written against them was false and nought, both for matter and manner."

And, worst of all, he had been ordained by a *bishop* (shock! horror! boo! hiss!). "And all this he did with as much fulness as

228

words and tears could express. After their trial and conviction, the court censured them to be expelled the place; Oldham presently, though his wife and family had liberty to stay all winter, or longer, till he could make provision to remove them comfortably. Lyford had liberty to stay six months. It was, indeed, with some eye to his release, if he carried himself well in the meantime, and that his repentance proved sound. Lyford acknowledged his censure was far less than he deserved." He went to Nantasket, then to Salem, and finally to Virginia in 1627, where he died.

A little before his banishment, Lyford's wife went to the Plymouth deacons and told them "he had a bastard by another before they were married, and she having some inkling of some ill carriage that way, when he was a suitor to her, she told him what she heard, and denied him. But she not certainly knowing the thing, otherwise than by some dark and secret mutterings, he not only stiffly denied it, but to satisfy her took a solemn oath there was no such matter. Upon which she gave consent and married with him; but afterwards it was found true and the bastard brought home to them." Bradford had his hands full.

FRIDAY, 14 MAY 1621

Problems with Wessagusset

Today's look gets complicated: which brings us to Thomas Weston again. Weston sent out his own group of colonists: turning a profit was the primary purpose of Weston's new colony, and this dictated how the colony would be assembled. Weston believed that families were a detriment to a well-run plantation, so he selected able-bodied men only—but not men experienced in colonial life. The final complement also included one surgeon and one lawyer (you can never have too many lawyers). The party was outfitted with enough supplies to last the winter.

An advance team of 60 settlers arrived at Plymouth in May 1622. They had sailed to the New World on the *Sparrow*, an English fishing vessel headed for the coast of Maine. The team travelled the final 150 miles down the New England coast in a shallop with three members of the *Sparrow*'s crew. These colonists stayed in Plymouth before scouting the coast to find a site for their colony. After finding one, they negotiated for the land with Chief Aberdecest and returned to Plymouth, sending the shallop back to the *Sparrow* and awaiting the rest of the colonists. The main body set off from London in April 1622 aboard the *Charity* and the

Swan. The group arrived in Plymouth in late June and moved into their settlement the following month. By the end of September, the colony was established, the *Swan* was moored in Weymouth (Fore) River, and the *Charity* returned to England.

Things did not start out well -- the new colonists ended scrounging off of the Plymouth colony's meagre resources, although they did help to bring in the harvest of 1622. Indians soon complained to Plymouth that the Wessagusset colonists were stealing their corn, but Plymouth had no authority over the new colony and could only send them a "rebuke." Wessagusset was consuming food too quickly because of disorder in the colony, as reported by Bradford, and it became apparent that they would run out before the end of the winter. In addition, Plymouth was also low on supplies since it was spending additional time during the growing season building fortifications, rather than growing crops. Bradford decided to assist the new colony, a decision which met with heavy criticism.

Tensions continued to build throughout the winter between the settlers and the Natives, and there was at least one instance where a Native was caught stealing from Plymouth. Near the end of the winter, the Natives near Wessagusset moved some of their huts to a swamp near the colony, and the colonists felt that they were under siege.

One colonist at Wessagusset saw these and other signs and indications of hostility, and fled to Plymouth to bring word of an imminent attack, pursued by Natives during his flight. He arrived at Plymouth on March 24 and met with Bradford. It is unclear whether this colonist's report was the tipping point or whether Plymouth had already decided to mount a pre-emptive attack. Edward Winslow had saved Massasoit's life, and the chief now warned him of a conspiracy among several tribes against Wessagusset and Plymouth. The threatening tribes were led by the Massachusetts but also included the Nauset, Paomet, Succonet, Mattachiest, Capawack, and Agawam tribes from as far away as Martha's Vineyard. Plymouth colony sent a small force under Miles Standish to Wessagusset, arriving on March 26.

Standish called all of the Wessagusset colonists into the stockade for defence. The following day, several Natives were at Wessagusset, including chief Pecksuot. Sources give different accounts of the killings, but four of the Natives were in the same room as Standish and several of his men. One source from the 1880s suggests that it was the Natives who arranged to be alone with Standish in order to attack him. Others sources state that Standish had invited them into the situation on peaceful pretences. Standish gave the order to strike, quickly killing Chief Pecksuot with his own knife. Several other Natives in the village were attacked next, and only one escaped to raise the alarm. As many as five colonists were also killed in the brief battle; one Native's head was cut off and displayed in Plymouth as a warning to others, which was a common practice in Europe at the time.

Following the brief conflict, the colonists divided, some returning to England in the *Swan*, others remained behind to join the Plymouth colony. By spring of 1623, the village was empty and the colony was dissolved. Thomas Weston arrived in Maine several months later, seeking to join his colony, only to discover that it had already failed. Because of the fighting at Wessagusset, Plymouth's trade with the Indians was devastated for years. Local tribes which had previously been favourable to Plymouth began to forge bonds with other more hostile tribes. Historians differ on whether the conflict could have been avoided or the colony saved.

The Council for New England gave Robert Gorges a patent for a settlement covering 300 square miles northeast of Boston Harbour. He was an English captain and son of Sir Ferdinando Gorges (remember him from last October?). This settlement was intended to be a spiritual and civic capital for the council's New England colonies. Gorges was commissioned Governor-General with authority over Plymouth and presumably future colonies. Weston had brought only working men, whereas Gorges brought entire families who would form a permanent settlement. He also brought two Anglican clergymen (!!), something of a red flag. Gorges arrived in Massachusetts in September 1623, only four months after Weston's colony collapsed. Instead of founding his colony at the location described in the patent, he chose the abandoned settlement at Wessagusset. It was rechristened Weymouth after Weymouth in Dorset, the town where the expedition began. Weston was charged with neglect of his colony and with selling weapons to the Indians which were supposed to have been used for the defence of the colony: he denied the first charge but confessed to the second. After a winter in Weymouth, Gorges abandoned his new colony in the spring of 1624 because of financial difficulties. Most of his settlers returned to England, but some remained as colonists in Weymouth, Plymouth, or Virginia. The remaining Weymouth settlers were supported by Plymouth until they were made part of the Massachusetts Bay Colony in 1630. In time, the location of the original settlement was lost to history and development: the original fort was rediscovered in 1891.

SATURDAY, 15 MAY 1621

Problems with Thomas Morton

I presented some background on Thomas Morton in my review of a recent book on this character for the last issue of the *Mayflower Quarterly*, a (slightly revised) excerpt of which follows. The book was Peter C. Mancall, *The Trials of Thomas Morton: An Anglican Lawyer, His Puritan Foes, and the Battle for a New England.* Mancall makes the claim that the *second* most influential book on the Plymouth Colony was Thomas Morton's *New English Canaan* (1637). Far less well known than Bradford's journal (which would be the first), and certainly far less read, the work requires a formidable knowledge of Classical literature to savour, or even to decipher. Morton produced in these three books a massive denunciation of Puritan government in the colonies and their policy of land enclosure and near genocide of the native population, who were described as a far nobler culture, and defined as a "Canaan" under attack from the "New Israel" of the Puritans.

Thomas Dudley termed Morton "a proud insolent man"; to Edward Winslow he was "an arrant knave" and a "serpent in the New England garden." For Bradford himself he was a man of "more craft then honestie, (who had been a kind of petie-fogger ...)" and an "instrumente of mischeefe." Puritan apologists Edward Johnson and Cotton Mather labeled him a "malignant adversary" and a "malicious calumniator." Charles Francis Adams, his first biographer, judged him in his final years "a broken down, disreputable sot," an interpretation that many historians have followed. Morton appears as a member of the "jury of the damned" summoned by the Devil in Stephen Vincent Benet's short story, *The Devil and Daniel Webster* (1936). In his own *New English Canaan*, Morton referred to himself as "Thomas Morton of Clifford's Inn, Gent.," and "the Sonne of a Souldier," and, in more recent times, he has had a veritable legion of defenders. An aristocrat by birth and a bon vivant by inclination, Morton was educated for the law at the Inns of Court and became a champion of the common law against the Crown and the Star Chamber; he was fond of falconry and foppery, bawdy puns and esoteric poetry. He was both an Elizabethan dandy and a Renaissance man.

Morton was most famous, or infamous, for dancing around the maypole at Merrymount in defiance of his (Puritan) neighbours; he was exiled three times from New England, frequently arrested, and placed on trial for sedition and accused of being a "Royalist agitator" (a trial that failed for lack of evidence). He was a High Church Anglican, intruding on a settlement of hundreds of people who had made a dangerous voyage of thousands of miles to get as far away from the Church of England as they possibly could. And, to top it all off, he sold liquor and firearms to the Indians -- and was proud of it.

Biographical details of Morton's life are spotty, and usually biased. Mancall treats Morton principally as spokesman for an alternative culture and vision of settlement in this "New" England, and does an admirable job of placing the two ideals side by side, and evaluating their foundations. The Plymouth and Bradford side of the story were deeply steeped in the Scriptures, and while modern authors tend to associate the Pilgrims with a very modern American sense of "religious freedom," it is also possible to see the main goal of the Separatists as simply to be left alone. This left them isolated, not only politically and culturally, but also religiously -- Plymouth was a complete failure when it came to attracting clergy. The Morton side of the story can be easily, although somewhat anachronistically, characterised as devoted to liberty, diversity, and multiculturalism. This is trumpeted as a "counter-narrative" to that of the Pilgrims and Puritans, and many reviewers have shed tears that this was "the road not taken." But two conclusions are somewhat glossed over in the book's comparison of these two visions: first, they are completely incompatible, and either one or the other must prevail; and second, because Morton's vision was extinguished so quickly, it is impossible to tell whether or not it was at all viable. The vast majority of those in New England at the time thought that it was not, however much it may appeal to twenty-first century political sensibilities.

SUNDAY, 16 MAY 1621

The Execution of John Billington

The last of the problems of Governor Bradford was the first execution in the colony.

William Hubbard, sometime in the mid- or late-seventeenth century, gave the fullest description of the event, from a letter written at the time. It begins, not surprisingly, with a Biblical reference to fraternal strife: "So when this wilderness began first to be peopled by the English where there was but one poor town, another Cain was found therein, who maliciously slew his neighbor in the field, as he accidentally met him, as he himself was going to shoot deer. The poor fellow perceiving the intent of this Billington, his mortal enemy, sheltered himself behind trees as well as he could for a while; but the other, not being so ill a marksman as to miss his aim, made a shot at them, and struck him on the shoulder, with which he died soon after. The murtherer expected that either for want of power to execute for capital offenses, or for want of people to increase the plantation, he should have his life spared; but justice otherwise determined."[163] Bradford's journal does not really describe the crime as much as he describes the procedure used to prosecute Billington: "This year John Billington the elder (one that came over with the first) was arraigned; and both by grand, and petty jury found guilty of willful murder; by plain and notorious evidence. And was for the same accordingly executed. This as it was the first execution amongst them, so was it a matter of great sadness unto them; they used all due means about his trial, and took the advice of Mr. Winthrop, and other the ablest gentlemen in the Bay of Massachusetts, that were then newly come over, who concurred with them that he ought to die, and the land be purged from blood. He and some of his, had been often punished for miscarriages before, being one of the profanest families amongst them; ... His fact was, that he waylaid a young man, one John Newcomen (about a former quarrel) and shot him with a gun, whereof he died." Bradford states Billington was approximately forty years of age; his burial location is unknown.

The execution did not end the family's troubles. Ellen Billington, John's widow, was sued for £100 by John Doane for

---

[163] Hubbard, *General History*, 101.

slander in June 1636 (what the slander was, was not recorded): Ellen was sentenced to sit in the stocks, be whipped, and pay a fine of £5. She married again, one Gregory Armstrong, in 1638. We will run across their sons again in a couple of weeks.

MONDAY, 17 MAY 1621

Why was Bradford not elected Governor five additional times?

As mentioned last week, William Bradford was elected governor of the Colony of New Plymouth thirty one times in thirty six years, from 1621 until his death in 1657. This must surely be a record in Colonial American annals, although, to be fair, many governors were appointed, so this electoral victory cannot really be compared with other colonies.

Caleb Johnson carefully analyses each of the five years in which Bradford was not elected:

1633-1634: "It is unclear whether (Bradford's not being elected governor) was voluntary, but it may have been the result of a perceived mishandling of Isaac Allerton, whom Bradford had trusted for many years, but who continually put his own financial advantage over those of the other shareholders, bringing trade goods for himself while giving the company leftovers and unwanted goods."[164] Edward Winslow was elected in 1633, and Thomas Prence in 1634; William Bradford had been elected every year for over a decade at that point.

1636: Edward Winslow was elected in this year after returning from a very successful business voyage to England.

1638: Thomas Prence was elected again.

1644: Edward Winslow was elected. "The year 1644 was a tough one for Plymouth, and Governor Winslow authorized an official investigation into whether or not Plymouth should be moved to Nauset, further out on the tip of Cape Cod. Bradford was a strong critic of the idea. In the end, the town would decide not to move, but many residents ended up moving there anyway, founding the town of Eastham, and further depleting Plymouth's resources."[165] Bradford was reelected in 1645, and would remain governor until the year of his death in 1657.

---

[164] Johnson, *Mayflower Passengers*, 86
[165] Johnson, *Mayflower Passengers*, 86-87

Was Plymouth Colony a failure?

1. Economic: The economy of Plymouth Colony was based on fish, timber, fur and agriculture. The colonists harvested trees for lumber, hunted beaver and otter for their pelts and fished for cod as well as hunted whales for their oil. They sent back all of the goods they harvested on ships and the Plymouth Company would sell the goods in England for a profit. The colonists struggled for many years to make any money and were deeply in debt to their investors, the Plymouth Company, who had paid for the voyage and the start-up money for the colony: The Plymouth Company initially invested about £1200 to £1600 in the colony before the *Mayflower* even sailed (A simple Purchasing Power Calculator would say the relative value of the larger figure is £336,000.00 in 2020, or US$477,083 at current exchange rates -- as before, this is difficult to calculate, and varies widely according to the scale used. The labour value, for example, would now be £4,648,000.00 [=US$6,597,907], using the wage index rather than the retail price index). The colonists eventually bought out the investors when these investors became unhappy with the lack of return they saw from their investment. But the fur trade had almost disappeared by 1640, and for the next 20 years, only further decline ensued. By the mid-1640s the town of Plymouth was virtually a ghost town; and economically the colony had become a backwater.

In 1627, the Plymouth Company investors were unhappy with the lack of return they saw from the colony and the colonists agreed to buy them out for £1800, which was to be paid in installments of £200 a year over nine years. Eight colonists pledged their personal credit to buy the investor's shares. These colonists were William Bradford, John Howland, Myles Standish, Isaac Allerton, Edward Winslow, William Brewster, John Alden and Thomas Prence. In reality, it took much longer than nine years to pay back the money and the pilgrims didn't finish paying it off until over 20 years later in 1648. The colony never became as economically successful as its northern neighbour and was merged with (or, perhaps better, was absorbed into) the Massachusetts Bay Colony in 1691.

2. Political: The government of Plymouth Colony originally ran as a charter government, even though they didn't actually have a charter from the Crown. A charter was official permission to establish a colony. It granted the colony the legal right to exist there and allowed it to establish a local government as long at the colony's laws didn't contradict the laws of England. The only permission that Plymouth colony had to establish itself in North America was a land patent issued by the New England Council in 1621 (and renewed and revised in 1630). This land patent did not give the colony the legal right to establish laws in the colony. Plymouth colony tried for many decades to obtain a charter from the Crown, but never succeeded. It eventually lost the right to self-govern entirely when it was merged with the Massachusetts Bay Colony in 1691 and became a royal colony.

Legal historians have stated that there were no lawyers in the Colony throughout the 17th century. However, by 1680, the General Court was sufficiently acquainted with attorneys to enact a limit on the fees they could receive in any case to five shillings.[166] The Governor and Assistants operated, through the Court of Assistants (also called the "Counsell"), to handle all matters on a subject-by-subject and case-by-case basis. They did not have the authority to enact comprehensive laws and ordinances, and rather issued orders on a limited array of subjects through the Court of Assistants. Only the General Court, attended by voting freemen, had the authority to enact such legislation, and it did not do so in a comprehensive manner until the codification of laws in 1636: this only lasted for a bit over 50 years.

Tomorrow we will look at the third, perhaps the cruellest, failure of all: the religious failure of Plymouth Colony.

WEDNESDAY, 19 MAY 1621

Religious Failure of Plymouth Colony

3. **Religious:** This is probably the longest answer, requiring more detail than time or space allows, but the religious failure of the Plymouth Colony can be summarised (if this is not too facile) under three headings:

a. *The impossibility of Separatism.* We have been programmed to see the Pilgrims as self-consciously working for religious freedom (in a twentieth or twenty-first century sense): this makes two assumptions which are questionable, at best, and erroneous, at worst. The first of these is that conscience, in general, and religion, in particular, are matters of private and personal opinion.

---

[166] PCR 11: 251

While that is certainly what modern secular and civil authority contends or perhaps assumes, in the sixteenth century, religion had a political and cultural and quite definitely a public character, and public activity definitely had a religious character. We use terms such as "separation of church and state" and "theocracy," but neither of those is appropriate or applicable to seventeenth century Plymouth – this would be looking at the colony with an exceptionally twentieth-century squint. Secondly, the Church of England was the *only* English institution that was in *every single community* in England -- neither the state nor the military had (or, indeed, has) the same or as widespread a presence in England. So to withdraw from the Church of England, of necessity, meant that one had to withdraw from England. As the Pilgrims noted, and in case they forgot, they were reminded by James I, the conclusion that the Church of England was not a true Church inevitably entailed the conclusion that the King of England was not a true King -- which was treasonous. This is seen even more clearly in the treatment of (Roman Catholic) recusants -- *no one* in England was executed simply for being a Catholic. Catholics were executed for treason (for which the normal form of execution was being hung, drawn, and quartered, since this offense was in the highest degree odious). Because Pope Pius V in his bull *Regnans in excelsis* (25 February 1570, excommunicating Elizabeth I) explicitly demanded that all Catholics rise up and overthrow the government, even calling on them to kill the Queen, he put English Catholics in a completely untenable situation: they had to choose between loyalty to their Church (which was treason) or loyalty to England (which was heresy). Both entailed death: either in this life or in the life to come. In a real sense, as I have suggested before, the principal desire of the Pilgrims was to be left alone, to live outside of both church and state. Which is neither viable, nor even particularly attractive.

b. I have also mentioned that the Plymouth Colony was woefully *unable to attract any clergymen to minister to them*, and thus they almost completely lacked religious leadership in America. Those clergy that came were either Anglicans (shudder -- that is what they travelled thousands of miles to get away from), or, in a slightly later period, clergy from Massachusetts Bay, particularly products of the newly established Harvard, who were not really in line with the religious tenets the Pilgrims held so dearly (both close to their

238

hearts, and at such a cost). This is connected with the fact that Plymouth was also never really able to attract settlers in large numbers; this is all the more obvious when compared with the experience north of the provincial line in Boston, which had thousands of people arriving by the boatload. It has been noted more than once that the diffidence of Plymouth Colony in not persecuting Quakers had everything to do with Quakers not wanting to settle there. There were Quakers (particularly around Sandwich), but never in very significant numbers -- and Plymouth could not afford to lose even the few people they had.

c. *Separatism could only work if the whole community was united*, as the *Acts of the Apostles* relates of the early Christian community: "And they continued stedfastly in the apostles' doctrine and fellowship, and in breaking of bread, and in prayers. And fear came upon every soul: and many wonders and signs were done by the apostles. And all that believed were together, and had all things common; And sold their possessions and goods, and parted them to all men, as every man had need" (Acts 2:42-45). As idealised as this picture is for the early Church, the Pilgrims consciously sought to imitate it sixteen centuries later. Much has been made of the tension between the Saints and the Strangers, but it has to be noted that the Strangers, with only a handful of exceptions, were willing to go along with the Saints, and conform to their activities and way of life, for the Colony to survive. If they were not willing to do that, they would not have made such a dangerous voyage in the first place. Bradford's very, very dark description of the disintegration of the religious life of the community (or, perhaps more accurately, the entropy of the community) highlights that he thought that the greatest, and gravest, failure of Plymouth, was neither economic nor political, as serious as those failures were, but religious. He took courage, however, from the fact that at least they tried.

THURSDAY, 20 MAY 1621

Marriage (part one)

About fifteen years ago, when I was pastor of a parish in New Hampshire, right on the Connecticut River, I was intrigued by the different ways the two neighbouring states dealt with the political struggle over the redefinition of marriage. In the People's Republic of Vermont, it was dealt with as a civil rights issue: aging hippies, with long grey ponytails down their backs, marched on the state capital in Montpelier singing "We Shall Overcome" -- they were thrilled that it was the 1960s all over again. In New Hampshire ("Live Free or Die"), the only state without a mandatory seatbelt law, it was considered a Libertarian issue: "How DARE the State say who can and cannot get married!" It was strange to see the two states come up with virtually the same answer from two directly opposite directions.

But it got me thinking -- when, exactly, did the state get in to the marriage business? How did that happen? What made anyone think that marriage was a state matter? In Roman law, marriage was not a civil matter, nor was it a contract: it was a *fact*. If two people treated each other as husband and wife (the technical term was *maritalis affectus*), then they were married. If they didn't, then they weren't: the question of whether they were married or not was investigated in exactly the same way as any other fact.

Judaism (and, centuries later, Christianity) had clear rules for who could get married and who could not. The question of what "made" marriage, in the Christian context, was settled in 1177 by Alexander III: consent makes marriage, but consummation gives it permanence. While the state dealt with property matters that arose out of marriage, marriage was only one of a large number of things that gave rise to property disputes that came before civil courts. But for about a millennium, marriage was seen as an ecclesiastical rather than a civil matter, and was regulated -- in English speaking lands, *exclusively* regulated -- by the Church.

This changed in England only in the eighteenth century: the Clandestine Marriages Act 1753 (long title: "An Act for the Better Preventing of Clandestine Marriage," popularly known as Lord Hardwicke's Marriage Act [26 Geo. II. c. 33]), was the first statutory legislation in England and Wales to require a formal ceremony of marriage. It came into force on 25 March 1754; civil marriage (i.e., marriage without any religious ceremony) did not come into existence for another hundred years (The Act for Marriages in England 1836, 6&7 Wm IV c. 85 [17 August 1836]).

The Pilgrims were thus, according to English law prior to Lord Hardwicke's Act, still able to exchange consent privately and be recognised as married. Since there were no clergymen in the

Plymouth Colony, there was no one who could officiate at a wedding. Thus far, no problem. But they took it one step further, as we shall see tomorrow, and that is what got them (in general) and Edward Winslow (in particular) into deep trouble.

FRIDAY, 21 MAY 1621

Marriage (part two)

The Pilgrims played a much smaller role in colonial development than the Puritans who settled in Massachusetts Bay a decade later, but their practices are important to this history because they show that the Pilgrims brought foreign marriage practises with them. Bradford's account of tomorrow's wedding underscores the importance of marriage and family to the colony, and confirms that the Pilgrims believed that marriage should be a civil matter: "According to the laudable custom of the Low Countries, in which they had lived, [it] was thought most requisite [for the marriage] to be performed by the magistrate, as being a civil thing [and] most consonant to the Scriptures (Ruth iv) and nowhere found in the Gospel to be laid on the ministers as a part of their office. 'This decree or law about marriage was published by the States of the Low Countries Anno 1590. That those of any religion (after lawful and open publication) coming before the magistrates in the Town, or State house, were to be orderly (by them) married one to another.' –Petit's History, fol. 1029." Bradford's account was not finished until 1646, when he added that civil marriage "hath continued amongst not only them, but hath been followed by all the famous churches of Christ in these parts to this time." Holland, the source of the Pilgrim's knowledge of civil marriage, had been heavily influenced by Luther as early as 1519, although in the 1550s, a form of Calvinism overtook Lutheranism as the dominant sect in the region. Consistories, like the one in Geneva, had also been established in most Dutch towns to supervise the lives of residents.

Note here that this was not simply a recognition of the fact that they had no one there to officiate at the marriage, not having any ordained clergy. They could have exchanged consent privately, or in front of witnesses alone, and it would have been perfectly legal in English law. This was, in fact, an attempt positively to *reject* the law of England on this matter by entrusting the office of officiating at a marriage to someone who was completely without any authority to do so in canon law, common law, or statutory law.

241

It was something of an "in your face" ceremony against both church and state.

The colonists' embrace of civil marriage did not sit well with leaders of the Anglican Church. In 1635, Edward Winslow returned to England to pay off debts the colony owed to its financial backers and to petition the Lord Commissioners for the Plantations to assist the colonists in resisting French and Dutch claims. Charles I, who became king in 1625, had established the commission in 1634 to oversee the colonies, and installed as its head William Laud, Archbishop of Canterbury, who was the scourge of Puritans because of his efforts to purge these ministers from the Church of England. Laud questioned Winslow, an act Bradford characterized as designed to "disturb the peace of the [colony's] churches." When asked about marriage, Winslow acknowledged that because he was a magistrate in Plymouth Colony, he had "married some." He defended his actions by arguing that "marriage was a civil thing and he found nowhere in the Word of God that it was tied to ministry." (Of course, he couldn't find the Word of God saying that "marriage was a civil thing," either, but that didn't suit his purpose.) Winslow also offered a second, more practical, reason for their recognition of civil marriage: the colonists "were necessitated so to do, having for a long time together at first no minister." Neither justification satisfied Laud, however, who arranged for Winslow to spend seventeen weeks in Fleet prison for illegally officiating at a marriage.

Law and government in the Plymouth colony, unlike most colonial law, derived from Reformation sources rather than from English law. Sectarian disputes between the Puritans and Anglicans were a major factor in the decision to leave England, as well as in their adoption of civil, or, better, community, rather than ecclesiastical control of marriage. To have permitted ministers to perform marriages in the new world would have risked giving too much control to Anglicans. It was safer to reserve marriage to magistrates who would ensure that Puritan values and Scripture shaped families in the colony. Community control of marriage also appealed to the new middle class that was beginning to dominate in England in the period surrounding their Civil War, although it was rejected in England after the Restoration. Note that civil marriage was not simply an option -- it was required, and ordained ministers were prohibited from officiating at marriages in the Plymouth Colony. The point was moot, however, in the early period, because there were few (or no) ordained ministers who could object.

This complex mix of sectarian differences and the absence of ecclesiastical courts explains the paradox that the United States, despite the religious zeal of so many of the original colonists, nonetheless was a pioneer in adopting civil marriage and divorce.

SATURDAY, 22 MAY 1621

First Marriage

[12 May o.s.] "The first Marriage in this Place is of Mr. Edward Winslow to Mrs. Susanna White, Widow of Mr. William White." Winslow's first wife was one of the last to die at the end of the winter, seven weeks ago; she and Edward had no children. There were few single women available, and Winslow, at twenty-five years old (remember his birthday on the *Mayflower*?) was certainly marriageable. Joining these two households brought infant Peregrine White and his brother Resolved. Edward and Susannah had five children together, of whom two have known descendants: Josiah Winslow (b. 1629, d. 1680) was the first native born governor of Plymouth Colony and commander of the united colonial forces during King Philip's War; and Elizabeth Winslow (b. ca. 1630, d. 1703), who had a total of eight children from the second and third of her three husbands: only one has descendants.

SUNDAY, 23 MAY 1621

How long is a generation?

In genealogy, the length of a generation in the past has been used principally as a check on the credibility of evidence — too long a span between parent and child, especially in a maternal line, has been reason to go back and take a more careful look at whether the received information reflects the actual reality, or whether a generation has been omitted or data for two different individuals attributed to the same person. For that purpose, the accepted 25-year average has worked quite acceptably, and birth dates too far out of line with it are properly suspect.

Several recent studies show that male-line generations, from father to son, are longer on average than female-line generations, from mother to daughter. They show, too, that both

243

are longer than the 25-year interval that conventional wisdom has assigned a generation. The male generation is at least a third longer; the female generation is about one-sixth longer. Of course, this is an average, and does not indicate that any particular, specific generation would be longer (or shorter, for that matter) than the average.

Using the accepted average, the "Five generation project" would have gone, more or less, from 1620 to about 1750: the original idea was to link the Pilgrims with those who were alive at the time of the American Revolution.

Having said that, some *Mayflower* lines have been very, very short, so that the fifth generation was reached before the end of the seventeenth century.

Other *Mayflower* lines are very, very long. As I was putting the names through the seventh generation on the spreadsheet I am using to assemble the Soule silver book, I started to notice a good number of death dates from the seventh generation in the twentieth century, and I flagged death dates in the seventh generation after 1935 -- there are about 25 of them, and the most recent death in the seventh generation is 1947. Although it was difficult enough work to catalogue descendants through the seventh generation (the full spreadsheet, containing all descendants, whether or not they had issue, and their spouses, has about 40,000 names), I would not be at all surprised if there were (are!) currently living Soule descendants from the ninth generation.

The recently published (2019) Winslow silver book benefitted from the Winslow family being very small, and thus they were able to document generations one through eight, naming generation nine. Thumbing through that book, I noticed more than one death date from the ninth generation in the twenty-first century (the most recent I found being 2009). I was unable to discover whether any individuals in the ninth generation were still living, but it would (theoretically) be possible. It might be somewhat startling for someone to pick up the book and see all of one's own vital statistics in print.

MONDAY, 24 MAY 1621

Worship

The colony (all fifty-odd of them) held two worship services each Sunday, one in the morning, and one in the afternoon: each one lasted for about three hours. They would also occasionally meet on a weekday to hear a sermon. They took their muskets with them, just in case, although they never had any occasion to use them. They filed in to the common house (at first) or to the fort (which doubled as a meetinghouse), men seated on one side, women and children on the other side, a configuration they called "dignifying the meeting." Before the fort was completed, they occasionally also met outdoors.

There was no ordained minister in Plymouth, since John Robinson was left in Leiden, and thus there was no pastor, teacher, or anyone who could administer sacraments or define doctrine. As the highest ranking layman, William Brewster presided over the congregation. He led the worship, preached (as he was able), and instructed the youth. He was responsible for the behaviour and morals of the colony, and issued warnings and admonitions as necessary.

There were two deacons: John Carver and Samuel Fuller. After Carver's death, Fuller was the only deacon left; he collected the offerings and was responsible for the care of the poor and the elderly, although at this stage pretty much everyone was poor, and William Brewster was as close as anyone was to "elderly." But Fuller tended to the sick, which was a significant job in that first year.

TUESDAY, 25 MAY 1621

Church

The building where the worship service took place was called the "meeting house," and doubled as a fort, a schoolhouse, a town hall, and probably as a jail, as well. The "pews" were probably benches. There was no standard posture for prayer: standing, sitting, kneeling were all practised. The pews probably ran the long way across the rectangular area, putting everyone closer to the pulpit (although there may, or may not, have actually been a pulpit). There was probably a communion table, but that was the extent of recognisable ecclesiastical furniture. Prohibited by the second commandment of the Decalogue were statues, crosses, icons, paintings, stained glass, and crucifixes.

WEDNESDAY, 26 MAY 1621

"Deliver us from evil ..."

If you recall several months ago, before contact was made with local natives, there was an eerie sense of isolation among the rapidly diminishing number of settlers, looking out into the dark woods, knowing that there were people there but not knowing who they were or what their intentions were. While contact with the Indians was vital to the survival of the colony (although the need to provide hospitality had its downside, as we shall see tomorrow), the colonists were exceptionally aware of the many, many threats (even if "enemies" is too strong a word) to their survival that surrounded them. The Indians decided, for their own reasons, to establish contact and provide support; the Pilgrims also realised that the natives outnumbered them by at least 100 to 1, they had real grievances (more about that next month when we encounter a lost Billington), and they could wipe them out whenever they wanted, upon a slight -- or even no -- provocation. Thus the settlers never, even years later, stopped strengthening the fort. So the Pilgrims thought; apparently the Indians believed that the Pilgrims had brought the plague-like disease with them, their own "weapon of mass destruction," and could obliterate them whenever they wanted.

The Pilgrims kept one eye open for threats from the land, but they had their other eye constantly trained on the sea for danger from that direction, as well. The Spanish claimed, by papal grant, all of North America, and the Spanish Inquisition was focussed on, not to say obsessed with, religious and political extremists just like the Separatists. The Dutch claimed land from the Hudson River to Cape Cod, and had refused the Pilgrims permission to settle in New Netherlands; the Dutch also were at war with England, off and on, for centuries. The French had colonies to the north along the Saint Lawrence and in what became Nova Scotia,[167] and their colonies dotted the eastern seacoast of the new world all the way down to Rio de Janeiro. There is an illuminating story of what happened when a French Jesuit (involuntary shudder) visited Plymouth in 1650, and how William Bradford and Edward Winslow fell all over themselves

---

[167] As an aside, I have recently started Conrad Black's *Rise to Greatness: The History of Canada. Volume I: Colony (1000-1867)* (Toronto: McClelland and Stewart, 2014). It presents a startling story of how very, very tenuous and tentative the settlement of New France really was, and how little support Champlain got from the French government, which went back and forth between wanting a large and successful colony on the one hand, and desiring to pull the plug on the whole venture on the other.

trying to be hospitable (maybe I should add that story in a couple of weeks). And almost any of these previous categories could be rolled together into the category of "pirates," who, in Glenn Alan Cheney's wonderful phrase, "might be interested in anything from gunpowder to women."[168] When the *Fortune* first appeared on the horizon in November 1621, that is what the Plymouth colony at first thought the ship carried. They also realised that their "dread sovereign" King James I and VI now knew exactly where they were and could round them up easily whenever he wanted to and imprison them -- or worse -- for sedition.

THURSDAY, 27 MAY 1621

The Burden of Hospitality

The settlers were, apparently, quite glad to receive visits from Massasoit and his brother Quadequina, Squanto, and Samoset. But the curiosity of many other natives became a serious burden: the Pilgrims were quickly exhausting the food that they had brought from England, and a harvest had not yet replaced their depleted stores. They had also run out of beer, which was Samoset's first, and only, request on his initial visit. *Mourt's Relation* continues: "But whereas [Massasoit's] people came very often, and very many together unto us, bringing for the most part their wives and children with them, they were welcome; yet we being but strangers [i.e., newcomers] as yet at Patuxet, alias New Plimoth, and not knowing how our corn might prosper, we could no longer give them such entertainment as we had done, and as we desired still to do." It is an ironic change of fate, that while they were friendless, isolated, and forlorn just two months ago, now the Pilgrims were over-run by visitors who were interested in every element of their life, and especially of their food.

FRIDAY, 28 MAY 1621

Intelligence

Another issue having to do with the large number of native visitors arriving at New Plimoth was the "gathering of intelligence." The visitors could see exactly how many (or how few) settlers there were, what they were doing, and what defences there were. The Pilgrims, on the other hand, had no idea at all about how many Indians there were, how far away they were,

---

[168] Cheney, *Thanksgiving*, 228

what they were doing, and how friendly, or unfriendly, they were. Official representatives of Massasoit, of course, were welcome, especially if they had furs to trade, but there simply was not enough food to go around, or enough time to entertain every visitor -- and their wives and children -- particularly if the curiosity of the visitors was not simply of the "let's get acquainted" variety. Massasoit had warned the Pilgrims that there were numerous tribes who were not friendly or well-disposed to either his tribe or to the Pilgrims, but the Pilgrims had no way of identifying who those were.

SATURDAY, 29 MAY 1621

Elections

References to elections are scattered throughout Bradford's journals and letters. It has been questioned whether Myles Standish was an elected or an appointed military commander. While it is probable that he was engaged by the leaders of the Separatist community in Holland to accompany the group and provide military expertise, it is clear that he had to receive at least confirmation in a vote from the settlers. Lyford, whose letters Bradford intercepted, wanted to stop any further immigration of Separatists from Leiden, giving a vote to those on his "particular" list as men who were likely to follow him, and outvoting Bradford's followers, so that they could choose a new captain in place of Standish. The colonists did not start keeping a record of elections until 1633, and they initially used discussion and consensus as well as a straight up-and-down vote. John Carver had been elected governor before leaving England, and this was "confirmed" upon arrival at Provincetown Harbour. While Carver's predecessor in that position, Christopher Martin, had an assistant, there is no mention of Carver having an assistant. When William Bradford was elected governor, he was given Isaac Allerton as an assistant, and all subsequent governors had at least one assistant -- and sometimes as many as seven. A Dutch visitor to Plymouth, Isaac de Rasieres, recorded that "the Governor has his council, which is chosen every year by the entire community, by election or prolongation of terms."[169] Voting was public -- no

---

[169] This quotation is from a fascinating little book called *Three Visitors to Early Plymouth*. The book puts together seven letters written in the 1620s by three visitor to Plymouth: Emmanuel Altham (one of the

secret ballots -- and usually either by calling out names or by a show of hands. Since Plymouth was so small at first, there was no need for a roll of voters or a census; these were more important when towns were established and the community became scattered. Religious qualifications for voting were introduced in the 1650s (no Quakers or Papists), and while they were discussed as early as the 1640s, property qualifications were settled in the 1670s: the requirement for voting was holding a minimum of a £20 taxable estate.

SUNDAY, 30 MAY 1621

The Governor

While the practise of voting in elections may make Plymouth appear to be a democracy, the exercise of actual power was something else. In the early years of the settlement, when disturbing reports about democracy in Plymouth were circulating in England, and when men could have gathered easily to discuss policy and make decisions either formally or informally, the decision making power was clearly exercised by Governor Bradford. Bradford, in a 1623 letter to calm the adventurers' apprehensions, stated that he seldom submitted matters to voters for a decision. While he was certainly trying to reassure the stockholders that the Plymouth settlement was not, in fact, democratic, there is no reason to doubt that what he wrote was true. The early settlers apparently agreed that the responsibility for governing the plantation rested with the governor, and that the purpose of government was, well, to govern. In 1623, when Bradford asked the General Court for a decision on policy toward the Massachusetts Indians, the Court referred the question back to the Governor. This was all in line with teaching by John Robinson that everyone must be subject to their rulers, as well as John Calvin's insistence on the supremacy of the civil governor. The first real challenge to Bradford's power came only after he had been governor for about four years (when Lyford and Oldham tried to stir up a revolt in 1625). No evidence of a further challenge to Bradford's authority came until the middle of the next decade. When one could stop and exchange pleasantries with him, and

---

Merchant Adventurers, who was also captain of the *Little James*), John Pory (an official from Jamestown in Virginia), and Isaac de Rasieres (a Dutch official from New Amsterdam).

when one could look up from work and see him working in the next field, it seemed foolish to worry about the extent of his power. But in 1636 the freemen called in General Court for a reading of the colony's laws, and a commission was established to codify them -- and this commission decided on a limitation of the power and authority of the governor and his assistants: the governor was specifically restricted from enacting legislation. Further curtailment of the power of magistrates followed in 1639, when the governor and his assistants lost the right to control the granting of land -- the magistrates noticeably dragged their heels about this. Colony law required a man elected governor to assume the office or to pay a fine, but between 1633 and 1639, when much of the changing of governors took place, it also allowed a man to decline election in successive years, and we know that Bradford asked not to be elected at least once. It is probably not a coincidence that after 1639, when this law was repealed, only once did an incumbent fail to be re-elected.

The Governor could summon the General Court into special session, when he deemed it necessary; he presided over it once it convened, and had a casting vote in case of a tie. He was also a judicial officer and could arrest and cast into prison, and responsible for the execution of all colony laws. There are several occasions on which the General Court refused to accept the Governor's recommendations, and some on which the Governor refused to accept the decision of the General Court (exercising something of a veto). But these were few and far between.

MONDAY, 31 MAY 1621

Shurtleff and Pulsifer

WARNING: The Geek Meter is Off the Chart on this Post!

My A-1 First Class Favourite Source for the Plymouth Colony is Nathaniel B. Shurtleff and David Pulsifer, eds., *Records of the Colony of New Plymouth, in New England*, in 12 vols. The Colony of New Plymouth (later called the "Old" Colony) became part of the Province of Massachusetts Bay under the Charter of 1691, but its records continued to be held in Plymouth successively by the last colonial secretary, the clerk of the Inferior Court, and the Plymouth County register of deeds. In the 19th century, concerns over the condition of and access to records led to their transcription by the Commonwealth, allowing the originals to remain in Plymouth. In 1853 the governor of Massachusetts called the attention of the executive council to the perishing condition of the early records and recommended that the two oldest volumes of the general court records should be printed at the expense of the state. Ephraim M. Wright and Nathaniel B. Shurtleff were appointed to take charge of the printing: Nathaniel Bradstreet Shurtleff, Sr. (b. 22 June 1810; d. 17 October 1874) was primarily a Know Nothing and Democratic politician, who served as the twentieth mayor of Boston (1868-1871). Most of the actual work in the compilation was done by David Pulsifer (b. 22 September 1802 in Ipswich; d. 9 August 1894 in Augusta, Maine), a historian and a preserver of old records; he had gone to Salem to learn bookbinding, where, in handling old records, his taste for antiquarian research was first developed. Subsequently, he served as a clerk in the county courts and transcribed several ancient books of records. Pulsifer was acknowledged to be especially skilful in deciphering 17th century handwriting, and was charged with the copying; he became the principal editor of the last four volumes.

The first six volumes are Court Orders from 1633 to 1691 (both the General Court and the Court of Assistants); volume seven, Judicial Acts, is a record of private lawsuits from 1636 to 1692; volume eight ("Miscellaneous Records") consists of vital records (birth, marriage, and death), treasury accounts, and lists of freeman; volumes nine and ten are the Acts of the Commissioners of the United Colonies (1643-1651 and 1653-1679); volume eleven consists of the Laws of Plymouth Colony from 1623 to 1682; volume twelve is our earliest records of Plymouth Colony deeds (1620 to 1651). These volumes were published in Boston by "the Press of W. White" from 1855 until the War Between the States brought the project to a halt in 1861.

While it is not exactly a secret, few people know that only about *half* of the total was actually published. An additional eleven volumes (!!) of manuscripts remain unpublished. These are mostly deeds, but also contain private letters entered into the court records. Jeremy Bangs has published a second volume of deeds (1651-1663 [Leiden: Leiden American Pilgrim Museum, 2016]) and the first part of a third volume (1664-1671 [Leiden: Leiden American Pilgrim Museum, 2017]): these would have been volumes thirteen and fourteen of the original series. This work was made possible in part by a grant from the Delano Kindred (thanks, folks!).[170]   I do not know if this transcription and publication project is continuing, but Bangs' work is a spectacular window into the colony. I would give my eyeteeth to work on that project.

Tomorrow I will talk about some of what can be discovered.

---

[170] Jeremy Bangs has also published other deeds in his *Indian Deeds: Land Transactions in Plymouth Colony* and his more recent *Josias Wompatuck and the Titicut Reserve of the Mattakeeset - Massachusetts Tribe.*

JUNE 1621

Land Sales

One of the particularly surprising discoveries made from reading the land and court records of the colony deals with the Indians. In almost every case, the initiative for land deals came from the Indians themselves, although (as Bangs points out in his *Indian Deeds*) in many, perhaps most, cases they were "invited" to sell by local settlers. One court case involves a land "gift pretended to be given by Phillip the sachem," which the Plymouth leaders were suspicious of: it is not certain that the colonist ever actually was granted this land. Still another case involves two settlers from other colonies who were jailed for obtaining Indian land without official permission, which is highly unusual in colonial history. And, of course, the Indians could always reject an offer to sell, as they did in a 3 October 1665 listing. The Plymouth leaders were particularly interested in making sure that the Indians did not sell too much land. On 2 July 1665, while giving permission for colonists to buy Indian land, the Plymouth magistrates specified that any such purchase "doe not cause or breed any desturbance amongst the Indians." It certainly appears that the colony's governors and assistants genuinely attempted to protect Indian land rights, in case after case.

This seems to have changed significantly around 1670, however. The Indians (both individually and as a community) had got so far into debt that land became the only substantial asset that they could produce to settle with their creditors. This is a sign of the tilt in the economic and political balance between the Indians and the settlers; perhaps it was inevitable, but it is also clear that there was no pattern of ruthless defrauding on the part of the colonists. The economic imbalance left the Indians with only their land to exchange for what had become necessities. The native leaders responded by establishing reservations, which seemed to be an effective way of limiting their losses.

Court Records

Land sales are not the only thing to show up in court records, although these land records highlight important areas, particularly where there was conflict between parties. But so much of the everyday life of the colony can be seen in these court records, as well: elections, weights and measures, permits for taverns (ordinaries), land grants, excuses from military service, fines for absence from church services, levying troops and equipment, public expenditures, taxes, apprentice and servant indentures, divorces, laying out streets and towns, regulation of wages and prices, the reaction against Quakers, and quite a bit more. And that does not touch on actual criminal trials, which were somewhat few and far between: as mentioned earlier, Plymouth went a good decade without a single jury trial.

These court records, however, need to be read carefully, because they are typically records of a decision or a final agreement, and what led up to that decision may not be written down. For that, the more narrative histories (Bradford, Winslow, Morton) may be able fill in the blanks. But this is why the use of these documents is both fun, in its detective-like work, and frustrating, because sometimes it doesn't tell us even half of what we want to know.

To my mind, the greatest advantage of these records is that they were made at the time, and thus they are mercifully free from the presumptions and assumptions of later periods of history. But we must be careful to ensure that we understand the circumstances of the time -- the capital offence of this type of scholarship is anachronism, or chronological inconsistency: the act of attributing a custom, event, intention, or object of one period (typically our own) to another period to which it does not belong.

3 JUNE 1621

Meanwhile, back in Europe ...

Today marks the four hundredth anniversary of the charter of the Dutch West India Company, chartered on 3 June 1621 by the Republic of the Seven United Netherlands. The company was given the exclusive right to operate in West Africa (between the Tropic of Cancer and the Cape of Good Hope) and the Americas. Willem Usselincx was one of the founders of the West India Company, and promoted the establishment of colonies in the New World as the company's principal purpose. In 1620, Usselincx made a last appeal to the States General, which rejected this vision as a primary goal. The legislators preferred trading posts with small populations and a military presence to protect them, which was working in the East Indies, as opposed to encouraging mass immigration and establishing large colonies. The company did not shift to colonization in North America until 1654, when it was forced to surrender Dutch Brazil and forfeit the richest sugar-producing area in the world.

Like the French in the north, the Dutch focused their interests on the fur trade. To that end, they cultivated relations with the Five Nations of the Iroquois to procure greater access to key central regions from which the skins came. In 1617, Dutch colonists built a fort at the confluence of the Hudson and Mohawk Rivers where Albany now stands. The Dutch claimed all territory from the end of the Delmarva peninsula to Cape Cod -- this would make Plymouth, at best, right on the border, if not within Dutch territory. In 1624, New Netherland became a province of the Dutch Republic, which had lowered the northern border of its North American dominion to 42 degrees latitude in acknowledgment of the claim by the English north of Cape Cod (Plymouth, for your information, is at 41° 57′ N). The population, even at its height, was very small and extremely contentious, and the Company provided little military support. In 1664, during a series of Anglo-Dutch conflicts, England moved to take over New Netherland; the Dutch colonists refused to fight, forcing Governor Stuyvesant's surrender. Although the Dutch briefly regained control of the territory in 1674, the English quickly consolidated their gains as the colony of New York.

Dutch continued to be spoken in the region for some time. President Martin Van Buren grew up in Kinderhook, New York, speaking only Dutch, becoming the only U. S. president not to have spoken English as a first language.

FRIDAY, 4 JUNE 1621

Holland v. the Hapsburgs

There was a brilliant presentation online yesterday from the New York State Archives on the 400th anniversary of the charter establishing the Dutch West India Company, about which I wrote yesterday morning. Related to this, however, is one of the reasons why the Pilgrims were so keen on leaving Holland when they did: the "Twelve Years' Truce" between the Habsburg rulers of Spain and the Southern Netherlands and the Dutch Republic was due to expire in 1621. There was continual contact between Stadtholder Prince Maurice of Orange and the government in

Brussels during 1620 and 1621 regarding a possible renewal of the Truce. Archduke Albert of Austria, Governor General of the Habsburg (Catholic) Netherlands and husband of Isabella Clara Eugenia, the daughter of King Philip II, was in favour of a renewal, especially after Maurice (falsely!) gave him the impression that a peace would be possible on the basis of a token recognition by the Republic of the sovereignty of the king of Spain. Renewal of the Truce had become less likely, as both in Spain and in the Republic more hard-line factions had come to power. The Spaniards demanded Dutch evacuation of the West and East Indies; lifting of the restrictions on Antwerp's trade by way of the Scheldt (through Dutch territory); and toleration of the public practice of the Catholic religion in the Republic. These demands were unacceptable to Maurice and the Truce expired in April 1621.

The war did not immediately resume, however. Maurice continued sending secret offers to Isabella after Albert died in July 1621, through the intermediary of the Flemish painter (!!) Peter Paul Rubens. Though the contents of these offers (which amounted to a version of the concessions demanded by Spain) were not known in the Republic, the fact of the secret negotiations became known. Proponents of restarting the war were disquieted, like the investors in the Dutch West India Company, which had just been founded with the main objective of bringing the war to the Spanish Americas. Opposition against the peace feelers therefore mounted, and nothing came of them.

Another reason the war did not immediately resume was that King Philip III died shortly before the truce ended. He was succeeded by his 16-year-old son Philip IV and a new government under Gaspar de Guzmán, Count-Duke of Olivares. The view of the Spanish government was that the truce had been economically ruinous to Spain, and had enabled the Dutch to gain very unfair advantages in trade with the Iberian Peninsula and the Mediterranean. The continued blockade of Antwerp had contributed to that city's steep decline in importance (hence the demand for the lifting of the closing of the Scheldt). The shift in trade between Spain and the Republic had resulted in a permanent trade deficit for Spain, because of a drain of Spanish silver to the Republic. The truce had also given further impetus to the Dutch penetration of the East Indies, and in 1615 a naval expedition under Joris van Spilbergen raided the West-Coast of Spanish South America. Spain felt threatened by these incursions and wanted to put a stop to them. Finally, the economic advantages had given the Republic the financial wherewithal to build a large navy during the truce and to enlarge its standing army to a size where it could rival Spanish military might. The three conditions Spain had set for a continuation of the truce had been intended to remedy these disadvantages (the demand for freedom of worship for Catholics being made as a matter of principle, but also to mobilise the still sizeable Catholic minority in the Republic and so destabilise it politically).

SATURDAY, 5 JUNE 1621

Babes in the woods

We have already seen the trouble Billingtons could get into: Francis Billington almost blew up the *Mayflower* before it even got to Plymouth, and climbed a tree to discover a large body of water that is known as Billington's Sea even now; John Billington, his father, was subject to the first criminal action in the colony (for insubordination against Myles Standish), and, as we have already discovered, came to no good end within a decade.

His sixteen year old son, John Billington [junior], at just about this time, wandered off to the south of Plymouth and got horribly, horribly lost. For five days John wandered aimlessly about, living on roots, berries, nuts and anything else that was even remotely edible.

Although Bradford in his journal records that the party sent to retrieve young John Billington left at the end of July, *Mourt's Relation* states that they left on 11 June (o.s., or 21 June in the Gregorian calendar we use). We learn from the earlier narrative that he had been held by the natives for some time before the Pilgrims were informed of his whereabouts, and that he had wandered around south of Plymouth for at least five days before he stumbled across the Indian settlement at Manomet. It would thus appear that John's disappearance happened just about now, and this fits into the timeline more easily at the beginning of June rather than the end of July, when Edward Winslow and Stephen Hopkins were going back and forth on their diplomatic trips to various local Indian tribes. It seems unlikely that the Pilgrims would have attempted any contact with tribes (and certainly not out to the Nauset, the natives of the "first encounter") while these

257

two were away or otherwise occupied.

The Billington family

The Billington family was one of the few families not touched by death in the first winter. John and Ellinor (whose maiden name is unknown) had two sons: Bradford's 1651 list of increasings notes that John Billington (the father) was "executed for killing a man," and we know that this took place in 1630. Bradford indicates that the elder son (whom we know to be John Billington, the younger -- the boy who yesterday got lost in the woods) died before his father. This John Billington was included in the division of cattle in 1627, so we know that he must have died between June 1627 and September 1630. He was born about 1604, so this would mean that he was between 23 and 26 at the time of his death. Bradford notes that Billington's second son (Francis) married and had children; the fact that he did not mention this about John as well would lead to the conclusion that John Billington (the younger) died unmarried and without issue.

Francis Billington did his best to make up for that. He married Christian Penn, who arrived on the *Anne* in 1623; Christian had married Francis Eaton as her first husband and had three children by him. My favourite quandary about the original manuscript of Bradford's *Of Plimmoth Plantation* has to do with the number of children Francis and Christian Billington had. There is smudge to the left of the number "8", so that it appears that Bradford recorded that they had 18 children, which, when the 3 Eaton children are added, would mean there were 21 -- a veritable colony of their own. Upon closer inspection, however, the smudge is, in fact, a smudge, and we can verify that there were only nine children of this union, one of whom was born after Bradford compiled his list. 11 children in this blended family is a big enough number.

MONDAY, 7 JUNE 1621

Wandering South

John Billington the younger's wanderings south would have taken him to the nearest native settlement to Plymouth, which is Manomet (about the location of the present Cape Cod Canal). Most of the descriptions I have seen of his wanderings suggest that he walked about 20 miles, which would have put him well past modern Manomet (as well as the Coast Guard station or the now shut down nuclear power plant). He probably had no idea of where he was going, of course, and thus his path would not have been in a straight line. The modern narratives tend to concentrate on his diet, which was minimal, rather than his route, which at this point is unknowable.

Emmanuel Altham, one of the Company of Adventurers for New Plymouth, in his "Letter to Sir Edward Altham" (1623) describes Manomet as the Indian settlement closest to Plymouth. He identifies not the location but the distance: "And now I will speak somewhat of the savages in the country about -- I mean the native Indians. The nearest that any dwell unto [Plymouth] is fourteen miles, and their town is called Manomet." This placemark indicates only a guess of where Manomet might have been

The Manomet location may have been a summer settlement: the natives are known to have moved closer to the coast, and their primary food sources, in the summer, and further inland in the winter. Young John may have been in luck in this timing, because if this had been earlier in the year, there might not have been any inhabitants even that close.

TUESDAY, 8 JUNE 2021

Arrival

Just about now, or perhaps in a day or two, John Billington the younger strolled into the Indian village at Manomet. What must have been going through his mind? The only Indians he had thus far met were friendly ones: Samoset ("Welcome, Englishmen!"), Squanto, Massasoit, Quidequina, and the *numerous* others that were overrunning the Pilgrim settlement and testing the limits of Pilgrim hospitality. He probably had every expectation that he would be taken care of, maybe fed well, and then sent back home, perhaps with an escort.

If that was his expectation, he was rather quickly disabused of it. The Manomet sachem, Canacum, could have had not even a slight doubt about where the boy had come from. But instead of returning the boy to the English, he sent him off to the Nausets on Cape Cod (near the modern Eastham). These were the very people who had attacked the Pilgrims on First Encounter beach back in December. They were also the ones whose graves and corn storage the Pilgrims had rifled in the starvation-fuelled search.

Why would Canacum do this? More on that tomorrow, but

259

ponder what this says about the relations among the natives until then.

WEDNESDAY, 9 JUNE 2021

Tribal Politics

Why did Canacum, the sachem of the Manomet Indians, send young John Billington to the Nauset Indians, several days' journey away, rather than straight home (where he knew he had come from) or to Massasoit and the Pokanoket Indians (whom he knew had a treaty with the Pilgrims)? The plagues that had decimated the Pokanoket Indians had, apparently, not been as disastrous to other tribes in the area, and by turning the Billington boy over to the Nausets instead of to the Pokanokets, Canacum made a conscious effort to defer to a neighbour whose relative strength had increased dramatically since the plague. It may also have been a way for Canacum to express his displeasure with Massasoit's decision to ally with the Pilgrims. The Nausets could pretty much do as they wanted in the area, while the Pokanoket, hemmed in by enemies on every side, had to be very, very careful. It is significant that the Nausets, from a position of strength, had early on taken the offensive against the Pilgrims, while Massasoit's Pokanokets, from a position of weakness, had tried to negotiate a deal. Massasoit's influence in the region was apparently not as dominant as he had led the Pilgrim leaders to believe -- this may also have been yet another reason why the settlers decided to send Winslow and Hopkins to meet with Massasoit on his home turf next month -- so they could see exactly how much of what he said was bluster, or a front, or a con job. It became crystal clear that Massasoit could not protect the Pilgrims. As Philbrick relates it, "With the boy in their possession, the Nausets were able to send an unmistakable message to the English: 'You stole something of ours; well, now we have something of yours'."[171]

These rivalries continue: as I mentioned in a recent review in the *Mayflower Quarterly*, the descendants of the Pokanoket Indians have exaggerated their tribe (under the name of Wampanoag, a name that only comes into use about fifty years after these events), and on the map produced by Plymouth 400 to show the location of various tribes, several of the more powerful tribes, such as the Massachusetts, are erased completely -- the

---

[171] Philbrick, *Mayflower*, 111

ultimate in cancel culture! The small, weak Pokanoket Indians are elevated by the phrase "Four Nations" to the level of a nation state such as England and Holland -- which they manifestly were not -- and they can finally take revenge on their neighbours by grabbing their land and erasing their names, even if it is 400 years later.

THURSDAY, 10 JUNE 2021

Native Government

The government of the various Indian tribes displayed a highly structured and rigid class structure. A chief, known as a sachem, was usually the largest property owner and the supreme ruler. The position of sachem (among the Pokanoket, this was Massasoit when the *Mayflower* arrived, and later his son, Metacom, who called himself King Philip) was inherited, usually passed on from father to son. In the absence of a son, a daughter could inherit the position -- which was exactly the same provision for succession as in most European monarchies. The sachem, once in place, had to prove himself: he could be replaced, or just ousted, for cowardice, poor judgement, ignorance, or a lack of leadership. The sachem ruled with a council, not unlike a parliament. The Manomet sachem Canacum had to show himself decisive, but also subordinate to his more powerful neighbours, and young John Billington was the perfect bargaining chip to show both of those things. The sachem had both a civil and a religious role (no separation of church and state here, either): as Glenn Cheney rather breezily notes, "To remain worthy of his title, [the sachem] had to keep the tribe in harmony with the spirits of nature. If the relationship between the tribe and nature went sour, it was his fault. The consequences could be anything from hunger to invasion. But as long as things went well, he was king."[172] The sachem exacted an annual tax in kind or in service from all members of the tribe, as well as any others dependant on his authority; this was a series of interconnections not unlike the feudal system in Europe in the Middle Ages.

FRIDAY, 11 JUNE 1621

Search parties

John Billington had now been gone for about five days, and the Pilgrims had looked as far as they could without getting too far

---

[172] Cheney, *Thanksgiving*, 211

from home. Today they sent Squanto out to see what he could find, but he, too, returned without any clue.

SATURDAY, 12 JUNE 1621

Travel by Water

Young Master Billington may have reached the Nausets by now, and word would have been sent to Massasoit about this new prize capture.

Although the natives had not yet developed such "technology" as the wheel, the arch, the sail, the rudder, or the firearm, they were able to use the natural resources around them to great effect. One example is the use of trees: in building houses, the bark supplied the shingles to place over a simple frame of bent green saplings. Walnut bark was especially good. A canoe could be built at the same time. Mud would be packed around the tree, leaving the lower part exposed; a fire would be lit around the bottom, until the tree fell over. It was much quicker, much less strenuous, and more efficient than using an axe. The fire could then be applied to hollow out the interior of the tree, and stone tools would be used to finish. The larger canoes were over forty feet long, and could hold more than forty men.

SUNDAY, 13 JUNE 1621

Why did the chicken cross the Atlantic?

Much has been made of the two dogs that came on the *Mayflower*, but it would appear that there were also chickens brought, as well. When Massasoit became ill in 1623, Edward Winslow came and -- I am not making this up -- wanted to bring him chicken soup. Winslow was with Massasoit at his winter encampment, and when the chief began to fail, Winslow sent a messenger back to Plymouth to get some chickens, STAT! By the time the messenger returned with the fowl, Massasoit had recovered sufficiently that he asked to be able to keep and breed the chickens rather than eat them. The natives did not have farm animals: this was very much a part of European diet. Whether Massasoit wanted them to eat, or just to have an exotic European bird as a status symbol, is unknown.

Although cows, pigs, and sheep came over several years later, having only chicken and dogs to start out with (as mentioned by John Smith) got me to think about what else they did not have. As far as drinks go, there was no beer after it ran out (as we have

262

mentioned several times), nor milk (as there were no cows or goats) or wine. There was no bread for quite some time, as the barley they brought over really did not take. Livestock as a source of food were a first priority; sheep (also as a source of wool for clothing) came several decades later. There was wildfowl, of course, as well as fish (once they got the hang of it, which was not for some time). But the diet was simple and extremely limited.

MONDAY, 14 JUNE 1621

Tobacco

Tobacco is an American plant, growing as far north as New England and as far south as South America. Natives used it for ceremonial purposes; Massasoit shared it with the Pilgrims as a way of cementing their alliance. The English observed at that time that Massasoit carried some in a pouch, and that his people awaited his permission before they smoked. Smoking thus was not casual -- one had to be invited by a superior. On other occasions, it could be used as a way of making amends. *Mourt's Relation* told of a party of Englishmen journeying through the country when they encountered a former guide who had previously abandoned them. The native tried to mend the relationship by sharing tobacco. The English declined, believing the tobacco had been stolen, but this incident showed the use of this gesture as a means of reconciliation or emerging friendship. It is likely that many, if not most, of the Pilgrims had smoked tobacco before coming to America; it may also have been useful for its appetite suppressing qualities.

By 1620, smoking (or "drinking tobacco," as the English idiom of the time had it) was well known in England, as well. By 1604, King James I and VI authored a pamphlet against the "loathsome custom," entitled *A Counterblaste to Tobacco*. But in the decade that followed, tobacco use skyrocketed, and the Virginia Company hit on tobacco as a major export crop from Virginia, so that by 1620 and thereafter, Virginia planters shipped massive amounts of the plant to be consumed in England.

TUESDAY, 15 JUNE 1621

Clothing

All clothing and shoes had to be imported into the colony at first. Without a shoemaker, a tanner to process the leather, and herds of cattle to slaughter for hides, shoes could only come from England -- and we have already noted the large amount of footwear brought over by William Mullins. Once that was gone, there was none other to be obtained on this side of the Atlantic. Clothing, for the first decade at least, was in perpetually short supply. In response to repeated requests for more clothes and more cloth, the merchant adventurers wrote in 1624 that they were sending cloth, socks, shoes, and leather. When a French ship foundered on the shore two years later, Plymouth got a share of what was salvaged from the wreck, but the one thing that was mentioned in the report was "clothing for the people." Clearly, Plymouth lacked ready access to even the most basic articles of attire.

This was particularly problematic for indentured servants, since their contracts frequently included a legal obligation for the master to supply the servants with clothing during their term of employment. At the end of the time, the master was not infrequently required to supply suits of clothing. Clothes as payment for years of labour might seem rather stingy to us today, but the scarcity of clothing and the distance new clothing had to travel to come to the colony made these hard to obtain articles essential and quite valuable. In one court case, Web Adey, having been placed in service as a punishment for "disorderly living in idleness & nastiness," was ordered to sell or lease his house in order to pay for proper clothing.[173]

WEDNESDAY, 16 JUNE 1621

Furs

Furs were the one locally available item that could be readily turned into money. Even before the Pilgrims arrived in New England, John Smith had identified the two principal products which could provide prosperity for New England as furs and fish. Fish were well known, and available in abundance: as we have mentioned already, there seems to have been a desire on the party of the financial backers of the Virginia Company and the Plymouth Company to link Jamestown and the prospective colony in "northern Virginia" (the Pilgrims' original destination) by having the northern settlement supply fish for the southern colony. The English were already quite active in the fish market, but Smith also saw the use of furs. He advised the English to drive the French out of the New England region in order to crush the competition, since "their rivals often afford better trading

---

[173] PCR 1:87, 91, 5 Jun 1638

terms."[174] When the settlers -- finally, after months of glimpses and one hostile encounter -- met the Natives, they carefully noted what furs the natives wore. They distributed a few trinkets and asked to start up a fur trade. Plymouth needed to generate income: they either had to extract or to grow something that could find a market in England. The Spanish had found mineral wealth in Central and South America, but the English never really found any mines, although that did not stop them from looking. The first major cash crop the English found, in Virginia, was tobacco. The second, suited to the colder climates further north, were beaver and otter pelts, along with other forest products, of which England, and particularly its navy, was in great need. In order to obtain fish, the settlers would need equipment, boats, tools, barrels, salt, and a lot of luck (and skill, of which they had almost none at the start). All they needed for furs was trading partners. This proved somewhat difficult to organise, as we shall see tomorrow, although not as difficult as getting fish, at which the Pilgrims failed miserably.

THURSDAY, 17 JUNE 1621

Trading

There were two significant difficulties that the Pilgrims encountered in trying to organise trade. As soon as Massasoit and Plymouth established an alliance, the settlers received a continual flow of visitors who came to check out the new settlement, and trade. This stream of prospective traders, as we have seen, proved disruptive and expensive: that is why, next month, the Pilgrims asked Massasoit to put an end to it (as we shall see). Instead of receiving one or two furs at a time, the Pilgrims wanted to negotiate a single price for the lot. This plan, however, assumed a level of organisation in the Native communities that did not exist. Hunting for the natives was an individual activity, and the mechanisms for collecting numerous pelts and trading for a bulk shipment did not conform to native practises.

Another challenge was settling on an item that could be given in exchange for the furs that the Pilgrims sought. At first, hunters accepted novelty items of European manufacture, valuable to them because they were rare: beads or other trinkets. As the

---

[174] Smith, *A Description of New England* [London, 1616], in Barbour, ed., *Complete Works of Captain John Smith* 1:323-324, 336

trade grew, however, and hunters grew used to having European goods, they demanded more: metal tools, European cloth, even firearms. Competitors for trade began arriving soon after the *Mayflower*, so that Plymouth found itself vying not only with the French to the north and the Dutch to the west, but with other Englishmen in their immediate area. More traders gave the local hunters power to pick their partners, which in turn placed demands on Plymouth to supply increasingly appealing trade items. Plymouth's traders quickly found local people engaging with increasing sophistication in this burgeoning market economy.

FRIDAY, 18 JUNE 1621

Trading Posts

Because bulky items (like furs and pelts) and people moved more easily along water, trading stations had to be set up along navigable rivers, like the Plymouth trading house in Kennebec (now in Maine). Plymouth, however, was not in a very good harbour, and did not have access to a very extensive river system, so the settlers' leaders had to look further afield, to the north and to the west, for better locations. Within fifteen years, however, Plymouth had only two remote trading stations, one of which was threatened by others moving in to its territory. Bradford complained of men who came to fish but turned to trading for furs. Thomas Weston himself set up a rival outpost in 1622. When this new outpost failed, Thomas Morton started another, and angered the colonists by trading guns for furs.

The demand for pelts led to overhunting, and the population of beaver and otter decreased dramatically; this also ended Plymouth colony's chance to make a profit. Within twenty five years of its start, the fur trade in Plymouth colony had ended, as a result of competition, conflict and poor resource management.

SATURDAY, 19 JUNE 1621

Massasoit learns

Massasoit must have learned about the captivity (not to say incarceration) of John Billington among the Nausets about today. This whole affair had become very convoluted, and the fact that the Nausets (or the Manomets) communicated with Massasoit rather than directly with the English settlers shows that this was, at least in part, about inter-tribal rivalries. A good deal of this is also, "Well, they are YOUR allies, not ours," as well. Massasoit must have decided to inform the settlers as soon as he found out, although *Mourt's Relation*, the only source to describe the events in detail, simply states that the colonists learned about Billington's captivity from Massasoit.

SUNDAY, 20 JUNE 1621

Plymouth learns

Plymouth must have heard the news of John Billington's capture at about this time, and immediately took steps to get him back. It was a sign of the dire straits of the community that the governor sent ten men -- just about half of the adult men of the entire colony -- to return young Billington. They must have remembered, and if it was not, their Indian allies would undoubtedly have reminded them, that these were the very natives whose graves they had rifled and who had attacked them at dawn in the first encounter. It must have been difficult to outfit the group -- too much armament would have been seen as going to war, too little would have appeared weak and courted disaster.

MONDAY, 21 JUNE 1621

Set sail to bring home John Billington

The Pilgrims' horrible string of luck with bad weather continued unabated, as *Mourt's Relation* described: "The 11th of June (o.s., 21 June n.s.) we set forth, the weather being very fair: but ere we had been long at sea, there arose a storm of wind and rain, with much lightning and thunder, insomuch that a spout arose not far from us: but, God be praised, it dured not long, and we put in that night for harbor at a place called Cummaquid," a shallow harbour on Cape Cod now known as Barnstable, "where we had some hope to find the boy. Two savages were in the boat with us, the one was Tisquantum (*Squanto*), our interpreter, the other Tokamahamon, a special friend. It being night before we came in, we anchored in the midst of the bay, where we were dry at low water." While *Mourt's Relation* described in some detail, and with frequent citation of exact dates, the activity of the *Mayflower* passengers from their arrival in New England until the death of John Carver and the election of William Bradford as governor, that regular chronicle ended abruptly at that point. There are five other, separate parts, however, about specific events in the life of the colony before the end of 1621, mostly describing visits to Indians: in addition to this trip to Nauset, the chronicle includes visits to Massasoit and the Pokanoket Indians, and to the Massachusett Indians thereafter. A concluding "letter" is given as a postscript. Activities which do not involve natives are mentioned rarely, if at all, in these parts, which almost function as appendices to the main narrative.

TUESDAY, 22 JUNE 1621

Visit to Cummaquid; on to Nauset

The Pilgrims spent the night, quite literally, "high and dry." "In the morning we espied savages seeking lobsters, and sent our two interpreters to speak with them, the channel being between them; where they told them what we were, and for what we were come, willing them not at all to fear us, for we would not hurt them. Their answer was, that the boy was well, but he was at Nauset; yet since we were there they desired us to come ashore and eat with them; which, as soon as our boat floated, we did, and went six ashore, having four pledges for them in the boat. They brought us to their sachem or governor, whom they call Iyanough, a man not exceeding twenty-six years of age, but very personable, gentle, courteous, and fair conditioned, indeed not like the savage, save for his attire; his entertainment was answerable to his parts, and his cheer plentiful and various."

The settlers also encountered disturbing evidence of the past here. "One thing was very grievous unto us at this place; there was an old woman, whom we judged to be no less than a hundred years old, which came to see us because she never saw English, yet could not behold us without breaking forth into great passion, weeping and crying excessively. We demanding the reason of it, they told us she had three sons who, when Master Hunt was in these parts, went aboard his ship to trade with him, and he carried them captives into Spain (for Tisquantum at this time was carried away also) by which means she was deprived of the comfort of her children in her old age. We told them we were sorry that any Englishman should give them that offense, that Hunt was a bad man, and that all the English that heard of it condemned him for the same: but for us, we would not offer them any such injury though it would gain us all the skins in the country. So we gave her some small trifles, which somewhat appeased her."

Iyanough and several others offered to accompany them to Nauset, about twenty miles to the east. Unlike the winter before, when Cape Cod had been completely empty of people, the Pilgrims now found Indians wherever they looked. "After dinner we took boat for Nauset, Iyanough and two of his men accompanying us. Ere we came to Nauset, the day and tide were almost spent, insomuch as we could not go in with our shallop, but the sachem or governor of Cummaquid went ashore and his men with him. We also sent Tisquantum to tell Aspinet, the sachem of Nauset, wherefore we came." They brought the shallop to within wading distance of the shore, and were soon approached by a huge number of Indians. Given what had happened at this very place last winter, the Pilgrims ordered the crowd to back away from the boat. Hoping that their alliance with Massasoit would ensure their safety, they also kept their weapons at the ready. "Because we had least cause to trust them, being they only had formerly made an assault upon us in the same place, in time of our winter discovery for habitation. And indeed it was no marvel they did so, for howsoever, though snow or otherwise, we saw no houses, yet we were in the midst of them. When our boat was aground they came very thick, but we stood therein upon our guard, not suffering any to enter except two: the one being of Maramoick, and one of those whose corn we had formerly found, we promised him restitution, and desired him either to come to Patuxet for satisfaction, or else we would bring them so much corn again, he promised to come, we used him very kindly for the present. Some few skins we got there but not many."

WEDNESDAY, 23 JUNE 1621

Reunited

It was still dark when the Nauset sachem, Aspinet, arrived with more than a hundred warriors, many of whom had undoubtedly been a part of the attack at First Encounter Beach in December. Half of the men stayed on the shore with their bows and arrows, while the other half (outnumbering the Pilgrims five to one) waded out unarmed. One of Aspinet's men carried John Billington in his arms; the youth wore a string of shell beads around his neck. "There he delivered us the boy, behung with beads, and made peace with us, we bestowing a knife on him, and likewise on another that first entertained the boy and brought him thither. So they departed from us."

Aspinet had some disturbing news: "Here we understood that the Narragansets had spoiled some of Massasoit's men, and taken him. This struck some fear in us, because the colony was so weakly guarded, the strength whereof being abroad: but we set forth with resolution to make the best haste home we could; yet the wind being contrary, having scarce any fresh water left, and at least sixteen leagues home, we put in again for the shore." The men knew that there were no more than half a dozen able-bodied men back at Plymouth to defend the colony. If Massasoit had, in fact, been captured, then according to the treaty, the Pilgrims were bound to attack the most powerful tribe in the region. "There we met again with Iyanough the sachem of Cummaquid, and the most of his town, both men, women, and children with him. He, being still willing to gratify us, took a runlet and led our men in the dark a great way for water, but could find none good, yet brought such as there was on his neck with him. In the meantime the women joined hand in hand and dancing before the shallop, the men also showing all the kindness they could, Iyanough himself taking a bracelet from about his neck and hanging it upon one of us. Again we set out, but to small purpose, for we gat but little homeward; our water also was very brackish, and not to be drunk."

THURSDAY, 24 JUNE 1621

Home again

The men spent last night in the boat again. "This morning Iyanough espied us again and ran after us; we being resolved to go to Cummaquid again to water, took him into the shallop, whose entertainment was not inferior unto the former. The soil at Nauset and here is alike, even and sandy, not so good for corn as where we are. Ships may safely ride in either harbor. In the summer they abound with fish. Being now watered we put forth again, and by God's providence, came safely home that night."

FRIDAY, 25 JUNE 1621

A sachem's troubles

While the Pilgrims, with Squanto and Tokamahamon, were on their way to return John Billington, Massasoit and several of his tribe were taken captive by the Narragansett. This was an opportunity for some of the "lesser" chiefs, particularly those who were opposed to the alliance with the English, to take things into their own hands. One "petty sachem" in particular, Corbitant, "ever fear'd to be too conversant with the Narragansetts, and no Friend to the English," used this opportunity to break the alliance. He arrived at the nearby village of Nemasket (now

270

Middleborough) and attempted "to draw the hearts of Massasoit's subjects from him." Corbitant "storms at the Peace between Nauset, Cummaquid and Us, and at Squanto the Worker of it, as also at Tokamahamon and Hobbamak." Bradford decided to send his two resident Indians, recently returned from accompanying them on the trip to Nauset, to Massasoit's headquarters at Sowams to see what was going on.

SATURDAY, 26 JUNE 1621

Hobomack

Hobomack was "a Pinese or chief Captain of Masassoit," who was living just outside the Plymouth palisade with his family, keeping an eye on the settlers, helping them to get along, and reporting back to Massasoit: he "continue[d] faithful as long as He live[d]." But he realised that if the various native tribes went to war with each other, Plymouth's pathetic little militia had to back up Massasoit. If Massasoit lost the support of the few villages who continued to support him, the Narragansett could easily take control of the whole area. The fifty two people in Plymouth would find themselves surrounded, their backs to the sea, no ship to take them away, and no friends to come to their rescue.

The Pilgrims probably knew only a small fraction of what was really going on. As Glenn Cheney quipped, "The complexity of the situation rivalled the political machinations of Europe."[175] While Tokamahomon went to see Corbitant, Squanto and Hobomack hurried to Namasket, where they thought Massasoit was being held.

And they were walking into a trap ...

SUNDAY, 27 JUNE 1621

The trap is sprung

Hobomack came back to Plymouth this afternoon, running hard, covered in sweat, and gasping for breath. Prince's *Annals* conflate from several sources what Hobomack told the startled Pilgrims: "[Hobomack and Squanto] are discover'd to Corbitant; who besets the House, [and] threatens to kill Squanto and Hobbamak for being Friends to us. [Corbitant] seizes Squanto and holds a Knife at his Breast, [and] offers to stab Hobamak, but being a stout Man, [Hobomack] clears Himself, concludes Squanto

---

[175] Cheney, *Thanksgiving*, 217

kill'd and flies to our Governor with the Information." Corbitant, who had been expecting Hobomack and Squanto to appear on just such an intelligence gathering mission, viewed Squanto as the instigator of Massasoit's shift toward the Pilgrims. If Squanto was dead, Corbitant told the Indians at Nemasket, "the English had lost their tongue." Unable to communicate with Massasoit, the Pilgrims would be useless as allies, and could be easily surrounded and eliminated.

Hobomack explained, the best he could, "in broken English and horrifically graphic sign language" what had happened.[176]

MONDAY, 28 JUNE 1621

Second Offence in the Colony

As if the brewing difficulties with and among the natives were not enough, there were more problems closer to home. The first breach of conduct had occurred in April, when John Billington (the elder) exchanged angry, insubordinate, and perhaps seditious, words with Myles Standish. Today, "the second Offence" in Plymouth was "the first DUELL fought in New England, upon a Challenge at single Combat with Sword & Dagger between Edward Doty and Edward Leister, Servants of Mr. Hopkins:" There is no record of the source or the nature of the argument, but both of the combatants clearly thought that death was the only thing that would settle it. "Both being wounded, the one in the Hand, the other in the Thigh; they are adjudg'd by the whole Company to have their Head and Feet tied together, and so to lie for 24 Hours, without Meat or Drink: which is begun to be inflicted, but within an Hour, because of their great Pains, at their own & their Master's humble Request, upon Promise of better Carriage, they are Released by the Governor." There was clearly a desperate and immediate demand for strong leadership.

TUESDAY, 29 JUNE 1621

Summertime, and the livin' is easy

Bradford actually sounded happy when he wrote about summer in Plymouth: the settlers "were all well recovered in health and strength and had all good things in plenty." They had actually learned how to fish and had all they could eat, the herring

---

[176] Cheney, *Thanksgiving*, 218

trick had worked with the corn, and in just one day four men shot enough fowl to feed everyone for a week. They ate lobsters that weighed several pounds, and found three varieties (count 'em!) of wild plums. Edward Winslow said that it was just like England, only with less fog.

WEDNESDAY, 30 JUNE 1621

Work

While yesterday's posting may have sounded pleasant, the Pilgrims certainly knew that they had only about four months, at most, remaining in which to prepare for winter. They had no ship to take refuge in, as they had last winter. There were no stores of food, and no cache of firewood. Over the course of the summer, they built seven dwellings for families, and four common buildings -- this was all that was available by the end of the fall, and all the habitation available for the upcoming winter. These would have to house everyone in the upcoming winter, and although the settlers did not know it now, their numbers would significantly increase in November. But they did know that there was no time to lose.

JULY 1621

Division of housing

William Bradford drew a somewhat crude map showing seven plots, all on the south side of "the streete" (there was no need to name it, as there was only one). The map showed garden plots for Peter Brown, John Goodman, and William Brewster on the east side of the "high way" that went from the street to the town brook. John Billington, Isaac Allerton, Francis Cooke, and Edward Winslow had plots on the west side. Most likely the five married men mentioned had houses, along with Bradford (the Governor) and Hopkins. Brown and Goodman had plots, but, being single, would not have had their own houses. There were seven houses, and about 49 people, yielding about seven people to a dwelling. The settlers were very, very suspicious of single men living alone (and with good reason), so all single men had to bunk with a family.

FRIDAY, 2 JULY 1621

Watching and Waiting

The settlers also spent the summer awaiting a relief ship from England. They had no way to know whether the *Mayflower* had made it back to England (it had -- it arrived on May 6/16, about a month and a half ago, but the Pilgrims had no way of knowing that). If it had not, no one would know where to find them: the supplies and new people needed so desperately would never arrive. Even if a ship sent to resupply them were to set sail across the ocean, it would be looking for them where they were supposed to be -- at the mouth of Hudson's River. And even if the *Mayflower* had made it back safely, there was no guarantee that the investors would send anything back: they might be (and they certainly were) angry that all they received back for their money was a boat load of ballast and some Indian trinkets. The fact that they had settled outside of any place to which they had a right to settle made any support from the merchant adventurers even more questionable.

SATURDAY, 3 JULY 1621

Ambassadors

The Pilgrims learned that Corbitant had released Massasoit

from captivity. The determination now turned to re-establishing communication with Pokanoket. Given the small size of the settlement, the question arose regarding whom the Pilgrims could send on what would likely be a long journey, particularly during the summer planting season. It was important that whomever they sent be comfortable in an Indian environment and capable of some conversation with the Indians. Stephen Hopkins, who had some familiarity with Indians in Virginia from his Jamestown experience was certainly one of them. Samoset had stayed with him the first night he spent in Plymouth. The other settler chosen was Edward Winslow. From the vantage point of four centuries later, while the choice of Stephen Hopkins makes perfect sense, it is obscure why Winslow was chosen as the other. He was 25 years old, newly married, and may have displayed particular interest in the Indians, their customs, and arrangements. He had two servants, but one (Elias Story) had died during the last winter, as had Ellen More, who had been entrusted to his care. His new wife, Susanna (Jackson) (White) Winslow, brought her two children, Resolved White, now about five or six, and eight month old Peregrine White. Winslow's servant, George Soule, would also have been part of this household, making the number of people in this house five, not far from our average of seven. There may have been another of the single men bunking with them; Winslow's plot could thus have been tilled in his absence, and there would be assistance for his wife.

SUNDAY, 4 JULY 1621

Planning the reconnaissance

Bradford wrote in his journal, "Having in some sort ordered their business at home, it was thought meet [*wise*] to send some abroad to see their new friend Massasoit, and to bestow upon him some gratuity [*gift*] to bind him the faster unto them; as also that hereby they might view the country and see in what manner he lived, what strength he had about him, and how the ways were to his place, if at any time they should have occasion." This was, however, only part of the reason for the expedition.

MONDAY, 5 JULY 1621

A new kind of pass

The Pilgrims had been beset by an interminable stream of Indians since the treaty with Massasoit had been concluded in the spring. If this continued, and it showed no sign of abating, they would have no food left by the time winter rolled around. But they also did not want to offend either their neighbours or their treaty partner, Massasoit. The second purpose of this proposed expedition was to propose an ingenious solution. The Pilgrims would present Massasoit with a copper chain; if the sachem had a messenger or a friend he wanted the Pilgrims to entertain, he would give that person the chain, and the Pilgrims would know that this was legitimate and would happily provide him with food and fellowship. All others would be denied.

TUESDAY, 6 JULY 1621

The Message for Massasoit

Winslow wrote in *Mourt's Relation* of the message they were instructed to carry to Massasoit: "The message was as followeth; that forasmuch as his subjects came often and without fear, upon all occasions amongst us, so we were now come unto him, and in witness of the love and good-will the English bear unto him, the governor hath sent him a coat, desiring that the peace and amity that was between them and us might be continued, not that we feared them, but because we intended not to injure any, desiring to live peaceably, and as with all men, so especially with them, our nearest neighbors. But whereas his people came very often, and very many together unto us, bringing for the most part their wives and children with them, they were welcome; yet we being but strangers as yet at Patuxet, alias New Plymouth, and not knowing how our corn might prosper, we could no longer give them such entertainment as we had done, and as we desired still to do: yet if he would be pleased to come himself, or any special friend of his desiring to see us, coming from him they should be welcome; and to the end we might know them from others, our governor had sent him a copper chain, desiring if any messenger should come from him to us, we might know him by bringing it with him, and hearken and give credit to his message accordingly. Also requesting him that such as have skins should bring them to us, and that he would hinder the multitude from oppressing us with them. And whereas at our first arrival at Paomet (called by us Cape Cod) we found there corn buried in the ground, and finding no inhabitants but some graves of dead new buried, took the corn, resolving if ever we could hear of any that had right thereunto, to make satisfaction to the full for it, yet since we understand the

276

owners thereof were fled for fear of us, our desire was either to pay them with the like quantity of corn, English meal, or any other commodities we had to pleasure them withal; requesting him that some one of his men might signify so much unto them, and we would content him for his pains. And last of all, our governor requested one favor of him, which was, that he would exchange some of their corn for seed with us, that we might make trial which best agreed with the soil where we live."

WEDNESDAY, 7 JULY 1621

Timeline

Mourt's Relation states that the Pilgrims left for Nauset in order to bring back John Billington on 11 June 1621: this is the only source to give an exact date for this event. Bradford, in his journal (written decades after the events) placed that expedition after the embassy of Winslow and Hopkins to Massasoit. Most modern writers (Philbrick, Cheney, et al.) have followed Bradford's order, even though he gave no dates and wrote many years after the fact: this is probably because the capture of Massasoit and Squanto can easily and logically be placed after the trip to Pokanoket. I have retained the chronology of *Mourt's Relation* in part because it was written several months after the events, rather than several decades, and because the emphasis on the return of the corn taken from Cape Cod makes more sense if the Pilgrims had already been to Nauset and had actually met the man whose corn they had taken in their hunger. Upon learning of Massasoit's release, which all sources agree took place after the Pilgrims were in Nauset, it would be only natural for the settlers to enquire after Massasoit's well being, as well as to look around and see what they could learn for themselves about their neighbours and to assure themselves of the state of their alliance.

THURSDAY, 8 JULY 1621

Bearing gifts

The section of *Mourt's Relation* on the visit to Pokanoket begins: "It seemed good to the company for many considerations to send some amongst them to Massasoit, the greatest commander amongst the savages bordering upon us; partly to know where to find them if occasion served, as also to see their strength, discover the country, prevent abuses in their disorderly coming unto us, make satisfaction for some conceived injuries to be done on our parts, and to continue the league of peace and friendship between them and us. For these, and the like ends, it pleased the governor to make choice of Stephen Hopkins, and Edward Winslow to go unto him, and having a fit opportunity, by reason of a savage called Tisquantum (that could speak English) coming unto us; with all expedition provided a horseman's coat of red cotton, and laced with a slight lace, for a present, that both they and their message might be the more acceptable amongst them." I was not all that sure what a horseman's coat was, so a little research on the internet (which, as we know, is never wrong) produced the following description from Wikipedia: "A duster is a light, loose-fitting long coat. The original dusters were full-length, light-colored canvas or linen coats worn by horsemen to protect their clothing from trail dust. These dusters were typically slit up the back to hip level for ease of wear on horseback. Dusters intended for riding may have features such as a buttonable rear slit and leg straps to hold the flaps in place. For better protection against rain, dusters were made from oilcloth and later from waxed cotton." Whether this even comes close to what Winslow and Hopkins brought to Massasoit, I leave to you to decide.

FRIDAY, 9 JULY 1621

First leg

While the Pilgrims had a horseman's coat, they did not (yet) have any horses, and so they had to walk the forty or so miles to Pokanoket. "With these presents and message we set forth, about nine o'clock in the morning, our guide resolving that night to rest at Nemasket, a town under Massasoit, and conceived by us to be very near, because the inhabitants flocked so thick upon every slight occasion amongst us: but we found it to be some fifteen English miles." Winslow recorded that along the way they came upon about a dozen men, women and children who were returning to Nemasket (modern Middleboro) after gathering lobsters in Plymouth harbour -- they "had pestered us till we were weary of them, perceiving that (as the manner of them all is) where victual is easiest to be got, there they live, especially in the summer: by reason whereof, our bay affording many lobsters, they resort every spring-tide thither; and now returned with us to Nemasket. Thither we came about three o'clock after noon, the inhabitants entertaining us with joy, in the best manner they could, giving us a kind of bread called by them maizium [*i.e., corn bread*], and the spawn of shads, which then they got in abundance, insomuch as they gave us spoons to eat them." With these they boiled "musty acorns, but of the shads we ate heartily." After this they desired "one of our men to shoot a crow, complaining what damage they sustained in their corn by them, who shooting some fourscore off and killing, they much admired it, as other shots on other occasions."

SATURDAY, 10 JULY 1621

Sharing food

"After this Tisquantum told us we should hardly in one day reach Pokanoket, moving us to go some eight miles further, where we should find more store and better victuals than there: being willing to hasten our journey we went, and came thither at sunsetting, where we found many of the Namascheucks (they so calling the men of Nemasket) fishing upon a weir which they had made on a river which belonged to them, where they caught abundance of bass. These welcomed us also, gave us of their fish, and we them of our victuals, not doubting but we should have enough where'er we came. There we lodged in the open fields: for houses they had none, though they spent the most of the summer there. The head of this river is reported to be not far from the place of our abode; upon it are and have been many towns, it being a good length. The ground is very good on both sides, it being for the most part cleared: thousands of men have lived there, which died in a great plague not long since: and pity it was and is to see so many goodly fields, and so well seated, without men to dress and manure the same." Bradford described it in far more sombre terms: "They not being able to bury one another, their skulls and bones were found in many places lying still above the ground where their houses and dwellings have been, a very sad spectacle to behold." Winslow continued, "Upon this river dwelleth Massasoit: it cometh into the sea at the Narraganset Bay, where the Frenchmen so much use. A ship may go many miles up it, as the savages report, and a shallop to the head of it; but so far as we saw, we are sure a shallop may." The Narragansett still lived on the other side of the bay, untouched by the plague, a continuing threat to the weakened Pokanoket and their allies.

SUNDAY, 11 JULY 1621

Tense encounter

Edward Winslow almost sounds like a television announcer: "But to return to our journey: the next morning we broke our fast, took our leave and departed, being then accompanied with some six savages. Having gone about six miles by the river side, at a known shoal place, it being low water, they spake to us to put off our breeches, for we must wade through. Here let me not forget the valor and courage of some of the savages on the opposite side of the river, for there were remaining alive only two men, both aged, especially the one being above threescore; these two, espying a company of men entering the river, ran very swiftly and low in the grass, to meet us at the bank, where with shrill voices and great courage standing charged upon us with their bows; they demanded what we were, supposing us to be enemies, and thinking to take advantage on us in the water: but seeing we were friends, they welcomed us with such food as they had, and we bestowed a small bracelet of beads on them. Thus far we are sure the tide ebbs and flows."

MONDAY, 12 JULY 1621

Views of the Country

I will let Edward Winslow speak for himself: "Having here again refreshed ourselves we proceeded in our journey, the weather being very hot for travel, yet the country so well watered that a man could scarce be dry, but he should have a spring at hand to cool his thirst, beside small rivers in abundance: but the savages will not willingly drink but at a springhead. When we came to any small brook where no bridge was, two of them desired to carry us through of their own accords, also fearing we were or would be weary, offered to carry our pieces, also if we would lay off any of our clothes, we should have them carried: and as the one of them had found more special kindness from one of the messengers, and the other savage from the other so they showed their thankfulness accordingly in affording us all help and furtherance in the journey. As we passed along, we observed that there were few places by the river but had been inhabited, by reason whereof much ground was clear, save of weeds which grew higher than our heads. There is much good timber, both oak, walnut tree, fir, beech, and exceeding great chestnut trees. The country, in respect of the lying on it, is

280

both champaign and hilly, like many places in England. In some places it is very rocky both above ground an in it: and though the country be wild and overgrown with woods, yet the trees stand not thick, but a man may well ride a horse amongst them."

TUESDAY, 13 JULY 1621

Fish Camp

"Passing on at length, one of the company, an Indian, espied a man and told the rest of it. We asked them if they feared any; they told us that if they were Narragansett men they would not trust them, whereat, we called for our pieces and bid them not to fear; for though they were twenty, we two alone would not care for them: but they hailing him, he proved a friend, and had only two women with him: their baskets were empty but they fetched water in their bottles, so that we drank with them and departed. After, we met another man with other two women, which had been at rendezvous by the salt water, and their baskets were full of roasted crab, fishes, and other dried shell fish, of which they gave us, and we ate and drank with them, and gave each of the women a streak of beads, and departed." The two messengers were clearly aware of the danger of making this trip so close to enemy territory; they also had to be careful about their food, since they were close to running out of the supplies they had brought with them, despite the generosity of everyone with whom they came in contact.

WEDNESDAY, 14 JULY 1621

Meeting with the Chief

"After, we came to a town of Massasoit's, where we ate oysters and other fish. From thence we went to Pokanoket but Massasoit was not at home." It was determined to send for the sachem, and when news was brought of his coming, "our guide Tisquantum requested that at our meeting we would discharge our pieces, but one of us going about to charge his piece, the women and children, through fear to see him take up his piece, ran away." They could not be brought back until the interpreter explained what was going on.

"Massasoit being come, we discharged our pieces, and saluted him, who after their manner kindly welcomed us, and took us into his house, and set us down by him, where, having delivered our foresaid message and presents, and having put the coat on his back and the chain about his neck, he was not a little proud to behold himself, and his men also to see their king so bravely attired."

In answer to the settlers' message, Massasoit told them that they were welcome, "and he would gladly continue that peace and friendship which was between him and us: and, for his men, they should no more pester us as they had done: also that he would send to Paomet, and would help us with corn for seed, according to our request."

"This being done, his men gathered near to him, to whom he turned himself, and made a great speech; they sometimes interposing, and, as it were, confirming and applauding him in that he said. The meaning whereof (as far as we could learn) thus; Was not he Massasoit, commander of the country about them? Was not such a town as his and the people of it? And should they not bring their skins unto us? To which they answered, they were his and would be at peace with us, and bring their skins to us. After this manner he named at least thirty places, and their answer was as aforesaid to every one: so that as it was delightful, it was tedious unto us. This being ended, he lighted tobacco for us, and fell to discoursing of England, and of the King's Majesty, marvelling that he would live without a wife." King James' wife, Anne of Denmark, had died in 1619 of dropsy, and had borne him three children, including the future Charles I. As an aside, a source of difference between Anne and James (and the Pilgrims) was the issue of religion; for example, she refused to receive the Anglican communion at her English coronation. Anne had been brought up a Lutheran, and had a Lutheran chaplain Hans Sering in her household, but she may have discreetly converted to Catholicism at some point, a politically embarrassing move which alarmed ministers of the Scottish Kirk and caused suspicion in Anglican England. Like James, Anne later supported a Catholic match for both their sons, and her correspondence with the potential bride, the Spanish Infanta, Maria Anna, included a request that two friars be sent to Jerusalem to pray for her and the King.

Massasoit also "talked of the Frenchmen, bidding us not to suffer them to come to Narraganset, for it was King James his country, and he also was King James his man. Late it grew, but victuals he offered none; for indeed he had not any, being he came so newly home. So we desired to go to rest; he laid us on the bed with himself and his wife, they at the one end and we at the other, it being only planks laid a foot from the ground, and a thin mat upon them. Two more of his chief men, for want of room, pressed by and upon us, so that we were worse weary of our lodging than of our journey." Lice and fleas pressed upon them two, and, apparently, the Indians sang themselves to sleep. Winslow and Hopkins probably got no sleep that night.

THURSDAY, 15 JULY 1621

Conclusion of meeting with Massasoit

"The next day, being Thursday, many of their sachems, or petty governors, came to see us, and many of their men also. There they went to their manner of games for skins and knives. There we challenged them to shoot with them for skins: but they durst not: only they desired to see one of us shoot a mark, who shooting with hail-shot, they wondered to see the mark so full of holes."

About one o'clock, Massasoit brought two fishes that he had shot; "they were like bream but three times so big, and better meat. These being boiled there were at least forty looked for share in them, the most ate of them: this meal only we had in two nights and a day, and had not one of us bought a partridge we had taken our journey fasting: very importunate he was to have us stay with them longer: but we desired to keep the Sabbath at home: and feared we should either be light-headed for want of sleep, for want with bad lodging, the savages' barbarous singing (for they use to sing themselves asleep), lice and fleas within doors, and mosquitoes without, we could hardly sleep all the time of our being there; we much fearing that if we should stay any longer, we should not be able to recover home for want of strength. " Pokanoket is probably not going to get a five star review for overnight accommodation from the Pilgrims.

FRIDAY, 16 JULY 1621

Heading home

On Friday morning, before sunrise, "we took our leave and departed, Massasoit being both grieved and ashamed that he could no better entertain us: and retaining Tisquantum to send from place to place to procure truck for us, and appointing another, called Tokamahamon, in his place, whom we had found faithful before and after upon all occasions."

At one of Massasoit's towns, where the messengers had previously eaten on their outward journey, "we were again refreshed with a little fish; and bought about a handful of meal of their parched corn, which was very precious at that time of the year, and a small string of dried shell-fish, as big as oysters. The latter we gave to the six savages that accompanied us, keeping the meal for ourselves; when we drank, we ate each a spoonful of it with a pipe of tobacco, instead of other victuals, and of this also we could not but give them so long as it lasted. Five miles they led us to a house out of the way in hope of victuals: but we found nobody there and so were but worse able to return home. That night we reached to the weir where we lay before, but the Namascheucks were returned: so that we had no hope of anything there. One of the savages had shot a shad in the water, and a small squirrel as big as a rat, called a neuxis; the one half of either he gave us, and after went to the weir to fish."

From that point, the two Pilgrims wrote to Plymouth, and sent Tokamahamon ahead of them to Nemasket, looking for him from to find someone to meet them with food at Nemasket. "Two men now only remained with us, and it pleased God to give them good store of fish, so that we were well refreshed. After supper we went to rest, and they to fishing again; more they got and fell to eating afresh, and retained sufficient ready roast for all our breakfasts. About two o'clock in the morning arose a great storm of wind, rain, lightning, and thunder, in such violent manner that we could not keep in our fire; and had the savages not roasted fish when we were asleep, we had set forward fasting, for the rain still continued with great violence, even the whole day through, till we came within two miles of home."

SATURDAY, 17 JULY 1621

Return

Being wet and weary, at length the messengers arrived at Nemasket; "there we refreshed ourselves, giving gifts to all such as had showed us any kindness. Amongst others, one of the six that came with us from Pokanoket, having before this on the way unkindly foresaken us, marvelled we gave him nothing, and told us what he had done for us. We also told him of some discourtesies he offered us, whereby he deserved nothing. Yet we gave him a small trifle, whereupon he offered us tobacco; but the house being full of people, we told them he stole some by the way, and if it were of that we would not take it, for we would not receive that which was stolen upon any terms; if we did, our God would be angry with us, and destroy us. This abashed him and gave the rest great content. But at our departure he would needs carry him on his back through a river, whom he had formerly in some sort abused. Fain they would have had us to lodge there all night, and wondered we would set forth again in such weather. But, God be praised, we came safe home that night, though wet, weary, and surbated."

SUNDAY, 18 JULY 1621

Back for the Sabbath

Note, in the quotations for the last week or so, the constant refrain that Winslow kept up about the repayment for the corn that was taken last November from the storage pits on Cape Cod. He not only met the man whose corn was taken during the expedition to Nauset to retrieve John Billington, but he also brought the matter up with Massasoit in their negotiations on this most recent trip. This shows not only that the Pilgrims did not come to the New World for the purposes of theft or destruction, and acted only out of the desperation of starving people, but it also shows that the Pilgrims wanted others to know this as well: Winslow wanted the repayment to be done by Massasoit, rather than by the settlers, even though Massasoit had not been responsible for the taking of the corn, so that all of the Indians would know that the Pilgrims had accepted this responsibility. This was also put in the description that was included in *Mourt's Relation*, which was intended for circulation in England and Holland, so that readers in the Old World would know that the Pilgrims intended to lead a godly life according to God's law. When Winslow spoke with sorrow to the Indians of the activity of the seizures and captivity of Captain Hunt, and included this in his chronicle, he surely was sending a notice, if not a warning, that this was exceptional, and should not be attempted again.

MONDAY, 19 JULY 2021

Results

In a letter written on 11 December, to go back to England with the *Fortune*, Edward Winslow wrote, "We have found the Indians very faithful in their covenant of peace with us; very loving and ready to [please] us; we often go to them, and they come to us; some of us have been fifty miles by land in the country with them. ... It had pleased God so to possess the Indians with a fear of us, and love unto us, that not only the greatest king amongst them, called Massasoit, but also all the princes and peoples round about us, have either made suit unto us, or been glad of any occasion to make peace with us, so that seven of them at once have sent messengers to us to that end." By the end of the year, for the first time in living memory, there was peace among all the tribes, and Winslow believed that this would not have happened without the arrival of the Pilgrims. There would be two significant encounters, however, before that: one at the end of August, in a strike against the rebellious chieftan Corbitant, and another in September as Winslow sought to make contact with the Massachusetts Indians.

TUESDAY, 20 JULY 2021

Looking back

With the return of Edward Winslow and Stephen Hopkins, things quieted down for the settlers in Plymouth to a regular rhythm. In trying to write about what happened exactly four hundred years ago on this day, for the next month or so there would be a string of "more of the same" posts. Because I started last September, on the day after the Speedwell sprung a leak (again!), there were a couple of months (or, more exactly, the forty-two days from 25 July 1620 until 6 September 1620) for which I had no posts. I propose to fill in that gap starting next Sunday, so these postings will cover what happened exactly four-hundred-and-one years ago. For a couple of days, in which we know things happened in 1621, I will have two parts for the post, but the only time that should happen would be in the strike against Corbitant towards the end of August. I will then pick back up with 1621 at the beginning of September. I still plan on ending this project when the Fortune sails back to England in December. But right now it is taking me more and more time to write less and less.

WEDNESDAY, 21 JULY 1621

Scarcity and Plenty

One last comment about the visit to Pokanoket -- despite the glowing reports of what was available for the taking in the wild and in the waters, this was clearly a subsistence economy: there was not much left over, and while the travellers regularly met natives who were happy to share with them, as the Pilgrims had been sharing with the hordes of visitors to their new settlement, there was nothing left over. This is a part of Massasoit's great embarrassment about their visit: he had been away, and thus there was nothing prepared for the entertainment. Each person probably brought his own food, and there was very little left over for the two messengers to share. There was only a limited means to preserve food, and the Pilgrims were constantly careful to put aside food for the winter, as well as having seed for the next spring's planting. And nothing, absolutely nothing, could go to waste; everyone had to be on the lookout for what use could be made of what God had provided.

THURSDAY, 22 JULY 1621

Survivors

As we prepare to step back in time to Holland on the eve of the Pilgrims' departure, we can see who was left a year later: of the one hundred and two passengers who had sailed from England and Holland, these were the survivors who saw the summer of 1621: John Alden; William Bradford; Isaac Allerton and his children: Bartholomew, Remember, and Mary; John and Eleanor Billington and their sons, John and Francis; William and Mary Brewster, their sons Love and Wrestling, and their charge, the bastard Richard More; Mary Chilton, orphaned at fourteen; Francis Cooke and his son John; Elizabeth Tilley, orphaned at thirteen, and her infant cousin, Humility Cooper; John Crackstone; Francis Eaton and his infant son Samuel; Samuel Fuller and his nephew (of the same name); Richard Gardinar; John Goodman and his buddy Peter Browne; Stephen and Elizabeth Hopkins and all of their children: Constance, Giles, Damaris and little Oceanus, and their two servants Edward Doty and Edward Leister; Priscilla Mullins; Joseph Rogers; Henry Samson; George Soule; Myles Standish; William Trevor; Richard Warren; Susanna White, her five year old son Resolved and her infant son Peregrine; Edward Winslow and his brother Gilbert; a servant known only as "Mr. Ely"; the Carvers' three servants, Desire Minter, a girl named Dorothy, and John Howland, who all survived the winter but were unemployed by May, when the last of the Carver family died.

FRIDAY, 23 JULY 1621

Survivors (part two)

Only the Hopkins, Billington, and Brewster families survived in their entirety -- actually it is not known when the youngest of the Hopkins family, Damaris and Oceanus, died. One or both had died by 1623, so it is possible that they did not survive the first winter at Plymouth. No other family had both father and mother living. Of the forty-one men who signed the Mayflower Compact, only nineteen still lived; of the nine who did not sign the Compact, there was a better survival rate; this may have made a difference in the community's interchanges: the number who signed the Compact slipped from 81% of the adult males to 70%. Eight children who had come with at least one parent now had none. Of eighteen adult women, only four survived. In the spring and the summer they planted their crops within a few hundred feet of the unmarked graves where their friends and family lay.

SATURDAY, 24 JULY 1621

Sabbath rest

Rested on the Sabbath. "They assemble by beat of drum, each with his musket or firelock, in front of the captain's door; they have their cloaks on, and place themselves in order, three abreast and are led by a sergeant without beat of drum. ... They march in good order, and each sets his arms down near him. They are constantly on their guard day and night."[177]

MONDAY, 26 JULY 1621

Continuing planting and construction.

TUESDAY, 27 JULY 1621

Continuing planting and construction.

WEDNESDAY, 28 JULY 1621

Continuing planting and construction.

THURSDAY, 29 JULY 1621

Continuing planting and construction.

FRIDAY, 30 JULY 1621

Continuing planting and construction

SATURDAY, 31 JULY 1621

Continuing planting and construction

---

[177] from a letter by Isaac de Rasieres, in *The Narratives of New Netherlands*, ed. J. Franklin Jameson, New York: Scribners, 1909

AUGUST 1621

SUNDAY, 1 AUGUST 1621

Kept the Sabbath.

MONDAY, 2 AUGUST 1621

Back to work in planting and construction.

TUESDAY, 3 AUGUST 1621

Continuing with planting and construction.

WEDNESDAY, 4 AUGUST 1621

Continuing with planting and construction.

THURSDAY, 5 AUGUST 1621

Continuing with planting and construction

FRIDAY, 6 AUGUST 1621

Continuing with planting and construction

SATURDAY, 7 AUGUST 1621

Continuing with planting and construction

SUNDAY, 8 AUGUST 1621

Kept the Sabbath,

MONDAY, 9 AUGUST 1621

Continuing with planting and construction.

TUESDAY, 10 AUGUST 1620

Continued planting and construction.

WEDNESDAY, 11 AUGUST 2021

Continued with planting and construction.

THURSDAY, 12 AUGUST 2021

Continued with planting and construction.

FRIDAY, 13 AUGUST 2021

Continued with planting and construction.

SATURDAY, 14 AUGUST 1621

Continuing planting and construction.

SUNDAY, 15 AUGUST 1621

Kept the Sabbath.

MONDAY, 16 AUGUST 1621

Resumed construction and planting.

TUESDAY, 17 AUGUST 1621

Continued construction and planting.

Meanwhile, back in England ...

A small relief ship named the *Fortune*, about the size of the *Speedwell*, is being loaded to sail to New England to increase the colony. Financed, as the *Mayflower* was, by Thomas Weston and others of the London-based Merchant Adventurers, the *Fortune* was to transport settlers to the colony on a ship that was much smaller than *Mayflower*. The *Fortune* required two months to prepare for the voyage, and was in some ways even more ill prepared than the *Mayflower*: Weston began preparations as soon as the *Mayflower* arrived back in England last May. More about this over the next few days.

WEDNESDAY, 18 AUGUST 1621

Continued construction and planting.

Fortune ready to depart

At 55 tons displacement, and about one-third the tonnage of the *Mayflower*, the *Fortune* was tasked with delivering thirty-five new settlers to the Plymouth Colony. The Master (captain) was Thomas Barton. Their leader was Robert Cushman who, in 1620, had been the Leiden agent in London for the *Mayflower* and *Speedwell*. It is believed that the majority of the passengers of the *Fortune* were gathered together in London by Thomas Weston and his partner.

THURSDAY, 19 AUGUST 1621

Continued planting and construction. Note that the settlers at the Plimoth Plantation had no idea that a relief ship was coming, nor were they expecting its arrival.

Departure of the Fortune from Southampton

The *Fortune* departs for New England. Recall that it took the *Mayflower* just over a month to return to England last April and May; the outward voyage to New England was sixty-six days, with another month of exploration elapsing before arriving at Plymouth. The *Fortune* was on the high seas for three months before sighting Cape Cod in November, and it took them some time to track down where, exactly, the Pilgrims were once they arrived, so that it was about *four whole months* in between the time of embarkation in England and arrival in Plymouth.

FRIDAY, 20 AUGUST 1621

Planting and construction continue.

Fortune passengers

Although Bradford notes that thirty-five persons were on *Fortune*, only the names of twenty-eight persons are listed in the 1623 Division of Land list and its distribution of lots. Eighteen persons are known to have been unmarried, eight married but emigrating without their families, and as far as can be determined, Mrs. Martha Ford, her daughter Martha, and Elizabeth Bassett wife of William Bassett were the only women on the ship. Records indicate that sixteen of the passengers were from the London area and three from Leiden. The origins of ten passengers could not be determined. A number of persons listed in 1623 do not appear in the 1627 Division of Cattle list and this may be due to death, removal to an area outside the colony or a return to England.

SATURDAY, 21 AUGUST 1621

Planting and construction continue.

Fortune passengers (part two)

As with the *Speedwell*, no actual passenger list survives for the *Fortune*. Charles Edward Banks compiled a list of likely passengers in his *Planters of the Commonwealth* based on a 1623 division of land in the colonys; the compiled list was later supplemented by entries in Eugene Aubrey Stratton's *Plymouth Colony: Its History and its People, 1620-1691*. I am compiling biographical sketches for all known or presumed passengers on the *Fortune*:[178]

1.   Adams John (From Wapping, Stephney, Middlesex, bound for Plymouth. Ref: Banks Mss. 36 pg 113)
2.   Basset William (From Bethnal Green, Stephney, Middlesex, bound for Plymouth. Ref: Banks Mss. 36 pg 113)
3.   Basset Elizabeth, wife
4.   Beale William
5.   Bompasse Edward

---

[178] For more complete information, see Becket Soule, *The Passengers of the Fortune – 1621* (Berwyn Heights, MD: Heritage Books, 2023).

6.   Brewster Jonathan, oldest son of Elder Brewster
7.   Briggs Clement (From Southwark, Surrey, bound for Plymouth. Ref: Pope. 36 pg 169)
8.   Bumpas Edward (From St Bartholomew, London, bound for Plymouth. Ref: Banks Mss. 36 pg 99)
9.   Cannon John
10.   Conner William
11.   Cushman Robert (From Canterbury, Kent, bound for Plymouth. Ref: Pope. 36 pg 76)
12.   Cushman Thomas, son abt 12 (From Canterbury, Kent, bound for Plymouth. Ref: Pope. 36 pg 76)
13.   Deane Steven (From Southwark, Surrey, bound for Plymouth. Ref: Banks Mss. 36 pg 169)
14.   Flavell Thomas & son (wife was on the *Anne*) (From Stephney, Middlesex, bound for Plymouth. Ref: Banks Mss. 36 pg 113)
15.   Ford _____ (presumably son William)(William. from Southwark, S Olave, Surrey, bound for Plymouth. Ref: Banks Mss. 36 pg 169)
16.   Ford Widow Martha, wife
17.   Ford Martha, daughter
18.   Ford John, son, born the day of arrival
19.   Hicks Robert (From Southwark, Surrey, bound for Plymouth. Ref: Pope. 36 pg 169)
20.   Hilton William (From Northwich bound for Plymouth 1623. Dover N.H. 1624. Ref: Banks, Mass. 36 pg 14)
21.   Morgan Bennet (Benedict, from Clerkenwell, St James, Middlesex, bound for Plymouth. Ref: Banks Mss. 36 pg 110)
22.   Morton Thomas - his son, Thomas Morton, Jr., arrived on the Anne
23.   Nicolas Austen
24.   Noye de la Philipe
25.   Palmer William (From Stephney, Middlesex, bound for Plymouth. Ref: Banks Mss. 36 pg 113)
26.   Palmer William, son
27.   Pitt William (From St Peter, Vincula Tower, London, bound for Plymouth. Ref: Banks Mss. 36 pg 103)
28.   Prence Thomas - Married Patience Brewster, the Elder's daughter (Prince, from All Hallows Barking, London or Stephney, Middlesex, bound for Plymouth and Eastham. Ref: Savage. 36 pg

98 & 113)
29.   Simonson Moses
30.   Statie Hugh
31.   Steward James
32.   Tench William
33.   Winslow John, brother of Governor Winslow (From Droitwich, Worchest. bound for Plymouth. Ref: Pope. 36 pg 184)
34.   Wright William (From Austerfield, Worchest. bound for Plymouth. Ref: Par Reg. 36 pg 184)
35.   ?

SUNDAY, 22 AUGUST 1620

From Mourt's Relation: "At our return from Nauset, we found it true that Massasoit was put from his country by the Narragansets. Word also was brought unto us that Corbitant, a petty sachem or governor under Massasoit (whom they ever feared to be too conversant with the Narragansets), was at Nemasket, who sought to draw the hearts of Massasoit's subjects from him, speaking also disdainfully of us, storming at the peace between Nauset, Cummaquid, and us, and at Tisquantum, the worker of it; also at Tokamahamon, and one Hobomok (two Indians, or Lemes, one of which he would treacherously have murdered a little before, being a special and trusty man of Massasoit's). Tokamahamon went to him, but the other two would not; yet put their lives in their hands, privately went to see if they could hear of their king, and lodging at Nemasket were discovered to Corbitant, who set a guard to beset the house, and took Tisquantum (for he had said, if he were dead, the English had lost their tongue) Hobomok seeing that Tisquantum was taken, and Corbitant held a knife at his breast, being a strong and stout man, brake from them and came to New Plymouth, full of fear and sorrow for Tisquantum, whom he thought to be slain." The plot thickens tomorrow.

The Ford Family on the Fortune

Young's list of Fortune passengers, revised by Stratton, and reproduced yesterday, only has thirty-four names, although all of the main sources (Winslow, in *Mourt's Relation*, Bradford, in his journal, and Captain John Smith) state that there were thirty-*five* passengers. Who is the missing passenger?[179]

One possibility is that reliance on the 1623 division of land has shortchanged the Ford family by one. This name of the male head of the household does not appear in any Plymouth Colony record, and therefore we do not know his first name and can only infer that there was a man with this surname on the *Fortune*. Alexander Young's *Chronicles of the Pilgrims*,[180] quotes a letter of Edward Winslow to a friend in England dated 11 December 1621: "The Goodwife Ford was delivered of a son the first night she landed and both of them are very well." It would be unlikely that a widow in the late stages of pregnancy would have been a passenger on the *Fortune* (or any other ship); therefore it seems more probable that her husband was with her on the voyage but died shortly after the date of Winslow's letter, since the 1623 division of land (apparently made about March 1623/4) allots *four* acres to "Widow Ford." The fact that Winslow calls her "Goodwife" and not "Widow" also supports this assumption.

The grant to the family of four acres in 1623 is subject to a number of interpretations. Barclay assumed that it encompassed the widow and three children, the husband having died by that date. Wakefield held instead that the grant was for the widow Ford, her deceased husband, and children John and Martha, the child born in 1621 having already died shortly after landing.[181] A third possibility is that the son John was the child born immediately after landing in 1621, and that the grant was for the two parents and the only two children of those two parents. This, however, would make John Ford only nineteen when he was granted land in 1640,[182] so if a person receiving a grant of land in Plymouth at this time was necessarily twenty-one, then this arrangement could not work.

There appears, however, to be a total of *five* people in the Ford family: (1) Mr. [unknown given name] Ford, who probably died within a year of landing, and definitely before the land

---

[179] Note, also, that the Stratton list, given above, counts some people twice (Edward Bompasse and Edward Bumpas are undoubtedly the same person).

[180] 1841, reprinted NEHGS 2016 with a preface by Robert Charles Anderson, p. 235

[181] MQ 40:55

[182] PCR 1:165

division of 1623, when his wife is referred to as "widow"; (2) Mrs. Martha (unknown maiden name) Ford; by the time of the 1627 Plymouth cattle division the widow Ford had married Peter Brown, and she appeared as the fifth person in the fifth company, and her children John Ford and Martha Ford as the seventh and eighth persons in that company;[183] (3) John Ford, b. say 1617; d. (or left Plymouth) between 5 January 1640/1[184] and 1643 (not in 1643 Plymouth list of men able to bear arms);[185] (4) Martha Ford, b. about 1619 (d. Plymouth 20 December 1683 "in her 64th year" [Plymouth Church Records 1:250]); m. Plymouth 29 October 1640 William Nelson;[186] (5) son Ford, born Plymouth, 9 November 1621, the day the *Fortune* arrived, and probably d. before 1623. I realise that this is a stretch, but if we include all five of these as passengers, the youngest one a passenger *in utero*, we can complete the number of thirty-five.

MONDAY, 23 AUGUST 1621

Meeting

Governor Bradford assembled his advisers on what to do about Corbitant. "It was conceiv'd not fit to be borne," Bradford wrote, "for if we should suffer our Friends and Messengers thus to be wrong'd, we shall have none to cleave to us, or give us Intelligence, or do us any Service, but would next fall upon us, &c." The council decided on quick and bold action; Myles Standish volunteered to lead ten men tomorrow with Hobbamock "to seize our Foes in the Night" in Nemasket. If Squanto had been killed, they were to seize Corbitant and cut off his head, and bring it back to Plymouth for public display. They were to harm "only those who had a Hand in the Murther, and retain Nepeof, another Sachim in the Confederacy, till we hear of Masassoit."

TUESDAY, 24 AUGUST 1621

Lost in the wet woods

Captain Standish set out with ten men armed, "who took their journey as aforesaid, but the day proved very wet. When we supposed we were within three or four miles of Nemasket, we

---

[183] PCR 12:11
[184] PCR 2:6
[185] TAG 42:39
[186] PCR 1:153; TAG 56:32-35

went out of the way and stayed there till night, because we would not be discovered. There we consulted what to do, and thinking best to beset the house at midnight, each was appointed his task by the captain, all men encouraging one another to the utmost of their power." That night the company's guide lost his way, "which much discouraged our men, being we were wet, and weary of our arms: but one of our men, having been before at Nemasket, brought us into the way again. Before we came to the town, we sat down and ate such as our knapsacks afforded. That being done, we threw them aside, and all such things as might hinder us, and so went on and beset the house, according to our last resolution."

WEDNESDAY, 25 AUGUST 1621

Attack!

Standish had briefed the men on the plan: Hobbamock was to lead the company to Corbitant's wigwam at midnight; once Standish had positioned them around the the outside, he and Hobbamock would charge inside and take Corbitant. The men outside were instructed to shoot any Indian who tried to escape.

The patter of the rain masked the sound of the Pilgrims taking their positions. Standish burst into the wigwam, shouting Corbitant's name. With Hobbamock acting as interpreter, they demanded to know where Corbitant was. Winslow wrote in *Mourt's Relation* that "Corbitant were not there: but fear had bereft the savages of speech. We charged them not to stir, for if Corbitant were not there, we would not meddle with them; if he were, we came principally for him, to be avenged on him for the supposed death of Tisquantum, and other matters: but howsoever, we would not at all hurt their women, or children. Notwithstanding some of them pressed out at a private door and escaped, but with some wounds: at length perceiving our principal ends, they told us Corbitant was returned with all his train, and that Tisquantum was yet living, and in the town, offering some tobacco, other such as they had to eat. In this hurley burley we discharged two pieces at random, which much terrified all the inhabitants, except Tisquantum and Tokamahamon, who though they knew not our end in coming, yet assured them of our honesty, that we would not hurt them. Those boys that were in the house, seeing our care of women, often cried, 'Neen squaes,' that is to say, 'I am a woman': the women also hanging upon Hobomok, calling him Towam, that is, "friend." But to be short, we kept them we

296

had, and made them make a fire that we might see to search the house."

In the meantime, Hobbamock pulled himself up through the widwam's smoke hole, and, balancing himself on the roof, called out for Squanto and Tokamahamon. The latter came, "accompanied with others, some armed and others naked. Those that had bows and arrows, we took them away, promising them again when it was day. The house we took for our better safeguard, but released those we had taken, manifesting whom we came for and wherefore."

The next morning, "we marched into the midst of the town, and went to the house of Tisquantum to breakfast," whither the Indians brought "the best food they have." "Thither came all whose hearts were upright towards us, but all Corbitant's faction were fled away. There in the midst of them we manifested again our intendment, assuring them, that although Corbitant had now escaped us, yet there was no place should secure him and his from us if he continued his threatening us and provoking others against us, who had kindly entertained him, and never intended evil towards him till he now so justly deserved it. Moreover, if Massasoit did not return in safety from Narraganset, or if hereafter he should make any insurrection against him, or offer violence to Tisquantum, Hobomok, or any of Massasoit's subjects, we would revenge it upon him, to the overthrow of him and his. As for those were wounded, we were sorry for it, though themselves procured it in not staying in the house at our command: yet if they would return home with us, our surgeon should heal them. At this offer, one man and a woman that were wounded went home with us, Tisquantum and many other known friends accompanying us, and offering all help that might be by carriage of any thing we had to ease us. So that by God's good providence, we safely returned home the morrow night after we set forth."

THURSDAY, 26 AUGUST 1621

A new era of peace

After the (unsuccessful) expedition to capture Corbitant, Governor Bradford received "many Gratulations from diverse Sachems and much firmer Peace." The show of force in the midnight raid, no matter how disorganised and confused, had won the Pilgrims some new respect. Epenow, the sachem in (what is now) Martha's Vineyard, and the leader who had attacked Dermer

297

several years ago, made overtures of friendship. Even Corbitant himself let it be known that he now wanted to make peace. Massasoit was by now back in Sowams, and now that the Pilgrims had proved themselves loyal and resolute supporters, a new era of peace settled over the region. Even Canonicus, chief sachem of the Narragansetts, sent a messenger to treat of Peace.

FRIDAY, 27 AUGUST 1621

Back to work: planting and construction continues.

SATURDAY, 28 AUGUST 1621

Construction and planting continue.

SUNDAY, 29 AUGUST 1621

Kept the Sabbath.

MONDAY, 30 AUGUST 1621

Resumed construction and planting.

TUESDAY, 31 AUGUST 1621

Continuing construction and planting.

SEPTEMBER 1621

WEDNESDAY, 1 SEPTEMBER 1621

Continuing construction and planting.

THURSDAY, 2 SEPTEMBER 1621

Continuing construction and planting.

FRIDAY, 3 SEPTEMBER 1621

Continuing construction and planting.

SATURDAY, 4 SEPTEMBER 1621

Continuing construction and planting.

SUNDAY, 5 SEPTEMBER 1621

Kept the Sabbath.

MONDAY, 6 SEPTEMBER 1621

Resumed planting and construction.

TUESDAY, 7 SEPTEMBER 1621

Planting and construction continue. By the middle of November, there were seven homes arranged along the central street, and there had been a reasonably plentiful harvest, enough to get them through the winter (or so they thought). While some crops prospered, many of the seeds that they had brought from England did not do as well: "our barley indifferent good, but our peas parched up with the sun." The unexpected arrival of 35 extra mouths to feed, also reduced their rations to almost starvation.

WEDNESDAY, 8 SEPTEMBER 1621

Families in Plymouth planted enough in their fields to feed themselves. Their main crop was a kind of corn they had never seen before. Because it was native to North America and grew better in America than English grains, the Pilgrims called it "Indian corn." All of this work had to be done with hand tools – tractors and automatic machines hadn't been invented yet. Indian corn was different from the sweet yellow corn that we eat today. It had various colours – reds, blacks, yellows and whites – on the same ear, and was not eaten fresh from the cob. Instead, Indian corn was dried and then pounded into flour and cornmeal for cooking and baking. Indian corn was part of almost every meal.

THURSDAY, 9 SEPTEMBER 1621

Along with Indian corn, the Pilgrims also grew some beans, pumpkins, wheat, barley, oats and peas in their fields. In the gardens near their houses, they grew many different kinds of herbs and vegetables, like parsley, lettuce, spinach, carrots and turnips. Salt, sugar, oil, and vinegar had to be imported from England.

FRIDAY, 10 SEPTEMBER 1621

The combination of available meat and shellfish, Indian corn and other field crops and garden plants made the Pilgrims' diet a rich and varied one through most seasons of the year. Like the natives, however, the colonists experienced seasonal variations. Not all foods were available at every season of the year. The Pilgrims tried to extend the life of their foods through preservation. Salting, the most common method of preservation, worked well for pork (meat from pigs) and fish. This method was sometimes combined with smoking for meats. Drying was also common. Vinegar pickles and sugar were also occasionally used to preserve foods.

SATURDAY, 11 SEPTEMBER 1621

We have spent plenty of time on what vegetables the Pilgrims ate, but what about meat? In New England, supplies of fish and shellfish were plentiful. Without hunting restrictions, deer, wild fowl, rabbits and other small animals were available to anyone who wanted to hunt them. We know that the Pilgrims brought with them farm animals -- unknown to the natives -- including pigs, chickens, and goats; sheep and cows came a couple of years later. These animals provided meat, eggs and dairy products for the colonists.

SUNDAY, 12 SEPTEMBER 1621

Kept the Sabbath. Note that church attendance was not mandated by law until 1650 in the colony of New Plymouth, but keeping the Sabbath by refraining from work and attendance at the two worship services was probably almost universal in this early period. The group had, after all, left England and undergone hardship for this very purpose, so it is likely that attendance did not need to be "enforced." The scriptures were the basis for worship, as for much else, and in the absence of any other written laws or regulations, the sacred writings also served as a legal code. The Pilgrims not only rejected the celebration of Easter, Christmas, and Saints' Days, but also hymns, the recitation of the Lord's Prayer, and creeds. Psalms were the only music allowed in service. Sabbath services were held twice on Sunday, from 9am to noon and from 2pm to 5pm, and sermons were often given on Thursdays and when Days of Thanksgiving or Days of Fasting and Humiliation were proclaimed.

MONDAY, 13 SEPTEMBER 1621

The principal texts used in Pilgrim worship were from the Book of Psalms. In their strictly literal reading of Scripture, it was noted that the only time that Jesus sang was on the night before he died, when he and the disciples sang psalms on the way to the Garden of Gethsemane: this was in contrast to the worship in the Temple, when only the priests and Levites sang. Thus the Pilgrims encouraged all to sing, but *only* the Psalms: this was also *a capella*, as the use of the organ and other instruments was proscribed in worship services. The Psalter used in the Church of England was Miles Coverdale's 1535 translation, used in the 1549 *Book of Common Prayer* (and all subsequent versions in the Church of England). Although the first complete metrical (or versified) Psalter in English was published in 1562, and was known as "Sternhold and Hopkins," Henry Ainsworth published his Psalter specifically for the Separatist Congregation in Holland. It remained as the main song book of the Pilgrims in Plymouth, although "The Bay Psalm-Book," published at Cambridge [Massachusetts] in 1640 and revised later, is better known. Ainsworth provided both a prose and a verse version of the psalms, and kept the two as close to each other as possible: the versified version is thus frequently garbled and unintelligible. More about the Ainsworth Psalter and Pilgrim worship and music can be found in the most recent issues of the *Mayflower Quarterly*, and I will add some more comments in the next few days.

TUESDAY, 14 SEPTEMBER 1621

Paul Jehle, in a blog post for the Plymouth Rock Foundation, identified three characteristics of the Ainsworth Psalter:

- **First**, its translation (and notes of interpretation) of the Scriptures kept the *lyrics* as close to the original text as possible. Henry Ainsworth's challenge was to take the Old Testament Psalms and turn the words into <u>prose</u> that could be set to an easy melody.
- **Second**, the prose of Scripture was inseparably connected

to the *melodies* employed by Ainsworth. These were taken from a blend of English, Dutch and French tunes used in the Reformed Churches in Amsterdam. Only the melodies are given in Ainsworth's *Psalm Book*, and the C-clef alone is used. There are forty-eight tunes and where there is no tune given, the book refers to a tune already used in another Psalm. Nine are duplicates so that only 39 needed to be memorized.

- **Third**, its *rhythm* was iambic (first beat on the second syllable). Trochaic (first beat on the first syllable) measures were not common until early in the 18th century. The tunes were often taken from folk songs and thus they were lively.

WEDNESDAY, 15 SEPTEMBER 1621

The Pilgrims noted a significant increase in visitation by Indians, and particularly by their leaders, in the month after the attack on Nemasket. Even though the foray did not capture Corbitant, the purpose of the expedition, and descended into comedy or farce at times, the local tribes began to recognise how the Pilgrims could be useful in their own plans to work together. This resulted not only in a treaty (to be discussed next week) but also in various tribes working together, which had not really been the case previously, and certainly not since the plague decimated the coastal tribes several years earlier.

THURSDAY, 16 SEPTEMBER 1621

About this time, Governor Bradford determined that an exploratory expedition should be sent north to the land of the Massachusetts. Squanto had warned them that the Massachusetts, who lived in the vicinity of modern Boston, "had often threatened us." It was time to bring them into the fold, as well. It is significant that in the modern maps of tribal lands in New England for the four hundredth anniversary of the *Mayflower*, the Massachusetts have been eliminated completely -- the ultimate in cancel culture -- and their land is currently identified as belonging to the Wampanoags, a name that is not found before King Philip's War. It appears that twenty-first century natives are not above continuing centuries old disputes (in this case, apparently, seizing another tribe's land in order to build a casino). The tiny, subordinate tribe is expanded to a "nation" in the 2020 banner of "Four Nations"; Massasoit's people, known as the Pokanokets for

302

the area they occupied at the head of Narragansett Bay, had been reduced to a few hundred warriors after the plague, and were considered the subjects of the Narragansetts, led by Canonicus.

FRIDAY, 17 SEPTEMBER 1621

Numerically, the Pokanokets were at a decided disadvantage. Struggling to maintain their existence as a separate and identifiable people, they were beginning to ally with the Massachusetts to the north and the Nausets on Cape Cod, who were also opposed to the Narragansetts. The Pilgrims had come along at a very opportune time: while it is often stated, to the point of cliché, that without the Pokanoket Indians, the Pilgrims would not have survived, it is also quite clear that without the Pilgrims, the Pokanoket Indians would not have survived. The presence of the Pilgrims enabled Massasoit and his tribe to break free from the Narragansetts, and extend their own control over the neighbouring tribes.

SATURDAY, 18 SEPTEMBER 1621

The paper trail

On board the *Fortune*, now about half way through its almost four month voyage across the Atlantic, was a very important document. When news from Plymouth returned to England in May 1620, along with the *Mayflower*, that the settlers had landed and established a home outside of the area in which they were authorised to do so, the Merchant Adventurers (i.e., the stockholders in the Plymouth Plantation) led by John Peirce went to the Council of New England to get the Pilgrims the rights to live and establish a government of their own at Plymouth. The result was the 1621 Pierce Patent, which supersedes the Mayflower Compact and gives them a much surer legal claim to the land they are living on. It is dated 1 June 1621; the Second Peirce Patent is thus the oldest existing state document of New England in the US. The remarkable document, signed by five Englishmen, gave each settler 100 acres of ground and "all such liberties, privileges, profits and commodities" as the land and rivers "shall yield." "Liberty" here is used in a technical, legal sense, and not, as we now tend to, meaning personal freedoms. It also references the "churches, schools, hospitals, townhouses, and bridges" the *Mayflower* passengers and subsequent English colonists would build in America. The 400-year old parchment document with four brown wax seals has been restored by specialists at the Northeast Document Conservation Centre in Massachusetts, and is on display at Pilgrim Hall in Plymouth. The conservators locally humidified and flattened small, folded areas of damage and repaired tears in the parchment. The document was then tension mounted to create a secure display and housing system that would account for the dimensional changes of parchment, the weight of the document, and the suspended wax seals. A number of linen threads were adhered to the edges of the parchment, wrapped around the edge of the mounting board, and secured to the reverse of the board. These linen threads, held in even tension around the parchment, expand and contract in an opposite manner to the parchment with changes in relative humidity. The threads were sewn through a layer of fine, lightweight linen to create the appearance that the object was floating within the mount. The full text is transcribed by Caleb Johnson, and a picture of the patent is shown, at http://mayflowerhistory.com/pierce-patent.

Special thanks to Donna Curtin, executive director of Pilgrim Hall, for showing and describing this to me last Thursday at Pilgrim Hall!

SUNDAY, 19 SEPTEMBER 1621

New neighbours

Thomas Prince, in his *Chronicles of the Annals of New England* (1755), records that on this day Sir William Alexander of Scotland, afterwards the Earl of Sterling, met with and prevailed on King James to assign Sir Ferdinando Gorges part of the New England Territory. Sir Ferdinando was entrusted "with the affairs of this Country, advising with some of the Company, yields that Sir William should have a Patent of the North Eastern Part of New England, to be held of the Crown of Scotland and called NEW SCOTLAND." The grant will be issued tomorrow, when we will describe the provisions and the territory of the Plymouth Colony's new northern neighbour.

MONDAY, 20 SEPTEMBER 1621

Northern Neighbours

Today King James gave Sir William Alexander, master of requests for Scotland, a Patent for New Scotland: "bounding the same from Cape Sables to the Bay of St. Mary, thence N. to the River St. Croix thence N. to Canada River, so down the River to

Gachep, thence S. E. to Cape Briton Islands and Cape Briton, thence round to Cape Sables again; with all Seas and Islands within six Leagues of the Western, Northern and Eastern Parts, and within 40 Leagues to the Southward of Cape Briton, & Cape Sables; to be called NOVA SCOTIA," The intriguing part of this grant is that James made it as King of Scotland, and not as King of England, the title under which he had made almost all previous grants (or using the consolidated "King of England, Scotland, France, and Ireland" or some combination of the above). As Alexander later recorded, his ambitions turned to the founding of a mainland colony; his previously granted lands in Newfoundland never again received extensive attention. This 1621 charter included lands in the New World that covered nearly all of the present-day Maritime provinces of Canada and the State of Maine. That this new endeavour was envisioned to be distinctly Scottish was later made clear and explicit: "My Countrimen would never adventure in such an Enterprize, unless it were as there was a New France, a New Spaine, and a New England, that they might likewise have a New Scotland, and that for that effect they might have bounds with a correspondencie in proportion (as others had) with the Countrey whereof it should beare the name, which might hold of their owne Crowne, and where they might bee gouerned by their owne Lawes."[187]

TUESDAY, 21 SEPTEMBER 1621

Northern Neighbours (part two)

By all appearances, Alexander had no personal experiences in the New World, and knew little about how make his new colony a reality. Neither could he point to active service in the remoter regions of the British Isles that had marked the careers of men like the third and fourth lords Ochiltree, Bishop Knox, Captain John Mason, Lord Falkland, or Lord Baltimore. However, he was not entirely unaware of the difficulty of the task he had set for himself. He had discussed the general points relating to plantation schemes with no less an authority than John Mason, who in 1620 had returned from Newfoundland, and had penned his observations on that country. Alexander was further

---

[187] William Alexander, *Encouragement to Colonies*, 32, in David Laing, ed., *Royal Letters, Charters and Tracts Relating to the Colonization of New Scotland* (Edinburgh: Bannatyne Club, 1867).

encouraged in his efforts by Sir Ferdinando Gorges, an officer of the (newly formed, as of last autumn) New England Company and someone involved with parallel efforts to plant settlements to the south of Alexander's mainland patent: in the Pilgrim's back yard.[188]

WEDNESDAY, 22 SEPTEMBER 1621

Founding a Colony

What was perhaps most telling was that Sir William Alexander understood that there was scant desire among his countrymen to abandon their native lands for the wilds of an unknown New World. As he wrote: "The sending forth of Colonies (seeming a novelty) is esteemed now to be a strange thing, as not only being above the courage of common men, but altogether alienated from their knowledge, which is no wonder."[189]   In actuality Alexander's grant overlapped with that of Gorges, and the latter had to approve the new delineation for New Scotland. This insight suggests that he had developed a reasonably clear sense of the challenges facing a would-be colonial planter within a few years of receiving his charter. He knew, or learned very quickly, that if he was going to found a colony, it would be a long- term enterprise.

THURSDAY, 23 SEPTEMBER 1621

Allegiance to King James

Nine Sachems subscribed an Instrument of Submission to King James I/VI: Oquamehud, Canacum (the sachem who had sent John Billington to the Nausets), Obbatinnua, Nattawahunt, Corbitant, Chikkatabak, Quadequina (Massasoit's brother), Huttamoiden, and Epenow.[190]   Morton's New England's Memoriall recorded, "Yea Masassoit in Writing under his Hand to Capt. Standish has owned the King of England to be his Master: Both He and many other Kings under Him, as of Pamet, Nawset, Cummaquid, Namasket, with diverse others who dwell about the Bays of Patuxet and Massachusett: and all this by friendly Usage, Love and Peace, just & honest Carriage, good Counsel." Tomorrow we will consider what the terms of this submission meant, and what the natives thought that they were

---

[188] See J.P. Baxter, ed., Sir Ferdinando Gorges and His Province of Maine, 55–6.
[189] Alexander, Encouragement to Colonies, 1
[190] PCR 1:133, 4:24-26, 5:76; Morton, New England's Memoriall 44-45

doing in signing it.

What did the Indians think that they were doing?

The initial treaty addressed Massasoit "friend" and "ally" of King James, not mentioning the word "subject" at all, a clear signal to the Indians that they would enjoy an alliance of equals with the English.[191] The stipulations of the original treaty implied reciprocity, or equality, despite some noted exceptions, such as the clause that that Indians deliver any offender against the English to English justice, but that lacked a reciprocal clause delivering offenders against the Indians to Indian justice. Nevertheless, the historical record makes it clear that Massasoit assumed reciprocity applied to every aspect of the treaty, stated or not. When Massasoit suspected Squanto of wrongdoing, he demanded the English turn him over to the Indians for judgment. When Plymouth's governor resisted, Massasoit protested vehemently, "demanding him ... as being one of his subjects, whom, by our first Articles of Peace, we could not retain."[192] In addition, the English asked no tribute of the Indians, as superior sachems traditionally did of their subjects. Rather, they gave and received gifts to solidify what they repeatedly referred to as a friendship (see, for example, Winslow's 1621 visit to Massasoit, in which he took "some gratuity to bind [Massasoit] the faster unto him" [Bradford, *Of Plimoth Plantation*, Morison ed., 87].)

SATURDAY, 25 SEPTEMBER 1621

What did the Indians think that they were doing [part two]?

At least nine Indian sachems, other than Massasoit, had signed their names to an agreement acknowledging themselves "to be the Loyal Subjects of King James." There is good evidence to believe that Massasoit and these other sachems understood and accepted this relationship. When Edward Winslow visited Massasoit 1621, for example, the sachem declared that he was "King James, his man," and that his land was "King James his country." While we cannot know the precise reasons the Indians may have decided to become subjects, we can discern some

---

[191] see Morton, *New England's Memoriall*, in *Chronicles of the Pilgrim Fathers*, 38

[192] Winslow, *Good Newes from New England*, 13-14

compelling possibilities. First, both Indians and English desired trade, and a treaty of peace would help ensure that. Second, a treaty with the English could offer the Pokanoket and the Massachusetts protection against their powerful neighbours, the Narragansetts. Plagues had decimated Massasoit's people in the years preceding Plymouth's settlement, while the Narragansetts had somehow avoided any infection. The resulting demographic imbalance made the already powerful Narragansetts threatening indeed. The fact that many surrounding sachems and sub-sachems entered into similar agreements with Plymouth implies that these other Indian chiefdoms also viewed submission to King James as a beneficial relationship.

SUNDAY, 26 SEPTEMBER 1621

Plymouth Colony treaties v. Massachusetts Bay Colony treaties

The shift from alliance to subjection became more pronounced with the arrival of English settlers in Massachusetts Bay in 1630. As they, too, began making formal treaties with the Indians, the new settlers introduced a very different style of subjection. Under the first treaty between the English and five Massachusetts sachems, the sachems agreed to "put ourselves, our subjects, lands, and estates under the government and jurisdiction of the Massachusets [Bay Colony]" and to "bee true and faithfull to the said government."[193] This treaty omitted any reference to the king, as did, by 1643, all other oaths and treaties used by the Massachusetts Bay colony. (As an aside: Connecticut, founded by settlers from Massachusetts, followed the same pattern. In contrast to its neighbour colonies, Rhode Island, whose settlers were religious and political dissidents from Massachusetts, openly proclaimed its loyalty to the king throughout this period.) The colony's choice to downplay its connection with royal authority reflected years of conflict between king and Parliament, which led in 1642 to the English Civil War. Massachusetts Bay, which saw Parliament's struggle as its own, justified striking the king's name from its official oaths because Charles I had "violated the privileges of parliament, and made war upon them, and thereby had lost

---

[193] Submission of the Massachusetts sub-tribes to the Massachusetts Bay Colony, 8 March 1644, in Alden T. Vaughan, *New England Frontier: Puritans and Indians, 1620-1675*, 3d ed. [Norman, 1995], 342

much of his kingdom and many of his subjects."[194] Thus, Massachusetts Bay's support for Parliament's war with the crown justified them in asserting direct rule over the Indians and making the Indians' inferior status explicit in their treaties, something that Plymouth had been attempting in practice, but not in its written agreements.

MONDAY, 27 SEPTEMBER 1621

Envoys to the Massachusetts

Although the Pilgrims had frequently been told by their Indian allies that the Massachusetts were often threatening them, "yet we should go amongst them, partly to see the country, partly to make peace with them, and partly to procure their trucks [*trading products, esp. furs*]. For these ends the governors chose ten men fit for the purpose, and sent Tisquantum and two other savages to bring us to speech with the people, and interpret for us" to go in the shallop (*Mourt's Relation*).

TUESDAY, 28 SEPTEMBER 1621

Are we there yet?

Winslow (in *Mourt's Relation*) writes that "We set out about midnight, the tide then serving for us; we supposing it to be nearer than it is, thought to be there the next morning betimes: but it proved well near twenty leagues from New Plymouth. We came into the bottom of the bay [*which we now know as Boston Harbour*], but being late we anchored and lay in the shallop, not having seen any of the people."

WEDNESDAY, 19 SEPTEMBER 2021

Sachem on the run

The travellers slept in the boat last night, and then went ashore. There they found a pile of lobsters "that had been gathered together by the savages, which we made ready under a cliff. The captain set two sentinels behind the cliff to the landward to secure the shallop, and taking a guide with him and four of our company, went to seek the inhabitants; where they met a woman coming for her lobsters, they told her of them, and contented her for them." She told them where the local Massachuset natives were; "Tisquantum went to them; the rest returned, having direction

---

[194] J. Hammond Trumbull, ed., *Public Records of the Colony of Connecticut* [Hartford, 1852], 1:25; *Journal of John Winthrop*, 432.

which way to bring the shallop to them. The sachem, or governor of this place, is called Obbatinewat, and though he lives in the bottom of the Massachusetts Bay, yet he is under Massasoit." He treated the visitors very kindly, but explained to them that he was scared, on the run, and "durst not then remain in any settled place, for fear of the Tarantines." The "Tarantines" were later identified as the Abenakis, who controlled all the land from Casco Bay (in what is now Maine) up to New Brunswick. This was a hard place to grow crops, so in the fall they headed south to steal corn: it appears that the starving Pilgrims' actions at Corn Hill last December were not at all unusual, or limited to the Pilgrims. Obbatinewat was also afraid of "the Squaw Sachem, or Massachusets queen," another enemy who was after him. "We told him of divers sachems that had acknowledged themselves to be King James his men, and if he also would submit himself, we would be his safeguard from his enemies, which he did, and went along with us to bring us to the Squaw Sachem. Again we crossed the bay, which is very large and hath at least fifty islands in it; but the certain number is not known to the inhabitants." Some islands had been cleared and recently inhabited, although the people had either died or moved away. It was dark before they arrived at the other side of the bay where the squaw sachem was supposed to be; the Indians went ashore to see if anyone was there, but they found no one. "That night also we rode at anchor aboard the shallop," safe but uncomfortable.

THURSDAY, 30 SEPTEMBER 2021

Encounter with the Massachusets

After another sleepless night, all but two of the travellers went ashore, and marched in arms for about three miles up into the country. They came to a place where corn had been newly gathered, a house pulled down, while all the people were gone. Winslow recorded that "a mile from hence, Nanepashemet, their king, in his life-time had lived. His house was not like others, but a scaffold was largely built, with poles and planks some six feet from ground, and the house upon that, being situated on the top of a hill. Not far from hence, in a bottom, we came to a fort built by their deceased king, the manner thus; there were poles some thirty or forty feet long, stuck in the ground as thick as they could be set one by another, and with these they enclosed a ring some forty or fifty feet over. A trench breast high was digged on each side; one way there was to go into it with a bridge; in the midst of this palisade stood the frame of a house wherein, being dead, he lay buried."

About a mile further, the travellers came to another platform surrounded by a trench, but this time it was seated on the top of a hill: "here Nanepashemet was killed, none dwelling in it since the time of his death. At this place we stayed, and sent two savages to look the inhabitants, and to inform them of our ends in coming, that they might not be fearful of us: within a mile of this place they found the women of the place together, with their corn on heaps, whither we supposed them to be fled for fear of us, and the more, because in divers places they had newly pulled down their houses, and for haste in one place had left some of their corn covered with a mat, and nobody with it."

The women entertained the Englishmen at first with great fear, "but seeing our gentle carriage towards them, they took heart and entertained us in the best manner they could, boiling cod and such other things as they had for us. At length, with much sending for, came one of their men, shaking and trembling for fear. But when he saw we intended them no hurt, but came to truck [trade], he promised us his skins also. Of him we inquired for their queen, but it seemed she was far from thence—at least we could not see her."

"Here Tisquantum would have had us rifle the savage women, and taken their skins and all such things as might be serviceable for us; for (said he) they are a bad people, and have oft threatened you: But our answer was; were they never so bad, we would not wrong them, or give them any just occasion against us: for their words, we little weighed them, but if they once attempted anything against us, then we would deal far worse than he desired." This is the first record of suspicion that Winslow notes about the possibility that Squanto had a "hidden agenda," and was manipulating the English settlers.

Having spent the day in exploration, the travellers returned to the shallop, this time almost all the native women "accompanying us to truck, who sold their coats from their backs, and tied boughs about them, but with great shamefacedness (for indeed they are more modest than some of our English women are). We promised them to come again to them, and they us, to keep their skins."

OCTOBER 1621

FRIDAY, 1 OCTOBER 1621

If only they had known ...

Since the travellers were now running out of food, the wind was fair, and there was a full moon, "we set out at evening and, through the goodness of God, came safely home before noon" this morning, after sailing all night. "Within this bay the savages say there are two rivers; the one whereof we saw, having a fair entrance, but we had no time to discover it. Better harbors for shipping cannot be than here are. At the entrance of the bay are many rocks; and in all likelihood very good fishing ground." They reported back to Plymouth that there was a considerable "Quantity of Bever, and a good Report of the Place, wishing we had been seated There." But, given the events of the previous year, it was immediately agreed that it was too late now to pick up and move. The site would be occupied nine years later by John Winthrop and the Puritans of the Great Migration, where they would build the "city on a hill."

SATURDAY, 2 OCTOBER 1621

Several comments arising from last week's trip:

1. The Pilgrims expressed no surprise that there was a female leader ("squaw sachem or Massachusetts queen") of the tribes, as they were perfectly used to having a female ruler. Various political activists have asserted, without any reference or source, that the Pilgrims could not have "wrapped their minds around" the possibility of a woman in authority, when in fact their experience in England, Scotland, and the Netherlands had included several woman rulers as queens and regents in the previous century. The fact that the Pilgrims despised Elizabeth I had much more to do with her theology and churchmanship (being, they thought, a crypto-papist) than with her being a woman.

2. The Pilgrims' actions not only brought peace to the region for the first time in living memory -- and the memory of the natives was notoriously long -- but enabled the warring tribes to live together in harmony, which had not been the case for hundreds of years. Native American society was just as warlike as any other in human history. The activists' vision of Native Americans as peace-pipe-smoking environmentalists which gained purchase in the

1970s has long since given way to a more Hobbesian portrait of pre-Columbian reality. In North America, most Natives were primitive farmers. This means that (with some exceptions) they had no permanent settlements: they farmed in an area for a few decades until the soil got tired, before moving on to greener pastures where the hunting was better and the lands more fertile. This meant that tribes were in constant conflict with other tribes. It also meant that chiefs were continually vying for power, creating confederations under themselves, and that the question of who owned the land was in a more or less constant state of flux. In most of North America, the idea that any one piece of land belonged to any one tribe, for more than 50 or 100 years, is therefore highly questionable. In short, if you looked at a map of Native America or Canada 200 years before Europeans arrived, it would have been entirely different. In the meantime, some groups of natives slaughtered, bullied or, yes, enslaved other natives, whenever they were strong enough. That ended, rather suddenly, when the Pilgrims arrived, because the balance of power shifted suddenly and permanently.

3. It appears that the starving Pilgrims' actions at Corn Hill last December, taking the corn they found because they had run out of food, were not at all unusual, or limited to the Pilgrims. What *was* unusual was that the Pilgrims eventually paid for the corn.

SUNDAY, 3 OCTOBER 2021

"All Summer no Want"

The Pilgrim chroniclers recorded, "All the Summer no Want: while some were Trading, others were Fishing Cod, Bass, &c We now gather in our Harvest: and as Cold Weather advances, come in Store of Water Fowl, wherewith this Place abounds; tho' afterwards they by Degrees decrease; as also abundance of Wild Turkies with Venison, &c. Fit out Houses against Winter, are in Health and have all Things in Plenty."

MONDAY, 4 OCTOBER 1621

When was the First Thanksgiving?

There are numerous celebrations this year of the four hundredth anniversary of the "first Thanksgiving," and many of them are thinly veiled substitutes for cancelled celebrations of the arrival of the Pilgrims in November 1620. But, leading up to the celebration of Thanksgiving next weekend (at least in Canada), I

313

think it appropriate to look at what we can glean of that first event. This holiday has sparked so much controversy in recent years, that one has to think twice before even calling it a celebration. Political activists have made the approval or the rejection of the holiday a litmus test for acceptability. And I am well and truly tired of hearing what everyone "was taught in school" -- which, in almost every case, seems to be what the speaker *wishes* he or she had been taught in school, to fit in with either their current personal grievance or reverence. But what can we get from the sources themselves?

The first question, and the one most easily answered, is when the first Thanksgiving was. We know that it took place before the arrival of the *Fortune* (remember them? They have been on that ship for three months now, and they still have another month to go before they arrive in Plymouth) in the middle of November 1621. The harvest itself, which produced the bounty spoken of in yesterday's post, would have started in mid to late September. In addition to this, the arrival of the *Fortune* almost doubled the population of the colony of New Plymouth, and everyone was promptly put on half rations, so the celebration, for such it was, must have taken place while they still had something to celebrate. The Canadian celebration of Thanksgiving as the second Monday in October, while it really has no explicit connection to Plymouth or the Pilgrims, may be fairly close to the timing of the 1621 event. The November date in the United States has more to do with Abraham Lincoln's proclamation during the War Between the States, and the timing of the Christmas shopping season, than it does with any memory of the "First Thanksgiving."

TUESDAY, 5 OCTOBER 1621

What was the First Thanksgiving?

Nearly all of what historians have learned about the first Thanksgiving comes from a single eyewitness report: a letter written on 12 December 1621 by Edward Winslow, and brought back to England on the *Fortune*: "Our harvest being gotten in, our governor sent four men on fowling, that so we might after a special manner rejoice together after we had gathered the fruit of our labors. They four in one day killed as much fowl as, with a little help beside, served the company almost a week. At which time, amongst other recreations, we exercised our arms, many of the

Indians coming amongst us, and among the rest their greatest king Massasoit, with some ninety men, whom for three days we entertained and feasted, and they went out and killed five deer, which they brought to the plantation and bestowed on our governor, and upon the captain and others. And although it be not always so plentiful as it was at this time with us, yet by the goodness of God, we are so far from want that we often wish you partakers of our plenty."

William Bradford passes over the celebration almost completely; he wrote over twenty years after the fact, and does not mention any specific celebration, but does give thanks for the bounty they enjoyed.

And that is about all we know from anyone who was there. It appears that this was a harvest festival, with thanksgiving to God in part for their survival and in part for the bounty of the harvest. There does not seem to be any intention to make this an annual commemoration, or any sign that this was, in fact, repeated later (for example, neither records this as the "first" time, suggesting that it happened again).

WEDNESDAY, 6 OCTOBER 1621

Who was at the First Thanksgiving?

Who was at the first Thanksgiving? Of the Pilgrims, the number included 22 men, four married women — including Edward Winslow's new wife — and more than 25 children and teenagers. These were the ones who had made it through the epidemic of disease that swept through the colony the previous winter. Some 78 percent of the women who had arrived on the *Mayflower* had died, a far higher percentage than for men or children. I am regularly astonished at the imbalance, and how four women (with help, presumably, from some of the younger folk) could feed about 150 people over three days. The men, we are told, engaged in military exercises, which is probably the seventeenth century equivalent of watching football. The other surprise is the number of at least 90 Indian warriors -- this does not look like a friendly visit, and there is nothing in the stories to indicate that their arrival was anticipated. What was such a large army -- probably most of the Pokanoket men -- doing in Plymouth? My speculations on that tomorrow.

THURSDAY, 7 OCTOBER 1621

What were the Native warriors doing at the First Thanksgiving?

Visits from natives, even native warriors and sachems, to Plymouth were not unusual -- in fact, there were so many of them that the Pilgrims last spring had to devise a way to limit them (by demanding a copper chain as a sign that this visitor had been approved by Massasoit). The Indians also brought their wives and children, so there was clearly a relationship of trust. But something was different about Massasoit's visit now.

First, there were 90 Pokanoket men, far larger than a usual friendly social call. They clearly outnumbered the Pilgrims (all of them, including women and children, not just the men) by about two-to-one. As I mentioned yesterday, it does not appear that this visit was expected, or that there was a special invitation to Massasoit. This was also most of the men of the Pokanoket tribe.

Second, they were all warriors, so this has something of a hostile tinge to it. Once they showed up, they had to be fed, although, to be fair, they did go out and kill five deer and bring them back, which is quite a substantial hostess gift.

Third, this occurred soon after the Pilgrims had established contact with the Massachusetts Indians in Boston Harbour. This tribe was outside of Massasoit's sphere of influence, and he may have been trying to assure himself that the Pilgrims were going to stay on his side of the fence. The Pilgrims were trying to connect and unite the Indians, in the interests of trade -- the more the tribes worked together, the more pelts that was for the English -- but this was very, very threatening to Massasoit and his plans to dominate the area.

Fourth, this may be related to a customary circuit which sachems would take of dependent and subordinate tribes while they readied themselves to withdraw inland for the winter. In a sense this was a show of force, and an attempt to put the Pilgrims in their place.

FRIDAY, 8 OCTOBER 2021

Pilgrim Mythology (part one)

"Until recent years, I think it fair to say that the Pilgrims suffered more at the hands of the historians and writers than they did at the hands of the Indians. Some writers have found the pure and undigested Pilgrim story of exile, emigration, and improvisation held together by a sinewy faith too unbelievable for consumption. So some of them dismissed it as a somewhat overgrown fairy tale: the type of story fit for company with the Easter Bunny at worse or Jonah in the belly of the whale at best. They then turned their energies to debunking the Pilgrim 'myths' and concentrated upon the more exciting and believable adventure in Boston such as witch hunts, blue laws, and triangular trade. And other historians, also finding the bare story too much for consumption, decided to embellish and improve upon the original, passing for concrete fact the romantic nostrums of tradition, thus earning for themselves and their subjects the eventual derision of a more discriminating and sophisticated audience."[195]

SATURDAY, 9 OCTOBER 2021

Pilgrim Mythology (part two)

Peter Gomes concluded his address on "What Can We Believe About the Pilgrims?" with this typical (for him) peroration: "We deceive ourselves if we attempt to embellish and adorn the narrative. After reading countless secondary sources, articles, and sermons, it is always so refreshing to read the homely and unadorned prose of Bradford. Here is an account of persistence, improvisation, and providence: a story each generation of Pilgrim finds relevant and compelling. Here too is an account of men and women, totally human and fallible, whose hopes and fears, ideals and foibles, doubts and joys are ancestors of our own. Their spirit of adventure and their prudent practicality are our birthright. Often their posterity are our neighbors and friends. Their religion was firmly rooted in the world in which they found themselves, and yet their homely prayers ring relevant three centuries later in our own bleak hours of despair,"[196]

SUNDAY, 10 OCTOBER 1621

American v Canadian Thanksgiving (part one)

The official celebration of U.S. Thanksgiving originated during the War Between the States -- both Presidents (Davis and Lincoln) established more than one national day of thanksgiving. Abraham Lincoln, urged by Sarah Josepha Hale (editor of *Godey's*

---

[195] Peter J. Gomes, "What Can We Believe About the Pilgrims?" NEHGR 124 (Apr 1970): 135f.
[196] NEGHR 124 (Apr 1970): 138.

Lady's Book, who wrote letters to politicians for 40 years advocating an official holiday), set a day of national Thanksgiving by proclamation for the final Thursday in November, explicitly in celebration of the bounties that had continued to fall on the Union and for the military successes in the war, and also explicitly in "humble penitence for our national perverseness and disobedience." It was both a day of thanksgiving and a day of humiliation and fasting -- an odd combination, given how the holiday has developed. Thanksgiving was a civic and civil day of celebration, and was only connected with the Pilgrims later on in the nineteenth century -- I am looking for a date range at which the Pilgrim celebration came to be seen as a proto-Thanksgiving Day, but have thus far not been able to discover when that happened. James Baker notes that while there are numerous Victorian pictures of Pilgrims (voyage of the *Mayflower*, landing on Plymouth Rock, courtship of Myles Standish, etc., etc., etc.) there are no nineteenth century paintings or engravings of a Plymouth "First Thanksgiving."[197]

MONDAY, 11 OCTOBER 1621

American v Canadian Thanksgiving (part two)

Canadian Thanksgiving, on the other hand, began as an explicitly religious observance: it dates back to the 1860s when Protestant ministers in Canada asked the government to declare an official holiday to remind people to thank God for the fall harvest each year. From 1879 onward, Thanksgiving Day was observed every year on a Thursday in November. After World War I, an amendment to the Armistice Day Act established that Armistice Day and Thanksgiving would, starting in 1921, both be celebrated on the Monday of the week in which November 11 occurred. Ten years later, in 1931, the two days became separate holidays, and Armistice Day was renamed Remembrance Day. From 1931 to 1957, the date was set by proclamation, generally falling on the second Monday in October, except for 1935, when it was moved owing to a general election. Canadian Thanksgiving has not been given any explicit connection to the Pilgrims, at least officially, although individual Canadians can obviously include the Pilgrims in their celebration.

---

[197] James Baker, *Thanksgiving.* 9.

TUESDAY, 12 OCTOBER 1621

Law and Government in the Plymouth Colony

With the exception of a few of their leaders it seems unlikely that the colonists were aware of any of the legal movements of the time, or even of the politics of the royal court. Most of them were small farmers or artisans. Their leaders were exiles because of their beliefs. "They were in respect of law and government footloose, maintaining with the homeland no more than a commercial relation with the group which financed them."[198]   The members of the Plymouth Colony produced four sets of written codifications of their laws over time, the first in 1636, followed by collections of laws published in 1658, 1672 and 1685. Yet it is vital to recognise that *none* of this law-making was based on authority granted expressly by royal charter, and Plymouth was fairly unique in its time for lacking such a charter: it was the only English colony in North America *never* to receive a royal charter. The colonists did possess "land patents," which conferred title in the new "plantation" land to William Bradford and his "associates." However, these land patents lacked the full grant of authorities that a charter would provide.[199] Such charters typically provided the recipients with the express authority to establish a colonial government and to exercise powers over the inhabitants of the colony. Royal charters also provided details as to sources for substantive law that should be utilized in the colony.[200] For example, John Winthrop obtained a Royal Charter from King Charles I in 1630 for establishing the Bay Colony, and that charter served "as the legal basis for the government of the Massachusetts Bay Colony for more than half a century."[201]

WEDNESDAY, 13 OCTOBER 1621

Laws, Human and Divine (part one)

Legal historians often emphasize that the Plymouth Colony applied a combination of English common law and Mosaic law in regulating the daily affairs of the settlers. This invocation of

---

[198] Goebbel, *King's Law and Local Custom in Seventeenth Century New England,* in *Essays in Early American Law,* 91.
[199] Langdon, *Pilgrim Colony: A History of New Plymouth, 1620-1691,* 40
[200] Chafee, *Colonial Courts and the Common Law,* in *Essays in Early American Law,* 56-57
[201] Powers, *Crime and Punishment,* 511

religious authority was also useful in establishing the Colony's own authority to govern: since it had no legislative or judicial authority from the Crown, Holy Writ was the only other option. What they lacked by royal charter was often obtained by invocation of the Colony's service of the greater "glory of God," just as the Monarch invoked this service of God ("by the grace of God") as a source of legitimacy for his own claim of power and authority. Whatever legislative powers were assumed depended therefore upon some view of the inherent capacity of the group. A necessary consequence of the Separatists' ideas of church forming was that a certain corporate quality attached to the congregation formed by covenant. [Note: There has never been a thoroughgoing study made of Separatism from the angle of corporate theory, and this is all the more remarkable because of the importance of the Congregational church in New England and the close relation of state and church in that region. To comprehend the steps by which the Separatists reached their views we must remember that in England their churches were beyond the pale of the law; that they rejected all ideas of hierarchical organization; and that the Protestant doctrines of the visible church made some form of organization essential. The central and most characteristic fact in Separatism was the covenant by which a church was organized. This was a dual act, a covenant with God -- a solemn promise by the body of believers to God to do his will -- and a second covenant, sometimes reduced to writing, made by the believers with one another, to work for the Lord, to avoid evil, to do good, and to stand together. Only in this way, they believed, could a visible church be established.]

THURSDAY, 14 OCTOBER 1621

Laws, Human and Divine (part two)

The law of God constituted the foundation for the legal system of *every* New England colony. The founders of New Haven provided, for example, "that the words of God shall be the only rule to be attended unto in ordering the affairs of government." The Connecticut General Court agreed that the duty of all New England judges was to do "justice according to our laws and the rule of righteousness" and "to settle" matters "as in equity and justice they shall see fit, that peace and truth may be continued." It followed "that the judicial laws of God, as they were delivered by Moses," were to be "a rule to all the courts" and that all judges had

320

a "duty to do the best they [could] that the law of God may be strictly observed." Interestingly, when Plymouth Colony's General Court later directed that towns should establish their own regulations for managing the local, day-to-day affairs of the townspeople, the General Court required that such local regulations be made with fidelity to the laws of the "Govern[ment]" of the General Court, and not to England itself. The Bradford land patent required that no law be established by the colonists which would be repugnant to the law in England. Historian George Langdon has emphasized that the Plymouth colonists resisted this restriction for some time, based on their view that "different circumstances" in the hazardous territory of the New World made "rigid adherence to English law" less impelling.[202] Governor Bradford and other prominent officers of the Colony realized the riskiness of proceeding without a royal charter for their venture. They instead possessed only a land patent issued by the New England Council, a private corporation which did not possess the authority to grant the colonists any right to self-governance.[203] Bradford, Isaac Allerton and others attempted repeatedly over the years of the Colony to obtain a charter from the Crown. They failed to do so, and Plymouth Colony ultimately lost its self-governance and was annexed as part of the Massachusetts Bay Colony in 1691.

FRIDAY, 15 OCTOBER 1621

Divine Law

Two books I am reading for review in upcoming issues of the *Mayflower Quarterly* have sections in them expressing outrage at the perceived invasion of individual privacy by colonial and religious authorities (and those two were basically the same people). There has been general agreement for the last century or so, settled in law in the United States since *Griswold v. Connecticut* (381 U.S. 479 [1965] with its infamous "emanations" of "penumbras"), that marital activity was essentially private; this has since been expanded to include most consensual sexual activity and, at about the same time, religious belief. I was somewhat startled by a matter-of-fact statement at the beginning of a recent book on ecclesiastical law in England that "everyone knows" (that

---

[202] Langdon, *Pilgrim Colony*, 93
[203] Langdon, *Pilgrim Colony*, 188

phrase usually covers over the absence of proof or argument, and is frequently connected to the phrase "of course") that religion is a private and personal choice -- and this in a country that has an established, state Church! It is vitally important to realise how complete a reversal this is from what was universally the case for thousands of years, and until quite recently in the West. In the seventeenth century, religious belief and sexual activity (the subjects of the next few posts) were seen by everyone, absolutely everyone, to be public, civil and civic matters, under law both human and divine, and part and parcel of the stability of the community, the family, the state, and the church (broadly conceived). This is not an argument that such a change is wrong, although we may realise that this shift has still not really been thought through completely, and that our modern concepts of privacy do not rest on very old precedents or foundations.

New Englanders who disagreed about the bearing of divine law were punished. Thus, one man in New Haven was fined for declaring that "the laws of the jurisdiction ... [were] the wills of men," while another was chastised for "reproach[ing] those that walk in the ways of God." Similarly, a Connecticut man who announced that "he hoped to meet some of the members of the Church in hell ere long, and he did not question but he should" was whipped, and one from Plymouth fined for speaking against the church's rule. Another Plymouth man was required to acknowledge his offense of blasphemy for saying "he neither feared God, nor the devil."

SATURDAY, 16 OCTOBER 1621

Faith in Practise

Except in Rhode Island, people were prosecuted for disagreeing publicly with official theological dogmas. Thus, the Plymouth Colony made it a crime to "deny the scriptures to be a rule of life." Pursuant to this and other legislation, one man was indicted in Plymouth for objecting that the churches in Massachusetts and Plymouth did not baptize infants and for criticizing the magistrates for failing to take the oath of supremacy, while a decade later a group was prosecuted for "continuing of a meeting upon the Lord's Day from house to house." Likewise, a woman guilty of "faulty" speeches during public worship had her whipping respited in the hope that she would "be warned by the present sentence and admonition to offend no more," but when she committed the same offense a second time, the whipping was administered. Pursuant to statute, innumerable individuals were fined for failing to fulfil religious duties, such as not attending church on Sunday, otherwise violating the Sabbath, or using profane language. A New Haven man was whipped for "a rash & sinful oath." Perhaps, the most infamous example after the 1630s of judicial activism to protect dominant religious beliefs was that of William Ledra, a Quaker who on pain of death was banished from Massachusetts Bay in 1660 after being banished earlier from Plymouth. Except in Rhode Island, Quakers were banished for "divers horrid errors," whipped, or fined. Viewing them as "subversi[ve] of the fundamentals of Christian religion, church, order, and the civil peace," the Plymouth Colony banished them, and the General Court set aside a day of fasting and humiliation to seek God's blessing in saving the colony from the "infection and disturbance" of those "fretting gangrenelike doctrines and persons commonly called Quakers."

SUNDAY, 17 OCTOBER 1621

Establishment

The liberty of individuals to work out their own relationship to God had led Anne Hutchinson, Roger Williams, and others to settle Rhode Island, and accordingly, they kept their churches entirely distinct from their government. Likewise, the leaders of the Plymouth colony strove to set up churches independent of government. Even more than the founders of Rhode Island, the Pilgrim fathers fit within a broad separatist tradition that directed true believers to keep themselves and their churches apart from the state and from state-supported churches, which by their inclusion of all subjects necessarily comprehended nonbelievers and other sinners. Rhode Island succeeded over time in maintaining the separation of church and state; Plymouth did not. Religious taxes were never imposed in Rhode Island, and the judicial records of the colony contain none of the cases of excommunication, schism, and subordination of the clergy that occurred in Connecticut and Massachusetts. Probably the ministers possessed less wealth.

MONDAY, 18 OCTOBER 1621

Fornication

The eradication of sin was seen as the goal and role of both ecclesiastical and civil authorities. A sin prosecuted with great frequency was fornication — a sin that, in the words of New Haven magistrates, "shuts out of the kingdom of heaven, without repentence." This was both a sin and a crime, as it not only defiled the perpetrator and the community, but ran the risk of a child born out of wedlock becoming a burden on the community's already tenuous resources. Large numbers of single women were punished for getting pregnant, and many young couples prosecuted for having a child less than nine months after they were married. In New Haven, a defendant and his wife were whipped "for their filthy dalliance together"; two servants were prosecuted "for diverse unclean filthy dalliances"; and a third servant whipped "for defiling himself by diverse unclean passages with one of his master's children." Similarly, in Plymouth a young couple was whipped "for unclean practices each with other." On the other hand, when Jane Powell explained that she had committed fornication with an Irish servant out of "hope...to have married him" and thereby escape her "sad and miserable condition by hard service," the Plymouth court ordered her "cleared for the present" and sent her home to see if she was pregnant.

On 3 March 1662/3, Elizabeth Soule (daughter of the pilgrim George) and Nathaniel Church were fined £5 for fornication. Elizabeth Soule thereafter sued Nathaniel Church for failure to marry her and won a partial judgement of £10 and costs in October 1663. The charge of fornication does not necessarily imply that the woman was pregnant; the fact that Nathaniel Church refused to marry Elizabeth Soule, and was not required to provide any child support or give any money to Elizabeth for any reason other than breach of contract, would indicate that there was a miscarriage, stillbirth, or an early infant death. There is no record of any birth of a child to Elizabeth Soule at or around this time. On 2 July 1667, Elizabeth Soule was again charged with fornication and was sentenced to be whipped; no male partner was named.

TUESDAY, 19 OCTOBER 1621

Fornication (part two)

Single men also were prosecuted for fornication, and a man would be required to support a child he was accused of fathering "if it shall appear to be his." But many prosecutions encountered difficulties. If a woman failed to prosecute a man, he would be "cleared." An accused father also was entitled to a trial by jury if he demanded it, and the courts treated men accused of fornication fairly and were careful not to convict the innocent. The judiciary's sympathy for men emerged with special clarity in the weird case of John Uffoote, who, after being divorced from his wife for "insufficiency," managed to get Martha Nettleton pregnant. Although "he was sorry for his sin," he was now convinced that he would not have suffered from impotence "if his wife had carried it toward him as she ought"; "finding the need of that help" from Martha, he "was by the power of temptation and corruption in his own heart overcome" and accordingly sought the court's permission to marry Martha. Although the court found "it is a strange thing that after all this he should miscarry in this manner," it allowed John and Martha to marry after fining both of them. Judges were much less sympathetic to women, as, for example, when Martha Richardson testified that a man unknown to her impregnated her after she had passed out in a fainting fit and the court ruled that it "could not but judge her guilty, both of known fornication and continued impudent lying, believing that no woman can be gotten with child without some knowledge, consent and delight in the acting thereof."

In the case of the Plymouth colony, one factor always in the background was the need for population growth. The colony was singularly unsuccessful in attracting immigrants and settlers; there was a need to balance the obligation to punish crime and sin and thus support the civic and moral foundations of society, against the pressing need for more people to survive.

WEDNESDAY, 20 OCTOBER 1621

Adultery

Another sexual sin prosecuted with some frequency was adultery. Death was the official penalty for adultery only in New Haven, although there is no record of it ever being inflicted there; elsewhere adulterers received lesser punishments. For example, a married woman in Plymouth who committed "uncleanness" with an Indian was only whipped at a cart's tail and required to wear a badge, while there is no record of the outcome of two other Plymouth cases — the first, in which a man was accused of "lascivious carriage" in grabbing a married woman's clothes and "enticing her by words, as also by taking out his instrument of nature that he might prevail to lie with her in her own house," and the second, in which a woman was presented for the "sin of fornication with her father in law."

Establishment (part two)

Perhaps because Plymouth never progressed beyond being a poor, agrarian outpost, its religious institutions proved unable to maintain themselves without the aid of the state. The inhabitants of Rehoboth, for example, found it necessary to petition the General Court "to assist them in a way according to the orders of other colonies about them" in raising money for a minister. The signers of the petition alleged that the nonsigners contributed nothing to the church. Initially, the matter was resolved on a voluntaristic basis, when the town's magistrate promised that, if petitioners would pay their share of the church's cost on the basis of value of their estates, the nonsigners would pay theirs or he would personally make up the difference. But elsewhere, the magistrates had to turn to more coercive approaches. When the town of Marshfield petitioned for help in supporting the ministry, the General Court sent Miles Standish and John Alden to call a town meeting and "signify unto them the Court's desire is, that the inhabitants of the said town would take notice of their duties so as to contribute according to their abilities freely to the maintenance of the minister." Two years later, in 1657, the General Court by statute declared that every town was "engaged" to "the public worship and service of God" and authorized the levy of taxes for that purpose. And, two years after that, outright coercion was applied to the town of Yarmouth, when the General Court directed the calling of a town meeting so that "each particular man will freely engage towards" support of the minister. This time, however, the court was explicit when it provided that, if everyone did not "freely engage," four men would be chosen to levy on those who refused to contribute, and the constable directed to distrain their goods. With this 1657 act and its subsequent enforcement, Plymouth was well on the path toward a religious polity nearly identical to that of its neighbour, Massachusetts Bay.

Magistrates

As a first step in organizing the government in 1620, those original settlers who concerned themselves with this effort convened and elected several "Assistants" and John Carver as the first Governor; this took place in Plymouth Harbour before the *Mayflower* departed for America. Carver died the next year, and William Bradford was elected as the next Governor and remained in that office for decades. These officers were elected again in each year by the General Court, which was convened on a fairly informal basis in the earliest years of the Colony. None of these officials were trained in the law, and there were no lawyers present in the Colony in these early decades. The Governor and Assistants operated, through the Court of Assistants (also called the "Counsell"), to handle all matters on a subject-by-subject and case-by-case basis. They did not have the authority to enact comprehensive laws and ordinances, but issued orders on a limited array of subjects actng as the Court of Assistants. Only the General Court, attended by voting freemen, had the authority to enact such legislation, and it did not do so in a comprehensive manner until the codification of laws in 1636[204] -- more on how, and perhaps more interestingly, why that happened tomorrow.

SATURDAY, 23 OCTOBER 1621

1636 Codification of Laws (part one)

A majority of the early settlers apparently agreed that responsibility for governing the plantation rested with the governor. In March 1623, when Bradford asked the General Court for a decision on policy towards the Massachusetts Indians, the Court in turn referred the question back to the Governor and his advisers (basically saying, "Do what you think is right": see Winslow, *Good Newes from New England*, ch. 5 [Appleton Books ed., p. 43]). Lyford and Oldham had tried to stir up a rebellion in 1625, but failed when a majority supported Bradford. No evidence exists of any further challenge to Bradford's authority for another ten years (!). Plymouth evidently knew -- and trusted -- its governor. But as settlement began elsewhere in the colony, and people arrived to whom Bradford was unfamiliar, some did begin to worry. In October 1636, when the freemen called in General Court for a reading of the colony's laws, "divers were fownd worthy the reforming, others the rejecting & others fitt to be instituted & made." The Court ordered a committee of eight freemen and eight magistrates to prepare a revision: "four for the

---

[204] PCR 11: 7, 11

town of Plymouth, two for Scituate, and two for Duxburrow."[205]
The eight freemen elected were William Brewster, Ralph Smith,
John Doane, and John Jenny (for Plymouth); Jonathan Brewster,
Christopher Wadsworth (for Duxbury); and Anthony Annabale
and James Cudworth (for Scituate). The committee met in
November, and in their sessions the magistrates and freemen
agreed to limit the power of the governor and assistants.
Henceforth, the freemen were to choose a governor and seven
assistants "to rule and governe the said plantacions within the said
limits for one whole yeare and no more."[206] But their authority to
govern did not extend to the enactment of legislation. All laws and
ordinances of the colony were to be voted on in the General Court
"by the freemen of the Corporacion and no other."[207] Neither law
altered accepted practise: since 1621, the General Court had
annually elected a governor and assistants. And since the
institution of colony records in 1633, the Court of Assistants,
which consisted of the governor and the seven assistants, had not
enacted legislation.

SUNDAY, 24 OCTOBER 1621

1636 Codification of Laws (part two)

Nevertheless, the 1636 legislation was an important
milestone, for no records now extant indicate that written law had
earlier guaranteed a check on the magistrate's authority. Further
curtailment of magisterial power followed when in 1639 the
governor and assistants lost the right to control the granting of
land. Seven years later the General Court ordered the governor
and assistants, when they sat as a court, to limit themselves to
judicial concerns.[208] As the governor and assistants sitting in the
Court of Assistants lost power, the General Court became the sole
governing authority in the colony. Consisting of the magistrates
and town deputies, and in June including all the freemen who
bothered to attend, the General Court governed almost without
legal restraint. Not only was it the legislative and taxing
instrument of the colony, but in addition it assumed responsibility
for "the management of the greatest concerns of this Common

---

[205] PCR 1:43
[206] PCR 11:7
[207] PCR 11:11
[208] PCR 11:54

Weale."[209]   Only the General Court could make war or enter an alliance; after 1640, it controlled the distribution of land; through its required approval of men desiring to become freemen, it supervised the granting of the franchise. Indeed, so extensive were its powers that it had the right to change the basic form of government, and it did so in 1685 when it established a county system. Not surprisingly, the magistrates resented the lessening or curtailing of their powers. When the freemen asked the governor and assistants to turn over control of the colony lands in 1638, the magistrates (principally Edward Winslow and William Bradford) dragged their heels. Seven years later, Winslow bitterly informed John Winthrop, "But we are so many (since we followed your example in one particular, which we too late repented) to consult, as 'tis very hard for any to say what will be done, though he should know what is most wholesome for us."   Bradford, too, felt dissatisfaction, but he and his colleagues always seemed to have the good sense to yield when they had to.

MONDAY, 25 OCTOBER 1621

1636 Codification of Laws (part three)

As the Governor and Assistants, sitting as the Court of assistants, lost power, the General Court became the sole governing authority in the colony. Consisting of the magistrates and town deputies, and in June including all the freemen who bothered to attend, the General Court governed without any legal restraint. Not only was it the legislative and taxing instrument of the colony, but in addition it assumed responsibility for "the management of the greatest concernes of this Common Weale," which covers quite a lot of territory. Before 1672, the only check on its power was the requirement in the Bradford Patent that no law could be made repugnant to the law of England. But this requirement could be, and was, ignored for, like Massachusetts Bay, Plymouth argued that "different circumstances" in America excused the colony from rigid adherence to English law.[210]   Even the General Court, however, apparently recognised the dangers inherent in governing without legal restraint, and so in 1672 it enacted legislation which (so it was hoped) would limit the authority of future courts. The first chapter of the Colony Book of General Laws printed that year

---

[209] Book of General Laws [1672], 15
[210] PCR 6:169

contained a bill of rights: annual free election of the governor and assistants by all the freemen; justice and right equally and impartially administered; no person damaged but by virtue or equity of some express law; the right of all men to a jury trial; the right of the defendant to challenge the jury for cause; and in a capital crime, the right to peremptory challenges and the prohibition of a death sentence without the testimony of at least two witnesses. Most of these rights the Pilgrims had brought with them from the Old World.

TUESDAY, 26 OCTOBER 1621

The General Court

Until 1645, the General Court met in March, June, October, and December of each year; thereafter the December session was omitted. During the first twenty years of the settlement, the election court was convened in March. But by 1640, some people were living too far away from the town of Plymouth to ask the freemen to tramp through the snow and ice of a New England winter, and in 1642, the colony made a law that June would be the month of the court for elections. The General Court was a judicial as well as a legislative body, and its records include judicial matters from the probating of wills to criminal trials for witchcraft and murder. The procedure followed by the court in the disposition of judicial cases is unknown. Undoubtedly the governor and the assistants sat as the bench, and the deputies may sometimes have acted as the jury. But, more probably, juries of laymen were impanelled to hear a particular case or cases, and the deputies were excused altogether from judicial deliberations. The evidence for this is, admittedly, fragmentary and consists only of the legislation guaranteeing trial under English common law procedures, and a law passed in 1649 directing that at the election courts, after the choice and swearing of magistrates, "the general ocations of the Country" requiring the presence of the deputies came next.[211]

WEDNESDAY, 27 OCTOBER 1621

The Governor and the Court

The most important man in the General Court was the governor, who could summon the court into special session when

---

[211] PCR 11:56

he deemed it necessary. He presided once the Court convened, and he had a casting vote in case of a tie. He was also a judicial officer and could arrest and commit to prison, and was responsible for the execution of all colony laws. He had no other statutory powers.[212] In October 1649, the deputies proposed that the majority of the Court order adjournment and dissolution and the making and repealing of laws. Bradford, however, persuaded them to postpone the question until the election court which convened the following June. This court appointed a committee of freemen and magistrates to consider the proposals, and "they (the said Comittie) declared their minds to be that things in respect of the aforesaid particular do rest unaltered as they are."[213] So it is clear that one of the governor's principal powers was the power of persuasion. The governor, through the prestige of his person and office, exercised a vigorous control over all colony policies.

THURSDAY, 28 OCTOBER 1621

The Governor's Leadership (part one)

It is unclear whether or not the town deputies and the magistrates voted on actions of the court separately, or as one (unicameral) body, although the latter seems to be more probable. Whatever their voting status in the General Court, the governor and assistants commanded the attention of the deputies. As the Court sat together, the governor, with the support of the other magistrates, could present an issue about which the most articulate and prestigious element in the Court could (and probably would) already have reached a decision. Their views carried great weight, for the notion that each individual's opinion with regard to declaring policy had equal weight was not yet a part of popular belief. The General Court's enactment of legislation in 1655 as a sequel of Governor Bradford's ultimatum (more about that later) is a case in point. If Bradford could dictate terms, he obviously could exercise a vigorous direction over the colony's affairs. While the moral persuasiveness of Thomas Prence was probably less, it assuredly was influential in the Court's proceedings. Although no court records exist which indicate who initiated legislation and colony policies, undoubtedly each governor was primarily responsible during his years in office.

---

[212] PCR 11:7, 81-82
[213] PCR 11:55-57

The Governor's Leadership (part two)

Occasionally, however, the General Court refused to accept a governor's leadership. Early in October 1645, a Court of Assistants met at Plymouth to consider "a matter of great concernment" -- the only account of this episode is found in Edward Winslow's letter to John Winthrop, 24 November 1645.[214] The colony records show that the matter "of great concernment" may have been the establishment by law of a standard bushel agreed upon by the New England Confederation. This law set a fine of twelve pence for failure to use the standard bushel in commercial transactions. The law was repealed in June 1646.[215] Bradford and three assistants, William Collier, Miles Standish, and Edward Winslow, were present, and the four magistrates agreed to present the issue and their decision to the adjourned session of the June General Court during the third week in October. After a full day of discussion, the Court voted the proposal into law; only one deputy voted against it. The last week in October, the regular October General Court convened and some of the magistrates and deputies who had not attended the earlier court appeared. The Court began a rather heated discussion of the law enacted the previous week, and after what Winslow described as "a tumultuous order," a majority of the Court demanded its repeal. Standish, who voted with Bradford earlier, reconsidered and voted with the opposition. Collier was gone, but Prence had arrived and stood with Bradford and Winslow against the rest of the Court; in spite of their arguments, the majority continued to press for repeal. Bradford, however, stood his ground and would not allow it. If, he stated, the law was found prejudicial, a future Court could reopen the issue. The Court then listened to the petition requesting toleration in religion for all men who were not disturbers of the civil peace. Outraged at this betrayal of the basic and foundational reason for the colony's existence, Bradford could hardly contain himself, and, supported vigorously by Prence and Winslow, spoke against allowing the petition even to come to a vote. Again, however, their arguments seemed to make little impression on the rebellious deputies, and, as a last resort,

---

[214] *Winthrop Papers* 5:55-56
[215] PCR 11:46

Bradford ordered the petition shelved. Winslow informed Winthrop of these disturbing events, and wrote that he was ready to move to Massachusetts.

How Bradford legally prevented the General Court from repealing a law enacted by a court a week earlier and forced the tabling of a petition is unknown. No grant of power under the colony's law enabled him to do either. Perhaps the deputies and the opposing magistrates acquiesced because they did not want to fight against Bradford's will; perhaps, unrecorded in law, he did possess a veto power. Apparently the colony's freemen thought Bradford's actions warranted, because they reelected him as governor the next June.

SATURDAY, 30 OCTOBER 1621

Bradford's Ultimatum (part one)

In June 1650, the General Court passed legislation punishing people who slandered a church or minister and ordered a fine of ten shillings or a whipping for persons profaning the Sabbath. The following year the Court voted to require people to attend church.[216] The new laws, however, seemed to give little check to the decline of religion. In 1653, William Leverich, the minister in Sandwich, carried out his earlier intention and left Sandwich for Long Island. Not long after his departure, John Mayo, minister of the Eastham Church, moved to Boston. Rehoboth petitioned asking that a way be found, as in other colonies, to compel recalcitrants to contribute to the support of the ministry. Dissension broke out in the Barnstable Church; even the Plymouth Church experienced trouble. In 1654, Plymouth asked John Reyner, minister to the church since 1636, to resign.

For Bradford, now past sixty and reaching the end of a life in which religion had been so important, such goings on were too much to endure. Bradford informed the General Court convening in June 1655 that unless it took "some speedy course" to halt the deteriorating state of religion in New Plymouth, he would resign as governor. He specifically wanted action taken to remedy the neglect of competent maintenance for the ministry and the failure to take measures for the suppression of error.[217]

---

[216] PCR 11:57-58
[217] PCR 3:80

Bradford's ultimatum (part two)

Bradford's prestige carried the Court. It ordered persons who denied the Scriptures as "a rule of life" to suffer corporal punishment at the discretion of a magistrate although such punishment might not extend to life or limb. And limited steps were taken to compel men to support the ministry[218]. A decade earlier the commissioners of the New England Confederation, a league linking Massachusetts, Connecticut, New Haven, and Plymouth, had recommended the four colonies bring the civil power of the state to bear upon those who would not contribute to the ministry. Requesting further time to consider the recommendation, one of the two Plymouth commissioners had refused to sign and nothing came of the proposal.[219] But in 1655, under the pressure of Bradford's ultimatum, the Court agreed to act. The new legislation still placed the primary reliance for support of the ministry upon voluntary contributions. Under the new law, no clergyman of any congregation could leave his church until he had complained to the magistrates and they had heard both sides. If the magistrates upon hearing a complaint believed the congregation was not properly supporting the minister, they should make every effort to persuade the congregation to do so. But if persuasion failed and "plaine Obstinacye against an Ordinance of God" continued, then the magistrates were "to vse such other meanes as may put them vpon theire duty."[220] In spite of Bradford's outburst and the legislation which followed, religion in some of the towns continued to languish and sectarianism spread. The decline of unity in religious life was aided and abetted by the arrival of Quaker missionaries whose effective proselytising and very presence was a test of the resolution of the colony to defend its churches.

---

[218] PCR 3:81, 11:64
[219] PCR 9:20
[220] PCR 11:64

NOVEMBER 1621

Protests from Towns

Protests of actions taken by the General Court sometimes came from the towns. Denied the right to participate directly in the colony government, the men who were not freemen but could vote for deputies sometimes tried to initiate or oppose policy through their elected representatives. Marshfield in 1645 bluntly informed the Court that it would not assent to a lease of the Kennebec fur trade to noncolony residents. Marshfield did not add what action the town planned if the Court ignored the town's instructions. Other towns similarly tried to influence legislation. Rehoboth in 1672 drew up a set of written instructions for its deputies, and in the following year Scituate proposed alteration or repeal of several laws. The Scituate townsmen urged amendment of the Court's authority to reject deputies at will and suggested legislating explicit reasons for not allowing elected representatives to take their seats. Establishment of a county system of government in 1685 and transfer of some taxing power to the new county courts brought vigorous protests from several towns. Duxbury declared itself "very much dissatisfied" with the new system and protested as well the severity of newly enacted laws tightening military discipline. Scituate men charged that giving rate-making power to the county courts was an infringement of their basic rights as Englishmen and looked for a threefold augmentation of the usual charges. Scituate also protested the new militia law. But the county system and the militia regulations stayed on the books.

TUESDAY, 2 NOVEMBER 1621

Election Campaigns

In spite of occasional protests from some of the towns, the same deputies seemed to return year after year to attend sessions of the General Court. Bridgewater, which (except in two years) sent only one deputy, had four representatives between 1656 and 1692; and one of the four served nineteen years. Duxbury elected the same two representatives for *twelve* consecutive terms. The extension of such a pattern throughout the colony meant that in any given year the personnel sitting on the Court were not likely to differ greatly from the previous court. This willingness to reelect incumbents was surely one sign of the existence of a surface equilibrium in the colony for in June 1682, when no significant political stresses were apparent, twenty-four of the twenty-seven deputies were holdovers from the preceding year. In contrast, in June 1692, when the colony was in serious political turmoil, nearly forty per cent of the deputies elected to the General Court replaced incumbents.

WEDNESDAY, 3 NOVEMBER 1621

Re-election

The significance of re-electing the same men should not be overestimated. Only freemen could hold the office, and possibly few among them wanted it: attending three general courts a year, and in some years four, could become all too burdensome. Moreover, in a small country town and in the absence of a formal party structure, certain difficulties clearly existed for those wishing to unseat the incumbent. Nor did the re-election of incumbents, when the presence of government did not normally intrude into the everyday life of the average citizen, necessarily indicate that politically all was well in the colony.

THURSDAY, 4 NOVEMBER 1621

Political Life in Plymouth Colony

Despite the transfer of power and responsibility from the governor and his advisers to the General Court (a transfer largely accomplished by 1640), in the seventeenth century Plymouth had moved away from, rather than toward, a wider and fuller participation by its inhabitants in the political life of the colony. Some shift of this sort was, of course, inevitable. The expansion and proliferation of settlement, which by 1638 required the establishment of a representative form of government, meant that government necessarily became less immediate and less responsive to the needs of its people. But the tightening of the qualifications required for participation in politics also suggests a conscious effort toward exclusiveness and a determination to preserve the internal mechanism of the state from disruptive elements. Less realistic than their predecessors, the men who initiated this policy seemed less aware that, in the absence of tradition and military power, a government must command the confidence of its people. Their failure to understand would eventually plunge the colony into political crisis.

FRIDAY, 5 NOVEMBER 1621

Freemen (part one)

Like Massachusetts, Plymouth began to use the word "freeman" to designate citizenship, including the right to vote for the governor and assistants and to hold colony office. But unlike the Bay Colony, Plymouth did not at first attempt to spell out statutory requirements for freemanship. Before 1656 no legislative statement of qualifications existed; and even thereafter candidates were required only to secure the approval of the freemen in their towns before presenting their names to the General Court. Additional legislation passed in 1658 excluded "opposers of the good and who some lawes of this Collonie or manifest opposers of the true worship of God or such as refuse to doe the Countrey seruice."[221] These conditions represent the extent of legislative disfranchisement until 1672.

SATURDAY, 6 NOVEMBER 1621

Freemen (part two)

Doubt exists that the opportunity for citizenship was always welcomed and exploited. Robert Carr, one of the Royal Commissioners visiting Plymouth in 1665, wrote home to Whitehall that he had been told that men sometimes did not want to become freemen, that the government in fact had to compel them. Although proof for Carr's assertion is lacking, there is evidence that people were occasionally laggard in exercising their political rights and fulfilling their political responsibilities. The colony government once or twice had to prod towns to send representatives to the General-Court. Even persuading men to attend, and remain at, town meetings, where issues affecting their own immediate interests were at stake, caused difficulties; to enforce attendance, the towns usually found it necessary to assess fines upon absentees.

SUNDAY, 7 NOVEMBER 1622

Freemen (part three)

For the vast majority of the adult males in early Plymouth, there seems to have existed at least a limited opportunity to

---

[221] PCR 11:65, 101

participate in the colony's political life, whether or not they were freemen or citizens. Bradford and other leaders of the plantation were not crusaders for democracy, but they knew that in America the restraints of tradition were an inadequate base upon which to build a civil order, that they needed the support of the people who had settled Plymouth. Moreover, the economic organisation of the plantation dictated the establishment of a pattern which extended the right to vote to a majority of the free adult males. This pattern, established for pragmatic reasons, persisted after the immediate reasons for it had disappeared. Thus in 1633 four of every five male taxpayers in the towns of Plymouth and Duxbury were or would become freemen. Of all the adult males present in the colony a decade later, one of every two eventually achieved freeman's status. After 1638 all the males who had taken the oath of allegiance and were heads of families and settled residents could vote in the election of representatives to the General Court. Finally, no one was excluded either from becoming a freeman or from voting for deputies by a property qualification (two different and not necessarily related things).

MONDAY, 8 NOVEMBER 1621

The End of the Plymouth Colony (part one)

The military failure at Quebec in the autumn of 1690 considerably aggravated the deepening financial crisis in Plymouth Colony. One of the four towns delinquent in paying its taxes earlier in the year subsequently sent in its arrears and the three other towns had probably also paid. But resistance to support of the war continued, and in February, Governor Hinckley informed Increase Mather that "some few leading men" were trying to persuade people neither to obey the present government nor to pay taxes assessed by it. Discounting the importance of this opposition and the shortage of hard money in the colony, the General Court in November ordered £1350 raised "for the payment of all known debts of the colony relating to the present war, and other- ways, excepting the charges about armes for the expedition to Canada." The Court ordered half of the tax paid in money. In November, "known debts" did not include soldiers' wages, since the Court apparently hoped that they would be paid in booty brought home from Quebec. The news of late November that the assault had failed disappointed this hope, and the Court agreed on 7 December to raise an additional £1350 for the payment of soldiers who fought in Canada and along the Maine frontier. The £2700 tax bill voted by the Court in November and December represented about seven and one-half per cent of the total assessed property valuation in the colony.

After the defeat in Canada opposition to the government increased, and in the early months of 1691 the colony seemed headed for a complete breakdown in authority. On 31 January, John Cotton wrote to his son Rowland that "our condition here calls with speed for a general court — if it would have been sooner it had been well." A few days later Cotton wrote Governor Hinckley: "Sir, I doubt not of your faithfulness and solicitous care to promote the best interest of this poor Colony, who hath not only deserved ill from the hands of God, but have so demeaned themselves to the authority of their own choosing as not to deserve from man to say 'I will be your Healer;' yet, good sir, I hope you will overlook all such discouraging considerations, and at this day stand forth and play the man." But Hinckley, discouraged by the failure of the inhabitants to support their soldiers in the field and their churches at home, had begun to lose heart and was either unwilling or unable to supply the leadership which the colony so desperately needed. By summer the situation had deteriorated further; when the annual Election Court met in June, representatives from Dartmouth, Swansea, Little Compton, and Freetown were absent. Three weeks later the town of Bridgewater voted it would pay nothing further towards the expenses of the colony until the other towns paid the taxes due for the previous year. Bridgewater's ultimatum stated what was already clear: the General Court had ceased to function as an effective instrument of government.

TUESDAY, 9 NOVEMBER 1621

The End of the Plymouth Colony (part two)

A number of towns wanted to try for a royal charter and agreed to provide limited financial support. Eastham, for example, voted their "unanimous minds" that efforts to secure a charter should be undertaken. And Major John Walley (commander of the Bristol County militia regiment), writing to Ichabod Wiswall (minister of the Duxbury Church) about this time, reported the people were very anxious to secure a charter and were prepared to raise a considerable sum if they were certain that the money would not be wasted; but Walley added they would not risk more than

£200 on an uncertainty. In spite of initial enthusiasm, raising £200 proved beyond the capability of the colony. While some men contributed liberally, others refused "partly by reason of the great charge of the war and their low condition, and partly and especially being discouraged by some leading men telling them that they would but throw away their money." Of the goal of £200, only £150 was collected, and although Hinckley himself urged sending this sum, the General Court reasoned that some men should not carry the whole burden while others did nothing. The Court, therefore, ordered the money returned.[222]

WEDNESDAY, 10 NOVEMBER 1621

Annexation

Progress on a Massachusetts Charter went forward, despite the Plymouth Colony's request for a charter stalling. On 1 January 1691, the king referred a new draft to the Committee for Trade and Plantations. Shortly thereafter, William III left for Holland. When he returned to England in April, the matter was discussed by the king in council, and in May the attorney general drew up a draft which reflected the decisions reached at this meeting. Through the summer months, hearings on the charter continued before the subcommittee of the Privy Council. In their testimony, Mather and his colleagues argued for including Maine, New Hampshire, and Nova Scotia in the Massachusetts Colony; there is no evidence they also argued for the annexation of Plymouth, although Wiswall later accused Mather of being one reason for the disappointment of Plymouth's hopes. A June draft of the charter included Maine and New Hampshire, but not Plymouth. Wiswall himself may have been the restraining influence in blocking the incorporation of Plymouth into Massachusetts in June, but Wiswall's influence waned during the summer, and on 2 September the Privy Council agreed to annex Plymouth to the Massachusetts Colony and instructed the attorney general to prepare a new draft of the charter. On 7 October 1691, with some further revision but with Plymouth annexed, the charter passed the Great Seal, and in the spring of the following year writs were sent from Boston to the Plymouth towns requiring the election of representatives to the Massachusetts Assembly scheduled to sit in June.

---

[222] *Hinckley papers*, 292-297

Thursday, 11 November 1621
Why did the Plymouth Colony Fail? (part one)

In the last analysis, the annexation of Plymouth took place for reasons beyond the colony's control. The failure to secure a charter before 1686 meant Plymouth was more vulnerable than either Rhode Island or Connecticut, and the absence of an interested and powerful supporter in England meant that no one who had personal contact with the men in power was prepared to argue its case. More important, the recurring reports of military failure in the war against the French indicated that consolidation was in the best interests of the crown and also of the inhabitants of New England: the charter itself stated that Plymouth had been incorporated into the Massachusetts Colony "to the end that our good subjects within our colony of New Plymouth in New England may be brought under such a form of government as may put them in a better condition of defense." There is little doubt that the Privy Council, in placing Plymouth under jurisdiction of the Massachusetts government and justifying its action in these terms, meant what it said. The council was in fact so alarmed by the military situation in New England that it urged the appointment of Sir William Phips, the new governor of the Massachusetts Colony, as commander-in-chief of all the militia of Connecticut, New Hampshire, and Rhode Island. The conclusion seems almost certain that Plymouth's case for a charter was lost in spite of any and all efforts that it could have made on its own behalf.

Friday, 12 November 1621
Why did the Plymouth Colony Fail? (part two)

Governor Bradford had known that for his little colony to survive, the government must retain the confidence of its people, that while strong executive leadership must be given, ultimately that leadership could function only within limits acceptable to the families living at Plymouth. Because Bradford accepted this, and because he proved a tower of strength in moments of crisis, Plymouth Plantation had survived to become the second permanent settlement of Englishmen in the New World. In part at least, because Governor Hinckley was not an equally forceful man, and because he did not seem to understand that governing in the absence of an efficient police force requires political sensitivity, a

341

government which had endured for seventy years collapsed in the years 1690 and 1691.

SATURDAY, 13 NOVEMBER 1621

Material Prosperity

Visitors to the Colony had high praise in the early days for its seriousness of purpose, but showed less enthusiasm for the colony's economic prospects. Basic to the existence of a settled family plantation in the New World was a soil sufficient for the raising of crops. The soil at Plymouth was not good. John Pory, accustomed to the black loam of Virginia, complained that he found the ground at Plymouth rocky; and even in comparison to the land a little further west in New England, it was poor. In fact, so disheartened did some become with farming at Plymouth that between 1631 and 1645 people were continually leaving the town to settle elsewhere in the colony. Yet the soil at Plymouth raised sufficient produce to keep the settlement going. When a few of the inhabitants moved in 1644 from Plymouth to Eastham, one who stayed behind noted that people left not because of want but because they sought better lands. Plymouth after 1623 grew its own food and had some corn left over to trade with the Indians. Nonetheless, the export of agricultural products could not alone provide the basis for substantial prosperity.

SUNDAY, 14 NOVEMBER 1621

Industry

Shipbuilding furnished a livelihood to a small number of persons. Materials needed for ship construction, timber, hemp, flax, and iron, could be obtained locally, and men who listed their occupation as "shipwright" lived in a number of colony towns. Scituate, in part because of its proximity to the Boston market, quickly became the major centre for the industry, and Scituate yards seem to have operated on a continuous basis in the last quarter of the seventeenth century and perhaps earlier. Vessels built here sailed chiefly in the coastal trade and seldom exceeded fifty tons; in most cases they were apparently sold to Boston owners. Taunton provided the site of the only major ironworks in the colony although several other towns tried to promote the industry. Shortly after the settlement of Taunton the inhabitants became aware of local deposits of bog iron. Undeterred by the difficulties experienced in the Massachusetts iron enterprise at

Saugus, twenty-two settlers formed a company to establish an ironworks on the Two Mile River. A full share cost £20, and the first stock offering brought in almost £300 subscribed in amounts from £5 to £20. The partners hired James and Henry Leonard of Braintree as bloomers (Henry soon left to begin the manufacture of iron in New Jersey), and by 1656 production at the ironworks had begun.

MONDAY, 15 NOVEMBER 1621

Prosperity

Until the settlement of Massachusetts opened up new markets and brought prosperity to Plymouth, the amount of acreage in use in the colony remained small. When the colonists met to liquidate the joint-stock company in 1627, they agreed to allow each adult male (servants were not included) to share in the distribution of land. The number of shares which an individual received was determined by the number of persons, excluding servants, who were resident in the household; each share entitled the owner to twenty acres of land. With marketing opportunities virtually nonexistent, however, and with the labour force extremely limited, there was little immediate pressure to take up land and place it in cultivation. For the purpose of keeping settlement intact, the planters therefore agreed that those men whose lots lay closest to the town would share their land with those whose lots were farther away. After 1630 the opening of new markets thirty miles to the north in the Massachusetts Bay Colony caused mounting opposition to a continuance of this policy. The settlers at Plymouth wanted more and better land, and they became anxious to take up the full acreage divided among them in 1627. Some of the lots granted in 1627 lay across Plymouth Bay and to farm them would require permanent settlement there.

TUESDAY, 16 NOVEMBER 1621

Division of Property (part one)

Liquidation of the joint-stock company in 1627 did not alter existing economic patterns at Plymouth; this change came four years earlier. Until 1623 the Pilgrims had attempted to live in a communal relationship of economic equality; individuals worked not for themselves but for the company and all assets were divided equally. But in 1623 the planters asked Bradford to permit men to work for themselves and pay a tax to the plantation. After

343

consultation with Brewster and others the Governor agreed and assigned each family a plot of land for present use; the extent depended upon the size of the family. All assets, however, continued to be held in common and land could not be conveyed by inheritance

WEDNESDAY, 17 NOVEMBER 1621

Division of Property (part two)

Bradford believed that the incentive of property was important. Communal ownership of property, he later wrote, had produced confusion and discontent and had not given the stimulus necessary for the physical improvement of the colony. At Plymouth some men had not exerted themselves because tangible evidence was lacking that their efforts in any way contributed directly to their personal well-being: "The experience that was had in the commone course, . . . may well evince they [the] vanitie of that conceite of Platos and other ancients, applauded by some of later times: that the taking away of propertie and bringing in communitie into a comonewealth, would make them happy and florishing; as if they were wiser than God." Bradford continued: "For the yong men that were most able and fitte for labour and service did repine that they should spend their time and streingth to worke for other mens wives and children with out any recompence." A system which permitted each man to work for himself, the Governor believed, proved more satisfactory for the individual and for the plantation; "for it made all hands very industrious, so as much more corne was planted than other waise would have bene by any means the Gov[erno]r or any other could use and saved him a great deall of trouble and gave farr better content." Bradford wrote long before anyone was interested in defending the free enterprise system. Moreover, "communism" in early Plymouth was not communism at all, but an extreme form of exploitive capitalism in which all the fruits of men's labor were shipped across the seas and from which there seemed little tangible benefit. In the sense that communal economic patterns had existed at Plymouth, Governor Bradford thought they had not been a success.

THURSDAY, 18 NOVEMBER 1621

Division of Property (part three)

First, the plantation divided the livestock. The settlers

were grouped in twelve companies totaling 156 people and including slightly less than forty families; each company received a cow and two goats. In January 1628 came an allotment or division of land. To forestall complaints, division was by lottery, and all acreage surveyed and considered adequate before distribution began. Since meadow was in short supply, all meadowland continued to be held in common. Fishing, fowling, and access to water remained free to all men. In the division of housing, the governor and four or five others were allowed to keep their homes; the rest of the dwellings were valued, and the man who lived in a better home paid an equalizing fee to the man who lived in a poorer one. Although such a property division could have sparked explosive dissension, Bradford handled the matter well. The decision to include persons who were not former members of the company and the attempt to divide equally undercut any basis for discontent. According to the Governor: "This distribution gave generally good contente and setled mens minds."

FRIDAY, 19 NOVEMBER 1621

Arrives a Ship at Cape Cod

A ship appeared at the tip of Cape Cod this afternoon -- the first in a year.

It was the *Fortune*, at the end of a four month journey. To summarise: the *Mayflower* had arrived back in England in May, virtually empty, with stories of a disastrous winter. Thomas Weston had scrambled to put together a group of additional settlers -- some had been passengers on the *Speedwell*, but had stayed in England because there was not enough room on the overcrowded *Mayflower* for them to make their intended journey last year. Others were those Weston could gather quickly from London. Since the Adventurers had learned that the colony was outside of their grant of land, a new patent was quickly obtained. Weston wrote a letter to the new colony, chastising them for their falling so far short of their agreement, addressed it to the man whom he thought was the leader (John Carver, who had died eight months ago), and bundled this all on a small ship and sent it to -- without supplies -- to -- he did not know where. When the *Fortune* arrived today at (what is now) Provincetown, they had only the vaguest ideas of where the Pilgrims were. No one on the ship had been to New England, much less Plymouth, before.

SATURDAY, 20 NOVEMBER 1621

News of a ship brought to Plymouth

On Saturday, "the Indians bring us Word of [the *Fortune*] being near, but think her a Frenchman: upon making for our Bay, the Governor orders a Piece to be fired to call Home such as are abroad at Work & we get ready for Defence." Not only did the *Fortune* not know where the Plymouth colony had set up, the Plymouth Colony had not known that Weston was sending another ship with further settlers.

SUNDAY, 21 NOVEMBER 1621

Hugging the Coast

The *Fortune*, after staying a couple of days near Provincetown and not sure where to go or what to do, starts to move slowly along the inner shore of Cape Cod, looking for signs of the *Mayflower* passengers. During the transit from Cape Cod to Plymouth the *Fortune* passengers were shocked by the barren and bleak shoreline, much as the *Mayflower* passengers had been. The *Fortune* passengers found it hard to believe that anything could exist in such a forbidding land. Bradford wrote that they "ther saw nothing but a naked and barren place."

MONDAY, 22 NOVEMBER 1621

Condition of the Fortune *Passengers*

Contrary to conditions on the *Mayflower* one year earlier, everyone on the *Fortune* seemed to be in good health upon arrival, despite having been on board for four months. One birth was recorded soon after arrival – Martha Ford gave birth to a son, although her husband may have died about that time. When the son died, and, indeed even the son's name, is unknown.

TUESDAY, 23 NOVEMBER 1621

Origin of the Fortune *Passengers*

It is believed that the majority of the passengers of the *Fortune* were gathered together in London by Thomas Weston and his partner. According to author Charles Banks, individual records show that sixteen of the passengers can definitely be assigned to London or districts of the city such as Stepney and Southwark. Ten more passengers, whose origins cannot be determined, either died early or left the colony as determined by who was listed in the 1627 Division of Cattle, which also doubled as a type of census.

WEDNESDAY, 24 NOVEMBER 1621

The Thirty Five Passengers

Both Bradford in his journal and Edward Winslow in *Mourt's Relation* state that there were thirty-five passengers on the *Fortune* when it landed in November 1621. As stated numerous times, there was no passenger list or manifest for this ship, or for any other ship that landed in Plymouth in the 1620s. Attempts to list the passengers of the *Fortune* and come up with thirty-five have thus far been singularly unsuccessful. Some commentators state that the number thirty-five does not include women or children, or is just an estimate, or was not remembered correctly; Stratton lists Edward Bumpas twice (with two different spellings), and still only comes up with 34. Winslow wrote his recollection a matter of days after they arrived, and while Bradford may have copied Winslow's number when writing his *Of Plimmoth Plantation* twenty years later, he was certainly there when the passengers landed and must have had a first-hand personal recollection with which to compare Winslow's number. Although Banks records that there was only one woman on the ship (Martha Ford), he notes that several of the passengers were married by 1623, although where they would have found brides is unknown -- all of the unmarried women in Plymouth are otherwise accounted for.

Tomorrow I will put together the list of thirty five, and this is the only way I can see that the records and the recollection of Winslow and Bradford can match. For the next few days I will go through those passengers about which we know anything: I have written genealogical sketches of all of the passengers in *The Passengers of the Fortune (1621)*, which I prepared for the Delano Kindred reunion last September.

There appear to be several families, or parts of families, which I list here to help expand the number:

(2) William **Bassett** and his wife Elizabeth **Bassett**

(1) Jonathan **Brewster**, eldest son of William Brewster (who was already in Plymouth)

(2) Robert **Cushman** and his son Thomas **Cushman** (more about them on Friday)

(2) Thomas **Flavell** and his **son** (name unknown). His wife arrived on the *Anne*, but they are not in the 1627 cattle division, and so they may have died or, more likely, returned to England.

(5) Mrs. Martha **Ford** (maiden name unknown), her **husband** (name unknown), John **Ford** (b. 1617), Martha **Ford** (b. 1619), **son** born when the *Fortune* arrived in Cape Cod (died soon afterward).

(2) William **Palmer** and his son William **Palmer**

(1) John **Winslow**, brother of Edward Winslow (who was already in Plymouth).

This accounts for fifteen persons (and three women), or 43% of the passengers. The following passengers appear in the 1623 Plymouth land division, but not in the 1627 cattle division or any other record, and thus they must have died or returned to England in the meantime: (8) William **Beale**, John **Cannon**, William **Conner**, Augustin **Nicolas**, William **Pitt**, Hugh **Stacy**, James **Steward**, William **Tench**, Each received a single acre in the 1623 land division, which would suggest that they were all unmarried men; some might have been servants for other investors who had not yet come to New England. That brings the total to 23 (66% of the total number of passengers).

THURSDAY, 25 NOVEMBER 1621

The list

The *Fortune* (1621):

1. John Adams
2. William Bassett
3. Elizabeth Bassett
4. William Beale*
5. Edward Bompasse (Bumpas)
6. Jonathan Brewster
7. Clement Briggs
8. John Cannon*
9. William Conner (Coner)*
10. Robert Cushman
11. Thomas Cushman
12. Stephen Deane
13. Philip Delano
14. Thomas Flavel
15. (son) Flavel
16. _____ Ford
17. Mrs. Martha Ford
18. John Ford
19. Martha Ford

20.   (son) Ford
21.   Robert Hicks (Hix)
22.   William Hilton
23.   Benedict Morgan
24.   Thomas Morton
25.   Augustine (Austen) Nicolas*
26.   William Palmer
27.   William Palmer (son)
28.   William Pitt*
29.   Thomas Prence
30.   Moses Simonson
31.   Hugh Stacy*
32.   James Steward*
33.   William Tench*
34.   John Winslow
35.   William Wright

This is the only way I can get the records to yield 35 names, and I believe that this accounts for everyone. With the exception of the eight men who are not mentioned other than in the 1623 land division (each given an asterisk in this list), all of the other passengers will be introduced in at least a summary fashion over the next few days. As I said yesterday, these eight each received a single acre in the land division, and were thus probably unmarried at the time, and are not recorded anywhere else in either New England or England; it is reasonable to assume that they either died after 1623 or returned to England.

FRIDAY, 26 NOVEMBER 1621

Fortune *Passengers: Cushmans*

One of the leading passengers on board the *Fortune* was **Robert Cushman**, accompanied by his son Thomas. Robert Cushman was baptized in Rolveden, Kent, 9 February 1577/8, son of Thomas and Elinor (Hubbard) Couchman;[223] he had been the London agent for the Leiden congregation and was involved in the *Mayflower* and *Speedwell* voyage preparations; by occupation he was a grocer in Canterbury and a woolcomber in Leiden. Cushman had planned to make the voyage across the Atlantic, but when the *Speedwell* had to be abandoned he was one of those who remained behind. This original intention of Cushman's and his

---

[223] NEHGR 68:181

many other services on behalf of the Pilgrims are undoubtedly the justification for the assignment to Cushman in 1623 of land in Plymouth as if he had been a passenger on the *Mayflower* (even though he wasn't). In 1620 Cushman had negotiated a financial support contract with the Merchant Adventurers; Bradford and others of the Leiden contingent refused to approve this contract at Southampton, with the Leideners saying the contract was all in the Adventurers' favour and to the settlers' detriment. One of Cushman's reasons for coming to Plymouth now, a year later, was to convince the Plymouth settlers finally to approve this agreement, which had been unsigned for over a year. Bradford realised that, so far, the Adventurers had nothing to show for their investment, and after assurances from Cushman that Weston could be counted on, Bradford and the others signed the agreement that Cushman had brought from the Merchant Adventurers. Lora Underhill has gathered together every record known to her of the life of Robert Cushman, and in the process has compiled the best biography available of the man. Her treatment also goes into great detail on the career of his son Thomas. Elizabeth French in 1914 published her research into the ancestry of Robert Cushman, including extensive transcripts of records of the family in Kent.[224]

Robert married Sarah Reder at St Alphege in Canterbury on 31 July 1606, and had three children with her, two of whom died young and are buried at the Pieterskerk in Leiden along with Sarah (who died in October 1616, probably in childbirth.[225] She apparently died before 1621, as there is no evidence she came to Plymouth with her husband and stepson. Thomas Cushman was on the *Fortune* with his father; he is the only surviving child of Thomas' first marriage and the only child known to have come to America and thus the ancestor of all of Robert Cushman's descendants in America. He had been baptised at St. Andrew,

---

[224] NEHGR 68:181- 85. Robert E. Cushman and Franklin P. Cole published *Robert Cushman of Kent (1577-1625) Chief Agent of the Plymouth Pilgrims (1617-1625)* (Plymouth: GSMD, 1995; reviewed in MD 45:173).

[225] Dexter, *The England and Holland of the Pilgrims*, 611; Bangs, *Strangers and Pilgrims*, 705). In June 1617, Robert remarried "Mary Shingleton from Sandwich in England, widow of Thomas Shingleton" [MD 10:193; NEHGR 68:183]

Canterbury, Kent, 8 February 1607/8;[226] William Beale & Thomas Cushman" received two acres in partnership in the 1623 Plymouth land division, as passengers on the *Fortune* -- Thomas would have been about fifteen years old at the time, which may explain the partnership;[227] in the 1627 Plymouth division of cattle, he was the sixth person in the eleventh company;[228] admitted freeman 1 January 1633/4,[229] he married by about 1636 Mary Allerton , daughter of Isaac Allerton, and herself a *Mayflower* passenger. Thomas in later life would become the church Elder for the Colony.

SATURDAY, 27 NOVEMBER 1621

The Adams Family [sorry, I couldn't resist]

John Adams' English origins are unknown. In the 1623 Plymouth land division John Adams was granted one acre, as a passenger on the *Fortune*.[230] Member of the 1626 Purchaser group,[231] in the 1627 Plymouth cattle division John Adams, "Eliner Adams," and James Adams were the second, third and fourth persons in the sixth company.[232] Based on his estimated date of marriage, John was probably born around 1600. About 1625, John Adams married Ellen Newton, a passenger on the *Anne*:[233] this identification, long in print, is based on the fact that she is the only Ellen in the 1623 land division, and there was no other known addition to the Plymouth population in the next few years. This makes her one of several unattached females who came over on the *Anne* and the *Little James*, without any obvious connection to any other passenger. Her English origins are unknown, although it is not impossible that John and Eleanor knew each other before coming to New England. This is similar to the identification of Mary Becket: this Mary, who came on the *Anne* and was not obviously part of any other group, is identified as George Soule's wife because there were only two Marys in

---

[226] NEHGR 68:183
[227] PCR 12:5
[228] PCR 12:12
[229] PCR 1:4, 21
[230] PCR 12:5
[231] PCR 2:177
[232] PCR 12:11
[233] PM 344

Plymouth in 1623 (the other being Mary Chilton, and she is otherwise spoken for), so by pure process of elimination, she must be the "Mary Soule" who was George's wife.

John and Eleanor Adams had three children: James Adams was born before 1627 (since he is included in the division of cattle); John Adams (who married Jane James in Marshfield in 1654) and Susan Adams (no further record), both of whom must have been born after the division of cattle, in which they are not mentioned. The widow Ellen Adams was named adminstratrix of John Adams' estate on 11 November 1633, the deceased having left no will; she was bound in the sum of £140, John Barnes surety, to provide £5 apiece to her three children by John Adams - James, John and Susan - when they came of age, if she should choose to remarry.[234] The payment to son James, made by Kenelm Winslow, was recorded on 26 December 1651,[235] when James was at least 25.

John Adams died between July and October 1633: he is assigned ground to be mowed in the earlier date,[236] and his estate is inventoried at the latter date.[237] "The widow Ellen Adams" married (2) Kenelm Winslow, brother of *Mayflower* passenger Edward Winslow, in June 1634,[238] and was buried at Marshfield 5 December 1681 "being 83 years old" (probably an inflated age).[239]

SUNDAY, 28 NOVEMBER 1621

Fortune *Passengers from Leiden: Delano, Bumpas, Morton, Simonson*

The *Mayflower* arrived back in England on 6 May 1621 (o.s.), and Thomas Weston wrote his scolding letter to the (now deceased) John Carver on 6 July 1621 (o.s.), and, presumably, put

---

[234] PCR 1:19

[235] PCR 2:176

[236] PCR 1:14

[237] MD 1:157-58, citing PCPR 1:14

[238] PCR 1:30, PM 518

[239] Marshfield VR 13. The best treatment in print of John Adams and his two sons is Robert S. Wakefield, "Men of the Fortune: John Adams," TAG 55 (1979):212-14. An earlier account is in NEHGR 33 [1879]:410-13.

the letter on the boat and immediately sent it down the Thames. That gave Weston less than 90 days to assemble as many people as he could to undertake a dangerous voyage across the Atlantic -- a voyage that lasted four months, with the first month having the *Fortune* stuck in the English Channel because of contrary winds.

An obvious source of passengers would be those who had come from Leiden on the *Speedwell*, but were unable to continue the journey when the *Speedwell* was abandoned, since there was not enough room on the horribly overcrowded *Mayflower*. A number of unmarried young men did go on the *Mayflower*, but these sailed for reasons such as family relationships with the other passengers, being hired because they had skills necessary to the new community, or being indentured to a passenger. We know that 20 people disembarked at Plymouth (England), and did not get back on the *Mayflower*. Six of these were Richard Warren's wife and five daughters: they were on the ill-fated *Paragon* and then on the *Anne*. Robert (and probably Thomas) Cushman were also in the group that stayed, and the Cushmans arrived a year later on the *Fortune*. A very, *very* obscure passage in a 1625 letter from Thomas Blossom to William Bradford *might* mean that Thomas Blossom and his (unnamed) son were on the *Speedwell*, but did not continue the journey [as an aside, Thomas Blossom is an ancestor of Barak Obama, both President Bushes, and Mr. Rogers]. That leaves ten *Speedwell*-but-not-*Mayflower* passengers to be accounted for.

We know of several members of the Leiden congregation who were on the *Fortune*: these were all unmarried young men, in their late teens or early twenties. If they had originally been on the *Speedwell*, and had remained in England because they could easily get work there and could take the next boat to America (whenever that would sail), it is reasonable to think that they would have stayed in touch with Thomas Weston and would have been able to leave at a moment's notice. Four of these are as follows:

1. Philip Delano (the anglicised form of Philippe de la Noye), whom Bradford notes as having French parents and who asked, on his own, to join the Leiden congregation. Philip's aunt was Hester (Mahieu) Cooke, wife of *Mayflower* passenger Francis Cooke ("the wife of Francis Cooke," Edward Winslow wrote, "being a Walloon, [who] holds communion with the Church at Plymouth, as she came from the French, by virtue of communion of churches"). Philip had been baptised in the Walloon Church in Leiden in December 1603, and so must have been about 18 when he boarded the *Fortune*. He would have been about the same age as his cousin John Cooke, who had accompanied his father Francis on the *Mayflower*.

2. In the land division of 1623, **Moses Simonson** was joined with Philip Delano in a grant of land, suggesting that they may both have come together from Leiden. It is assumed that he was about Philip's age (and several sources guess that he was born at about 1605). In the 1623 Plymouth land division "Moyses Simonson & Philipe de la Noye" jointly received two acres;[240] in the 1627 Plymouth cattle division Moses Simonson was the eighth person in the first company (headed by Francis Cooke).[241] In 2004 Jeremy Bangs published a number of intriguing records for the family of Simon Moseszon of Leiden and explored the possibility that he might be father of Moses Simonson. Although such a connection is possible, it is far from proven.[242]

3. Also in the land division of 1623, and in the tax lists of 1633 and 1634, **Edward Bumpas** was adjacent to Philip Delano. The two men at a later date held adjacent land.[243] The last three sons of Bumpas were Philip, Thomas and Samuel, names also used by Delano. These items suggest that Eduard Bompasse (anglicised as Edward Bumpas) came from Leiden with Delano in 1620 or 1621, that the two may have had some association there before that date, and that Bumpas was also a member of the Walloon community there. He was about the same age as Moses Simonson (based on his age at marriage).

4. **Thomas Morton** was quite possibly the witness to the marriage of George Morton and Juliana Carpenter in Leiden on 6 July 1612 [n.s.].[244] Juliana Carpenter's sister Alice was William Bradford's second wife. This identification, if true, shows another member of the Leiden congregation. His age at first marriage would suggest that he was in his late twenties when he was a passenger on the *Fortune*. There is a possibility that he was married, perhaps around 1617, but his wife's name is unknown, and she appears in

---

[240] PCR 12:5
[241] PCR 12:9
[242] *New England Ancestors* 5 n. 3:54-55
[243] PCR 1:59, 66, 67
[244] MD 11:193

no New England record. The (younger) Thomas Morton who came on the *Anne* might be this Thomas' son, but it is just as possible that he was his nephew.

If we add those related to *Mayflower* passengers (Jonathan Brewster, eldest son of William Brewster; John Winslow, younger brother of Edward Winslow), that leaves only four passengers of the *Speedwell* unaccounted for. This is a long way from George Willison (and many commentators who follow him) in *Saints and Strangers*, who theorises that there was a veritable riot when large numbers of people demanded to be let off the *Mayflower* and *Speedwell*, abandoning the trip when the ships put in to Plymouth. From what it appears, most of those that stayed in England because there was no room for them on the *Mayflower* were those most able to support themselves individually; they stayed in close touch with the Merchant Adventurers for news of the new colony, and they got on the first ship they could that would take them to New England.

MONDAY, 29 NOVEMBER 1621
Searching for Plymouth

Although the *Fortune* arrived in the Cape Cod area last Friday, the ship strangely remained at the tip of the Cape for some time which caused the natives to be alarmed, thinking it might be a hostile French vessel. Upon hearing reports of this strange vessel, Governor Bradford had Myles Standish arm his militia and load the cannon on Burial Hill in case of an attack by the French. It took the ship weeks to find Plymouth, and it is not recorded when, exactly, it arrived.

And when they saw the depressing conditions within the colony (such as the limited provisions, the high mortality, and the threadbare clothing) being experienced by the settlers, they became quite panicked. The passengers were so disheartened and had such misgivings about this place they even advised the ship's master they wanted to reembark and leave if the colony did not meet their expectations, but were talked out of such action by the master and ship's crew, although they were promised that, if need be, they would be taken down the coast to Virginia.

TUESDAY, 30 NOVEMBER 1621
Additions to the Colony

On the ship were a large number of non-religious

passengers having been given the sobriquet of "Strangers," many of them single men who would greatly out-number the single, marriageable females in the colony: the non-religious passengers probably outnumbered the godly passengers -- but the non-religious were probably the few who could be collected and shipped off on such short notice. With arrival of the Fortune the colony had a total of sixty-six men and just sixteen women. This situation regarding the shortage of women came about partly as a result of the many deaths in the winter of 1620/21. For every eligible female, there were six eligible men. Another problem that concerned the Fortune arrivals was that there were no accommodations for them in the little colony. Bradford was forced to divide the Fortune passengers among the pre-existing seven houses and four public buildings, some of which were converted into virtual male dormitories for the many young men.

December 1621

Premonitions of Starvation

The problem that most concerned the colony was the continuing shortage of food made more severe by the arrival of the *Fortune*. Weston had not provided *any* provisions for the settlement on board the *Fortune*. And instead of making the colony situation stronger, the arrival of thirty-five more persons to feed, with the second severe winter for the colony coming on, had put things in what would be a disastrous situation. Bradford calculated that even if their daily rations were reduced to half, their store of corn would only last for six more months. And after having worked tirelessly this year and experiencing extreme hardships since their arrival one year earlier, they now would face another hard winter with a shortage of provisions. Bradford wrote, "They were presently put to half allowance, one as well as another, which begane to be hard, but they bore it patiently, under hope of (future) supply."

THURSDAY, 2 DECEMBER 1621

Planning for the Return

The *Fortune* did not even carry food to sustain the crew on the return trip. The Adventurers also sent a letter castigating the Planters for the fact that the *Mayflower* had arrived in England with an empty hold and demanding that the *Fortune* return immediately filled with valuable goods. The return trip, as it turned out, took a lot longer than anyone had anticipated.

FRIDAY, 3 DECEMBER 1621

Return Trip Cargo

To prove to the Adventurers that they were serious about repaying the debt owed to Weston, the colony spent two weeks in December 1621 loading the *Fortune* with hogsheads of beaver skins, otter skins, sassafras, and clapboards made from split oak to be used in the making of barrel staves. The value of the cargo was about £400-500, which would come close to reducing the colony's debt to the Adventurers by half. If only it had arrived ...

SATURDAY, 4 DECEMBER 1621

Summary of 1621

Thomas Prince summarised the events of 1621 from Bradford's journals and letters in his *A Chronological History of New England, in the Form of Annals*: "We have built 7 Dwelling Houses; 4 the Use of the Plantation, and have made Provision for diverse others. Both Masassoit, the greatest King of the Natives and all the Princes and People round us have made Peace with us. Seven of them at once sent their Messengers to this End. And as we cannot but account it an extraordinary Blessing of GOD in Directing our Course for these Parts, we obtain'd the Honour to receive Allowance of our Passing and Enjoying thereof under the Authority of the PRESIDENT and COUNCIL for the Affairs of NEW ENGLAND." The last part is a reference to the second Pierce Patent (see my post for 18 September 1621), whereby the settlers were authorised to plant their colony in New England; they still lacked a charter to form a government: they never received one, which is probably the main reason for the failure of the colony.

SUNDAY, 5 DECEMBER 1621

Jonathan Brewster

Two of the passengers on the *Fortune* were closely related to settlers already in Plymouth: John Winslow was the brother of Edward and Gilbert Winslow (more about him tomorrow), and **Jonathan Brewster** was the eldest son of William Brewster, elder of the Plymouth community.

Jonathan was born 12 August 1593 in Scrooby, Nottinghamshire, the son of William and Mary (_____) Brewster,[245] making him 28 when he arrived in Plymouth. Records documenting his education have not been found, but the proof that he had received study in reading and writing while he was living in England and Holland is well documented. He is noted as a "ribbon maker" in Leiden; once he arrived in New England he worked as a merchant and operated a ferry. Jonathan's name was among the "Purchasers" named of fifty-three men from the plantation, who with five Englishmen, agreed to discharge the financial debts of Plymouth Colony. "Jona. Brewster" was also one

---

[245] MD 1:7, 32:2

of the colony subscribers or purchasers who signed the agreement or trade monopoly partnership arranged between James Sherley (goldsmith), John Beecham/Beauchamp (salter), and Richard Andrews of London, merchants, and William Bradford, Edward Winslow, Thomas Prence, Myles Standish, William Brewster, John Alden, John Howland, and Isaac Allerton of Plymouth. These partners were called "Undertakers" and their purpose was to assume responsibility for repaying Plymouth Colony's debt of £1800 that was owed to the Merchant Adventurers of London for supplies and transportation of the Pilgrims to Cape Cod in New England in 1620.[246]

Jonathan married Lucretia Oldham "of Darby," daughter of William and Phillipa (Sowter) Oldham on 10 April 1624 in Plymouth.[247] She was baptised at All Saints, Derby, Derbyshire, 14 January 1600/1, and thus must have been about 23 when she arrived on the *Anne* with her brother John and Jonathan Brewster's sisters, Patience and Fear Brewster. Lucretia and her brother have not been documented to have been members of a Separatist congregation or to have lived in Leiden. The settlement of Elder William Brewster's estate in 1645 mentioned the discharge of Jonathan's alleged debts "in regard of his greate charge of children..." and Bradford's History made reference to Jonathan's 9 or 10 children without naming them, so it is possible that all have not been identified at this time. Jonathan entered the names of his children twice in the Brewster Book in his own handwriting, each time, once with names only and then with places and dates of birth; he recorded only eight children who can be positively identified.

In 1985 and 1986, Jeremy Bangs published a three part article presenting and discussing all known documents naming Jonathan Brewster in Leiden.[248] Bangs examined the claim made by the Dexters that Jonathan Brewster had an earlier wife and child while residing in Leiden and determined that the records cited by the Dexters did not pertain to Jonathan Brewster. Bangs, *Strangers and Pilgrims*, 438-441 provides a discussion of the Brewster-Brewer Company, including Jonathan's occupation and trade business.

---

[246] PCR 2:177
[247] MD 1:8
[248] MQ 51:161-67, 52:6-16, 57-63

Jonathan died on 7 August 1659 in New London, Connecticut. The record of Jonathan's death was entered in "The Brewster Book" by his son Benjamin Brewster. Jonathan was buried in Brewster Cemetery on Brewster's Neck (now Preston, Connecticut). The original headstone marking the Brewster burial plot broke into fragments many years ago, leaving only a small footstone of red sandstone with a harp engraved over the lettering bearing Jonathan's name, In 1855, an obelisk with a plain granite shaft about eight feet high was erected to mark the family burial plot.

MONDAY, 6 DECEMBER 1621

John Winslow

The other close relative of a Plymouth settler is Edward Winslow's (slightly) younger brother John. He was born in Droitwich, Worcestershire, 16 April 1597 and baptized there 18 April 1597, the son of Edward and Magdalen (Oliver) Winslow.[249] He was presumably educated as well as his siblings, and certainly well enough to be successful in trade. In the 1623 Plymouth land division **John Winslow** received one acre as a passenger on the *Fortune*.[250] In the 1627 Plymouth division of cattle John Winslow and Mary Winslow were the fifth and sixth persons in the sixth company.[251] He married Mary Chilton, daughter of James Chilton (and herself a *Mayflower* passenger) in Plymouth by 22 May 1627.[252] For this reason, John Winslow and his family are treated in the silver books, in the volume on James Chilton.[253] She died between 31 July 1676 (date of will) and 1 May 1679 (renunciation of executorship). John moved to Boston in the 1650s, where he became a very successful merchant. He died between 12 March 1673/4 (date of will) and 21 May 1674 (probate of will). The inventory of the estate of John Winslow, taken 27 October 1674, totalled £2946 14s. l0d., of which £450 was real estate: "the dwelling house, garden & land adjoining to it"; most of the value was in shares in vessels, hard currency, debts due

---

[249] NEHGR4:297, 21:120
[250] PCR 12:5
[251] PCR 12:11
[252] PCR 12:11; MF 15:5-7
[253] MF 15:5-7, 10-19

and trade goods.[254] He and Mary had a whopping ten children, at least eight of whom have descendants. Bradford, in his list of increasings, says that John and Mary Winslow had nine children, but Benjamin Winslow was born in 1653, after Bradford's list was compiled.

The varied abilities of the five Winslow brothers are interesting to observe. Gilbert left too slight a mark on the records to judge. Edward, the eldest, was also the ablest. The second brother, John, was also quite talented, but was not inclined to public service; he died as one of the wealthiest merchants in Boston. The two younger siblings, Kenelm and Josiah, remained in Plymouth Colony, were publicly visible so long as their two elder brothers were still present, and then faded slowly from sight.

John was 24 when he came on the *Fortune*, almost exactly the age his brother Edward was when he made his *Mayflower* journey (Edward celebrated his 25th birthday during the crossing). I have been unable to find any information on what John did before coming to New England.

TUESDAY, 7 DECEMBER 1621

Bassett and Briggs Family

1. In the 1623 Plymouth land division "William Bassite" received two acres as a passenger on the *Fortune*.[255] In the 1627 Plymouth division of cattle, the sixth company included **William Bassett**, Elizabeth Basset, William Basset Jr. and Elizabeth Basset Jr..[256] We know he was a blacksmith,[257] because the first five lines of his inventory included blacksmith's tools, including a pair of bellows, an anvil, a vice, tongs and hammers and coal shovels, and "all the rest of the smith shop."[258] His inventory also included more than twenty books, listed by title, mostly theological.[259] William was probably born about 1596, based on the date of his first marriage, and died between 3 April 1667 (date of will) and 12 May 1667 (date of inventory). He married twice: (1) By 1623 (and probably by 1621) Elizabeth _____, probably also a passenger on the *Fortune*

---

[254] MD 3:133-34
[255] PCR 12:5
[256] PCR 12:11
[257] PCLR 3:66
[258] PCPR 2:2:37-38
[259] MD 16:163

in 1621. She appears in no record after 1627 and may have died anytime between 1634 (birth of her last child) and the date of her husband's second marriage. (2) After 1651 and before 12 December 1664 Mary (Tilden) Lapham, daughter of Nathaniel Tilden and widow of Thomas Lapham. She was living at Bridgewater as late as 28 March 1690.[260] William and Elizabeth had six children: the third, Sarah Bassett, married Peregrine White, the first Englishman born in New England (while the *Mayflower* was at anchor in Provincetown).

In 1611 a William Bassett, formerly of Sandwich in England, widower of Cecily Light, was twice betrothed at Leiden in Holland. His first bride-to-be died, but he succeeded the second time.[261] Some have held that this was the man who came to Plymouth, but this seems unlikely given the ten-year gap before the arrival in Plymouth in 1621, and the lack of evidence for children of the Plymouth man born before that date, assuming that he had been married at least twice before. It is also possible that the William Bassett of Leiden in 1611 was the father of the immigrant to Plymouth in 1621, but there is no evidence directly favouring this hypothesis.[262]

If the two-acre grant to William Bassett in 1623 was for William and his wife Elizabeth, then the first child would not have been born until 1624, three years after William's arrival in Plymouth. It is possible (though not likely) that the marriage took place in Plymouth, and Elizabeth came on the *Fortune* as a single woman. Savage has misread the 1627 Plymouth cattle division, somehow including daughter Sarah Bassett in this list, when in fact only two children, William and Elizabeth, were included.[263] Sarah must have been born soon after 1627, however, to have married by the end of 1648.

On 6 March 1648/9, William Bassett was fined 5s. "for not mending of guns in seasonable time," and, on 9 June 1653, he was fined 10s. "for neglecting to publish and make known an order directed to him from the council of war, prohibiting provisions for being transported out of the colony" [PCR 2:137, 3:36].

2. **Clement Briggs** was from Southwark, on the south bank of the

---

[260] Bridgewater VR 1:320
[261] Plooij VI, VIII
[262] See discussion in Stratton 242-43.
[263] Savage, *Genealogical Dictionary*, 1:136

Thames, and is one of the few passengers of the *Fortune* whose origins are known. In the 1623 Plymouth land division, "Clemente Brigges" was granted one acre "beyond the first brook to the wood westward."[264] In the 1627 Plymouth cattle division, "Clemont Briggs" was included in the company of John Howland.[265] He was born by about 1600 (a deposition of 1638 implies that in 1616 Briggs had already been a servant of Mr. Samuel Latham for a few years). On 29 August 1638, "Clement Briggs of Weymouth, fellmonger," deposed that "about two and twenty years since this deponent then dwelling with one Mr. Samuel Lathame in Barmundsey Street in Southwarke, a fellmonger, and one Thomas Harlow then also dwelling with Mr. Rob[er]te Reeks in the same street, a fellmonger, the said Harlow and this deponent had often conference together how many pelts each of their masters pulled a week." Briggs goes on to tell in detail how many pelts had been handled a week "for the space of three or four years," possibly implying that he had in 1616 been servant to Samuel Latham since about 1612. The deposition was apparently taken at the request of Robert Hicks, who may have been involved in a lawsuit in England.[266]

   Clement also married twice: (1) By 1 March 1630/1, Joan Allen (on 1 March 1630/1, "Mr. Tho[mas] Stoughton, constable of Dorchester, was fined £5 for taking upon him to marry Clement Briggs & Joane Allen").[267] She died by 1640. (On 6 March 1637/8 at a Quarter Court at Cambridge, Clement Briggs gave a bond of £10 for the appearance of his wife at the next court; at the same court Arthur Warren was presented "for keeping company with Clement Briggs's wife, [which] was found to be true."[268] At a Quarter Court on 5 June 1638, Clement Briggs's wife was "enjoined not to come into the company of Arthur Warren."[269]) Clement and Joan had two children. (2) By 1640 Elizabeth _____. She died between 11 November 1685 (date of codicil) and 11 August 1691 (probate of will). Clement and Elizabeth had four children.

---

[264] PCR 12:5
[265] PCR 12:10
[266] PCR 12:34-35
[267] MBCR 1:83
[268] MBCR 1:219
[269] MBCR 1:233

In 1966 Edna Anne Hannibal, with the assistance of Claude W. Barlow, published a solid genealogy of the descendants of Clement Briggs.[270] This volume presents evidence supporting the interesting hypothesis that the widow of Clement Briggs was the "widow Briggs" residing in the early 1650s at Southampton [p. 4].

WEDNESDAY, 8 DECEMBER 1621

Thomas Prence

Thomas Prence was the first man elected Governor of the Plymouth Colony (1634-1635, 1638-1639, 1657-1673) who was not a passenger on the *Mayflower*. He was born about 1600 (based on age at death), son of Thomas Prence, carriage-maker. In his will, dated 31 July 1630 and proved 14 August 1630, Thomas Prence, carriage-maker, of Lechlade, Gloucestershire, left a legacy to his son Thomas Prence "now remaining in New England in the parts beyond the seas." The Prence family moved to the London parish of All Hallows Barking, near Tower Hill, at some time before Thomas came to America. In the 1623 Plymouth division of land Thomas Prence received one acre as a passenger on the *Fortune*.[271] In the 1627 Plymouth division of cattle Thomas Prince, Patience Prince and Rebecca Prince are the tenth, eleventh and twelfth persons in the fifth company.[272] An early settler of Duxbury (by 1637), in 1644 he moved to Eastham, which he helped found, returning later to Plymouth. He married probably four times: (1) Plymouth 5 August 1624 Patience Brewster, daughter of William Brewster. She died late in 1634 (in a letter to his son John Winthrop Jr. dated 12 December 1634, John Winthrop reported that "the pestilent fever hath taken away some at Plimouth, among others Mr. Prence the governor his wife"[273]). (2) Plymouth 1 April 1635 Mary Collier, daughter of William Collier.[274] She died perhaps by 1644. (3) After 1 July 1644 (when she witnessed Rev. George Phillips's will as Apphia Freeman in Watertown[275]) and certainly some considerable time before 8 December 1662 (when

---

[270] *Clement Briggs of Plymouth Colony and His Descendants, 1621-1965*
[271] PCR 12:5
[272] PCR 12:10
[273] *Winthrop Papers* 3:177
[274] PCR 1:34
[275] NEHGR 3:78

Thomas gave land to her son) Apphia (Quick) Freeman, former wife of Samuel Freeman [1630, Watertown],[276] daughter of William Quick of London.[277] (4) After 26 February 1665[/6] and by 1 August 1668 Mary L Howes, widow of Thomas Howes.[278] She died on 9 December 1695.[279] He had four children with his first wife, two with his second wife, and probably three with his third wife.

Prence was involved in the colony's disputes over control of settlements on the Connecticut River. As part of the colony's fur trading operations, a trading post was established at Matianuck [now Windsor], Connecticut, in the early 1630s. This was done over objections by the Dutch of New Netherland, who had established their own trading post at present-day Hartford not long before. Discontented colonists from the neighbouring Massachusetts Bay Colony settled in the same area 1634, seeking to escape what they perceived as the harsh rule of "King [John] Winthrop". Although Jonathan Brewster, head of the Matianuck post, gave some assistance to the needy Massachusetts colonists, the Plymouth government protested that the settlers were occupying land that they had rightly acquired from the local natives. The matter was also bound to a conflict between the two English provinces over the Maine fur trade and became further complicated by the outbreak of the Pequot War. Prence negotiated the agreement that in 1637 resolved the dispute: most of the land was purchased by the Massachusetts arrivals, and Plymouth retained the trading post and several smaller plots of land. Prence was also involved in an unsuccessful attempt to gain Massachusetts assistance in the recovery of the Pentagoet trading post in Maine.

On 6 March 1637/8, having been elected governor, Thomas Prence was excused from the requirement that the governor live in Plymouth, and was permitted to retain his residence in Duxbury.[280] When he was again elected governor, in 1657, he was allowed to maintain his residence in Eastham, but in 1663 the court ordered that the governor's house at Plymouth be enlarged, and by 1665 Prence again became a resident of

---

[276] GM1 1:698-700
[277] TAG 11:178
[278] MD 6:157-65, 230-35
[279] MD 6:230, citing Yarmouth Town Records 3:328
[280] PCR 1:79

Plymouth. Thomas Prence died in Plymouth 29 March 1673, in his 73rd year ("Thomas Prence, Esquire, Governor of the jurisdiction of New Plymouth, died the 29th of March, 1673, and was interred the 8th of April following. After he had served God in the office of Governor sixteen years, or near thereunto, he finished his course in the 73 year of his life. He was a worthy gentleman, very pious, and very able for his office, and faithful in the discharge thereof, studious of peace, a wellwiller to all that feared God, and a terror to the wicked. His death was much lamented, and his body honorably buried at Plymouth the day and year above mentioned").[281] His inventory included a long list of books valued at £14 2d., including two great Bibles and "100 of psalm books." Most of the books were theological, but other titles included *New England's Memorial Culpepper's London Dispensatory* and *Blunt's Law Dictionary.*[282] There were also "1 midwife's book" and "44 school books."[283] He is buried on Burial Hill in Plymouth.

There is much, much more to say about Prence's active life, particularly his Quaker policies, but perhaps due to the fact that he had no grandsons that carried the Prence surname, little attention has been directed to this family.[284]

THURSDAY, 9 DECEMBER 1621

Deane and Hicks Family

1. In the 1623 Plymouth division of land, one acre "beyond the first brook to the wood westward" was granted to **Stephen Deane** as a passenger on the *Fortune.*[285] In the 1627 Plymouth division of cattle, Stephen Deane was the twelfth person in the twelfth company [].[286] On 7 January 1632/3, he was granted permission by the General Court to set up his corn mill "upon the brook adjoining to the town of Plymouth" and to receive as a toll one pottle of each bushel ground; from the terms of the agreement, it is clear that Deane already had a functioning mill farther from

---

[281] PCR 8:34; see also MD 3:203-4
[282] MD 3:208-9
[283] MD 3:212, 213
[284] A brief account of his family was prepared in 1852 by David Hamblen and a more substantial treatment was published in 1931 by Mary Walton Ferris (*Dawes-Gates Ancestral Lines*, 2:682-94).
[285] PCR 12:5
[286] PCR 12:13

town.[287] He was born by about 1605, based on estimated date of marriage, but his English origins are unknown. By about 1630, Stephen married Elizabeth Ring, daughter of widow Mary Ring (and possibly the Elizabeth Ring, daughter of William & Marie Ring, baptised at Ufford, Suffolk, 23 February 1602/3)[288]). She married (2) Plymouth 16 September 1635 Josias Cooke.[289] Stephen and Elizabeth had three daughters. Stephen died in Plymouth between 10 March 1633/4 (purchase of Godbert Godbertson's house) and 2 October 1634 (date of inventory), and probably closer to the latter date. (Secondary sources claim that he died in September 1634, which is reasonable but not proved.) The best treatment of the family of Stephen Deane may be found in John I. Coddington's article on the widow Mary Ring and her children.[290]

2. In the 1623 Plymouth division of land, "Robart Hickes" was granted one acre as a passenger on the *Fortune*, and his wife and children were granted four acres as passengers on the *Anne*.[291] In the 1627 Plymouth division of cattle, **Robert Hicks**, Margaret Hicks, Samuel Hicks, Ephraim Hicks, Lydia Hicks and Phebe Hicks were the sixth through eleventh persons in the twelfth company.[292] He came from London, and his occupation is given as a fellmonger. He was born about 1598 (based on the estimated date of his marriage), and he married by 1603 Margaret ____. She died at Plymouth between 8 July 1665 (date of will) and 6 March 1665/6 (probate of will). They had eight children. Hicks' youngest son married Elizabeth Howland, daughter of John Howland. Robert Hicks died in Plymouth 24 May 1647 (from inventory). Savage and Pope both give this date as 24 March, apparently based on the abstract of the inventory published in 1850.[293] On the original, the month of death is in the upper right corner of the page, and is worn, so that only "Ma" can now be read on microfilm. Bowman saw this as May.

In 1938 Louis Effingham deForest compiled a

[287] PCR 1:8, 22
[288] TAG 42:197-99
[289] PCR 1:35
[290] TAG 42:193-205
[291] PCR 12:5, 6
[292] PCR 12:13
[293] NEHGR 4:282

comprehensive summary of all that was known about Robert Hicks at that date.[294] This summary includes children Elizabeth and Daniel, for whom there is no evidence. The major breakthrough on this family was made when Robert S. Wakefield discovered additional baptismal entries in the St. Mary Magdalen, Bermondsey, register.[295]

Several sources give Robert Hicks two wives: Elizabeth Morgan and Margaret Winslow. No record has been found of *any* marriage for Robert Hicks, and his only known wife was Margaret; the argument that Margaret was a Winslow has little basis.[296]

Clement Briggs of Weymouth, fellmonger, deposed 29 August 1638 that "about two and twenty years since this deponent then dwelling with one Mr. Samuell Lathame in Barmundsey Streete in Southwarke a fellmonger and one Thomas Harlow then also dwelling with Mr. Rob[er]te Reeks in the same street a fellmonger the said Harlow and this deponent had often conference together how many pelts each of their masters pulled a week. And this deponent deposeth and saith that the said Rob[er]te Reeks did pull three hundred pelts a week and diverse times six or seven hundred & more a week in the killing seasons, which was the most part of the year (except the time of Lent) for the space of three or four years. And that the said Rob[er]te Reeks sold his sheep's pelts at that time for 40s. a hundred to Mr. Arnold Allard, whereas this deponent's Mr. Samuell Lathame sold his pelts for 50s. per hundred to the same man at the same time and Mr. Heeks pelts were much better ware."[297]

On 13 July 1639, Robert Hicks of Plymouth, "citizen & leatherseller of London," by a bill dated 6 July 1618 was indebted to Thomas Heath, citizen and cooper of London, for £180, which amount was demanded by letter of attorney made by Hannah Cugley but Hicks showed an acquittance of all debts to Heath, having paid it long ago.[298]

---

[294] *Moore Ancestry.* 295-308
[295] TAG 51:57-58
[296] TAG 54:31-34
[297] PCR 12:35
[298] PCR 12:43

368

FRIDAY, 10 DECEMBER 1621

Flavel and Ford Family

1. In the 1623 Plymouth division of land, "**Thomas Flavell** & his son" were granted two acres as passengers on the *Fortune*, and "Goodwife Flavell" one acre as a passenger on the *Anne* (1623).[299] As this family is not found in the 1627 division of cattle, or in any other New England records, we must assume that they all died, or, more likely, returned to England. Willison gave Flavell's wife's name as Elizabeth, and was followed in this by Robert S. Wakefield, in his analysis of the 1623 land division,[300] but there is no documentary support for this name. Elsewhere Flavell's wife's name is given as Anne,[301] but this would seem to be a confusion with the name of the ship on which she arrived.

2. In the 1623 Plymouth land division "Widow Foord" received four acres as a 1621 passenger on the *Fortune*.[302] By the time of the 1627 Plymouth cattle division the widow Ford had married Peter Brown, and she appeared as the fifth person in the fifth company, and her children John Ford and Martha Ford as the seventh and eighth persons in that company.[303] Mr. Ford (his first name is unknown) was born around 1592 (based on his estimated date of marriage), and died between 11 December 1621 (Winslow's letter [Young's *Pilgrim Fathers* 235-36]) and late 1623 (wife appears as "Widow Foord" in land division). His wife's name is Martha (although her maiden name is unknown), and they married by about 1617. She married (2) in Plymouth by 1626 Peter Brown of the *Mayflower*. She had two children with Peter Brown and died by 1630.[304] This man's name does not appear in any Plymouth Colony record, and therefore we do not know his first name and can only infer that there was a man with this surname on the *Fortune*. Alexander Young's *Chronicles of the Pilgrims*[305] quotes a letter of Edward Winslow to a friend in England dated 11 December 1621: "The Goodwife Ford was delivered of a son the first night she landed and both of them are very well." It would be

---

[299] PCR 1:5
[300] Willison, *Saints and Strangers* 449; MQ 40:58
[301] *Genealogical Bulletin* 1:173
[302] PCR 12:5
[303] PCR 12:11
[304] TAG 42:39-40
[305] Young, *Chronicles*, 235

unlikely that a widow in the late stages of pregnancy would have been a passenger on the *Fortune* (or any other ship); therefore it seems more probable that her husband was with her on the voyage but died shortly after the date of Winslow's letter, since the 1623 division of land (apparently made about March 1623/4) allots four acres to "Widow Ford." The fact that Winslow calls her "Goodwife" and not "Widow" also supports this assumption.

The grant to the family of four acres in 1623 is subject to a number of interpretations. Barclay assumed that it encompassed the widow and three children, the husband having died by that date. Wakefield held instead that the grant was for the widow Ford, her deceased husband, and children John and Martha, the child born in 1621 shortly after landing having already died.[306] A third possibility is that the son John was the child born immediately after landing in 1621, and that the grant was for the two parents and the only two children of those two parents. This would make John Ford only nineteen when he was granted land in 1640,[307] so if a person receiving a grant of land in Plymouth at this time was necessarily twenty-one, then this arrangement could not work.

In 1966 Florence Barclay treated this family definitively, and the conclusions presented here on the Ford children and what is known about the immigrant head of family follow that article.[308] Barclay's most important conclusions were that the husband of Martha and the father of these three children sailed on the *Fortune* and arrived in Plymouth where he soon died, and that William Ford of Marshfield was not a part of this family. Robert S. Wakefield also wrote about this family, with the emphasis on the daughter Martha and her Nelson descendants.[309]

I have counted five people in this family: Mr and Mrs Ford and all three children; that is the only way that I can obtain the full 35 passengers on the *Fortune*.

SATURDAY, 11 DECEMBER 1621

Hilton Family

William Hilton may get the award for being the most

---

[306] MQ 40:55
[307] PCR 1:165
[308] TAG 42:35-42
[309] TAG 56:32-35

colourful passenger on the *Fortune*. In the 1623 Plymouth division of land William Hilton received one acre as a passenger on the *Fortune* and "William Hilton's wife & 2 children" received three acres as passengers on the *Anne*.[310] In his discussion of the controversy surrounding Rev. John Lyford and his followers, William Hubbard noted that "the first occasion of quarrel with them was, the baptizing of Mr. Hilton's child, who was not joined to the church at Plymouth;"[311] this event apparently took place in 1624. He was a tavern keeper and ferry operator (at Kittery, Maine). On 27 June 1648, "Mr. William Hilton being licensed for to keep the ordinary at the mouth of the river of Pascataquack and that none other shall keep any private ordinary there, nor to sell wine, beer nor liquor upon any pretence."[312] On 16 October 1649, "Mr. William Hilton presented for not keeping victual and drink at all times for strangers and inhabitants, admonished."[313] On 15 October 1650, "for as much as the house at the river's mouth where Mr. Shapleigh's father first built and Mr. William Hilton now dwelleth; in regard it was first house there built and Mr. Shapleigh intendeth to build and enlarge it, and for further considerations, it is thought fit it should from time to time be for a house of entertainment or ordinary with this proviso, that the tenant be such a one as the inhabitants shall approve of."[314] William was born by about 1591 (based on estimated date of marriage), son of William Hilton of Northwich, Cheshire,[315] and died between 28 June 1655 (when he was appointed to a committee[316]) and 30 June 1656 (by which date his widow had remarried[317]). He married (1) By 1616 _____ _____, who came with two children to Plymouth in 1623 on the Anne. She died by about 1636. (2) By about 1636 Frances _____, born about 1618 (deposed on 27 February 1687/8, aged about seventy, regarding events that had taken place forty-six years earlier involving

---

[310] PCR 12:5, 6
[311] Hubbard, *General History*, 93-94
[312] MPCR 1:125
[313] MPCR 1:135
[314] MPCR 1:147
[315] GDMNH 334
[316] MPCR 2:38
[317] MPCR 2:47

William Hilton[318]). She survived him and married again by 30 June 1656 Richard White.[319] In a footnote in his MPCR series, Charles Thornton Libby remarked: "This woman's [Frances's] court records serve to illustrate the social distinctions of the period. While married to Mr. William Hilton she was always entitled 'Mistress,' even when called into court for rude behaviour, but after his death and upon her marriage to Goodman Richard White, she promptly dropped to 'Goody'."[320] He had four children with each of his wives, for a total of eight.

In a letter written in November 1621, soon after his arrival at Plymouth, and published the following year by Captain John Smith, William Hilton wrote to a cousin in England saying "Our company are for the most part very religious honest people, the word of God sincerely taught us every Sabbath, so that I know not anything a contented mind can here want. I desire your friendly care to send my wife and children to me, where I wish all the friends I have in England."[321]

William's wife and two children (son William and daughter Mary) arrived in 1623. A third child was born soon, probably in 1624, and Rev. John Lyford's baptism of this child was the opening shot in a series of disruptions at Plymouth revolving around Lyford and John Oldham."[322] William Hilton and his family soon left Plymouth, but his place of residence in the next few years is not certain, and is intertwined with the career of his brother Edward Hilton. A useful document in this regard is the petition of William Hilton, eldest son of the immigrant William Hilton. Although the petition itself is not dated, it was discussed at court in Massachusetts Bay in late May and early June of 1660. William Hilton tells us that "your petitioner's father came over into New England about the year Anno Domini 1621; & your petitioner came about one year & an half after, and in a little time following settled ourselves upon the River of Pischataq[ua], with Mr. Edw[ard] Hilton, who were the first English planters

---

[318] NEHGR 31:181, citing York Court Files.
[319] MPCR 2:74
[320] MPCR 1:267
[321] Barbour, ed., *Works of Captain John Smith*, 430-31; Young, *Chronicles*, 250-51; NEHGR 31:179
[322] PM 345

there."[323] The petition goes on to claim land up the Merrimack River, which had been granted to William Hilton Senior and William Hilton Junior by the local Indian sachem; the petition was only partially successful.

Edward Hilton settled on the Piscataqua sometime between 1625 and 1628, and the petitioner is here claiming that the Hilton brothers made the settlement simultaneously. One possibility, then, is that William Hilton left Plymouth in later 1624 or early 1625, after the baptism incident, and joined his brother Edward about that time in settling what would become Dover. This would not require any residence between Plymouth and Dover.

Noyes, Libby and Davis state that Hilton "left Plymouth and joined [David] Thomson at Little Harbor with the purpose of starting salt works," and apparently did this in partnership with Gilbert Winslow.[324] This would provide William Hilton and his family with a home prior to the arrival of Edward Hilton, assuming the latter did not come so early as 1625.

Noyes, Libby and Davis note that "(b)esides the wife who followed him to Plymouth, and Frances, possibly a widow with children when he married her about 1651, there may have been others," suggesting that "if one of his wives should prove to have been a Winslow it would explain his letter writing with Edward Winslow, his association with John Winslow, his removal to Piscataqua with Gilbert Winslow and the marriage of two of John Winslow's sons to his relations."[325]

On 16 October 1649, Mrs. Hilton was presented and admonished for fighting and abusing her neighbours with her tongue. At the same court Mr. William Hilton was presented for breach of the Sabbath in carrying of wood from the woods and for failing to keep food and drink on hand for strangers and inhabitants.[326]

On 15 March 1649/50, Mr. William Hilton brought cases against Hatevell Nutter, Thomas Hanscom and Robert

---

[323] SJC Case #362; NEHGR 36:41-42
[324] GDMNH 334-35, 765 (no documentary evidence provided)
[325] GDMNH 335 (without, unfortunately, documentary support for the Winslow associations)
[326] MPCR 1:135

Mendam.[327] He was still suing Hanscom and Mendam on 11 March 1651[/2].[328] On 15 October 1650, Mr. William Hilton and Frances his wife were sued by Mr. Georg Moncke for slander.[329] On 11 March 1651[/2], Jeremy Sheires reviled Mr. William Hilton when Hilton was foreman of the jury, and Sheires was fined £2.[330] On 14 October 1651, Mr. William Hilton posted bail for Clement Campion, sued Thomas Way for debt, and sued Michaell Powell for debt.[331]

On 30 June 1653, "William Hilton Senior" sued Samuell Allcocke for cutting and carrying away his timber.[332] On 25 October 1653, Mr. William Hilton Senior sued Ann Mason of London and, in a separate action, sued Sir Ferdinando Gorges, for damage done against him.[333]

On 28 June 1655, the court found Frances Hilton, the wife of William Hilton, guilty of "railing at her husband and saying he went with Joane [sic, John in the blotter] his bastard to his three halfe penny whores and that he carried a cloak of profession for his knavery." For this offense she was sentenced to have "twenty lashes upon the bare skin, only the execution thereof upon her husband's request to be respited upon her good behaviour until the next county court, except any just complaints come in against her. In the meantime, which if they do unto authority then the punishment to be inflicted upon her by order of the commissioners of York at what time they shall see cause to order it."[334]

At the same court in which Richard White became William Hilton's administrator, White also brought a charge of slander against Rice Jones for an offense against his wife, Frances White.[335] As the court dragged on, Frances White was countersued for "causelessly abusing" the wife of Rice Jones with opprobrious and disgraceful speeches and was sentenced to

---

[327] MPCR 1:138
[328] MPCR 1:156
[329] MPCR 1:145
[330] MPCR 1:160
[331] MPCR 1:169
[332] MPCR 2:11
[333] MPCR 2:19
[334] MPCR 2:43-44
[335] MPCR 2:47

acknowledge her offence in court, 3 July 1656.[336] On 6 July 1657, Joan Andrews was presented for "threatening Goody Whitte at York in a profane manner saying that she would swear herself to the devil but she would be avenged of her."[337]

In 1877 John T. Hassam published "Some Descendants of William Hilton" and in 1882 "The Dover Settlement and the Hiltons."[338] Although these articles contain some errors (and in fact the second corrects some items in the first), they are filled with useful information on both brothers.

SUNDAY, 12 DECEMBER 1621

Palmer and Wright Family

1. In the 1623 Plymouth division of land **William Palmer** received two acres as a passenger on the *Fortune*, and "Franc[e]s wife to William Palmer" received one acre as a passenger on the *Anne*.[339] In the 1627 Plymouth division of cattle William Palmer, Frances Palmer and William Palmer Junior were the eighth, ninth and tenth persons in the seventh company.[340] William was born by about 1581 (based on estimated date of first marriage) and died in Duxbury between 7 November 1637 (date of will) and 13 November 1637 (date of inventory]). William was a "nailer": his inventory included a bellows, anvil, vice and all the tools necessary for nailmaking.[341] He married (1) By about 1606 Frances ____ . She arrived on the *Anne* in 1623 and had died by 1637. (2) By 1637 Mary ____. She married (2) by 20 October 1646 Robert Paddock.[342] She married (3) Plymouth 24 March 1650/1 Thomas Roberts.[343] William had four children by his first wife, and one child (probably posthumous) by his second wife.

On 23 July 1633, William Mendlove, the servant of William Palmer, was whipped for attempting to force his affections on the maid servant of the same Palmer, and for running away from his master and having to be brought back "forcibly" by

---

[336] MPCR 2:50
[337] MPCR 2:56
[338] NEHGR 31:179-87, 36:40-46
[339] PCR 12:5, 6
[340] PCR 12:11
[341] MD 2:150
[342] PCR 2:109; TAG 32:42-43
[343] PCR 8:11; TAG 32:44

Penwatechet, a Manomet Indian; Palmer sold his service to Richard Church.[344] On 25 July 1633, William Palmer, nailer, of Plymouth, purchased the time of Robert Barker, the apprentice of the late John Thorpe, and promised to teach him the trade of "nailing & at the end of his time to give him only two suits of apparel".[345] On 2 January 1637/8, Mr. Hopkins was presented for allowing excessive drinking in his house. "Old Palmer" was one of the three men said to have been drunk there, and "widow Palmer" and "widow Palmer's man" were two of the witnesses.[346]

In 1956 Florence Barclay produced the definitive article on William Palmer, resolving many of the outstanding problems, outlining the careers of the two sons of the immigrant named William, and pointing out several errors in Savage, particularly the mixing of William (b. 1612) with the man of that name who went to Newtown, Long Island.[347] In 1976 Paul Prindle also published a brief account of William Palmer.[348] Carlton A. Palmer Jr, has published several articles attempting to outline the three Williams and their wives and arriving at conclusions contrary to those of Florence Barclay.[349] Unfortunately, his misunderstanding of the meaning of "son-in-law" undermines his own arguments.

2. In the 1623 Plymouth land division **William Wright** and **William Pitt** were paired in the receipt of two acres of land.[350] In the 1627 Plymouth cattle division William Wright was the fifth person in the company of John Howland.[351] William was born about 1600 (based on estimated age of wife), and died in Plymouth between 16 September 1633 (date of will) and 6 November 1633 (date of inventory). He married Priscilla Carpenter in Plymouth between 1629 and 1633. She m. (2) Plymouth 27 November 1634 John Cooper (who settled in Scituate in 1634).[352] William had no recorded children, making it more difficult to determine the date of his marriage.

---

[344] PCR 1:15
[345] PCR 1:16
[346] PCR 1:75
[347] TAG 32:39-45
[348] Prindle, *Gillespie Ancestry*, 354- 56
[349] *The Augustan Society Omnibus* 9:101-3, 107; MQ 50:188-90
[350] PCR 12:5
[351] PCR 12:10
[352] PCR 1:32; GM 2:2:200-2

In his will of 30 July 1633, Samuel Fuller makes several references to "my brother William Wright," including a bequest of "one cloth suit not yet fully finished lying in my trunk at town."[353] Fuller and Wright had married sisters. William Wright appears alone in both the 1623 land division and the 1627 cattle division. This indicates that Priscilla Carpenter did not come to Plymouth until the remnant of the Leiden congregation arrived in 1629 and 1630. William and Priscilla were no doubt married sometime not long after her arrival, and certainly before 30 July 1633. In the inventory, listed in the loft over the bedchamber, were many carpentry tools: one broad ax, two felling axes, two hand saws, one thwart saw, three augers, one chisel, one gouge, one drawing knife, one "prser" [piercer], one gimlet, two hammers, one pair of old hinges, two chest locks, one padlock, one splitting knife.[354] These may point to his occupation. On the other hand, the average husbandman may have needed many such tools during the early years of settlement, when everyone had to have a newly built house. He signed his will, indicating his literacy; his inventory included, in the bedchamber, "one great Bible & a little Bible. 1 Greenham's works. 1 psalm book with 17 other small books," valued at £1 3s.[355]

MONDAY, 13 DECEMBER 1621
"Threats against us"

The Pilgrims began to realise that their alliance with the Pokanokets had created a serious problem, particularly with the more powerful Narragansetts. Winslow wrote, in his *Good Newes from New England* (which picked up just where *Mourt's Relation* left off, and was published in 1624) that "soon after the Ship's [i.e., the *Fortune*] Departure, that Great People of the Narragansetts, said to be many Thousands strong, and can raise above 5000 Fighting Men, notwithstanding their desired and obtained Peace with us in the foregoing Summer, begin to breath forth many Threats against us; so that 'tis the common Talk of all the Indians round us, of their Preparations to come against us. In reason a man would think they should have now more cause to fear us than before our supply came." The previous summer (1621),

---

[353] MD 1:24-27
[354] MD 1:205
[355] MD 1:205

Bradford had exchanged what he felt were positive and hopeful messages with the Narragansett sachem, Canonicus. Since then, however, Canonicus had grown increasingly jealous of the Pokonoket-Plymouth alliance. The Narragansetts, it was rumoured, were preparing to attach the English.

TUESDAY, 14 DECEMBER 1621

Symbolic Threats

Bradford noted that, "At length Canonicus their chief Sachem in a braving manner sends us a Bundle of Arrows tied with a Snake Skin, which Squanto tells us it is a Challenge and Threatning." This mysterious object was intended for Squanto, but when the Narragansett messenger discovered that he was away, he hurriedly handed it over to the Pilgrims. When Squanto arrived back, he explained its meaning. Winslow recorded that "our Governor with Advice of others, sends them an Answer, That if they had rather War than Peace, they might Begin when they wou'd; we had done them no Wrong, nor do we fear them, nor shou'd they find us unprovided. By another Messenger we send back the Snake-Skin charg'd with Powder and Bullets: But they refuse to receive it, and Return it to us. Since the Death of so many Indians they tho't to Lord it over the Rest, conceive we are a Bar in their Way, and see Massassoit already take Shelter under our Wings." Philbrick adds that "the powder-stuffed snake skin was passed like a hot potato from village to village until it finally made its way back to Plymouth."[356]

WEDNESDAY, 15 DECEMBER 1621

"Impaling" the Village

The presentation of a challenge and threat from the Narragansetts made the Pilgrims realise that their little village (with only seven houses) was wide-open to attack. Their muskets were cumbersome, and their big guns, while they might blow a ship in the harbour out of the water, were of little use against a rapid Indian attack, especially if they attacked at night. "This makes us more carefully to look to ourselves, and agree to enclose our Dwellings with strong Pales, Flankers, Gates, &c."

THURSDAY, 16 DECEMBER 1621

The Wall

---

[356] Philbrick, *Mayflower*, 127

The wall had to be at least half a mile in length; hundreds, if not thousands, of trees had to be felled, their trunks stripped of branches and chopped or sawed to the proper length, then set deeply into the ground. The tree trunks of the fort had to be set so tightly together that a man could not get between them. Standish also insisted that they must construct three protruding gates, known as flankers, that would also serve as defensive shooting platforms. For a work force of fewer than fifty men, living on a starvation diet, this was an almost impossible task. One of the remarkable things about the small village is that it had been able to survive for almost a year without any stockade or wall -- enemies and friends could, and did, simply walk straight into the village, where the only place of defence was the fort, which also served as a church, meeting hall, storehouse, and dormitory. It took them more than a month to finish the stockade around the village.

FRIDAY, 17 DECEMBER 1621

Letter sent back to England

Bradford composed a letter to Thomas Weston in answer to his letter to Governor Carver, carried on the *Fortune*: "Sir: Your large letter written to Mr. Carver, and dated the 6. of July, 1621, I have received the 10. of November, wherein (after the apology made for your self) you lay many heavy imputations upon him and us all. Touching him, he is departed this life, and now is at rest in the Lord from all those troubles and encumbrances with which we are yet to strive. He needs not my apology; for his care and pains was so great for the common good, both ours and yours, as that therewith (it is thought) he oppressed himself and shortened his days; of whose loss we cannot sufficiently complain. At great charges in this adventure, I confess you have been, and many losses may sustain; but the loss of his and many other honest and industrious men's lives, cannot be valued at any price. Of the one, there may be hope of recovery, but the other no recompence can make good. But I will not insist in generall, but come more particularly to the things themselves. You greatly blame us for keeping the ship so long in the country, and then to send her away empty. She lay 5. weeks at Cape-Codd, whilst with many a weary step (after a long journey) and the endurance of many a hard brunt, we sought out in the foul winter a place of habitation. Then we went in so tedious a time to make provision to shelter us and our goods, about which labour, many of our arms & legs can tell us to

379

this day we were not negligent. But it pleased God to visit us then with death daily, and with so generall a disease, that the living were scarce able to bury the dead; and the well not in any measure sufficient to tend the sick. And now to be so greatly blamed, for not freighting the ship, doth indeed go near us, and much discourage us. But you say you know we will pretend weakness; and do you think we had not cause? Yes, you tell us you believe it, but it was more weakness of judgment, then of hands. Our weakness herein is great we confess, therefore we will bear this check patiently amongst the rest, till God send us wiser men. But they which told you we spent so much time in discoursing & consulting, &c., their hearts can tell their tongues, they lie. They cared not, so they might salve their own sores, how they wounded others. Indeed, it is our calamity that we are (beyond expectation) yoked with some ill conditioned people, who will never do good, but corrupt and abuse others, &c."

SATURDAY, 18 DECEMBER 1621

Cushman's sermon

Robert Cushman had brought the sober news that those who had financed the voyage were displeased and required the Pilgrims to sign an amended contract. Cushman and Bradford convinced them to sign. The amended contract greatly benefitted the Pilgrims with additional support from their financiers. During his short visit to New England he would make a contribution of a spiritual nature, as well: Cushman was committed to the extreme Protestantism the Pilgrims espoused, and spent time in prison in England for it. In 1619 he wrote a book about his experience called *The Cry of a Stone*, on how the Church of England was no church. The title of his sermon in Plymouth this weekend was "The Sin and Danger of Self-Love and the Sweetness of True Friendship," with teaching and exhortation as to the danger of selfishness and how to live a godly, unselfish life. Although the language is somewhat difficult for us to read today, it's an excellent sermon, and parts are quite moving. It is credited with changing the settlers' minds so that they finally agreed to the contract. And undoubtedly occasioned complaints that all sermons are about money.

Portions of this sermon tomorrow.

380

Self-Love

The text on which Cushman's sermon was preached was, *Let no man seek his own, but every man another's wealth* (I Corinthians 10:24). "The occasion of these words of the Apostle Paul, was because of the abuses which were in the Church of Corinth. Which abuses arose chiefly through swelling pride, self-love and conceitedness. ... It is lawful sometimes for men to gather wealth, and grow rich, even as there was a time for Joseph to store up corn, but a godly and sincere Christian will see when this time is, and will not hoard up when he seeth others of his brethren and associates to want, but then is a time, if he have anything to fetch out and disperse it. ... bear ye therefore one another's burthen, and be not a burthen one to another, avoid all factions, frowardness, singularity and withdrawings, and cleave fast to the Lord, and one to another continually; so shall you be a notable president to these poor heathens, whose eyes are upon you, and who very brutishly and cruelly do daily eat and consume one another, through their emulations, ways and contentions; be you therefore ashamed of it, and win them to peace both with yourselves, and one another, by your peaceable examples, which will preach louder to them, then if you could cry in their barbarous language, so also shall you be an encouragment to many of your christian friends in your native country, to come to you, when they hear of your peace, love and kindness that is amongst you: but above all, it shall go well with your souls, when that God of peace and unity shall come to visit you with death as he hath done many of your associates, you being found of him, not in murmurings, discontent and jars, but in brotherly love, and peace, may be translated from this wandering wilderness unto that joyful and heavenly Canaan."

Cushman's audience had been struggling in the wilderness under the burdens of the London contract for an entire year. But like Winthrop's much more famous *Modell of Christian Charity* a decade later, Cushman's sermon exhorted its listeners to Christian love and selfless cooperation for the welfare of the whole. In Cushman's case the good of the whole would be achieved by sacrificial and charitable attitudes and actions toward both fellow settlers at Plymouth and unreliable partners in London. But, as it turned out, Christian love and charity, under the restraints of an unfavourable business contract, were a mixed blessing for ordinary people of mean estates. Such virtues may have been the way to heaven but were decidedly not the way to a full belly, and Plymouth's people were eager for both rewards. This was not clear to Robert Cushman; it was only too clear to Governor Bradford: most settlers in Plymouth were poor, and the partnership with Londoners kept them so. The Pilgrims' purpose in America could be served in several ways, but the colonists quickly concluded that the "common course and condition" laid down by the investors in London was not one of them. Circumstances in early Plymouth dictated a rough equality. Curiously, it was at odds with conventional thinking about God's design for his people, and it tended to erode as conditions first worsened and then, through individual effort, improved. Bradford concluded that because all of Plymouth's settlers were treated alike and were expected to respond alike, "they thought themselves in the like condition, and one as good as another" -- a condition Cushman in London would have applauded, were Christian virtue the motive. But, the governor went on, although the equalitarian tendency did not altogether erase those arbitrary distinctions that "God hath set amongst men, yet it did at least much diminish and take off the mutual respects that should be preserved amongst them." To Bradford this was a fundamental contradiction; the "common course and condition" worked against divine doctrine about human differences that existed for the common good. Cushman's sermon contained repeated warnings that selfish individualism, a shifting for oneself, could only destroy the spiritual league and covenant of love and sacrifice and lead to the colony's demise. The Pilgrims' response to Cushman's plea was almost immediate, and positive: the settlers accepted the offered contract. But absolute commitment to the "common course and condition" for the good of the whole soon faded before more secular realities of the New World struggle. Bradford with a great deal of sorrow explained that "God in His wisdom saw another course fitter for them." Given the abundance of land and resources -- once settlers learned to use them -- there probably was no other way.

Cushman's sermon was first printed in England (1621) and later in America (Boston, 1846). The latter half of the sermon, on the sweetness of friendship, does not seem to have been included in either of the publications. I have spent some time trying to see

382

if any of that part of the sermon has survived, and it does not appear that any of it has.

MONDAY, 20 DECEMBER 1621

Cushman Monument on Burial Hill

By far the most conspicuous memorial on Burial Hill is to someone who is not buried there. The Cushman memorial, a twenty-five foot obelisk erected in 1858, is to Robert Cushman, his son Thomas, and Mary (Allerton) Cushman, Thomas' wife. Robert Cushman returned to England on the *Fortune*, and never came back to New England; he died in London during the Great Plague of 1625. On the west side of the memorial is this touching inscription: "He died, lamented by the forefathers as 'their ancient friend, - who was as their right hand with their friends the adventurers, and for divers years had done and agitated all their business with them to their great advantage. And you, my loving friends, the adventurers to this plantation, as your care has been first to settle religion here before either profit or popularity, so, I pray you, go on. -- I rejoice -- that you thus honor God with your riches, and I trust you shall be repaid again double and treble in this world, yea, and the memory of this action shall never die.'" The monument makes special mention of yesterday's sermon, so that this may very well be the only monument in America to a Sunday sermon.

Robert Cushman's son Thomas became the ruling elder of the Plymouth church, and married Mary Allerton , the last surviving of the passengers of the *Mayflower* (depending on how one considers Peregrine White). Robert's 1691 grave marker is one of the half dozen seventeenth century gravestones on Burial Hill; the original was removed to make room "for a more enduring memorial" and placed next to the newer (and more showy) granite obelisk.

TUESDAY, 21 DECEMBER 1621

Christmas at Plimoth Plantation: Saints v Strangers

The differences between the Separatists and the newcomers did not wait for long to manifest themselves after the *Fortune*'s departure. It took the settlers a little more than a month to impale the town; the chopping and sawing was back-breaking and time consuming, made all the more difficult by the lack or deficiency of their equipment. Without oxen to help drag the tree

383

trunks in from the forest, they were forced to lug the ten to twelve foot lengths of timber in by hand. They dug a two- to three- foot trench, first using picks to break through the frozen topsoil and then a large hoe-like tool to dig a trench that was wide and deep enough to accommodate the ends of the pales. Adding to the difficulties was the lack of food. Some of the labourers grew so faint from hunger that they were seen to stagger on their way back to their homes after a day's work.

And then came the twenty-fifth of December, a day like any other for the previous inhabitants of Plymouth, although it did mark the first anniversary of the arrival of the *Mayflower* at Plymouth. There was probably a gasp of unbelief when several of the newly arrived passengers from the *Fortune* stated flatly that they would not work today, because it was "against their consciences" -- an excuse that was quite clearly aimed to carry the most weight with the Pilgrims. Bradford, begrudgingly, gave this suddenly pious minority the day off, and headed out to the fields to work with most of the settlement's men. Coming back at mid-day, however, he was horrified to see that those who had stayed behind were not engaged in prayer, but in playing games. If they wanted to spend Christmas praying at home, that was fine with the Governor; "but there should be no gaming or reveling in the streets" -- freedom of conscience did not extend to stool ball (a game like cricket that was popular in the west of England). While I do know some people who treat cricket like a religion, a rough modern equivalent of this behaviour might be eating pork in a synagogue. Bradford confiscated the balls and bats and declared that is was not fair if a few healthy men played while everyone else worked.

The Pilgrims had come to the New World to live according to the Gospel, and were now confronted with a noisy minority that were doing what they could to make that impossible, or at least unlikely. Bradford was thus presented not only with an impending attack on the settlement by hostile Narragansetts, but also with a visible and growing hostile divide among his own people: an internal attack on the very reason for this settlement. Bradford had to make it clear that no matter how things were done in England, Plymouth would follow God's law, to which everyone would be expected to conform. For many of the new arrivals, however, this must have been astonishing, to say the least. While some of the passengers on the *Fortune* knew the Leiden congregation well, others probably had little knowledge of, or appreciation for, the project being lived out in Plimoth Plantation. Almost half of the thirty-five passengers of the *Fortune* were on the 1623 land division but are not on the 1627 division of cattle, suggesting that they either died in the meantime, or, perhaps more likely, had returned to England, finding that life in New England was not what they had bargained for at all.

WEDNESDAY, 22 DECEMBER 1621

Departure of the Fortune

After a stay of just two weeks, the *Fortune* left to return to London on 23 December 1621 (n.s.). Robert Cushman returned, carrying the signed agreement of the settlers with the London Merchant Adventurers (which may have been the primary purpose of the *Fortune*'s voyage), as well as a manuscript account of the first year of the Pilgrims in New England that would become known as *Mourt's Relation*. We have been sampling longer and shorter excerpts of this work, written by Edward Winslow and William Bradford, for the past thirteen months -- it contained the brief summary of what later generations called "the first Thanksgiving," and painted a rosy picture of bounty and good, which would soon -- very soon -- disintegrate, as the settlers entered a winter which, if anything, was more difficult than the last. Robert Cushman left his son Thomas in the care of William Bradford, who gave him a home, educated him, and treated him as a son. The last letter written by Cushman to Bradford, dated "London, December 22, AD 1624," concluded: "Lastly, I must intreat you still, to have a care of my son, as of your own; and I shall rest bound unto you. I pray you let him sometime practice writing. I hope the next ships to come to you." Bradford replied: "Your son and all of us, are in good health (blessed be God). He received the things you sent him. I hope God will make him a good man." But Cushman had died before the comforting message reached him.

THURSDAY, 23 DECEMBER 1621

The misfortune of the Fortune

The *Fortune* departed Plymouth for England today, but fortune was not with the ship of that name on the return. Apparently due to a major navigation error, the ship sailed hundreds of miles off course from England, south-east into the Bay of Biscay off the coast of Vendee, north of La Rochelle. About five weeks into her voyage, on 19 January 1622 and not far from the fortified Ile d'Yeu, a French warship (or, according to other accounts, French pirates) overtook the *Fortune* which was off-course about 350 sea miles southeast of where they should be – Land's End and the English Channel. It seems the *Fortune's* master mistook the long peninsula of Brittany in western France for the Lizard Peninsula on the southwestern end of England and then strayed off down the French Atlantic coast to be taken by the French. Although the *Fortune* was not considered an enemy ship, France at this time was undergoing Huguenot rebel activities and any English vessel coming close to their shore was suspected of aiding the rebels and was liable for search and seizure. The French stopped and boarded the *Fortune*, which was then seized. Although the *Fortune* was not carrying contraband, the French governor seized her guns, cargo and rigging. The governor locked the ship's master in a dungeon and kept Cushman and the crew on board under guard. After thirteen days they were freed, but without its cargo of valuable beaver skins, otter pelts, and wood. The *Fortune* finally arrived back into the Thames on 17 February 1621/22.

The loss of the *Fortune's* valuable cargo dealt a severe financial loss to the Merchant Adventurers who by this time had little hope of recouping their investment in either the *Fortune* or the *Mayflower*. Due to this, the Merchant Adventurers were reorganized in 1626 in conjunction with Plymouth Colony leaders, in an effort to restructure financial agreements and for Plymouth Colony eventually to pay its creditors. The colonists didn't have the money but agreed to pay £200 instalments for nine years -- this might have been the first debt management program in American history. Like just about everything else in this tale, it didn't go quite as planned. The Pilgrims ended up taking 23 years to pay off their debt.

* * * * *

This marks the 518th post on the **Mayflower, Day-by-Day,** starting on 24 July 1620, the day before the *Mayflower* departed London to rendezvous with the *Speedwell* in Southampton, and ending on 23 December 1621, the day the *Fortune* departed Plymouth to return to England. I actually started with the post for

6 September 1620, so the posts from 24 July 1620 through 6 September 1620 are "double posts" on those days alongside the posts for 1621. If you count only the actual, individual posts (and don't separate the double posts, where I wrote about 1621 and 1620 on the same day), this is post number 474.

This is the **last post** (cue the bugle): I have to stop somewhere, and the return of the *Fortune* is as good a place as any. I am astonished that I have lasted this long, and managed to post every single day, mostly between 6:00 AM and 7:00 AM, for well over a year. Thank you all for your kind wishes and comments.

MEMBERS OF THE LEIDEN, HOLLAND CONGREGATION

Note: An asterisk on a name indicates those who died in the winter of 1620–21.

- Allerton, Isaac (possibly Suffolk).
  - Mary (Norris) Allerton*, wife (Newbury, Berkshire)
  - Bartholomew Allerton, 7, son (Leiden, Holland).
  - Remember Allerton, 5, daughter (Leiden).
  - Mary Allerton , 3, daughter (Leiden). She died in 1699, the last surviving *Mayflower* passenger.
- Bradford, William (Austerfield, Yorkshire).
  - Dorothy (May) Bradford*, wife (Wisbech, Isle of Ely, Cambridgeshire).
- Brewster, William (possibly Nottingham).
  - Mary Brewster, wife.
  - Love/Truelove Brewster, 9, son (Leiden).
  - Wrestling Brewster, 6, son (Leiden).
- Carver, John (possibly Yorkshire).
  - Katherine (Leggett) (White) Carver, wife (probably Sturton-le-Steeple, Nottinghamshire).
- Chilton, James* (Canterbury, Kent).
  - Mrs. (James) Chilton*, wife.
  - Mary Chilton, 13, daughter (Sandwich, Kent).
- Cooke, Francis.
  - John Cooke, 13, son (Leiden).
- Cooper, Humility, 1, (probably Leiden) baby daughter of Robert Cooper, in company of her aunt Ann Cooper Tilley, wife of Edward Tilley
- Crackstone/Crackston, John* (possibly Colchester, Essex).
  - John Crackstone, son.
- Fletcher, Moses* (Sandwich, Kent).
- Fuller, Edward* (Redenhall, Norfolk).
  - Mrs. (Edward) ___Fuller*, wife.
  - Samuel Fuller, 12, son.
- Fuller, Samuel (Redenhall, Norfolk), (brother to Edward).
- Goodman, John (possibly Northampton).

- Priest, Degory*
- Rogers, Thomas* (Watford, Northamptonshire).
  - Joseph Rogers, 17, son (Watford, Northamptonshire).
- Samson, Henry, 16, (Henlow, Bedfordshire) child in company of his uncle and aunt Edward and Ann Tilley.
- Tilley, Edward* (Henlow, Bedfordshire)
  - Agnes/Ann (Cooper) Tilley* (Henlow, Bedfordshire) wife of Edward and aunt of Humility Cooper and Henry Samson.
- Tilley, John* (Henlow, Bedfordshire).
  - Joan (Hurst) (Rogers) Tilley*, wife (Henlow, Bedfordshire).
  - Elizabeth Tilley, 13, daughter (Henlow, Bedfordshire).
- Tinker, Thomas* (possibly Norfolk).
  - Mrs. Thomas Tinker*, wife.
  - boy Tinker*, son, died in the winter of 1620.
- Turner, John* (possibly Norfolk).
  - boy Turner*, son, died in the winter of 1620.
  - boy Turner*, younger son. died in the winter of 1620.
- White, William* William White's sister Bridget was John Robinson's wife. John Robinson was Pastor of the Pilgrim Fathers leading the Separatists since his days at college at Cambridge
  - Susanna White, wife, widowed February 21, 1621. She subsequently married Pilgrim Edward Winslow.
  - Resolved White, 5, son, wife was Judith Vassal.
  - Peregrine White, son. Born on board the *Mayflower* in Cape Cod Harbor in late November 1620. First European born to the Pilgrims in America.
- Williams, Thomas
- Winslow, Edward (Droitwich, Worcestershire).
  - Elizabeth (Barker) Winslow*, wife.

SERVANTS OF THE LEIDEN CONGREGATION

- Butten, William* (possibly Nottingham), "a youth",

indentured servant of Samuel Fuller, died during the voyage. He was the first passenger to die on November 16, three days before Cape Cod was sighted.

- ___, Dorothy, teenager, maidservant of John Carver.
- Hooke, John*, (probably Norwich, Norfolk) age 13, apprenticed to Isaac Allerton, died during the first winter.
- Howland, John, (Fenstanton, Huntingdonshire), about 21, manservant and executive assistant for Governor John Carver.
- Latham, William, (possibly Lancashire), age 11, servant and apprentice to the John Carver family.
- Minter, Desire, (Norwich, Norfolk), a servant of John Carver whose parents died in Leiden.
- More, Ellen (Elinor)*, (Shipton, Shropshire), age 8, assigned as a servant of Edward Winslow. She died from illness sometime in November 1620 soon after the arrival of *Mayflower* in Cape Cod harbor and likely was buried ashore there in an unmarked grave.
- More, Jasper*, (Shipton, Shropshire), age 7, indentured to John Carver. He died from illness on board *Mayflower* on December 6, 1620, and likely was buried ashore on Cape Cod in an unmarked grave.
- More, Richard, (Shipton, Shropshire), age 6, indentured to William Brewster. He is buried in the Charter Street Burial Ground in Salem, Massachusetts. He is the only *Mayflower* passenger to have his gravestone still where it was originally placed sometime in the mid-1690s. Also buried nearby in the same cemetery were his wives Christian Hunter More and Jane (Crumpton) More.
- More, Mary*, (Shipton, Shropshire), age 4, assigned as a servant of William Brewster. She died sometime in the winter of 1620/1621. She and her sister Ellen are recognised on the Pilgrim Memorial Tomb in Plymouth.
- Soule, George, 21–25, servant or employee of Edward Winslow.
- Story, Elias*, age under 21, in the care of Edward Winslow.
- Wilder, Roger*, age under 21, servant in the John Carver family.

PASSENGERS RECRUITED BY THOMAS WESTON OF LONDON MERCHANT ADVENTURERS

- Billington, John (possibly Lancashire).
  - Eleanor Billington, wife.
  - John Billington, 16, son.
  - Francis Billington, 14, son.
- Britteridge, Richard* (possibly Sussex).
- Browne, Peter (Dorking, Surrey).
- Clarke, Richard*
- Eaton, Francis (Bristol, Gloucestershire/Somerset).
  - Sarah Eaton*, wife.
  - Samuel Eaton, 1, son.
- Gardiner, Richard (Harwich, Essex).
- Hopkins, Stephen (Upper Clatford, Hampshire).
  - Elizabeth (Fisher) Hopkins, wife.
  - Giles Hopkins, 12, son by first marriage (Hursley, Hampshire).
  - Constance Hopkins, 14, daughter by first marriage (Hursley, Hampshire).
  - Damaris Hopkins, 1–2, daughter. (She died soon in Plymouth Colony and her parents later had another daughter with the same name.)
  - Oceanus Hopkins, born on board the *Mayflower* while en route to the New World.
- Margesson, Edmund* (possibly Norfolk).
- Martin, Christopher* 38 (Great Burstead, Essex). *Mayflower* Governor & Purchasing Agent.
  - Mary (Prowe) Martin*, wife.
- Mullins, William* (Dorking, Surrey).
  - Alice Mullins*, wife.
  - Priscilla Mullins, 18, daughter.
  - Joseph Mullins*, 14, son.
- Prowe, Solomon* (Billericay, Essex). Son of Mary Prowe
- Rigsdale, John* (possibly Lincolnshire).
  - Alice Rigsdale*, wife.
- Standish, Myles (Standish, Wigan, Lancashire). Military Expert for Colony.
  - Rose Standish*, wife.
- Warren, Richard (Hertford, England).

- Winslow, Gilbert (Droitwich, Worcestershire), brother to Pilgrim Edward Winslow but not known to have lived in Leiden.

SERVANTS OF MERCHANT ADVENTURERS PASSENGERS

- Carter, Robert*, (possibly Surrey), teenager, servant or apprentice to William Mullins, shoemaker.
- Doty, Edward, (possibly Lincolnshire) age probably about 21, servant to Stephen Hopkins.
- Holbeck, William*, age likely under 21, servant to William White.
- Langemore, John*, age under 21, servant to Christopher Martin.
- Leister, Edward, also spelled Leitster, (possibly vicinity of London), aged over 21, servant to Stephen Hopkins.
- Thompson (or Thomson), Edward*, age under 21, in the care of the William White family, first passenger to die after the *Mayflower* reached Cape Cod.

BIBLIOGRAPHY

Allan, Sue, *In the Shadow of Men*: The Lives of Separatist Women. Burgess Hill: Domtom Publishing, Ltd., 2020.

Allan, Sue, *In Search of Governor William Bradford of Austerfield*. Burgess Hill: Domtom Book Publishing, 2020.

Anderson, Robert Charles, ed. *Puritan Pedigrees: The Deep Roots of the Great Migration to New England*. Boston: NEHGS, 2018.

Anderson, Robert Charles, ed. *The Great Migration Begins: Immigrants to New England, 1620-1633*. Boston: NEHGS. [GM1]

Anderson, Robert Charles, ed. *The Great Migration: Immigrants to New England, 1634-1635*. Boston, NEHGS. [GM2]

Anderson, Robert Charles, ed. *The Mayflower Migration: Immigrants to Plymouth, 1620*. Boston: NEHGS, 2020 [MM]

Anderson, Robert Charles, ed., *The Pilgrim Migration: Immigrants to Plymouth Colony, 1620-1633*. Boston, NEHGS, 2004 [PM]

Arber, Edward, *The story of the Pilgrim fathers, 1606-1623 A.D.: as told by themselves, their friends, and their enemies*. Boston : Houghton, Mifflin, 1897. [Arber, *Pilgrim Fathers*]

Baker, James, *Thanksgiving: The Biography of an American Holiday*. Durham, NH: University of New Hampshire Press, 2009. [Baker, *Thanksgiving*]

Bangs, Jeremy D., *Indian Deeds: Land Transactions in Plymouth Colony*. Boston: NEHGS, 2002, rev. 2008. [Bangs, *Indian Deeds*]

Bangs, Jeremy D., *Intellectual Baggage*. Leiden: Leiden American Pilgrim Museum, 2020.

Bangs, Jeremy D., *Josias Wompatuck and the Titicut Reserve of the Mattakeeset - Massachusetts Tribe*. Leiden: Leiden American Pilgrim Museum, 2021, Available from lulu.com.

Bangs, Jeremy D., *Pilgrim Edward Winslow: New England's First International Diplomat, A Documentary Biography*. Boston: NEHGS, 2004.

Bangs, Jeremy D., *Plymouth Colony's Private Libraries*. Leiden: Leiden American Pilgrim Museum, rev. ed. 2018. Available from lulu.com [Bangs, *Plymouth Private Libraries*]

Bangs, Jeremy D., *Strangers and Pilgrims, Travellers and Sojourners: Leiden and the Foundations of Plymouth Plantation*. Plymouth, MA: GSMD, 2009. [Bangs, *Strangers and Pilgrims*]

Banks, Charles, *The English Ancestry and Homes of the Pilgrim Fathers*. Baltimore: Genealogical Publishing Company, 1929, reissued 2006. [Banks, *English Ancestry*]

Barbour, Philip L., ed., *The complete works of Captain John Smith (1580-1631)*. Published for the Institute of Early American History and Culture, Williamsburg, Va. by Chapel Hill, NC: University of North Carolina Press, 1986. [*Works of John Smith*]

Bradford, William, *Of Plymouth Plantation, 1620-1647*. ed. Samuel Eliot Morison. New York: A. A. Knopf, 1952.

Bradford, William, *Of Plimoth Plantation by William Bradford: The 400th Anniversary Edition*. ed. Kenneth P. Minkema, et al. Boston: NEHGS, 2020. [*Of Plimoth Plantation – 400*]

Vital records of Bridgewater, Massachusetts, to the year 1850. Boston: Published by the New England Historic Genealogical Society, at the charge of the Eddy Town-Record Fund, 1916. [Bridgewater VR]

Bowman, George Ernest, *Mayflower Reader: A Selection of Articles from the Mayflower Descendant*. Baltimore: Genealogical Publishing Company, 1978. [*Mayflower Reader*]

Cambers, Andrew, *Godly Reading: Print, Manuscript and Puritanism in England, 1580-1720*. Cambridge: Cambridge University Press, 2011. [Cambers, *Godly Reading*]

Chaffee, Zechariah, Jr., *Colonial Courts and the Common Law*, in *Proceedings of the Massachusetts Historical Society*. Third Series, Vol. 68 (Oct. 1944 - May 1947), 132-159; reprinted in *Essays in Early American Law*, 1969, 53-82.

Cheney, Glen A., Thanksgiving: The Pilgrims' First Year in America. New London, CT: New London Librarium, 2013 (2nd ed.). [Cheney, *Thanksgiving*]

Cushman, Robert E. and Franklin P. Cole, *Robert Cushman of Kent (1577-1625) Chief Agent of the Plymouth Pilgrims (1617-1625)*. Plymouth: GSMD, 1995.

deForest, L. Effingham, and Anne Lawrence deForest, *Moore and Allied Families: The Ancestry of William Henry Moore*. New York: The deforest Publishing Company, 1938. [*Moore Ancestry*]

Dexter, Henry Martyn, and Morton Dexter, *The England and Holland of the Pilgrims*. London, 1906; reprint, Baltimore: Genealogical Publishing Company, 1978. [Dexter and Dexter: *England and Holland*]

Ferris, Mary Walton, *Dawes-Gates Ancestral Lines: A Memorial Volume containing the American Ancestry of Rufus Dawes*. 2 volumes. [Milwaukee]: Privately printed. [Wisconsin Cuneo Press], 1931-43. [*Dawes-Gates Ancestral Lines*]

Fraser, Rebecca, *The Mayflower: The Families, The Voyage, and the Founding of America*. New York: St Martin's Press, 2017.

Genealogical Dictionary of Maine and New Hampshire. ed. Noyes, Sybil, Charles Thornton Libby, and Walter Goodwin Davis. Originally published in five parts, Portland, ME, 1928-1939; reprint Baltimore: Genealogical Publishing Company, 1972; Boston: NEHGS, 2012. [GDMNH]

Goebbel, Julius, *King's Law and Local Custom in Seventeenth Century New England*, in *Essays in the History of Early American Law*. New York: Foundation for Research in American Legal History, 1931.

Goodwin, John Abbott, *The Pilgrim republic : an historical review of the colony of New Plymouth, with sketches of the rise of other New England settlements, the history of congregationalism, and the creeds of the period*. Boston: Houghton Mifflin, 1899. [Goodwin, *Pilgrim Republic*]

Griffis, William Elliott, *The Pilgrims in Their Three Homes* Boston: Houghton Mifflin, 1900. [Griffis, *Three Homes*]

Hannibal, Edna Anne, *Clement Briggs of Plymouth Colony and his descendants, 1621-1965*. Palo Alto, CA: E. A. Hannibal, 1966.

[The] Hinckley papers: being letters and papers of Thomas Hinckley, governor of the colony of New Plymouth, Boston: Massachusetts Historical Society, 1861.

Hubbard, William, *A general history of New England: from the discovery to MDCLXXX*. Cambridge, MA: Hilliard & Metcalf, 1815. [Hubbard, *General History*]

James, Sydney V., ed., *Three Visitors to Early Plymouth*. Plymouth: Plimoth Plantation, 1963. [*Three Visitors*]

Johnson, Caleb H., *The Mayflower and Her Passengers*. [Philadelphia, Pa.], Xlibris, 2006. [Johnson, *Mayflower Passengers*]

Langdon, George D., *Pilgrim Colony: A History of New Plymouth, 1620-1691*. New Haven, CT: Yale University Press, 1966. [Langdon, *Pilgrim Colony*]

Mancall, Peter C., *The Trials of Thomas Morton: An Anglican Lawyer, His Puritan Foes, and the Battle for a New England*. New Haven CT: Yale University Press, 2019.

[The] Mayflower Descendant: a quarterly magazine of Pilgrim genealogy and history (1899-1935, 1937, 1985 -). [MD]

Mayflower Quarterly [1935 -]; after 2016, *Mayflower Quarterly Magazine*. [MQ]

Morton, Nathaniel, *New-Englands memoriall: or, A brief relation of the most memorable and remarkable passages of the providence of God, manifested to the planters of New-England in America; with special reference to the first colony thereof, called New-Plimouth*. Cambridge [MA]: Printed by S.G. and M.J. [i.e, Samuel Green and Marmaduke Johnson] for John Usher of Boston, 1669. [Morton, *New England's Memoriall*]

(Mourt's Relation) *A Relation or Journal of the Beginning and Proceedings of the English Plantation Settled at Plimoth in New England*. London: John Bellamie, 1622; reprinted by New York: Applewood Books, 1986.

New England Ancestors (Vol. 1, no. 1 [2000] - v. 10, no. 4 [fall 2009]; continued as *American Ancestors* with vol. 11, no. 1 [winter 2010]).

New England Historic & Genealogical Society Register [1847 -]. [NEHGR]

Nickerson, W. Sears, *Land Ho! 1620: A Seaman's Story of the Mayflower, Her Construction, Her Navigation, and Her First Landfall.* East Lansing, MI: Michigan State University Press, 1997. [Nickerson, *Land Ho! 1620*]

Philbrick, Nathaniel, *Mayflower: A Story of Courage, Community and War.* New York: Viking, 2006. [Philbrick, Mayflower]

Plooij, Daniel, and D. Rendel Harris, *Leyden documents relating to the Pilgrim fathers, permission to reside at Leyden and betrothal records: together with parallel documents from the Amsterdam archives.* Leiden: Brill, 1920. [Plooij]

Vital records of Plymouth, Massachusetts to the year 1850. Ed. Lee van Antwerp. Camden, ME: Picton Press, 1993. [Plymouth VR]

Pope, Charles Henry, *The Plymouth scrap book: the oldest original documents extant in Plymouth archives printed verbatim, some reproduced, with a review of Bradford's History of Plymouth plantation.* Boston: C. E. Goodspeed, 1918.

Powers, Edwin, *Crime and Punishment in Early Massachusetts, 1620-1692. A Documentary History.* Boston: Beacon Press, 1966. [Powers, *Crime and Punishment*]

Prindle, Paul W., *Ancestry of Elizabeth Barrett Gillespie (Mrs. William Sperry Beinecke).* New Orleans: Polyanthos, 1976. [Prindle, *Gillespie Ancestry*]

Province and Court Records of Maine, 6 vols. Ed. Neill W. Allen and Robert Earle Moody. Portland, ME: Maine Historical Society, 1928-1975; vols. 1-3 reprinted Newburyport, MA, 1991. [MPCR]

Roberts, Gary Boyd, *The Mayflower 500: Five Hundred Notable Descendants of the Founding Families of the Mayflower.* Boston: NEHGS, 2020. [Roberts, *Mayflower 500*]

Russell, William Shaw, *Pilgrim memorials, and guide to Plymouth: with a lithographic map and eight copperplate engravings.* Boston : Crosby, Nichols and Co., 1855. [Russell, *Pilgrim Memorials*]

Savage, James, *A Genealogical Dictionary of the First Settlers of New England, Showing Three Generations of Those Who Came Before May, 1692, on the Basis of Farmer's Register.* 4 volumes; Boston: Little, Brown and Co., 1860-1862. [Savage, *Genealogical Register*]

Savage, James, Richard S. Dunn and Letitia Yandle, *Journal of John Winthrop, 1630-1649.* Cambridge, MA: Harvard University Press, 1996. [*Journal of John Winthrop*]

Seelye, John, *Memory's Nation: The Place of Plymouth Rock.* Chapel Hill, NC: University of North Carolina Press, 1998. [Seelye, *Memory's Nation*]

Shurtleff, Nathaniel B., and David Pulsifer, edd. *Records of the Colony of New Plymouth.* 12 vols. Boston: Press of William White, printer to the Commonwealth, 1855-1861. Vols. 1-8 edited by Nathaniel B. Shurtleff; v. 9-12 by David Pulsifer. [PCR]

v. 1-6. Court orders [being the proceedings of the General Court and the Court of Assistants] 1633-1691

v. 7. Judicial acts [of the General Court and Court of Assistants] 1636-1692

v. 8. Miscellaneous records [including births, marriages, deaths and burials, treasury accounts, and lists of freemen and others] 1633-1689

v. 9-10. Acts of the Commissioners of the United Colonies of New England, 1643-1679

v. 11. Laws, 1623-1682

v. 12. Deeds, &c., 1620-1651; book of Indian records for their lands

Shurtleff, Nathaniel B., ed., *Records of the Governor and Company of the Massachusetts Bay in New England, 1628-1686,* 5 volumes in 6 parts.. Boston, W. White, Printer to the Commonwealth, 1853. v. 1. 1628-1641; v. 2. 1642-1649; v. 3. 1644-1657; v. 4, pt. 1. 1650-1660; v. 4, pt. 2. 1661-1674; v. 5. 1674-1686. [MBCR]

Stowell, William Hendry and Sir Daniel Wilson, *A History of the Puritans and Pilgrim Fathers: The Puritans in England*. London: Thomas Nelson, 1849. [Stowell and Wilson, *Puritans and Pilgrim Fathers*]

Stratton, Eugene Aubrey, *Plymouth Colony, its history & people, 1620-1691*. Salt Lake City, UT: Ancestry Publishing Company, 1986. [Stratton, *Plymouth Colony*]

The American Genealogist (1922 --). [TAG]

The Genealogical Bulletin (1903-1905)

The Genealogist. Journal of the American Society of Genealogists. (1980 -). [TG]

Tomlins, Christopher, "Reconsidering Indentured Servitude: European Migration and the Early American Labor Force, 1600–1775," *Labor History* 42 (2001): 5–43.

Willison, George, *Saints and Strangers - Being the Lives of the Pilgrim Fathers & Their Families, with Their Friends & Foes: & and Account of Their Posthumous Wanderings in Limbo, Their Final Resurrection & Rise to Glory, & the Strange Pilgrimages of Plymouth Rock*. London: William Heinemann, Ltd., 1945.

Winslow, Edward, *Good Newes from New England: or a true Relation of things very remarkable at the Plantation of Plimoth in New-England*. London: Printed by I. D. for William Bladen and John Bellamie, 1624; reprinted by Bedford, MA: Applewood Books, 1986; ed. Kelly Wisecup, Amherst, MA: University of Massachusetts Press, 2014.

Winslow, Edward, *Hypocrisie unmasked: by a true relation of the proceedings of the Governour and company of the Massachusets against Samuel Gorton (and his accomplices), etc.* London : Printed by Rich. Cotes, for John Bellamy at the three Golden Lions in Cornhill, neare the Royall Exchange, 1647. [Winslow, *Hypocrisie unmasked*]

Winthrop Papers. 6 volumes. Boston: Massachusetts Historical Society, 1929 - . v. 1. 1498-1628; v. 2. 1629-1630; v. 3. 1631-1637; v. 4. 1638-1644; v. 5. 1645-1649; v. 6. 1650-1654.

York Deeds, 18 volumes. Portland, ME: John T. Hull, 1887-1910.

Young, Alexander, *Chronicles of the Pilgrim fathers of the colony of Plymouth, from 1602 to 1625: now first collected from original records and contemporaneous printed documents, and illustrated with notes.* Boston: Charles C. Little and James Brown, 1841, reprinted with a preface by Robert Charles Anderson, Boston: NEHGS, 2016.

About the Author

Warren Becket Soule attended schools in North Carolina and New Jersey before graduating from Davidson College in Davidson, North Carolina. He attended the Episcopal Divinity School in Cambridge, Massachusetts; and has also received degrees in Classical Philology from Harvard University, in Philosophy and History from the University of Dallas, and the certificate in genealogical research from Boston University.

Fr. Soule was ordained to the priesthood in the Episcopal Church by Bishop Robert E. Terwilliger in 1982, and served parishes in North Carolina, Texas, England, and Pennsylvania. After being received into full communion with the Catholic Church, he entered the Dominican Order and was ordained to the priesthood in the Catholic Church by James, Cardinal Hickey in 1993. He received the licentiate (1992) and doctorate in canon law (1994) from The Catholic University of America; his research centred on the Anglo-Norman school of canonists in the Middle Ages.

Fr. Soule has taught Latin, Greek, and canon law at The Catholic University of America and at the Dominican House of Studies (1988-1989, 1992-1994, 2000-2002, 2003-2007), and mediaeval history and Law at Oxford University, as well as Roman Law and English Constitutional History at Cambridge University (1994-1999). He has been visiting lecturer at the L'viv Theological Academy in L'viv, Ukraine, Visiting Fellow in Mediaeval Thought at Durham University (England), has taught and lectured at other institutions of higher studies in the United States, Canada, and Great Britain, and has served as an official for the Congregation for the Eastern Churches in Vatican City (2002-2003). His articles and reviews have appeared in *The Jurist*, *The Thomist*, *Studia Canonica*, *New Blackfriars*, *Orientalia Christiana Periodica*, *Kanon*, *Folia Canonica*, *The Mayflower Quarterly*, *The North Carolina Genealogical Society Journal*, *The Genealogical Magazine of New Jersey*, and the *Ecclesiastical Law Journal*; his recent publications include a translation of the *Sentences* of the mediaeval theologian Peter Lombard, a commentary on the law on clergy in the Code of Canons of the Eastern Churches, *A Documentary History of the Diocese of Charlotte 1972-2022* (Lulu, 2022), and *Passengers of the Fortune -1621* (Heritage Books, 2023), The Centennial History of the Society of Mayflower Descendants in the State of North Carolina 1924-2024 (Heritage Books, 2024), and over 100 entries in the fourth edition of the *Oxford Dictionary of the Christian Church* (2021). He is currently editing Peter Lombard's magisterial twelfth-century commentary on the Psalter for publication.

Fr. Soule has served as a judge for the Archdiocese of Washington (1992-2002; Adjutant Judicial Vicar, 1999-2002), the Diocese of East Anglia, the Ukrainian Catholic Eparchy of Saint Josaphat of Parma, the Maronite Eparchy of Saint Maron of Brooklyn, and is currently a judge for the Diocese of Charlotte (NC). He served the Catholic Campus Ministry at the College of William and Mary (2003-2006) and was weekend assistant at parishes in Williamsburg and Richmond, Virginia; he continues to be in demand internationally as a lecturer, preacher, and retreat master.

Fr. Soule became the Bishop James A. Griffin Professor of Canon Law at the Pontifical College Josephinum (2010-2017), after serving as Associate Professor of Canon Law and Dean of the Pontifical Faculty of the Immaculate Conception (Dominican House of Studies) in Washington, D.C. (2003-2007), pastor of Saint Denis' Catholic Church in Hanover, New Hampshire (2008-2010) and of Saint John the Evangelist Catholic Church in Waynesville, North Carolina (2017-2018). He has taught law at Saint Paul University in Ottawa, Ontario, from which he retired in 2020; Fr. Soule continues to teach, write and supervise. He served as the first Judicial Vicar and Episcopal Vicar for Canonical Affairs for the Personal Ordinariate of the Chair of Saint Peter, the jurisdiction established by Pope Benedict XVI for those of the Anglican tradition in the United States and Canada entering into full communion with the Catholic Church. He presently serves as pastor of Saint Margaret of Scotland Catholic Church in Maggie Valley, North Carolina (2020 -).

Proud of his *Mayflower* ancestry (George Soule [three lines], Bradford, Alden, Allerton, Browne, Doty, Eaton, Fuller, Howland, and Warren [three lines], as well as Philip Delano of the *Fortune* [two lines]), he has been researching his family history for over thirty years. A life member of the NC Society of Mayflower Descendants, where he is co-Historian and Governor, he also serves as Elder, Deputy Governor General, and Deputy Governor of the Canadian Society of Mayflower Descendants. He has served on the Board of Directors and as President of Soule Kindred in America and Delano Kindred, and served on the Editorial Review Committee of the General Society of Mayflower Descendants as well as the book review editor of the *Mayflower Quarterly*. Fr. Soule is the book review editor for the North Carolina Genealogical Society *Journal* and has served as Secretary and Historian of the NCGS. He is Chaplain of the Society of Colonial Wars in the State of North Carolina, and is a General Executive Counsellor of the Military Order of the Stars and Bars (Army of Northern Virginia) and is a member and chaplain of Major General W. H. C. Whiting Chapter #305. He is also active in the United Empire Loyalist Association of Canada (Sir Guy Carleton Chapter). He sings Gilbert and Sullivan constantly in private and occasionally in public, specialising in roles that are long on humour and short on vocal demands.

Current and Ongoing Projects:

Descendants of George Soule of the Mayflower [1620], in five volumes. Volume 1 (the first five generations, naming the sixth) should be published in 2025.

Descendants of Philip Delano of the Fortune [1621], in five volumes (known as "The Emerald Books"). Volume 1 (the first five generations, naming the sixth) should be published in 2025.

Descendants of Abraham Sampson in four volumes (known as "The Crimson Books"). Volume 1 (the first five generations, naming the sixth) should be published in 2026.

Mayflower Loyalists: is a growing published list of Loyalists who descend from *Mayflower* passengers. The intent is to study migration patterns and build a bridge between the Loyalists identified by the United Empire Loyalists Association and their *Mayflower* ancestors.

Mayflower in Grey: producing a database of all *Mayflower* descendants who served in the armed forces or in the government of the Confederate State of America (1861-1865).

Any information or documentation related to any of these projects is most welcome; Becket Soule can be reached at wbsoule1620@gmail.com *or* wbsoule@rcdoc.org

INDEX

Authors are only included in the index if their names occur in the text, rather than citations in footnotes.

The ship *Mayflower* is not indexed, as it occurs on almost every page.

Garfield, James A., 41, 214
Gates, (Sir) Thomas, 89, 90
General Court, 237, 249, 250, 251, 320, 323, 326, 327, 328, 329, 330, 331, 332, 333, 335, 336, 337, 338, 339, 340, 366
General Society of Mayflower Descendants, 402
George I, 11
Gere, Richard Tiffany, 216
German Ocean, 5
Gilbert, (Sir) Humphrey, 86
Gilbert, John, 85
Gilbert, Raleigh, 85
Godbertson, Godbert, 129, 367
Godbertson, Samuel, 129
Godbertson, Sarah (Allerton) (Vincent) (Priest), 129, 130
Gomes, (Rev.) Peter J., ix, 36, 317
Goodman, John, 39, 134, 135, 136, 137, 138, 274, 287, 388
Goodwin, William, 4
Gorges, Robert, 231
Gorges, Sir Ferdinando, 10, 73, 75, 76, 83, 183, 231, 304, 306, 374
Gosnold, (Capt.) Bartholomew, 82
Graham, Martha, 218
Grant, Ulysses Simpson (born Hiram Ulysses), 220
Gravesend, 1
Greene, William, 77
Greenland, 25
Gregorian calendar, viii, 44, 45, 123, 194, 257
Gregory XIII, 44
Gulf Stream, 54, 74, 98

Habsburg, 255
Hacker, Sarah, 35
Hale, Sarah Josepha, 317
Hamble minor, 2
Hamilton, George, 215
Hamlin, Ellen Vesta (Emery), 219
Hampton, 6
Harlow, Thomas, 363
Harvard College, 36, 49, 221, 238, 401
Harwich, 25, 391
Hawke, Ethan Green, 221
Heale, Giles, 29, 143, 155, 197
Hefner, Hugh, 215
Hemingway, Ernest, 221
Henlow, Bedfordshire, 165, 167, 168, 389
Henry VIII, 108
Hepburn, Katharine Houghton, 216
Hetfield, James (Metallica), 215
Hicks (Hix), Robert, 292, 349
Hilton, Edward, 372, 373
Hilton, William, 292, 349, 370, 371, 372, 373, 374, 375
Hinckley, Thomas, 338, 339, 341
Hoar, George Frisbie, 200
Hobbamock, 271, 272, 295, 296, 297
Holbeck, William, 60, 157, 392
Hooke, John, 60, 162, 180, 181, 390
Hopkins, Constance, 35, 42, 391
Hopkins, Damaris, 35, 287, 391

May, Henry, 225
mayflower (Epigaea repens), 180
Mayflower Compact, viii, 41, 60, 64, 86, 89, 91, 92, 93, 107, 115, 122, 124, 137, 140, 148, 149, 150, 153, 169, 172, 173, 176, 181, 199, 200, 208, 224, 288, 303
Mayflower Families in Progress (MFIP), 175
Mayflower Families through Five Generations ("Silver Books"), 158, 174, 175, 176, 244
Mayflower II, 33
Mayflower Quarterly, 401, 402
Mayo Clinic, 217
Mayo, (Rev.) John, 333
McClellan, George C., 220
McClintock, Barbara, 217
McCullough, David, 221
Merchant Adventurers, 26, 27, 38, 77, 131, 227, 249, 290, 303, 350, 355, 359, 385, 386, 391, 392
Merry Mount, 28, 233
Metacom ["King Philip"], 261
Meyrick, Sir Gelli, 19
Minter, Desire, 163, 171, 172, 173, 287, 390
Mitchell, Elizabeth Trumbull (Miller) [Mrs. "Billy"], 220
Monhegan Island, Maine, 182
Monroe, Marilyn (neé Norma Jean Baker), 217
More, Edward, 108
More, Ellen (Helen, Elinor), 62, 64, 275, 390

More, Jasper, 38, 62, 108, 171, 173, 390
More, Katherine, 108
More, Mary, 62, 390
More, Richard, 43, 50, 62, 78, 108, 109, 287, 390
More, Samuel, 50, 108
More, Thomas, 108
More, William, 108
Morgan, Benedict/Bennet, 292, 349
Morison, Samuel Eliot, 208, 221
Morton, (Rev.) John, 226
Morton, George, 198, 225, 354
Morton, Nathaniel, 72, 92, 199, 205, 307
    New England's Memoriall, 72, 92, 157, 199, 205, 306, 307, 366
Morton, Thomas, 28, 145, 232, 266, 292, 349, 354, 355, 396
    New English Canaan, 232
Mourt's Relation, 20, 21, 27, 29, 57, 89, 94, 105, 109, 114, 133, 140, 142, 146, 182, 183, 185, 189, 197, 198, 199, 224, 225, 247, 257, 263, 267, 276, 277, 285, 293, 296, 309, 347, 377, 385
Weld, Susan Ker "Tuesday" (Mrs. Dudley Moore, 216
Mullins, Alice (____), 158, 159
Mullins, Elizabeth, 159, 160
Mullins, Joan (Bridger), 157
Mullins, John, 157, 158
Mullins, Joseph, 159, 161, 391

414

Mullins, William, 20, 23, 29, 38, 45, 60, 155, 156, 157, 158, 159, 160, 197, 221, 264, 391, 392

Mullins, William (son of William Mullins), 158, 159, 160

Nanepashemet [Native chief], 310, 311

Nantucket Sound, 82

Narragansett [Natives], 183, 186, 192, 270, 271, 279, 281, 298, 303, 308, 377, 378, 384

Nauset [Natives], 183, 185, 230, 257, 259, 260, 262, 266, 303, 306

Neal, Simon, 50, 156, 170, 177

Nemasket (Middleboro), 270, 272, 278, 279, 284, 293, 295, 296, 302

Netherlands, 2

Nettleton, Martha, 325

New Amsterdam [New York], 17, 66, 249

New Brunswick, 310

New England Confederation, 332, 334

New Netherland, 66, 67, 72, 255, 365

New Netherland Company, 67

Newcomen, John, 234

Newport, (Sir) Christopher, 85

Newton, Ellen, 351

Nichols, Christopher, 25

Nicolas, Augustine/Austen, 292, 348, 349

Nimitz, Catherine Vance (Freeman) [Mrs. Chester], 220

Nixon, Richard M., 214, 218

Nova Scotia, 180, 202, 220, 246, 340

Old Colony Club, 115

Oldham, John, 228, 229, 249, 327, 372

Overschie, 4

Oxford University, 401

Palmer, William, 292, 348, 349, 375, 376

Paomet [Natives], 93, 230, 276, 282

Parker, John, 29

Patuxet [or Apaum], 182, 189, 247, 269, 276, 306

Pecksuot [Native chief], 230, 231

Perry, Matthew Calbraith, 219

Perry, Oliver Hazard, 219

Pershing, Helen Frances (Warren) [Mrs. John], 220

Philbrick, Nathaniel, 17, 33, 69, 90

Philip III, 256

Phillips, John, 61

Pickering, Edward, 77

Picton Press, 174

Pierce Patent [1621], 92, 303, 358

Pierce, John, 66, 73

Pilgrim Hall [Plymouth, MA], 14, 304

Pitt, William, 292, 348, 349, 376

Plymouth [England], 15, 16, 18, 20

Plymouth Company, 73, 83, 109, 236, 264

Plymouth Rock, 93, 115, 116, 210, 301, 318, 398

Pokanoket [Natives], 183, 186, 187, 192, 260, 261, 268, 275, 277, 278, 279, 281, 283, 284, 286, 303, 308, 315, 316

Pontifical College Josephinum, 402

Popham Colony, 83, 84, 85, 86

Popham, (Sir) John, 85

Popham, George, 85

Portland Bill, 11

Pory, John, 342

Post, Emily, 218

Pound, Ezra Weston Loomis, 221

Powell, Philemon, 77

Pratt, Mary (Priest), 129

Pratt, Phineas, 78, 129

Prence, Thomas, 141, 226, 235, 236, 292, 331, 349, 359, 364, 365, 366

Presley, Priscilla Ann (Wagner) [Mrs. Elvis], 215

Priest, Degory, 23, 42, 128, 129, 130, 162, 214, 215, 389

Priest, Mary, 42

Priest, Sarah, 42

Prince, Thomas, 41, 122, 140, 141, 142, 201, 304, 358, 364

Pring, Martin, 97, 142

Provincetown Harbour, 82, 93, 94, 100, 198, 206, 248

Prowe, Solomon, 391

Prower, Edward, 124

Prower, Mary, 124

Prower, Solomon, 62, 123, 124, 125, 132

Pulsifer, David, 202, 250, 251

Quadequina, 189, 190, 191, 247, 306

Quakers, 148, 210, 239, 249, 254, 323, 334, 366

Raleigh, (Sir) Walter, 40

Records of the Colony of New Plymouth, 24, 203, 250

Reeve, Christopher D'Olier, 216

Rehnquist, William, 215

Rehoboth, Massachusetts, 326, 333, 335

Remington, Eliphalet, 218

Reyner, (Rev.) John, 333

Reynolds, Burt, 216

Reynolds, John, 63

Reynolds, Master (of the *Speedwell*), 11, 19

Richardson, Martha, 325

Rigdale, John, 39

Rigsdale, Alice (Gallard), 150

Rigsdale, John, 150, 153

Roberts, Gary Boyd, 214, 217

Robinson, (Rev.) John, 1, 2, 3, 6, 8, 9, 10, 14, 49, 147, 165, 170, 181, 223, 245, 249, 389

Rogers, Elizabeth, 42

Rogers, Joseph, 42

Rogers, Margaret, 42

Rogers, Thomas, 39, 42, 169, 215, 220, 222, 389

Rolfe, John, 35

Roman Catholic, 41, 125, 238

Roosevelt, Franklin Delano, 34, 214

Roosevelt, Sara (Delano), 214

Roosevelt, Theodore, 34

Sagadahoc [Maine], 71, 72, 84

Salem, Massachusetts, 43, 154, 162, 229, 251, 390

Samoset, 182, 184, 185, 187, 189, 191, 193, 247, 259, 275

Sampson, Abraham, 167, 168

Sampson, Deborah, 219

Samson, Henry, 165, 167, 168, 214, 219, 220, 287, 389

Schie, 4

Scituate, Massachusetts, 147, 148, 328, 335, 342, 376

Scrooby, 49, 52, 86, 156, 223, 358

Sea Venture, 85

Seabury, (Bishop) Samuel, 218

Second Virginia Company, 73, 76

Separatists, 26, 48, 77, 84, 116, 157, 209, 210, 233, 246, 248, 320, 383, 389

Sewall, Samuel, 28

shallop, 94, 98, 99, 100, 101, 102, 103, 105, 106, 109, 111, 112, 113, 114, 118, 120, 121, 132, 138, 141, 182, 188, 229, 269, 270, 279, 309, 311

Shepard, Alan B., 218

Short, Thomas, 25

Shurtleff, Nathaniel B., 250, 251

Simonson, Moses, 293, 349, 354

Smith, (Capt.) John, 12, 15, 21, 24, 69, 81, 82, 95, 118, 264, 265, 293, 372

A Description of New England, 81, 265

Smith, Joseph, 34, 218

Snow, Rebecca (Brown), 138

Snow, William, 138

Society for the Propagation of the Gospel in New England, 160

Society of Mayflower Descendants in the State of North Carolina, vii

Solent, 2, 10

Soule Kindred in America, vii, 176, 402

Soule, Benjamin, 52, 62, 102

Soule, Elizabeth, 324

Soule, George, 52, 62, 64, 65, 102, 175, 176, 177, 178, 179, 215, 217, 219, 220, 221, 275, 287, 351, 390, 402

Soule, Henchman, 36

Soule, Mary (Becket or Bucket), 62, 65

Soule, Warren Becket, i, 401

Soule, Zachariah, 65

Souter, David H., 215

Southampton, 1, 2, 3, 4, 5, 6, 7, 8, 9, 10, 12, 29, 57, 93, 224, 290, 350, 364, 386

Southampton Water, 2, 5, 10

Southworth, Constant, 28

Southworth, Edward, 12, 225

Spanish Armada, 18

Sparrow, 229

Speedwell, 2, 4, 5, 6, 7, 9, 10, 11, 12, 13, 14, 15, 16, 17, 18, 19, 22, 74, 195, 214, 224, 286, 290, 291, 345, 349, 353, 355, 386

Spencer, Arlene, 26

Spock, Benjamin, 34, 217

Spooner, William, 129

Squanto, 183, 186, 189, 190, 191, 193, 203, 207, 247, 259,

www.ingramcontent.com/pod-product-compliance
Lightning Source LLC
Chambersburg PA
CBHW060131280326
41932CB00012B/1480